The
Counterfeit Ark

Before the Flood

And, God said unto Noah
The end of all flesh is come before me
For the earth is filled with violence through them
And, behold
I will destroy them with the earth

Make thee an ark of gopher wood
Rooms shalt thou make in the ark
And shalt pitch it within and without with pitch

And of every living thing of all flesh
Two of every sort
Shalt thou bring into the ark
To keep them alive with thee
And take unto thee of all food that is eaten
And thou shalt gather it to thee
And it shall be food for thee and for them

The Flood: During and After

And it came to pass after seven days
That the waters of the flood were upon the earth
And the rain was upon the earth
Forty days and forty nights
And every living substance was destroyed
Which was upon the face of the ground
Both man and cattle
And the creeping things
And the fowl of heaven
And they were destroyed from the earth
And only Noah remained alive
And they that were with him in the ark

And God remembered Noah
And every living thing
And all the cattle that was with him in the ark
And God made a wind to pass over the earth
And the waters assuaged
And it came to pass at the end of the forty days
That Noah opened the window of the ark which he had made
Also he sent forth a dove from him
To see if the waters were abated
From off the face of the ground
And he stayed yet another seven days
And again he sent forth the dove out of the ark
And the dove came in to him in the evening
And in her mouth was an olive leaf plucked off
So Noah knew the waters were abated from off the earth
And in the second month
On the seventh and twentieth day of the month
Was the earth dried.

—Genesis 6, 7, 8

AND GOD GAVE NOAH THE RAINBOW SIGN
NO MORE WATER
THE FIRE NEXT TIME

—"I've Got a Home in That Rock"

The Counterfeit Ark

CRISIS RELOCATION FOR NUCLEAR WAR

Edited by
Jennifer Leaning and Langley Keyes

A PHYSICIANS FOR SOCIAL RESPONSIBILITY BOOK

Ballinger Publishing Company
Cambridge, Massachusetts
A Subsidiary of Harper and Row, Publishers, Inc.

International Standard Book Number: 0–88410–940–2 (c)
0–88410–941–0 (p)

Library of Congress Catalog Card Number: 83–15519

Printed in the United States of America

Library of Congress Cataloging in Publication Data
Main entry under title:

The Counterfeit ark.

"A Physicians for Social Responsibility book."
Includes index.
1. United States—Civil defense—Addresses, essays, lectures. 2. Atomic warfare—Addresses, essays, lectures. 3. Evacuation of civilians—United States—Addresses, essays, lectures. I. Leaning, Jennifer. II. Keyes, Langley Carleton, 1938—
UA927.C65 1983   363.3'5'0973   83–15519
ISBN 0–88410–940–2
ISBN 0–88410–941–0 (pbk.)

Contents

PART II: THE FLOOD: DURING AND AFTER   129

List of Figures

List of Tables

Foreword

This is a book written about one vital but often ignored part of the nuclear arms debate: the effort to save civilian lives in the event of a nuclear attack. Civil defense against nuclear attack has taken many forms. In 1957 the Gaither Panel recommended a massive shelter program to President Eisenhower. After extensive review by the President and the National Security Council, the proposal was rejected for several reasons. Most important, it was judged that the program would not save a large enough fraction of the population to justify its cost. Second, any survivors of a nuclear exchange would emerge into a totally devastated society lacking all of the support systems required to keep them alive even if they escaped injury. President Eisenhower summed up his views in a few cryptic observations: "You can't have that war," he said, "The living would envy the dead. There would not be enough bulldozers available to scrape the bodies off the streets." John Foster Dulles added that such a program would demoralize our allies, as we proceeded to provide even a limited measure of protection for ourselves while ignoring their safety. The shelter idea, however, did not stay dead. A civil defense craze in 1961 ended when President Kennedy came to the same conclusion arrived at by Eisenhower. The lesson learned both times was that the bulk of the civilian population could not be protected from the effects of nuclear war.

An obvious extension of this conclusion is that nations cannot fight nuclear wars. However, if one's goal, like that of the present administration, is to create a war-winning military capability, one must at least pretend to protect the civilian population. The current result is crisis relocation planning (CRP). Even though this plan has been discredited by many and ridiculed in the popular press, the administration still presses on with budgetary requests for the Federal Emergency Management Agency (FEMA) to pursue this program.

The Counterfeit Ark, written by people with experience in the technical areas that surround the CRP concept, asks hard questions about the validity of the assumptions that undergird the CRP planning process. The book constitutes an effort to nail the lid on the coffin of civil defense, to enable us to understand the inadequacy of the CRP concept, and get back to the fundamental reality obscured by the CRP smoke screen: the total unacceptability of any kind of nuclear war under any set of assumptions.

Several themes run through the book, unify the diverse technical areas under consideration, and make clear the inadequacy of CRP. Crisis relocation planning is morally wrong; it is strategically wrong; and it is operationally wrong. It promises what it can't deliver—survival for 80 percent of the relocated population. It lulls the U.S. into the belief that it can withstand a nuclear assault and go on to win the war while providing a signal to the Soviet Union that we harbor a first-strike strategy, thus encouraging the very thing CRP is promoted to preclude—a preemptive Soviet strike. Operationally, the planning to date by FEMA has rivaled the Keystone Cops in performance. If the context were not so serious, the FEMA agenda for postal service after the bomb and the provision of food for abandoned pets would be hilarious. I find it hard to believe that its promoters really take it seriously.

A central theme of morality and politics that runs through many of the essays is that of "choosing": Who shall go into the blast-hardened shelters; who shall be given medical treatment; which shelters shall be given food and water? The moral dilemma of the choosers is not mentioned by the FEMA planners. "Sophie's Choice" will be multiplied to the nth power. Who has the right to make these choices? Do any of us want to be put in the position of so choosing? CRP is about allocating life or death to millions. Nowhere do the planners deal with the moral horror of this fact.

The disaster resulting from a nuclear attack on the scale envisaged by FEMA (6000 megatons) represents a "singularity"—a disaster without precedent in form, scale, and impact. Experience with other kinds of disaster provides no precedents. No previous event can begin to prepare us for the horror, complexity, and devastation of nuclear attack. Dr. Howard Hiatt, dean of the Harvard School of Public Health, has aptly called such a war "the last epidemic."

The studies undertaken by think-tanks for FEMA and its predecessors are the ultimate examples of technical rationality and system analysis gone amuck. Intelligent people end up saying wild things because of their willingness to accept "leaps of faith" that common sense would indicate are highly suspect if not nonsensical.

Serious analysis of any one of the sets of assumptions upon which FEMA planners are operating produces questions and reveals outright fallacies in the methodology, analysis, and conclusions upon which the FEMA crisis relocation scenario is based.

It is imperative to understand that despite the serious shortcomings of CRP, which some FEMA people are willing to admit, the administration goes forward with the concept (granted amid great congressional hostility). Why? Because CRP allows the administration to say the U.S. population can be "saved," at least most of it, in a serious nuclear exchange. CRP is *central* to a war-fighting, first-strike, limited nuclear war—call it what you want—strategy. A civil defense plan, even one as poor as CRP, is needed as an integral part of the first-strike policy.

Without the smokescreen provided by CRP, the administration would have to admit that the vast majority of Americans would be killed in a nuclear exchange. With that admission, nuclear war remains unthinkable. Once this is thoroughly understood by citizens and officials alike, the government can get down to the serious business of halting the futile arms race through such actions as a moratorium on further weapons building, a negotiable freeze, or one of the many plans that have been advocated as a substitute for the present madness. Present force levels far exceed what is needed for a deterrent, so there is a great flexibility in choosing a route to much lower levels of arms.

The Counterfeit Ark demonstrates clearly that a civilian population cannot be protected against the effects of a nuclear attack. Eisenhower came to this conclusion. Kennedy did as well. Given the facts, these leaders made the only reasonable assessment. In these times of even greater peril, we must demand the same discernment from our own.

Jerome Weisner
1983

Introduction

Jennifer Leaning and Langley Keyes

In recent years we have seen the federal government respond to burgeoning technological developments in nuclear weapons systems with a policy advocating the use of nuclear weapons as instruments of war. Increased funding is being sought for all methods to improve what is called our "destructive advantage." Two strategic systems are at work in this concept. The first, our offensive weapons system, is designed to reduce the opponent's capacity to retaliate against either our population centers or our military and industrial installations. The second, our civil defense system, is designed to pro'ect our populations from the effects of a nuclear attack. To the extent that both can be perfected, the U.S. supposedly secures a greater destructive advantage—seen as a survival edge—in the projected conflict with the Soviet Union.

The erosion of deterrence, a policy based on the nonuse of nuclear weapons, and the introduction in its place of a policy based on using nuclear weapons, now *requires* a civil defense plan that would, according to President Reagan's directive, "provide for the survival of a substantial portion of the U.S. population."[1] As the current director of the Federal Emergency Management Agency (FEMA) described the evolution in policy: " . . . [T]his Administration has categorically rejected . . . the short-war, mutually assured destruction, it'll all be over in 20 minutes so why the hell mess around spending dollars on it. We're trying to inject long-war mentality."[2] Civil defense, long respected as a source of relief in the context of natural and technological disasters, has thus become enmeshed in the strategic systems that support nuclear war fighting. Because of this entanglement, it has become the focus of much public controversy.

FEMA was formed in 1979, consolidating in one agency the various federal bureaucracies involved in disaster management. Charged with disaster planning for all peacetime and "attack-related" emergencies,

FEMA has actively promoted crisis relocation planning (CRP), the government's current choice for surviving nuclear war. In 1983, responding to growing popular debate about the feasibility of CRP and the concept of survival after nuclear war, FEMA subsumed this program under the more general category of "integrated emergency management," declaring that civil defense for nuclear war embodies disaster management strategies that are applicable to a range of natural and technological disasters. Crisis relocation, FEMA now suggests, can be used for many contingencies, so long as planning and programming activities for disasters other than nuclear war do not "detract from attack-related preparedness."[3] Although packaged somewhat differently than before, the 1984 federal budget for CRP indicates that only the posture, not the policy, has changed. As Jerome Weisner says in his Foreword, CRP remains an essential element in the government's pursuit of its strategy to fight a nuclear war and, if not to win, at least to prevail and certainly to survive. The notion of survivability lies at the heart of current efforts to persuade the public that the use of nuclear weapons presents us with plausible policy options. It is imperative that this link in strategy and public persuasion be appreciated, because as long as people allow the government to say that our society can survive the use of nuclear weapons—that nuclear war is just war writ larger and a good plan will help us cope with its effects—people will also acquiesce to policies that promote an escalation of the arms race and an intensification of the risk of war. Cloaked in less obtrusive language for 1983, CRP persists, continuing to shore up dangerous illusions.

The central components of CRP are population evacuation and shelter, in anticipation of a 6559 megaton attack on the United States by the Soviet Union.[4] Beginning from the acknowledgment that any preparedness plan, to be effective, must be preceded by some period of warning, civil defense planners have hypothesized a five- to seven-day period of "heightened international tension," during which the president, after evaluating intelligence reports, may decide to order crisis relocation into effect. The actual time for population evacuation, accounting for time taken by national security deliberations, may thus be reduced to a period of three to five days. Approximately two-thirds of the U.S. population is thought to reside in areas considered to be at high risk of direct thermal and blast effects. During the initial phase of crisis relocation, these 150 million Americans are expected to travel between 50 and 300 miles to designated low-risk rural areas. Civil defense planners estimate that approximately 80 percent of the population at risk will ultimately make this trek. They will join the approximately 75 million people in areas of relatively low risk for direct effects, comprising a potential shelter population of 195 million people. In the early stage of crisis relocation, as people are moving in from urban areas, they are expected to find lodging with friends or relatives, or to congregate in schools or meeting halls. During the later phase, the urban evacuees and their rural hosts are expected to upgrade existing shelters or build expedient ones. In the event of nuclear attack, these 195 million people are to be prepared to spend from one to four weeks in these improvised shelter conditions. A subset of 30 million people, called essential workers, will be asked to commute daily into the major urban areas from blast-protected shelters located nearby, in order to maintain the urban infrastructure during the crisis period.

According to FEMA, an adequate evacuation and shelter program such as CRP will result in the survival of 80 percent of the population after a major nuclear attack on military and industrial targets. Under congressional questioning, however, Charles F. Estes, Jr., director of strategic policy in the Office of the Undersecretary of Defense for Policy, revealed that this 80 percent survival figure was not derived from computer simulations but rather entered as an initial assumption:

> It was assumed at the outset that 80 percent of the population of hypothesized target areas would in fact have been evacuated and would survive. . . . [T]his was an entering assumption rather than one of the study's analytically derived findings. . . .
> It is important . . . to note that the survivability assumptions . . . of the computer model were derived from opinions of interested civil defense program managers, academics, and contractor personnel. These opinions were obtained through use of accepted opinion survey techniques.[5]

In subsequent testimony, John McConnell, a member of FEMA's national policy staff, amplified Estes's remarks:

> The 80 percent evacuation assumption was believed to be reasonable if not conservative by a panel of social scientists who participated in support of the . . . study. These persons were familiar with studies of and experience in both wartime and peacetime evacuations, and believed . . . that there was no reason to believe that crisis relocation would display characteristics different from those encountered in natural disaster evacuations.[6]

Hence, the assurance of an 80 percent survival fraction is thus merely an assumption based on an 80 percent evacuation fraction that is, in turn, an assumption based on a sample of expert opinion. The opinions themselves are based upon a cascade of other assumptions buried in the several stages of the plan.

Assumptions about the feasibility of evacuation and shelter are:

• The targeting scenario, including a presumed warning period and no retargeting of enemy warheads, is accurate.

• Evacuation of 150 million people from all major urban areas in three to five days is logistically possible.

• The population will remain orderly, obedient, and psychologically stable.

• Essential workers will remain at assigned posts near targeted areas and commute to them daily.

• Shelters of adequate protection, equipped with necessary life supports, can be provided for the necessary minimum period.

• Command, control, and communications centers will function as planned.

Regarding survival in the post-attack world, the following assumptions are made: The remaining population will survive, in terms of biological persistence over time, because the ecosystem will not be so seriously disrupted as to exert a significant constraint on human survival; the incidence and virulence of infectious disease will not outstrip the resistance of the surviving population and the potential for medical care; the intermediate radiation effects will not prove incapacitating or lethal and will not significantly impair fertility; and a psychological will to live and engage in relationships will endure. This series of assumptions culminates in the notion that reducing survival to a state at best defined in terms of biological persistence of the species is an outcome sufficiently acceptable to risk its occurrence.

Critics of crisis relocation maintain that the strategic scenario is unrealistic, the evacuation and shelter plans are unfeasible, and the long-term questions of biological and social survival remain unaddressed. In response, FEMA has defended the components of its plan as both possible and plausible, citing extensive research that government consultants have conducted on all aspects of the proposed program. As William K. Chipman, director of FEMA's population protection division, declared in House testimony: "We have . . . conducted rather extensive research concerning many aspects of crisis relocation—feasibility of actual relocation; the sort of planning that has to be done; the problems relating to medical emergencies, to food, to movement, communications, to communicating in the psychological sense with people—many of those things. . . ."[7] Louis Giuffrida, director of FEMA, declared in Congressional testimony that "The Civil Defense Research Program provides the scientific, analytical, and technical basis for the entire Civil Defense program. It is necessary to assure that the basic facts and relationships upon which rest the plans, policies, procedures, and procurement for civil defense are sound, well documented, and thought through properly and objectively."[8]

As debate on crisis relocation has intensified at many levels of our society, those professionals whose expertise lies in the fields of transportation, urban life, systems analysis, public health, medicine, ecology, and military strategy have been called upon by the public to express their views on current government civil defense plans. Familiarity with the research base behind FEMA's plan has thus become necessary. From what sources has FEMA derived its assertions that densely settled urban areas can be successfully evacuated in three to five days? Has FEMA adequately assessed the data on evacuations before declaring that the vast majority of Americans will obey civil defense directives during the relocation and shelter periods? What are the assumptions behind FEMA's estimates of casualties? On what analysis do they base their claims of survivability?

Reviewing the research behind crisis relocation involves identifying those consultant reports that discuss the issues of strategic doctrine and civil defense, moving and sheltering populations over time, and population casualty consequences. A computer printout of over 2000 reports is obtainable from FEMA headquarters. Much of this research focuses on detailed models of physical weapons effects, prototype shelter constructions, and civil defense organization. Dating from the early 1960s, it has cost the federal government well over $200 million.[9] Several hundred of these reports address the larger issues of feasibility of crisis relocation and survival potential after nuclear war. Mr. Chipman submitted a selected list of approximately 100 "salient" studies on these issues to the 1981 Congressional Record;[10] FEMA refers elsewhere to a group of 370 such reports;[11] and annotated bibliographies have been compiled.[12] These several hundred research reports that address issues of feasibility and survival originate from a few main consulting centers. The authors of these reports cross reference each other, share a distribution list, attend the same government-sponsored seminars, and over time have developed a hermetic consensus on their topic. Their work has never been subject to independent academic review.

With this book we begin that process. We have invited authors from a range of academic disciplines to address a variety of issues raised by the concept of crisis relocation for nuclear war. Each author was asked to consider a topic most relevant to his or her area of expertise and to evaluate what had been written on the topic by the government-sponsored civil defense research. We set for them the conditions: a full-scale nuclear war consisting of a 6559 megaton attack on the continental

United States by the Soviet Union, in anticipation of which the federal government was to execute its crisis relocation plan. We asked our authors to evaluate, from the perspective of their disciplines, FEMA's claims that CRP was feasible and if effective would result in the survival of 80 percent of the U.S. population.

Each chapter but one begins with several excerpts from the civil defense documents analyzed in the chapter's subsequent discussion. These introductory quotations are intended to acquaint the reader with the wide spectrum of approaches taken by the research literature.

The documents evaluated in this book do not comprise an exhaustive, let alone an inclusive, list of all that has been written under government contract. Our criteria for selection were that each document contribute one or more of the following features:

1. The document focused on issues of feasibility and survivability of civil defense for nuclear war.

2. The document was sufficiently recent to include the concept of crisis relocation as a major civil defense policy option.

3. The document was cited by more than one subsequent author or by FEMA as an authoritative source.

4. The document was written by consultants who had already authored several previous reports.

5. The document was a concise or vivid expression of a representative point of view.

By making these selections we sought to acquaint the academic community with this federally financed research base that for the past twenty years, proceeding without restraint of outside review, has been instrumental in defining a most controversial national policy.

The chapters cover a wide variety of issues. In Part I, "Before the Flood," an initial series of four chapters discuss the concepts of disaster management, the nature of social science research, the uses of language, and the concepts of military strategy reflected in crisis relocation for nuclear war. The subsequent three chapters assess the factors involved in realistically preparing to evacuate a population of this magnitude and complexity. Part II, "The Flood: During and After," looks at the consequences of nuclear war and implications for population survival from the differing perspectives of shelter requirements, social control, immediate casualties, radiation effects, agricultural potential, ecological destruction, urban resettlement, and psychological life.

While the authors in this book make substantial contributions to the current debate about the efficacy of civil defense for nuclear war, we would like to point out areas where work still needs to be done, thereby encouraging others to direct their attention to this issue. In addressing some topics—for example, the evacuation of special populations—a chapter anticipates the need for a wider discussion. Chapter 7 opens the subject by examining how children might fare in crisis relocation. Related problems would be incurred by attempts to evacuate people who are physically handicapped, housed in institutions (nursing homes, hospitals, prisons, or mental health facilities), or, as with many of the elderly, living in relative social isolation with few resources. Such problems have not been explored.

Regarding the issue of infectious disease, we have not attempted to carry the analysis beyond the ground-breaking work already done. Hence, it is essential that experts in epidemiology, infectious disease, and demography continue to address the potential for increased incidence of infectious disease and epidemics, as well as the impacts these effects might have on population growth after nuclear war. A pioneering work by Herbert L. Abrams and William E. Von Kaenel[13]—cited frequently in this book—made plain just how many questions remain unanswered and suggested how serious the problem might be: In the post-attack world, what factors deplete immunity; how do diseases progress through populations; what impact does disease have on fertility and infant survival; how are disease patterns transformed by changes in both host and parasite?

This book mentions only in passing the issue of central command, control, and communications. Much of the civil defense research in this area is classified. To evaluate what is available requires the time and attention of those with expertise in the field. A similar commitment of expert time would be necessary to describe the ways in which radioactivity produced by nuclear war damages the environment and migrates through the food chain to threaten various life systems. This subject, discussed only briefly in this book, is enormously complex and merits further study.

Despite our recognition that there are more documents to read and more subjects to discuss, we have discerned, in this first formal public scrutiny of the federal civil defense literature, a mode of analysis and a world view that consistently dominate the reports. These themes, which characterize the nature of the research, warrant review because they affect the content and direction of government policy on nuclear war.

A Reductionist Pattern of Analysis

Civil defense researchers employ the techniques of modeling theory, referral-to-precedent, and best-case examples to develop their arguments. A reliance on models reduces discussion to the weighting of variables, each taken one at a time, plucked from a complex context. Hence, the whole is fragmented, dimensions simplified, and ramifications ignored. Referral-to-precedent allows nuclear war to be viewed as just one more disaster—albeit bigger—and population response is thus predicted as a function of previous experience. Using the best case to exemplify what might happen contributes to the bounded reality in which modeling theory and reference-to-precedent can be used with a minimum of cognitive dissonance. By not dealing with the uncertainties unleashed by nuclear war, the troubling potential for chaos, and the disquieting potential for horror, this pattern of analysis serves an important if unconscious purpose. It allows both researcher and policymaker to maintain a certain distance from the subject and sustain an aura of control.

A Minimalist View of Survival

Crisis relocation can be seen as effective only by defining survival after nuclear war in severely restricted terms. The civil defense research uses the term "survival" as if it were merely a computation of the numbers of individuals alive after nuclear war. The conditions that allow for persistence of life over time, or that maintain a recognizable quality of life, are not discussed. This research literature reflects a truly astounding capacity to dismiss without mention the destruction of human civilization and expresses no doubts about the stability of the natural environment or human psychological will. The world of nature and the world of our psyche are seen as constants—nature persistently bounteous and our spirits continuously resilient. In this view, the world after nuclear war is merely less complex and less populated. Recovery efforts are suspended in abstraction, performed by factors of production spaced on a grid without place names. A minimalist view of survival can be evaluated in one of two ways. It is either a coping mechanism allowing one to bear loss with equanimity (if you don't ask for much, you won't miss much); or it is a disturbing indication of diminished perception (if what we had now were really understood, this civil defense research would not settle for so little afterwards).

An Aversion To Hard Questions

The hard questions raised by the concept of civil defense for nuclear war—who decides who survives, who survives for how long, what is the meaning of survival—are not explicitly asked in the civil defense literature. Yet by accepting the parameters of their assignment, the researchers have accepted certain answers. To accept the survival of 80 percent of the U.S. population as a reasonable policy goal is also to accept as reasonable the deaths of 45 million people. To accept that the federal government has different plans for its leaders than for its public, and different plans for some members of the public than for others, is also to accept that—in this regard at least—the government is not "for the people." To accept as a sufficient definition of survival the numerical sum of those alive immediately after nuclear attack is also to accept as inessential the loss of our cultural and natural inheritance and the loss of everyone's dreams. Avoiding the hard questions has protected these researchers not from making hard choices but from recognizing that they have done so.

The claim that nuclear war can be survived—given adequate civil defense—supports a doctrine of nuclear war fighting. This claim rests on an unexamined body of civil defense research accumulated over many years. We hope that by submitting this research to independent academic review, we can help the public and policymakers assess the extent to which the claim is well-founded. To set forth the flaws in the existing research literature is to pose a fundamental challenge to the theoretical basis of official strategic policy. We have enlisted our colleagues and embarked upon this endeavor in order to promote a more informed, clear-sighted, and fearless public debate. Failure to engage in this debate carries high costs.

ACKNOWLEDGMENTS

The editors would like to thank Lisa Peattie and Aron Bernstein for their constant encouragement and moral support, Doris Kanin for her catalytic role in helping us initiate this project, Ruth A. Barron for her sustaining editorial counsel, and Karen Pratt for her invaluable help in manuscript preparation.

PART I

Before The Flood

1

The Singularity of Nuclear War: Paradigms of Disaster Planning

Jennifer Leaning and Langley Keyes

For man also knoweth not his time:
as the fishes that are taken in an evil net,
and as the birds that are caught in the snare;
so are the sons of men snared in an evil time,
when it falleth suddenly upon them.
                                        Ecclesiastes 9:12

Someone once suggested that Noah, with his ark, was the first disaster planner. He anticipated a threat, having a somewhat unusual and personalized warning system. Certain consequences seemed probable. Thus, Noah developed his response to the potential danger and implemented it by building his shelter and equipping it. He projected his manpower needs and had the capability to mobilize the necessary personnel. When the threat was realized, he rode out the storm in reasonable safety and, in not too many days, was ready to start on the recovery stage—to begin to pick up the pieces to start a new world.

While Noah's story has been well remembered in subsequent years, his actions were not too different from the actions of many contemporary persons who one way or another, are engaged in planning for emergencies in many different types of communities around the world. They too attempt to recognize threats that are likely. Efforts are made to anticipate probable effects of a range of dangers and what countermeasures can be made to neutralize or soften disaster impact. Consideration is given to the difficulties associated with mobilizing persons and resources to deal with multiple pre- and post-impact needs. The ultimate goal in such planning is to enable an effective and efficient start towards the restoration of normal routines. . . .

We also assume that any kind of planning has to be realistic. It has to be built upon real knowledge—thus our assertion that our observations do not stem from theoretical speculations but studies of actual disasters. Disaster planning has to be realistic also in that it cannot presuppose an ideal situation but the probable situation. This is why we stress throughout this report that good disaster plans are developed so that they can be adjusted to people rather than attempting to force people to conform to planning. Finally, disaster planning has to be realistic in the sense that it is taken for granted that planning can be undertaken. Persons with vivid imagination can always come up with hypothetical possibilities so horrendous that they serve to immobilize any effort at planning.

An example of the latter would be where a potential planner visualized a situation where his community would have to handle 10,000 casualties. Such a problem boggles the mind. A catastrophe of this magnitude could conceivably happen but it is very unlikely in American society. The largest number of deaths in any given disaster were the 5,000 or so killed in the Galveston hurricane-flood of 1900. In only three other disasters have casualties reached the 1,000 figure. Moreover, in recent years, the total average deaths in the United States in major disasters have averaged around 200 a year. A single major disaster is, therefore, extremely likely not to cause more than 100 deaths. This is a more realistic estimate, something that is more manageable and more amenable to planning. Our general point is that anyone can sit around and dream up all sorts of catastrophes which would defy almost any kind of planning. It is far more realistic to assume probable situations because that is what is likely to occur and for which community planning can be undertaken. . . .

SOURCE: Russell R. Dynes, E.L. Quarantelli, and Gary A. Kreps, *A Perspective on Disaster Planning*, prepared for the Defense Civil Preparedness Agency, Washington, D.C., December, 1972, pp. 1, iv.

It has been argued above that one appropriately can examine nuclear attack within the same conceptual and analytic framework as any other disaster, whether natural or man-made. The same basic definition encompasses all of the events and when defining characteristics are examined, we find that natural hazards differ as much among themselves as they are different from nuclear attack. Therefore, a careful examination of the problem reveals no significant reason for treating nuclear attack as a phenomenon totally different from other events characterized as disasters in the scholarly and research literature.

Furthermore, it should be stressed that the concern in this book is with the *threat* of nuclear attack and with people's likely response to a request to relocate when CRP is executed. Our primary concern is therefore with response to warnings about a hazard that allows time to warn the threatened population and has other characteristics similar to some natural hazards. At the *level of warning response*, nuclear attack may be treated like other disasters that have similar defining characteristics. Hence one may, with a minimum of interpretation, apply findings about human reactions to natural hazards to the problem of nuclear attack, as long as careful attention is paid to matching along the defining characteristics.

UNIQUE ASPECTS OF NUCLEAR ATTACK

The preceding arguments were meant to demonstrate that logical and appropriate comparisons can be made between warning response in natural hazards and nuclear attack. It was argued that *analytically*, in terms of the present state of hazards' research, there is no justification for isolating nuclear disasters in a class by themselves. This is not to say, however, that nuclear attack—like *all* other hazards—does not involve some unique characteristics. Indeed, there are several aspects of nuclear attack that are unique and do demand attention when applying data on natural-disaster warning response to the environment in which crisis relocation would be executed.

Both nuclear attack and natural disasters can—and should—be characterized in terms of the same key defining properties: scope of impact, speed of onset, duration of impact, secondary impacts, and social preparedness. Furthermore, one can describe many generic functions that may be the same for nuclear and natural disaster: the organization of warning systems may be the same, similar principles of warning-message construction may apply, certain protective strategies—for example, evacuation—may be the same. The unique aspect of nuclear attack (and all nuclear disasters for that matter) is that a nuclear component is involved, and special consideration is necessary because in terms of the way people *perceive* the situation, such circumstances are different from other types of disaster agents. Research indicates that much of the public views nuclear energy, and most things related to it, as a particularly threatening hazard with the potential for extraordinarily long-term negative effects—literally the power to irreversibly destroy generations. Of course, the idea—or realization—that people have a different mind set for disasters where the hazard agent is nuclear certainly does not preclude comparisons with natural disasters. Instead, it only requires that this emotional dimension be recognized at the outset and that the necessary qualifications be made when such perceptual differences may have some bearing upon expected human performance. . . .

It was argued that nuclear attack can appropriately be examined within the same conceptual and analytic framework as any other type of disaster agent, whether natural or man-made. The same basic definition of disaster encompasses a variety of disaster events and when defining characteristics are examined, it was pointed out that natural disasters differ at least as much among themselves as they are different from nuclear attack. Thus, from a theoretical point of view, there appears to be no substantial reason for treating response to nuclear attack as a phenomenon totally different from other events characterized as disasters in the research literature. . . .

Whether one is a researcher, emergency manager, or citizen, an uncomfortable feeling is generated when the possibility of nuclear attack and strategies for preparing for it are written down and discussed as events that may well occur. Some people feel that by discussing and preparing for a disaster we somehow risk predisposing it to happen. Such rationalizations have been used to justify not thinking about and preparing for natural hazards for many years. This practice has not, however, stopped natural disasters or reduced death, injury, or property-damage rates. Unfortunately, in the case of nuclear attack, unlike natural disasters, there is a political dimension to preparedness that may indeed lend some credibility to such arguments. The logical conclusion, however, is not that preparedness should be abandoned. The absolute horror and almost unimaginable destructiveness of a nuclear attack, coupled with the idea that U.S. political leaders would have limited options in the short run for stopping an attack in progress, make it unreasonable—if not immoral—to fail to develop some preparedness plan to at least forestall total destruction of the civilian population.

SOURCE: Ronald W. Perry, *The Social Psychology of Civil Defense*, Lexington Books, Lexington, Mass., 1982, pp. 32, 34, 98, 108.

INTRODUCTION

The theoretical underpinnings upon which the Federal Emergency Management Agency (FEMA) builds its model of crisis relocation planning (CRP) are to be found in the research of Ronald Perry, Russell Dynes, and E.L. Quarantelli. Perry's study, published as *The Social Psychology of Civil Defense*, constitutes a review of the disaster planning and management literature and attitudes toward nuclear catastrophe. Dynes and Quarantelli's *A Perspective on Disaster Planning* presents a detailed account of how people have actually behaved in and responded to various types of natural disasters.

At the heart of the argument supporting CRP for nuclear war lies the belief that the disaster resulting from a nuclear attack is fundamentally similar to other kinds of natural and manmade disasters. In *The Social Psychology of Civil Defense*, Perry espouses this philosophy and states its fundamental axiom as follows: "In the case of nuclear attack versus natural and technological disasters, the *within-category* variation is *at least equal* to the *between-category* variation." (Italics added.)[1] In other words, in terms of scale and impact, there is as much difference between large and small hurricanes as exists between nuclear war and other types of disaster. The implication of the argument is that a nuclear exchange may result in far more damage than a flood, but conversely, a massive tornado may produce greater destruction than a nuclear attack.

If nuclear war is then but a variation on natural and other manmade disasters, it follows that the planning techniques used to deal with such catastrophes are applicable to the nuclear war situation. According to

Perry, this would be the case but for the one way in which nuclear war *is* different from other kinds of disasters. He says that "the *unique* [italics added] aspect of nuclear attack (and all nuclear disasters for that matter) is that a nuclear component is involved, and special consideration is necessary because in terms of the way people *perceive* the situation, such circumstances are different from other types of disaster agents"[2]—that perception evokes fear and uncertainty primarily because of anxiety about the effects of radiation.[3] According to Perry, it is deeply held negative perceptions that get in the way of CRP. He asserts that as long as people maintain such views of nuclear attack, they will not engage in preparing for such a disaster in the same cooperative way in which they would prepare for a non-nuclear catastrophe. For Perry, then, what makes CRP unique is *not* the nature of the disaster being prepared for, but rather the impact of the *perceptual difference* between nuclear war and other disasters on the way people are likely to behave.

Thus, to carry out relocation planning for nuclear attack successfully, the federal government must change peoples' views of the character and consequences of such a catastrophe. The average citizen must come to view nuclear attack as simply a variation of disaster—albeit a serious one.

If people's perceptions can be brought around to this view, successful CRP can be carried out. For, the argument continues, past experience with natural disasters and the average citizen reaction to them reveals that the "popular image" of panic, people out of control, and the dissolution of order is not born out in reality.[4] *A Perspective on Disaster Planning* by Dynes, Quarantelli, and Kreps is a study undertaken for the Defense Civil Preparedness Agency (FEMA's predecessor); it paints a picture of low levels of panic, extensive cooperation, minimal vandalism, and heightened morale and selflessness. Dynes is talking specifically about natural disasters. However, this distinction is easy to overlook in the rush to evoke a positive image of CRP. Combining Dynes' assertions of the "positive response" to catastrophe with Perry's view that nuclear attack is like any other major natural or manmade disaster produces an upbeat scenario of CRP and nuclear war.

The response Dynes posits for natural disaster will be the same for a nuclear attack given that the structure and defining characteristics of such an event, perceptual differences aside, are similar to a natural disaster. Since people respond well to natural disasters, one can posit that they will react equally well to the survival demands of nuclear war.[5]

Having established that perception is all that stands between the theory of crisis relocation and its successful implementation, Perry moves on to the moral imperative of such planning: not only can crisis relocation be carried out, but normatively such planning is categorically requisite. As long as there is the possibility of saving any lives, there is a role for CRP.

> The critical question is not can one imagine a nuclear attack that could destroy all life; instead we must inquire whether one can imagine any instance of nuclear attack that would fail to destroy all life. If one can visualize a single attack situation in which some people somewhere in the United States could survive, then there is a role for emergency managers and consequently for a civil-defense program.[6]

He states also that "as long as *all* of the United States is not attacked simultaneously there is at least the possibility, if not the moral obligation to make some plans to protect and/or care for the parts of the population that are not directly attacked."[7]

The argument is now complete. CRP is not only possible; it is morally the only defensible strategy to undertake. All we have to fear is fear itself or, in this case, perception. Change that perception of the impact of nuclear war and CRP can be effectively implemented.

The justification for crisis relocation outlined above is fundamentally flawed in the following four ways:

1. The disaster flowing from nuclear attack is *not* like other kinds of natural or manmade disaster. Nuclear war is a "singularity"—a unique event that has the real potential and high probability of provoking a level and form of disaster totally without precedent or analogue in our experience of the natural or manmade world.

2. A strong case exists for the role of CRP in *furthering* rather than lessening the likelihood of nuclear attack.

3. Rather than being rooted in irrational fear and ungrounded dread, peoples' perceptions of the dangers of nuclear war are in fact highly sensible and a reasonable response to the realities of the situation.

4. The moral imperative of saving whatever lives may remain after a full-scale nuclear attack must be weighed against the moral imperative of avoiding the assault in the first place.

To develop the arguments that lie behind these four conclusions, this chapter will:

1. Examine the characteristics of disasters to test the validity of the assertion that "in the case of nuclear attack versus natural and technological disasters, the within-category variation is at least equal to the between-category variation."[8]

2. Analyze the conceptual framework used to structure the stages of disaster planning and the belief system underlying that framework.

3. Explore the relationship between risk assessment and the perception of disaster.

CHARACTERISTICS OF DISASTER

Perry and Dynes, Quarantelli, and Kreps list a number of characteristics of disaster. Three of these that are particularly relevant to our analysis are: scope of impact, secondary impacts, and predictability. To explore Perry's assertion that "the within-category variation is at least equal to the between-category variation," we need to look at the meaning of these three defining characteristics in each of three disaster settings: natural, technological, and nuclear attack.

Our central argument is that nuclear attack constitutes a singularity because of the huge scope of impact in terms of geographic area and people; the uncertain extent of secondary impacts—that is, radiation and the effects on the ecological system; and the degree to which predictability of nuclear attack is a function not of technology or natural forces to which probabilities can be assigned but rather of the unique dynamics of two factors: the international political system and the enormous unknowns surrounding the effects of these weapons. The radical difference between nuclear attack and all other types of disaster in the content of these three defining characteristics constitutes the basis for our argument that nuclear attack is a unique form of disaster—a singularity for which there is no parallel in the natural or manmade world.

Scope of Impact

Perry defines *scope of impact* as "a geographic reference indicating that impact involves a small area or only a few people (narrow impact) or a larger area or number of people (widespread impact)."[9] The meaning of "widespread" takes on a singular quality for a sustained nuclear attack in which the potential size of the affected area and the potential number of people involved have no historic precedent.

In his discussion of natural disasters, Dynes cautions that "disaster planning has to be realistic. . . . Persons with vivid imagination can always come up with hypothetical possibilities so horrendous that they serve to immobilize any effort at planning."[10]

Dynes' idea of "vivid imagination" is that of a "planner [who] visualized a situation where his community would have to handle 10,000 casualties. Such a problem boggles the mind. A catastrophe of this magnitude could conceivably happen but it is very unlikely in American society. The largest number of deaths in any given disaster were the 5,000 or so killed in the Galveston hurricane-flood of 1900."[11] A natural calamity that brings a hundred deaths is considered by Dynes to be a "major disaster."

The magnitude of the immediate deaths from a nuclear attack dwarfs to insignificance our experience with natural disasters. The vivid imagination of Dyne's disaster planner can be unleashed with no fear of underestimating reality. In a case study of the impact of a one-megaton bomb exploding over Detroit, the Office of Technology Assessment indicates that the attack will result in the instant death of 220,000 people. The figures rise if one considers a larger bomb and daytime conditions, when there are more people in the center of the city.[12]

It takes little imagination to see the enormous gap between the meaning in human terms of the scope of a natural disaster and a nuclear attack. Dynes' 10,000 person "fantasy" becomes but a small fraction of the deaths in a single isolated nuclear bomb explosion over Detroit. One bomb over one city is the lower end of the continuum for nuclear warfare. Colin Gray, now a member of the President's General Advisory Committee on Arms Control, has indicated that the loss of twenty million Americans "is an acceptable price for creating a post-war world order compatible with Western values."[13]

At the lower end of the nuclear attack continuum one *might* make the case that a single bomb attack on Detroit is like a nuclear plant accident that races to meltdown with little warning. However, it is variously estimated that even under the worst of circumstances, a disaster such as Three Mile Island threatened to be might result in the immediate deaths of 3,300 to 45,000 people living in the surrounding area.[14] The disjuncture in loss of life is between the smallest attack and the worst nuclear plant disaster imaginable. When one moves into war-fighting scenarios involving more than one bomb and more than one city, the comparison with the plant disaster loses all meaning. One enters a realm in which the scope of destruction resulting from nuclear attack is a singularity, a magnitude, and a dimension unique to itself.

As Perry is willing to admit:

In the case of a limited nuclear exchange, one might even argue that nuclear attack and hurricanes are similar in scope and impact. . . . [T]he destructive potential of a full-scale nuclear war, however, greatly exceeds the scope of impact for every other conceivable hazard agent. To the extent that a nuclear attack can result in the simultaneous destruction of many communities . . . it is a unique hazard event.[15]

Yet this recognition of the singularity represented by a full-scale nuclear attack on the United States does not inform Perry's general argument that nuclear war fighting is just another form of disaster. He does not acknowledge that in the case of an extended nuclear exchange between the superpowers the consequences would at minimum be a radical transformation of society. No other known form of disaster has even the remotest probability, let alone the distinct possibility, of producing such a singular transformation.

Secondary Impacts

Disasters leave secondary impacts in their wakes. As Perry points out, these are often "more devastating than the initial impact."[16] Floods result in debris and silt; earthquakes create fires and public health risks. However, disasters resulting from unleashed nuclear force have a chillingly unique characteristic: they involve radiation. Radiation is an issue in both nuclear attack and nuclear plant disasters. What makes the radiation component of a nuclear attack different from that of a plant accident is its potential scope. Even a moderate nuclear attack on the United States would blanket the continent with potentially lethal levels of radiation.[17] As Perry acknowledges, "while most disasters involve secondary impacts, the nature of those posed by nuclear attack is unique both in form (radiation) and also in the very long time frame during which it continues to constitute a hazard or threat."[18] Once again, the logic of his own argument about the uniqueness of nuclear attack eludes Perry. He goes on in the next paragraph to postulate that disasters differ "as much among themselves as they differ from nuclear attack."[19]

In addition to radiation, however, it is important to mention the potential secondary effects of a major nuclear attack on the entire ecological system. While the debates continue as to the magnitude of these impacts (e.g., what percentage of the atmospheric ozone layers will be destroyed?),[20] few would dispute that there is the potential for a devastating impact on the ecosystem; that the uncertainties surrounding such impacts are of a singular nature; and that the possibilities are high for serious long-term damage to that system.

Predictability

Predictability is that disaster characteristic dealing with the degree to which "the current level of technology permits us to anticipate or predice a threatened disaster impact."[21] Two aspects of predictability are embedded in this definition. The first is the predictability of the disaster occurring. We can predict a flood if the water level gets above a known point. Certain geographic areas at particular times of the year have a high probability of hurricanes. As Dynes pointed out, "for some weather phenomena, it is possible to obtain for specific localities the gross probabilities of a particular disaster agent striking the given area."[22] A nuclear plant can be predicted to malfunction if specific elements go awry in combination with each other. Predictability has to do with probability of occurrence—probability informed by experience and scientific indication.

The second aspect of predictability focuses on the level of impact of a disaster. Based on experience, one can estimate a relationship between severity of flood—i.e., how high, how fast, how wide—and the destruction that the deluge leaves in its wake. There is a predictability about what elements will be entrained in a disaster and the boundaries of its impact. In the years of flooding in the Tennessee Valley area prior to the establishment of the Tennessee Valley Authority, it was estimated that there were limits beyond which even the worst floods would not go.

In summary, one can predict with measured probability the outer limits of natural and manmade disaster impact. The exceptional hurricane, the monster cyclone, the totally uncontrolled nuclear plant meltdown constitute end-game situations. Yet even these events can be estimated from experience or derived from principles of science and comparison.

Predictability of both the occurrence and impact of nuclear attack is different from other kinds of prediction for two fundamental reasons: (1) It is human decision rather than the whim of nature or the failure of technology that initiates the disaster of nuclear attack and determines how wide its scope will be, and (2) predictability implies some set of events from which to establish probabilities. However, we have no experience with nuclear fighting and therefore no empirical basis upon which to ground that prediction.

Whether or not a nuclear attack will occur and how wide its scope will be is a function, in the first instance, not of rampant nature or technical miscalculation, but rather the political processes governing international relationships. One looks not to the meteorologists, the engineers, or the scientists for estimates as to when and how big a nuclear attack will be, but rather to the diplomats involved in the complex human drama of superpower diplomacy.

Human intentionality determines the timing, the speed of onset, and the initial scope of impact. The extended scope of impact and the duration of the disaster it produces are a function of complex unknowns. The characteristics of a natural disaster are locked into the forces of nature; the logic of physics determines the characteristics of a nuclear power plant failure. The characteristics of a nuclear war begin in the hands of the war fighters and then extend beyond control and predictability.

The experience we have had with using nuclear weapons in wartime is summed up in two words: Hiroshima and Nagasaki. Those events have been studied with all the devices of modern science to determine the impact of the bombs on people and property. But as to the predictability of the scope, duration, and impact of nuclear war fighting, we have no empirical knowledge. All of these take place in the unknown. Nuclear attack represents a singular event about which we can only guess, surmise, and project our own view of probability. As James Fallows points out in *National Defense* when discussing the likely impact of nuclear weapons in a first strike scenario: "The overwhelming impression that comes from talks with those who design, maintain, and test nuclear weapons . . . is the uncertainty of it all. The most important questions about how weapons work cannot be conclusively answered until they are fired."[23]

Fallows is focusing specifically on the issue of weapon accuracy, but his emphasis on the "uncertainty of it all" applies to all aspects of nuclear war fighting. What is the true impact of a 6,000-megaton attack on the environment, the tree cover, the ozone layer? What are the long-term effects of the radiation released by such an attack? What will determine whether the nuclear attack will be limited or protracted? One can only speculate about these questions. The nuclear theologians, as Fallows calls them, have their internally consistent scenarios, but nuclear attack doctrines and their assigned probabilities are, according to Fallows, "an act of faith, for the doctrines and theories are pure theology."[24] Speculation and opinion rather than probability is at the center of prediction about the nature and impact of nuclear war, thus making the meaning of the term "prediction" categorically different from its usage in other forms of disaster.

CONCEPTUAL FRAMEWORK OF
DISASTER PLANNING

Disasters as we have experienced them arise from natural events or technological failures. Organizing society to deal with the effects of disasters on people and property has become increasingly sophisticated as concepts of "good" disaster planning have emerged and the public and private roles in that planning have developed.

Four stages of disaster planning are posited in the literature: mitigation, preparedness, response, and recovery.[25] Actions appropriate to each phase are articulated as follows:

Mitigation focuses on what can be done to prevent a disaster from taking place. Mitigation efforts include analyzing hazards and vulnerability (e.g., how likely it is that a flash flood will occur in a certain canyon), establishing warning, communications, and public information systems so that the occurrence of an event can be predicted and announced at the earliest possible point, and elaborating legal and technical constraints aimed at prevention—for example, land-use laws, building codes, and insurance requirements.

Preparedness efforts are directed at minimizing the impact of a disaster should mitigation fail and a disaster indeed occur. Elements of preparedness planning include deciding what resources are needed for a given disaster, organizing liaison teams, defining emergency procedures, developing and disseminating information to the public about how to respond to a range of disasters, and developing fail-safe technologies designed to intervene sequentially in the event of an initial systems failure.

Response efforts are invoked once a disaster has occurred. Their form and content are determined by the preparedness planning that has taken place. As the elements of response evolve, they become the major determinants in reducing the immediate impact of the disaster. Response efforts include assigning equipment to tasks (demolition, extraction, fire fighting), maintaining public order and law enforcement, and gathering and releasing public and technical information in ways that reduce disaster impact and speed relief efforts.

Recovery marshals resources from the outside to the disaster area in order to return the environment, infrastructure, economy, and population to their pre-disaster state as quickly and efficiently as possible. Components include evaluating capability (what can the outside bring in), assessing damage (what has taken place and what is needed), and defining and setting up an organizational locus and liaison network to direct and coordinate recovery efforts.

A complex set of factors influences the relative weight given to each of the four stages in a particular disaster situation. Common to all four stages of disaster management, however, are four assumptions about the nature of disasters and the world in which they occur. Derived from our experience with disasters, the following assumptions undergird the way we frame the problem of disaster planning:

1. Predictability of disaster characteristics;
2. Applicability of technical rationality;

3. Opportunity for sequential intervention; and

4. Persistence of a world outside the disaster area.

Central to the argument that nuclear attack constitutes a singularity is the view that neither the conceptual framework structuring the stages of disaster planning nor the belief system underlying that framework can "work" as described above when the disaster under consideration is a nuclear attack.

Predictability of Disaster Characteristics

We assume, on the basis of past experience, that there is a known probability about the likelihood of disaster occurring in a given setting and a predictability about the disaster's characteristics: scope of impact and secondary impacts. As discussed, the meaning of these characteristics for the disaster ensuing from a nuclear attack is qualitatively and quantitatively different from that of other categories of disaster. Prediction about the characteristics of a nuclear attack is based not on experience but rather on induction from a set of political and military assumptions.

To regard the disaster resulting from nuclear war as the end of humanity is as reasonable a view of outcome as is to argue that nuclear war can be limited and contained. Predictability is in the eye of the predictor. The limits of our experience with natural and technological disasters do not help to frame the defining characteristics of the disaster of nuclear war.

The uncertainties involved in predicting the characteristics of nuclear war throw the process of civil defense planning into equal uncertainty. What assumptions should planners make about the size of a nuclear attack, the speed of its onset, its duration, its impact on the natural environment? In the absence of logical self-limits to nuclear war, other than total destruction, one set of assumptions seems as valid as another. This lack of natural boundaries makes those that are established subject to critique. The uniqueness of the nuclear attack scenario lies in the fact that if one prepares for anything but the worst case, the consequences of being wrong would be enormous. The level of death and destruction, should a limited nuclear exchange escalate to sequential retaliation, is without parallel.

All four stages of disaster planning are plagued by the issue of predictability, for the fact is that the timing, scope, and duration of a nuclear attack are a function not of natural events or technological malfunction with precedents in past experience, but rather of complex political interactions and weapons effects which, once unleashed, enter a realm we have not seen and so do not understand.

Applicability of Technical Rationality

In conventional disasters, planning can be viewed as a rational response to a natural or technologically induced event. Good disaster planning constitutes the application of the best-known theories of organization, mobilization, and communication to the actual practice of disaster management. CRP is presented as a technical means of coping with the set of institutional, economic, and public health issues involved in planning for a nuclear attack disaster—an instrumental, politically neutral response to the demands of a particular kind of catastrophe. In fact, however, CRP participates in creating the political climate that increases the probability of nuclear war.

A critical aspect of disaster planning for nuclear attack that is mentioned only in passing by Perry and not at all by Dynes is the relationship between that planning and the disaster itself. Does *planning* for an orderly response to disaster in some way affect the likelihood or the character of the disaster being planned for? Philip Herr (see Chapter 5) makes the following points regarding this issue:

> Hurricanes clearly are not made more or less likely by planning response to them. Flooding, however, *may* be made more likely if reliance on . . . an evacuation plan substitutes for developing structural control, such as dams. Acceptance of unworkable paper plans for emergency response allows nuclear plants to be built and thereby increases the very risk the plans are designed to reduce.

There is a close analogy between the acceptance of unworkable paper plans for emergency response, which allows a nuclear plant to be built and "thereby increases the very risk the plans are designed to reduce," and the acceptance of CRP as a defense against nuclear attack, which thereby makes nuclear war fighting seem all the more survivable. CRP for nuclear attack is not simply a technical response to a potential disaster; it is directly related to the disaster it has been created to prevent. This direct relationship is most acutely found at the mitigation stage.

Since mitigation focuses on what can be done to prevent a disaster, those who argue for CRP posit that the existence of such a plan will decrease the likelihood of nuclear attack. They believe that a fully developed plan will convey to the Soviet Union the seriousness of our intention to proceed with the use of nuclear weapons, if necessary, and the comprehensiveness of our capacity to withstand and survive an attack, if forthcoming.[26] Thus, such planning is seen to reinforce our strategic bluff—the perceptual slight of hand that constitutes deterrence. The argument can be made with at least equal merit (since we are dealing in the realm of theory and speculation) that because the Soviet Union may perceive our planning as provocative, CRP may positively influence, or increase, the probability of nuclear war. Strengthening a strategic bluff only reduces the probability of war if the other side is less willing than we are to go to war to attain its goals. And in a world where the doctrine of deterrence is being eroded by notions of nuclear war fighting, the existence of a U.S. plan, touted as promoting survival after nuclear attack, might be viewed by the Soviets as an indication that the United States is entertaining thoughts of launching a first strike. It could also reinforce a tendency in Soviet thinking that if destructive advantage had any validity at all, it would lie in a surprise Soviet attack, prior to initiation of U.S. evacuation measures.

One cannot think of a disaster situation other than nuclear attack in which efforts undertaken to lessen the likelihood of the disaster occurring can be argued to increase the probability of such an event. As Herr points out, one can envisage a situation in which faulty mitigation strategies contribute to the impact of a disaster. The dam does not work as predicted. The floodplain is too narrowly defined, and zoning permits construction in a vulnerable area. But nowhere except in nuclear attack disaster planning can one make a strong case for the view that the more successful the mitigation strategy—that is, the better and more complete the overall CRP planning—the greater the likelihood of triggering disaster.

Perry acknowledges that "unfortunately, in the case of nuclear attack, unlike natural disasters, there is a political dimension to preparedness that may indeed lend some credibility to such arguments,"[27] that is, that planning influences the likelihood of disaster.

The "political dimension of preparedness" for nuclear attack is a critical issue. To the degree that both the federal government and the American people come to believe they have a preparedness system that can adequately blunt the impact of nuclear attack, they may be willing to participate in a nuclear war. The probability of war is increased to the degree that disaster planning is perceived as being effective.

Opportunity for Sequential Intervention

We assume that a natural or technological disaster takes place in stages, which can be defined in terms of time and space. On the basis of empirical observation, we assume that there is an ultimately self-limiting quality about disasters; they can be seen as having a beginning, a series of evolving characteristics, and a finite duration. However divergent their manifestations, disasters are also understood as occurring within a limited geographical area. Disaster management plans assume this limited, sequential nature of disasters. All mitigation, preparedness, and response-recovery efforts are based on the assumption that some disasters can be prevented from spreading; were they to occur, preparation can reduce consequences because there would be time to marshal resources between occurrences and full impact; response-recovery efforts have relevance because at some point, within the geographical confines of the disaster site, the disaster can be said to "be over." In the case of floods, heavy rains begin; a high water alert is given; dams upstream are assessed; in apprehension, people begin to leave downstream areas; the dams break; a flood occurs; flood waters spread to adjacent areas; depending on response efforts and further rains, the waters recede; recovery measures continue. During all four stages of disaster management, the opportunity exists for intervention and for focused allocation of community resources designed to reduce impact. The singularity of a nuclear attack disaster invalidates this concept of sequential intervention for two reasons: the instantaneous magnitude of destruction and the political rather than technical nature of such intervention.

If a full-scale nuclear attack were to occur, continental or global devastation would be accomplished in a matter of hours or, at most, days. In a surprise first strike, the stages of preparedness and response would be melded together in the heat of the thermonuclear blast. The nature of total devastation surrounding ground zero would render meaningless the concepts of intervention and responsiveness central to ordinary disaster planning. Orderly progression of stages of disaster planning would fall by the wayside. Efforts to reduce the impact of the nuclear attack through prompt responsive measures would be of minimal value. Unlike technological disasters that might be modified by intervention after the onset of occurrence (such as a nuclear power plant accident), nuclear attack allows for no such phased interaction with the cause of the disaster.

Intervention to slow down or stop a nuclear assault is a function not of technical expertise, as in the case of nuclear plant malfunction, or of nature taking its course, as with a flood, but rather the political agenda of the United States, and Soviet Union, and other possible combatants. Whether the bombs keep dropping or the rubble is bounced another time, the disaster area widens as a function of diplomatic and military interactions over which the disaster planners have no control. Intervention to limit the scope of the catastrophe is a function not of disaster planning and execution of those plans, but rather of a distant and unrelated set of actors. Until that system successfully concludes the hostilities, disaster management will be frozen in the response phase—the phase least able to cope, given the nature of the devastation wrought by the nuclear weapons.

Persistence of a World outside the Disaster Area

We assume, in all disaster planning, that there remains an outside, unaffected world from which to launch disaster management. Particularly at the response-recovery stage, planning presumes the persistence of an outside source of supplies and personnel. This outside is also assumed to be larger in area, richer in resources, and more capable of organized relief effort than is the area hit by disaster. In past experience the outside source of relief, when compared to disasters creating even the most staggering misery, has always had the capacity to respond at some level to the demands of the stricken area. In all disasters of recent history for which there has been access to sufficient information, there has always remained an outside, which supplied and supported response and recovery efforts. In isolated areas of devastation (concentration camps, cities under siege, riots along the Hindu-Moslem borders at Partition, famine in the Sahel), the perception of an outside source of relief may have waned and the effectiveness of intervention appeared meager. Had political realities permitted the world to concentrate relief efforts on those areas of distress, however, the calamities need not have been so severe and protracted. The extent to which the immediate or full transfer of resources may not take place reflects geopolitical constraints, not demand reaching the ultimate limit of supply. In all disaster management, the potential to transfer sufficient resources from an outside remains assumed. To paraphrase Gertrude Stein, there is always a "there" there.

A nuclear war on the scale envisioned both by those who plan to fight one and those who plan to prevent one would engulf entire continents in destruction of unsurpassed extent and intensity, obliterating persistence of an outside. All those who survived the immediate effects would be trapped in the same grim circumstances. Survivors could not look to the arrival of equipped and trained personnel bringing resources from unaffected areas. Flight would hold no options, all regions having suffered attack. All factors sustaining essential components of society—industry, transport, communications, medical care, agriculture—would have been extensively damaged or destroyed.

From the standpoint of either scale or time, there exists no precedent in world history for such a disaster. The historical record indicates that the plague took the lives of approximately one-third of the population of Europe over a five-year period; in six years, World War II claimed the lives of thirty to forty million people. In both instances, the environment and social and economic infrastructure, except for discrete, isolated areas when viewed on the global scale, remained relatively intact. The deaths and the devastation took place in different areas at different times, and response and recovery could be organized from regions outside the perimeter of acute effects.

From the perspective of the response and recovery stages of disaster planning, the absence of an outside from which help can be drawn constitutes the most fundamental way in which nuclear attack differs from all other forms of disaster. One cannot overstate the degree to which nuclear attack obliterates these two stages of disaster management. The singularity of catastrophe represented by protracted nuclear exchange finds its ultimate symbol in the obliteration of the concept of a helping external world.

RISK ASSESSMENT AND THE PERCEPTION OF DISASTER

Assessing disaster management strategies of mitigation, preparedness, response, and recovery culminates in perceptions of risk. Perceptions of risk in turn determine the stance we take toward a particular disaster, whether it is associated with the use of a particular technology or with settlement of an environment. We define the term "risk" as a weighted summation of the assumed characteristics of a particular disaster. People assess the risk of a disaster by considering, on the basis of their experience, the probability of occurrence, the predictability of its impact, our capacity to intervene, and the availability of outside resources. In this assessment, people weigh the finite risk of disaster they assume is associated with choosing to reside in an area or choosing to use a technology, and the benefits they assume are bestowed by those choices. The fact that tornadoes occasionally sweep Kansas has not prevented settlement; despite varying estimates of earthquake probability along the San Andreas Fault, people are not leaving California; nuclear power plants are still in operation with the probability of a severe core meltdown estimated from 0.1 to 10 percent per power plant by the year 2000.[28]

In all these disaster situations, our assumptions about the characteristics of disasters and our capacities to cope shape our perceptions of risk and allow us to calculate whether, on balance, using a technology or settling in an environment is worth the risk of whatever disaster might be associated with that choice.

These calculations of risk are not simply scientific exercises. People have different interests in calculating risks of a disaster. If a particular interest group stands to gain by the use of a technology or settlement of an environment, both the actual risk and the perception of risk can be altered. Serious mitigation and preparedness efforts can reduce the probability of occurrence and consequences of impact and thus reduce the actual risk of a disaster. A campaign that minimizes probability of occurrence, exaggerates capacity to intervene, and magnifies the domain of the outside can alter perceptions of risk and persuade people to adopt a course more filled with actual risk than they perceive it to be. Such a campaign might have the adverse effect of influencing either the probability that a disaster will occur or the extent to which the disaster will be devastating. For example, if people were persuaded to believe that nuclear power plants operated without high probability of accident, regulator vigilance would abate and the possibility of an accident occurring would increase.

In the context of nuclear weapons, definitions of benefits and risks derive from sources very different from those that define these factors for other technologies. The benefit, or utility, of a nuclear power plant rests in its use, not its possession. It is the use of this technology, not its mere presence on the landscape, that is considered a benefit to society. According to the doctrine of deterrence, the benefit, or utility, of nuclear weapons lies not in their use, which was conceded to have horrible consequences, but in their possession, backed, to a varying degree, by implicit or explicit threats of use. The possession of this technology, not its use, was seen as ensuring conditions for world peace. Current concepts of nuclear war strategy, however, relying on the use of nuclear weapons as the source of security, erode deterrence theory. Nuclear weapons are viewed increasingly as simply one more technology whose use, in certain circumstances, might represent a rational option.

As current political considerations in the U.S. government have begun to alter perceptions of the utility of nuclear weapons, CRP has been introduced to alter perceptions of risk. Perceptions of the risk in using a technology are based in part on assessments of the probability that in its use the technology will result in disaster and in part on the extent to which mitigation and preparedness efforts can reduce both the probability that a disaster will occur and its impact if it were to occur. Perceptions of risk and perceptions of benefit also interact in that the more useful a technology is perceived as being, the greater the tendency to discount concerns that it might be unsafe.

The perceived safety of a nuclear power plant lies in estimates that the probability of disaster is low, not in assessments of how well interventions and preparedness can compensate for the disaster that might occur. Phrased in these terms, if the Nuclear Regulatory Commission were to acknowledge that the probability of a severe core meltdown from the use of nuclear power were one in ten, or even one in one hundred, it is highly unlikely that popular resistance to the use of this technology could be assuaged by detailing plans to cope with the results of the disaster that would probably occur.

Since it is clear to all that the use of nuclear weapons carries an overwhelming probability of enormous disaster—not one in one hundred or one in ten but one in one—it would appear impossible to perceive any safety in the use of this technology. Because the government has acquired an enhanced strategic perception of the utility of using these weapons, however, it becomes in its interest to discourage public perception that the use of this technology might also be associated with profound risk. CRP, viewed as a program of public education, is one of the ways in which perceptions of risk, as they apply to the use of nuclear weapons, are being redefined. From the standpoint of civil defense planning for nuclear war, no claims are made that the risk in the use of nuclear weapons is slight or that the disaster of nuclear war can remain very limited. What is claimed, however, is that with effective preparedness, the consequences of the disaster can be so reduced and recovery so ensured that the use of nuclear weapons, if not perceived as safe, can at least be viewed as acceptable.

We can see in Perry's discussion of perception the critical way in which CRP has become an exercise in reducing the perception of risk rather than the actual level of risk associated with nuclear war. He minimizes the significance of this perception difference on the questions of disaster similarity by stating:

> Of course, the idea—or realization—that people have a different mind set for disasters where the hazard agent is nuclear certainly does not preclude comparisons with natural disasters. Instead, it only requires that this *emotional* dimension be recognized at the outset and that the necessary qualifications be made when such perceptual differences may have some bearing upon expected human performance. (Italics added.)[29]

His message is clear: From a planning perspective, the real difference between nuclear attack and other kinds of disasters lies not in objective differences but rather in the domain of emotions, of perception. The difference is in the eye of the beholder, not in the disaster itself. From a planning perspective, he appears to be less interested in whether CRP is a realistic disaster management strategy for nuclear war than he is in persuading people to go along with it. To get people to participate in CRP requires that the perception be changed. In Perry's judgment people misperceive the nature of nuclear attack and are in error to shrink from it in fear.

We come to a very different conclusion. To perceive nuclear war as terrible and destructive is not illusory or grandiose. This perception is rooted in a fundamental, common sense evaluation of the potential total holocaust associated with a major nuclear attack. The initial destruction, the secondary impacts, the unknown effects on the ecological system, and the uncertainty about how devastating the impact of radiation will be all combine to make fear a legitimate response. What needs to be changed is not popular perceptions about the risks of nuclear war, which are quite accurate, but the political climate promoting the probability that we might try to fight one. Contributing to that climate are sophistic arguments that blur the singularity of nuclear war and attempt to hide it among the crowd of ordinary disasters.

In summary, CRP is a flawed, unworkable, and dishonest response to the threat of nuclear war. To the extent that it is all these things it cannot defend against the ravages of that disaster. Worse, however, is that if people become convinced, that is, perceive, that CRP reduces the risk of nuclear war, their anxieties may be diminished. They may acquiesce to war-fighting strategies and not insist that the nation's leaders engage in the only mitigating strategy that makes sense for the disaster of nuclear war. Faced with a disaster of overwhelming consequences, the appropriate mitigation strategy is not to pretend to develop a preparedness plan that in reality cannot cope. In the setting of nuclear war, the only mitigating strategy is prevention. To prevent nuclear war from ever taking place, nuclear weapons must be reduced in number and their use eliminated. CRP, far from presenting a valid disaster management strategy for nuclear war, distracts us from the only one there is.

2

Faith in the Rational Leap: Social Science Research and Crisis Relocation Planning

Donald A. Schön

Who is it that darkeneth counsel
by words without knowledge?
                    Job 38:2

Our purpose, as we have said, has been to develop a perspective against which to view the *amount* of destruction, but we have also wanted to develop one that will serve when we come to consider the sorts of imbalances, or disparities, that nuclear attacks might produce. In this latter connection, we wanted especially to take note of disasters that involved survival disparities of varied sorts. Those just reviewed meet this second objective along with the first. We shall return to the disparities involved later.

We shift our attention, now, from catastrophes that have actually been experienced to some purely hypothetical ones of the kind that nuclear war might produce. The similarities and contrasts are of some interest. . . .

For introductory purposes the magnitudes of the disasters implied by our hypothetical nuclear attacks can perhaps best be conveyed in terms of a single dimension. We shall eventually discuss each of 28 dimensions (i.e., populations) for which attack outcomes have been calculated with our apparatus. But to begin with we limit our exposition to the one most frequently discussed in other studies: the number—or, alternatively, the proportion—of people surviving.

Since even the brief sketches that we have just presented of historic catastrophes provide much richer detail than this, readers may feel uncomfort-

24

able with the change. Some may even suspect that description in only one dimension is utterly unsuitable for such a complex subject, and hence bound to be unfruitful. (It is, indeed, a little like restricting a description of apple pie to specifics about what fraction of the apple is used.) There are some advantages to beginning this way, however. Doing so will make it possible to appraise the influences of some important variables before these are obscured by clutter. And, after all, in this report the limitation will be temporary.

SOURCE: Norman Hanunian, *Dimensions of Survival: Postattack Survival Disparities and National Viability*, Rand Corporation, Santa Monica, Calif., 1966, pp. 19–20.

Although the studies done by the Disaster Research Center and others have dispelled the myths associated with peoples' behavior during a disaster, if the causative agent of the incident were radiation, would peoples' reactions be substantially different? The conclusion drawn by many is that because radiation is largely an unknown quantity, imperceptible to the ordinary senses, inherently, the fear of the unknown and its consequences would cause a different behavior pattern—perhaps similar to popular notions. This would, in turn, have a dramatic effect on evacuation involving a release of radioactivity.

Dr. Russell R. Dynes, Co-Director of the Disaster Research Center, was asked if he thought people would react differently—panic—because of a radiation threat. Dr. Dynes' reply was that there has been an overemphasis placed on the qualitative difference between radiation and other threats by both public officials and anti-nuclear groups, "What was assumed was that the nuclear advent represented some new juncture in human history and, therefore, it would evoke and demand a quite different level of human behavior." Dr. Dynes continued, "As I read history, there is not reason to suggest that because of the presence of a new 'order' of threat that human behavior would disintegrate into 'uncivilized' behavior."

The summation of Dr. Dynes' reply is that there is not reason to expect that people will react any differently because the disaster agent is radiation than they would for a flood, fire, or any other type of causative agent. This "normal" behavior is amply documented and does not include panic.

Dr. Dynes further states:

If your concern is primarily with evacuation, there is good reason to suggest that the problem in evacuation is not one of panic flight but the problem of getting people to move at all. The question of the perception of threat is a very complicated one and is not as obvious as many people assume it to be.

SOURCE: Joseph M. Hans, Jr., and Thomas C. Sell, *Evacuation Risks—An Evaluation*, U.S. Environmental Protection Agency, Las Vegas, 1974, p. 47.

INTRODUCTION

The government-sponsored literature on the impacts of nuclear war, the possibilities and problems of crisis relocation, and the policies and programs of civil defense all reveal, in a particularly vivid manner, the salient features of what, in the 1950s, 1960s, and 1970s, and still to some extent at present, has been the main way of applying social science research to social problems.

In the context of nuclear cataclysm, the outlines of applied social research methodology stand out in relief: its questionable premises and doubtful assertions, its unstated articles of faith, its blithe dismissal of important sources of uncertainty. Thus, to analyze the government-sponsored literature on nuclear cataclysm is to analyze the prevailing paradigm of applied social research—and especially, the particular form taken by that paradigm in the hands of the systems analysts. It is not at all clear that the defects of the paradigm—that is, of applied social research as a form of Technical Rationality—are any more significant for our appreciation of the issue of nuclear cataclysm than they are significant for any other social issue. But they are more nakedly visible. Their incongruity with common sense is more apparent and far less tolerable. The pretensions of professional expertise, based upon that paradigm, are far more offensive and far less believable.

Similarly, the necessary second question—"What else is there?"—is no more imperative in the case of nuclear cataclysm than in any other case. Yet our need to ask it is far more intense because of the overwhelming, very nearly unbearable magnitude of the question. What is the alternative to the technical-rational paradigm of the applied social researchers? If we reject the systems analysts' approach to the problem, what alternative approach remains? Are we thrown back on "common sense," "humanitarian feeling," and "natural intuition"? What kind of thinking is left to us? What way of reasoning? What approach to the gathering and interpretation of data, the framing of policy questions and problems, the recognition of and response to unpredictability, uncertainty, indeterminancy, and uniqueness?

Martin Rein and I have attempted to wrestle with these questions in the relatively quiet backwaters of social policy. Our work together has led us to pay attention to the ways in which social questions and problems are framed—that is, how social policy analysts and advocates construct coherent meanings for the problematic situations with which they deal, how they identify and group the "things" to which they pay attention, how they set the problems to which their analyses represent strategies of solution. We have argued for a kind of social research more nearly grounded in the practice of policy debate; on the one hand, more closely connected to practice, and, on the other, more reflective on the divergent frames that constitute the structure of policy controversy. We have called this sort of social research "frame-reflective." (Rein, in some of his writings, has used the closely allied term "value-critical.")

My long-term goal is to undertake a frame-reflective analysis of the controversy over the impacts of nuclear war and, more specifically, over the feasibility of relocation and sheltering under conditions of nuclear attack. My ultimate intent is twofold—first, to surface the divergent frames inherent in the controversy, and second, to propose frame-reflective research as a way of doing social research alternative to the ways of research and framing the question implicit in the writings of the applied social researchers and systems analysts. For purposes of this paper, however, I will focus on the survivalist studies and the way in which their authors "frame" their research agendas.

THE CONTROVERSY

In the controversy over the impacts of nuclear war, lines are closely drawn between the "survivalists," who see nuclear war as one disaster among others, and those who see nuclear war as a singular, cataclysmic event. Prominent among the survivalists are those who write, under government contract, in support of the main tenets of current U.S. government policy: they argue for the necessity of a strong civil defense program that would promote crisis relocation for large-scale populations, in anticipation of a nuclear attack. On the whole, they are systems analysts and applied social researchers who have framed the issue in terms of their disciplines and research methodologies. They differ in the particular topic to which they pay attention (severity of the impact of a nuclear attack, for example, or feasibility of evacuation in a nuclear crisis), and they differ in the particular discipline or methodology they employ (economic analysis, for example, or social psychology). Nevertheless, they are strikingly similar in their ways of framing the problem and in their main lines of argument.

Proponents of the "cataclysmic" view come from various disciplinary and professional backgrounds. Some are journalists, physicians, physical scientists; others are social scientists, or planners. They write, without government support, against current government policy and against the survivalist essays of their social scientific colleagues.

Of the many survivalist writings, I have selected three that appear to be reasonably good specimens of the genre: *Dimensions of Survival: Postattack Survival Disparities and National Viability*, a Rand Corporation report written by Norman Hanunian for the Technical Analysis Branch of the United States Atomic Energy Commission; *Evacuation Risks—An Evaluation*, a report to the U.S. Environmental Protection Agency's Office of Radiation Programs, by Joseph M. Hans, Jr. and Thomas C. Sell; and *The Social Psychology of Civil Defense*, a study by Ronald W. Perry, based on research supported by the National Science Foundation's Division of Civil and Environmental Engineering.

THE SURVIVALIST STUDIES

Each of the studies I shall consider addresses a specific topic drawn from the family of topics central to the survivalist point of view. Moreover, each was written at a different time in the period from 1966 and 1979. The Hanunian report, published in 1966, explores "the *compositional* changes that massive nuclear attack might produce in America's societal structure."[1] The study by Hans and Sell, written in 1974, analyzes the risks of "death, major injury and cost" associated with the evacuation of population groups from a nuclear "impact area."[2] Perry's report, first published in 1979, is "an attempt to determine what can be learned from studies of evacuation in natural disasters that is of use in understanding citizen warning response in connection with nuclear attack."[3] Considering the different times at which they were written, the different topics they address, and the different backgrounds of their authors, the three studies demonstrate impressive homogeneity and continuity in the survivalist writings of applied social researchers.

The Hanunian Report

Hanunian places his study in the context of a growing social scientific literature concerned with "predicting whether a postattack society would be viable."[4] His contribution, as he sees it, will be to provide "a much more elaborate appreciation of what might survive than can be gotten by reference to analyses so far reported."[5] His concern is specifically directed to the question of the survivability of the U.S. economy in the aftermath of a nuclear attack and, more specifically still, to the "compositional changes" that a massive nuclear attack might produce.

To begin with, he locates his question in the context of other great calamities—the fourteenth century plague, Japan's wartime losses, wartime losses in Eastern Europe—all of which the affected societies have endured and survived. His primary methodological tool is a model. Simulated nuclear attacks of various magnitudes and directions are launched against plausible simulated targets consisting of a geographic distribution of various populations (humans, animals, and capital goods) in the United States. Estimates are then made of survival rates of capital equipment and of the various populations, by such categories as young and elderly, urban and rural, income levels, and geographic region. These direct demographic effects of simulated nuclear attacks are then translated into estimates of survival rates, under various attacks, of certain "broad economic entities"—that is, labor and capital in regional and sectoral economies. A "well-tried production function"—the Cobb-Douglas function—is used to calculate the "outputs that could be produced if labor and capital were no longer available in their usual amounts."[6]

Conclusions from Hanunian's "runs" of his model are of the following sorts:

• Capital would "tend to fare (much better) than labor under any attack where fallout had to be contended with," with the "interesting result" that "output per worker could be much larger than in preattack circumstances."[7]

• "[I]nsofar as output on the farm is determined by the availability of farm labor and farm capital, it is only an exceptional attack that would discriminate against it."[8]

• "[A]griculture's fate would not be overly dependent on the level of survival elsewhere in the U.S. economy."[9]

A careful reading of Hanunian's report creates a strong sense of paradox. On the one hand, he goes to great pains to present his enterprise as a technical, scientific one; he sees himself as a competent professional conforming to the methodological canons of his profession. He wants to make his methods of analysis explicit, to tailor his conclusions to his data, to make the residual uncertainties clear. Moreover, he seems not to be willing to function merely as an instrument of the sponsoring bureaucracy. He appears to take pleasure, for example, in criticizing Herman Kahn's doctrine of the "two countries" in *On Thermonuclear War*— Country A and Country B, the one destroyed by a nuclear attack, the other surviving it.[10] Hanunian uses his data to show that the surviving "country" may be in many respects not a country at all—whole regions, income groups, age groups, and even family members being likely to be torn from the whole.

On the other hand, Hanunian allows himself to draw survivalist conclusions of the sorts illustrated above in the face of uncertainties, many of which he lists explicitly, that would appear to make such inferences totally unfounded. How does he reconcile his claims to scientific reasoning with his willingness to make shockingly unfounded inferences? He employs a variety of procedural, theoretical, and methodological "moves" that are worth documenting in some detail.

To begin with, he sets a very special problem. He does not attempt to estimate the magnitude of the impact of nuclear attacks on the U.S. economy, but only to estimate the *relative* impacts of such attacks, especially on farm and nonfarm sectors of the economy. His main analytic thrust is directed against those who argue that the vulnerability of the farm economy to nuclear attack would undermine the survivability of the economy as a whole. His final claim is not that our economy as a whole is likely to survive such attacks, but that its survival is not preferentially dependent on the limiting vulnerability of the farm economy. In effect, he decomposes the global problem of socioeconomic survival in order to structure a professionally manageable task—a specialized task that he can see himself performing credibly without having to work out the global question. "While estimates of conceivable postattack states of the economy are subject to many reservations," he says, "most of the reservations are of relatively little concern so long as our interest is in the unevenness of survival and not in its absolute kind."[11]

He eschews the worst case on the grounds that there would be nothing left to analyze. "Our interest was directed," he points out, "at evaluating the spectrum of possibilities and we were constrained from extending the range of attack weights considered only by the futility of analyzing cases in which virtually everyone, or no one, would survive."[12]

In his modeling of the interaction of "attack patterns" and "target systems," he identifies a number of potentially confounding uncertainties, which he then dismisses either by making radically simplifying assumptions about them or by deciding to ignore them. For example:

• In his simulation of "attacks," he assumes the strategic rationality of the enemy decisionmakers who choose what kinds and scales of attacks to launch.

• He decides not to consider certain kinds of damage—damage due to firestorms and conflagrations, for example—because these are "overwhelmingly complex." Similarly, he dismisses certain secondary effects—those affecting climate and ecology, in particular—because these are "imponderables."

• He chooses not to consider the effects of wind patterns on the distribution of radioactive fallout, or the long-term residual hazards created by radioactive elements that may become lodged in the fields, affecting farm workers and entering into the food chain.

• He makes radically simplifying assumptions about the existence of fallout shelters, accepting their existence (although he appears to have some doubts) on the basis of a government report.

• He recognizes, but decides to ignore, the fact that "social organization" will affect the likelihood that urban workers will get access to and make use of nuclear fallout shelters. Similarly, he ignores the critical questions of the willingness and psychological ability of urban workers to return to productive work after nuclear attack. His entire analysis of the impact of nuclear attack on the economy is based on an estimate of the workers' *availability;* he does not consider the question of their motivation to return to work or the persistence of the patterns of social organization that would enable the economy to continue to function. All such questions "lie beyond the scope" of models such as his; until there are advances in our understanding of "socioeconomic organization," he says nothing can be done about the matter.[13]

• He employs measures, algorithms, equations, and other analytic tools, because they make analysis manageable; at the same time he dutifully recognizes the existence of controversy over their reliability. He decides to employ the Cobb-Douglas production function, for example, in spite of his inclusion of a quotation by Leontieff, in which Leontieff argues forcefully that this function has no other virtue than simplicity.[14]

All such acts of simplification and selective inattention are justified—usually implicitly and at times explicitly—by reference to a normative view of systems modeling as a form of scientific inquiry. Hanunian sees himself as a modeler of economic systems, engaged in a salutary effort to advance the state of the art. Others before him (Herman Kahn, for example) have attempted to model the impact of nuclear attack on our economy, and he has improved on their efforts. His simplifications and selective negligence are justifiable because other investigators will improve upon *his* efforts. Indeed, he treats the principal contribution of this study as one of showing specialists who have not yet entered into this inquiry how their contributions may help to dispel residual pockets of uncertainty.

> If we can acquaint enough such specialists with the nature of the context within which modeling work would be useful, and if we can supply these people with points of departure (both in terms of problem areas that are recognizably related to their specialties and in terms of data to support such investigations), we may succeed in stimulating fruitful bits of work suitable for eventual integration into a grand model that would genuinely be applicable in the large. Any model we could construct today would have only pretensions to such applicability. Our main hope, then, is that we have highlighted enough separate facets of

the general problem—the impact of nuclear war—so that specialists who have not previously become professionally involved will now see ways in which they can contribute something toward ultimate solutions.[15]

This is nothing less than a confession of faith in a particular view of scientific progress. The researcher is under an obligation to analyze that which is analyzable and to draw what conclusions one can from analysis. That which lies beyond one's current analytical capacity should be set aside. So long as the relevant uncertainties are identified, one is justified in purging them from the model. That model is an "input to further analysis.[16] Other "specialists" can then take up the cause, "professionally" contributing something toward the cumulative development of "ultimate solutions."

The picture is that of a scientific inquiry conceived as continuing, cumulative, and convergent. Hanunian can justifiably ignore "social organization," for example, because it is not his department and is little understood anyway, even though it is absolutely central to the argument for economic recoverability. As he says, "we have not come to grips at all with severe organizational problems that would inevitably be present after attacks as disruptive as those with which we have concerned ourselves."[17] But what if "social organization" does not lend itself to the sort of cumulatively convergent social scientific research that Hanunian has in mind? That question does not arise. Either "social organization" will be taken up and solved, in time, by the appropriate specialists, or else it falls into the category of "imponderables." And about imponderables one cannot argue rationally; the burden of proof, Hanunian implies, lies with those who choose to discuss them. As he says of the analysts he appears to take as his main adversaries,

> analysts who continue to view agriculture as the critical sector—the sector more likely than any other to jeopardize the economy's postattack viability—must be content to support their belief mainly by allusion to imponderables (*e.g.*, induced changes in climate, or in ecology). Otherwise, the burden is on them to generate the sort of meticulous analysis that is capable, if anything is, of convincingly contradicting the indications described above.[18]

The message is clear. Just as one is justified in modeling what one can model, setting residual uncertainties aside for future modeling, so one is justified in ignoring those imponderable effects that *may* lead to catastrophic outcomes. The burden of proof lies with those who allude to them. Thus, one need not ask, "What ought our policy to be in the face of overwhelming uncertainty?"

The Hans and Sell Study of Evacuation Risks

This is a report to the Environmental Protection Agency, and the authors frame their study in terms of the regulatory responsibilities of that agency. Given that applicants for a license to operate a nuclear power plant must "submit detailed plans for coping with emergencies and accidents which could affect members of the public around power plant sites,[19] the authors want to determine the *risks* of evacuation—that is, "the risk of death, major injury and cost associated with an evacuation; what parameters in an evacuation affect risk; and, if such parameters exist, can they be used to prognosticate risk."[20] From such analyses, they hope to contribute to a procedure for deciding what "projected absorbed dosages" (PAGs) should be taken as criteria for evacuation and what "counter measures" other than evacuation may be appropriate for impact situations.

The weight of their remarks, however, suggests a rather expanded scope and a rather different thrust. While they begin with nuclear power plant accidents, their conclusions are stated in terms of nuclear impact in general and even (as we shall see) in terms of *any* impact relevant to a possible evacuation. Further, their underlying intention seems to be one of puncturing certain myths of chaos and panic commonly associated with large-scale evacuations.

Their basic methodology is that of risk analysis. The risk of damage to the health of a population, attendant on a nuclear accident, is to be weighed against the risks and costs of evacuation. Risks and costs of evacuation are set by investigating "individual events of the past which required evacuations and estimating the risks associated with the movement of these people."[21] Specifically, they list 500 such events, all in the period after 1960, including evacuations in the case of flood, hurricane, transportation of hazardous materials, tidal wave, dam break, nuclear test, landslide, and fire. From this list, they select fifty-nine events which they describe in terms of parameters they consider relevant to evacuation risk, namely, weather, time of day or year, and road conditions—all of which "could also be related to the conditions which might exist at a nuclear power plant."[22]

On the basis of a questionnaire distributed to individuals who were directly involved in these events (participants or persons in charge), they conclude that only ten deaths were reported in toto and that the National Motor Vehicle Accident (NMVA) death rate—2.4×10^{-8} deaths per evacuation mile, or 0.07 deaths per day per 100,000 persons—would be a "reasonable predictive value."[23] Later, to be on the safe side, they multiply this value by a factor of two. Part of their justification for acceptance of the NMVA death rate is their finding that evacuations are *not* characterized by "panic" or by reckless, high-speed, or drunk driving.[24]

In order to test their formula, they apply it, retrospectively, to the case of Hurricane Carla. Here, they find, to their surprise, that in this "wettest dry run in mass evacuation in the history of America [there was] not a single fatality attributable to the evacuation, including some 500,000 people."[25] The probability is low, they conclude, that "deaths or injuries occurring in a specific event would be higher than that predicted using the NMVA Death and Injury Rate."[26]

When they turn to estimates of the costs of evacuation, they consider urban and rural situations. For both, they decide to use "average" values. In the urban case, "given the tremendous range of variables directly related to the production of goods and services and their impact on each other and the community," they use "as a first approximation of cost, average values of costs or losses which could be applied across the nation."[27] And in the case of farms, they observe that

> it is not realistic to base the costs of the evacuation on the worst possible situation—which would indicate a catastrophic initiating event—although this would in fact estimate an upper limit for a particular area. Rather, it seems more logical to establish as an average evacuation cost for a farm, only the additional cost of the loss of income based on the value of the farm product on a yearly basis.[28]

They ask how much time it is likely to take to set an evacuation in motion, because "the population in the affected area may receive a dose commitment because evacuations require a finite time to accomplish."[29] Based on their sample of past cases, they conclude that an evacuation may take from two to eighteen hours, depending on the density of the population.

They devote several pages to "dispelling the myths of panic," showing through their own studies, and others like it, that flight, panic, immobilization, ineffectiveness of local organizations, antisocial behavior, low morale, and the like are all highly improbable under conditions of actual crisis. In summary, they find that "large or small population groups can be effectively evacuated from impact areas with minimal death and injury risks, and in most cases they can take care of themselves, provided adequate plans are developed and executed to minimize potential problems."[30] People will tend to use their own transportation, will attend to their own food and shelter, and are unlikely to display panic or hysteria, even in massive population movements. The key to good evacuation policy is "advanced planning."

In the final analysis, then, the authors are not merely estimating the "risks and costs" of evacuation of populations from the area of a nuclear power plant accident; they are attempting to lay to rest a number of disquieting myths about such evacuations, putting in their stead the comforting thought that all such evacuations can be accomplished with minimal casualties and little or no disruption. Moreover, as they slip from the language of "power plant accidents" to the language of "impact areas," they suggest that their conclusions may be applicable to nuclear-related evacuations in general. Several principal moves, and several less important ones, allow them to progress more or less smoothly to these conclusions.

Their risk analysis depends crucially on their assumption that they are dealing with a general *type* of event—evacuations—of which nuclear-related evacuations are a special case. Generalizations and rules of thumb derived from a sample of past events of this type they apply to the case of nuclear-related evacuations, of which they have no examples. It is this assumption that nuclear events belong to general types of phenomena, and are subsumable under the causal and descriptive generalizations constructed from the empirical analysis of past examples of those types, that makes their sort of analysis possible. Otherwise, they might have to say, "This is an unknown, possibly unique case, about which we know little or nothing before the fact." Or if they were to base their conclusions on the two best-known examples of nuclear incidents—Hiroshima and Nagasaki—what would they say?

In their descriptions of disasters and evacuations, they employ a highly technical language—"deaths per evacuation mile," "PAGs"—which has the effect of distancing the reader from the experience under discussion.

In the interest of simplification of "a tremendous range of variables," or in the interest of "realism," they eschew consideration of worst cases (those associated with a "catastrophic initiating event," for example) and stick to "averages" derived from a sample of past events—"average evacuation costs" or "average losses."

They are selectively inattentive to considerations slightly beyond the scope of their immediate argument. Having noted that evacuations will take from two to eighteen hours, during which time "the population in the affected area may receive a dose commitment," they do not pause to consider the meaning of their observation. After all, their concern is with the risks and costs of *evacuation*.

Finally, they rely, when it suits them, on outside authorities whose pronouncements they accept without question. At one point in their report they do consider this central question: "If the causative agent of the incident were radiation, would people's reactions be substantially different?" Their response is to fall back on the writings of Dr. Russell R. Dynes, codirector of the Disaster Research Center. This individual believes "there has been an overemphasis placed on the qualitative difference between radiation and other threats."[31] He thinks the likely problem will not be "panic flight" but "getting people to move at all." Dynes has an interesting line of reasoning: he uses the same proposition to motivate opposite conclusions. When he is concerned with panic, he states that "the freedom to escape from the threat of death or injury has a calming effect on the population"; but when he is concerned with the "problem of getting them to move," he notes that "because the disaster agent is radiation . . . that, in itself, will provide a sufficient motivation to move."[32] Between panic in flight and immobility in the face of impending disaster there would appear to be little choice, but Dynes seems to find solace in both conditions.

It is also interesting that the authors do not feel the need to make a critical examination of Dynes' reasoning. Like medieval theologians arguing for the existence of God, they find authority alone sufficient if it points in the right direction.

Perry's Book

Ronald Perry's *The Social Psychology of Civil Defense* also qualifies as a prime example of the survivalist literature of applied social research. Like the authors we have already considered, Perry addresses himself to a specialized question in his capacity as a specialized social scientist: "The question of whether citizens would respond to CRP (Crisis Relocation Planning)—and hence whether that aspect of the U.S. civil defense program would work—can be at least in part answered social scientifically."[33] But Perry's analysis differs in several important ways from the two earlier studies. First, Perry is a social psychologist, and he seeks to work from social psychological theory; as a consequence, he is particularly concerned with arguments based on judgments about the consequences of our *perceptions* of matters related to the efficacy of civil defense. Second, because his book was written in the late 1970s, it reflects a greater awareness of the opposing views already put forward. It is therefore a more sophisticated variant of the survivalist-researcher's view. Indeed, Perry's writing might serve as a model of the genre. His argument is transparent and appealing in its simplicity. Given his principal question—Would citizens respond to CRP?—he frames the problem as one of empirical investigation and theoretical analysis.

Empirically, he is able to draw on a sample of relevant past experiences by assimilating nuclear-related crisis relocation to "evacuation plans and practices in certain natural hazards [which] share . . . characteristics with crisis relocation."[34] Granted that "there are places where radical differences exist between anticipated nuclear attack and natural disasters, particularly in the nature of the consequences associated with impact," it is still possible "after identifying and taking into account these unique features of nuclear attack, to make carefully qualified comparisons between warning response in natural disasters and likely warning response under CRP."[35]

Several assumptions are key to this claim. First, Perry considers only those cases in which there is sufficient advance warning of an attack. He follows the federal government's crisis relocation plan in adopting the assumption that warning will be given five to seven days "before the bombs begin to fall."[36] He adopts, "for analytical purposes,"[37] a set of conditions that are, for his purposes, "ideal": that adequate warning can be given ahead of time, that relocation ahead of any attack is logistically possible, and that there will be "a so-called safe location anywhere on the planet."[38] All of these best case assumptions are made with the justification that they make *analysis* possible.

Armed with these assumptions, Perry goes on to consider social responses to warning in cases of natural disasters, and then in manmade and war-related disasters. Here, his argument is twofold: first, that these cases and nuclear disaster fall equally under the general category of "disaster", and second, that past experience of social response to warnings of disaster confirms the view that citizens will comply.

With respect to the first point, he frames his inquiry as a counterattack on the "mystique" of nuclear war. Empirically, he argues, "there is as much variation among the three natural hazards (riverine floods, earthquakes and hurricanes) as there is variation between the natural hazards and nuclear attack."[39] Considering duration of the disaster, speed of onset, and scope of impact, there is "no significant reason for treating nuclear attack as a phenomenon totally different from other events characterized as disasters in the scholarly and research literatures."[40] It is true that nuclear disaster poses the "specific threat of radiation,"[41] but this (as we will see) affects the likelihood of compliance with warning mainly through the mediation of social *perception* of the threat. And there is also the issue, in the case of a nuclear attack, of the scope of the disaster and the immense scale of evacuation. This difference can be mitigated, however, by considering a massive evacuation as "simultaneous evacuation of a large number of communities across the U.S." Although many more people will be involved, shelters will have to be constructed hastily, absences will be extended, and logistics of provision will have to be managed without outside dependence, evacuation under nuclear attack "while certainly more complicated under CRP, poses only slightly different requirements than in other settings."[42] From all of this, Perry concludes the following:

> It has been found that nuclear and natural disasters can be grouped easily under the same definition. . . . [S]ome nuclear disasters are classifi-

able as very similar to non-nuclear disasters . . . and . . . the variation between two nuclear disasters is nearly as great as that between nuclear and non-nuclear disasters. . . . [O]ne can appropriately examine evacuation in response to nuclear attack, floods and reactor incidents within the same conceptual and analytic framework."[43]

The "some" nuclear disasters that Perry chooses to consider in this way are, of course, those compatible with his best case assumptions: the ones where there is adequate warning before attack and where attack is of a magnitude consistent with the existence of "safe shelter" within range of feasible evacuation.

Having set the stage for examination of the general category of disaster, Perry's empirical analysis yields predictable results. In the case of natural disasters, he finds that "massive numbers of killed or injured people rarely result and the length of time spent in a public shelter is usually less than two weeks."[44] With respect to wartime attacks, he argues that, "contrary to beliefs held in the 1960s—by such diverse personalities as New Left radicals and U.S. government officials—social structures rarely collapse as a function of bombs or frontal attacks from outside . . . one should not expect widespread panic, anarchy, or a decay of traditional U.S. values."[45] Indeed, he continues, such attacks tend rather to "increase popular support of the existing government." Perry quotes a study done for the Institute for Defense Analyses by Charles E. Fritz to the effect that

> the day after the atomic bombing, the Governor of Hiroshima Prefecture observed that the people were aroused with 'a spirit to destroy utterly the American devils and to bring to completion the work of restoration of war damage'. . . . [T]wenty-four hours after the bomb was dropped, the local Japanese government had met to plan the relief effort, electric power was partially restored, banking operations were undertaken, car lines were cleared. Considering that this was the first atomic bomb the world had ever seen . . . such rapid recovery is remarkable. . . . [T]he use of the atomic weapon did not destroy totally the people's will to resist or their capacity to rebuild. It is not reasonable to expect that a U.S. population, or any other for that matter, would be any more terrorized or debilitated than the Japanese.[46]

This "lesson of Hiroshima" is interestingly in contrast with the lessons drawn by such commentators as Hersey, Lifton, and Schell.

From such analyses as these, Perry answers the question "Would citizens comply?" with a resounding "Unquestionably yes!"[47] Yet he does allow for a possibly significant difference between the cases of social response to past disasters and possible U.S. response to a future nuclear disaster. This difference has to do with the complementary questions of citizen perception of a warning of nuclear attack and with the adequacy of civil defense planning for such an attack. It is here that his theoretical superstructure comes into play.

Perry draws on two bodies of social psychological theory: "emergent norm theory" and "decision theory." Emergent norm theory proposes that, in case of a crisis, social collectivities go through a process of "social milling," in which individuals seek "collective meaning" by working collectively to "resolve ambiguities"; out of this process a new social normative structure may "emerge."[48] On the contrary, in some cases, "crises are followed by the invocation of *standby mechanisms* that avert the necessity for new norms. Standby mechanisms are institutionalized mechanisms that permit individuals faced with crisis to opt for an *alternate* normative structure (previously devised and held, so to speak, in reserve) as a means of dealing with the crisis."[49] Perry's argument, in brief, is that CRP can provide such an alternate mechanism, obviating the need for "emergent norms" just to the extent that two conditions are fulfilled: warning of attack is credible and citizens believe that "alternate norms will promise successful coping." Both conditions are matters of social perception, and they operate within the "bounded rationality" of an individual's calculus of decision, given a warning and a request to relocate. There are four essential conditions, Perry asserts,

> that insure a decision to relocate on request: (1) the individual must have an adaptive plan; (2) he must perceive that the personal risk involved in not relocating is high; (3) he must believe that the threat is real; and (4) he must either have his family (household) assembled to evacuate as a unit, or know that missing members are accounted for and not in danger.[50]

Conditions (2) and (3) depend on the credibility of warning. Here, Perry argues simply that, "in a situation where the president of the U.S. announces the warning to relocate and newspapers publish full-page evacuation instructions . . . the source is unimpeachable and contributes positively to a definition of the threat as real."[51] He contrasts this ideal situation with the "contradictory" and "confusing" warnings issued in connection with the nuclear accident at Three Mile Island. The message is that a warning will be credible so long as the trumpet announcing it is not uncertain.

Conditions (1) and (4) depend on two factors: first, that the individual does *not* perceive nuclear disaster as unimaginably different from other disasters (in which case he might unfortunately believe that no plan for it can be "adaptive") and, second, that the individual believe in the adequacy of CRP. The latter condition depends both on the adequacy of planning and on the individual's belief in it. Perry clearly believes that CRP *can* provide the "alternative social structure" that will lead individuals to believe that "they have an adaptive plan." But their actual belief will depend, at least in part, on the adequacy of governmental planning and implementation—that is, on the adequacy of governmental planning, and execution, with respect to detection of the threat well in advance, initiating crisis relocation, warning the population to be relocated, communicating instructions to potential evacuees, moving the population out of the risk area, supervising the risk area once evacuated, and providing reception and shelter in the host area.[52] Here, Perry allows himself a negative observation: the current state of the art of governmental CRP planning is woefully inadequate. Plans are not implementable because they are "top down" and fail to take account of grass-roots problems and responses.[53]

The entire argument leads, therefore, to a twofold moral. CRP can be an effective means of protection against (best case) nuclear attack if, on the one hand, we perceive things properly, and if, on the other, we plan and execute CRP appropriately. But here the argument turns back on itself in a remarkable way. We "perceive" properly when we regard nuclear disaster as significantly like other disasters and when we believe in the possibility and necessity of effective CRP. We are more likely to plan and execute CRP effectively under the very same conditions. But these are the subjects to which Perry, in his theoretical and empirical investigation, has addressed himself. There is a prophecy at stake and, Perry tells us, it may be self-fulfilling or self-defeating. Perry's claims will be true if, in our collective wisdom, we believe them. They may become false if, through the elaboration of the so-called nuclear mystique, we are led to doubt them.

From this self-motivating argument, it is a very small step to an argument based on a conception of morality. Perry is aware that the entire fabric of his reasoning depends on his best case assumptions. But, given the argument from collective perception, it is, in his view, immoral to make any other assumptions. He states that "if one can visualize a single attack situation in which some people somewhere in the U.S. could survive, then there is a role for emergency managers and consequently for a civil defense program."[54] Emergency planners must consider not just the worst case (total nuclear war, where no one would survive) but the entire range of possible outcomes of nuclear attack. "It is at least possible that nuclear weapons might be used" in limited ways; and this possibility "is what demands the attention of emergency managers and requires the development of some civil defense program."[55]

> The absolute horror and almost unimaginable destructiveness of a nuclear attack, coupled with the idea that U.S. political leaders would have limited options in the short run for stopping an attack in progress,

make it unreasonable—if not immoral—to fail to develop some preparedness plan to at least forestall total destruction of the civilian
population.[56]

Thus, Perry turns the cataclysmic argument around. Grant that a nuclear
attack *may* be cataclysmic; if there is any chance that it may *not* be—that
some limited attack could occur—then it is unreasonable, and immoral,
to deny the need for CRP. And the effectiveness of this planning, to close
the loop, depends on the public's perception of its adequacy. The public
will not comply and cooperate unless individuals believe in the reality of a
threat significantly *like* other threats of disaster and in the potential
efficacy of evacuation and relocation. Ergo, we must plan and implement
effectively. Ergo, as well, we are bound by reason and morality not to
undermine the beliefs on which such planning and action will depend.

THE STUDIES RECONSIDERED

In the end, we are led to ask what it means to be reasonable and
moral about the possibility of nuclear disaster. The survivalist answer to
these questions, as enunciated by applied social researchers, depends
upon their underlying adherence to the canons of Technical Rationality.

Each of the three studies we have considered approaches a special
question in a special way, but each contains as "subtext" an underlying
argument of global import. This argument is substantially the same in
each of the three cases. It follows from a shared way of framing both the
global policy question and the kind of inquiry appropriate to it.

Hanunian asks, "What are the likely impacts of a nuclear attack on
the U.S. economy?"; he then applies a form of economic modeling and
concludes both that there are "attack scenarios" under which the economy could remain viable and that the farm economy is not preferentially
vulnerable to attack. Hans and Sell ask, "What are the likely costs and
risks of a nuclear-related evacuation?"; they then apply an empirical
analysis of "similar" disaster-related evacuations and conclude that the
risks of nuclear-related evacuations would be small. Perry asks whether
citizens would comply with an order to evacuate and relocate in advance
of a nuclear attack; he then draws on an empirical analysis of disaster- and
war-related evacuations and makes use of selected bodies of social
psychological theory. He concludes that citizens would undoubtedly
comply with such an order so long as they perceived the reality of the
threat and the credibility of the crisis relocation plan.

Underneath these specialized arguments there is a global argument.
It is more or less submerged in the reports by Hanunian and Hans and

Sell, and it is quite close to the surface of Perry's book. It has to do with the "big questions"—to paraphrase Perry: Is nuclear war possible? Can anyone survive it? Is crisis relocation planning an effective means of protection against it?

The thrust of this argument is demystification of nuclear disaster. The claim is that nuclear attack, its likely impacts, and the remedial measures we might adopt to mitigate its impacts are all inherently understandable. They are not qualitatively different from other crises and disasters whose impacts nations have suffered, survived, and in some cases mitigated through remedial action. Some aspects of the problem of nuclear disaster are inherently analyzable, some consequences of nuclear attack are inherently predictable, and some remedial measures are inherently plannable. It is prudent and reasonable, indeed morally imperative, to analyze what is analyzable, predict what is predictable, and plan what is plannable; to do otherwise would be both unreasonable and immoral. Exactly at this point the argument about the big questions joins an underlying methodological and epistemological perspective, for it is the authors' unquestioning allegiance to Technical Rationality that shapes their view of what is analyzable, predictable, and plannable and their attitude toward reason and morality in the face of possible nuclear disaster. Their allegiance to Technical Rationality reveals itself in the following moves, all of which are closely interlocked:

Decomposition and Specialization

The global, enormously complex problem of nuclear disaster is decomposed into manageable parts, each of which lends itself to specialized analysis. It is assumed, for the most part tacitly, that the separate parts of the problem *can* be sensibly considered apart from the whole—for example, that economic impacts can be sensibly considered in the absence of an analysis of impacts on large-scale social organization, or that the risks of evacuation can be sensibly considered apart from the risks inherent in a period of delay prior to evacuation. The specialized contributions to analysis of parts of the problem are assumed to be recomposable, ultimately (in Hanunian's happy phrase), into an aggregate picture of likely impacts and possible mitigation.

Proceduralization

Just as the global problem of nuclear disaster is decomposed into manageable parts, so the complex human processes of response to disaster are treated as procedures and decomposed into manageable and analyzable sequences. Hans and Sell break evacuation into "outer" and "inner," and describe the conditions affecting each. Perry carefully identifies the elements of a calculus of decision to evacuate and spells out the five stages of implementation of a crisis relocation plan. Hanunian seeks to identify and sequence the component processes and stages of economic recuperation from nuclear attack. The point of such exercises in procedural decomposition of complex processes is to make collective human behavior amenable to strategies of analysis, prediction, and control. Again, the analysts assume, but do not justify their assumption, that accurate descriptions of whole complexes of collective behavior can be validly constructed by recomposing the descriptions of their component parts.

Distancing Through Technicization

The introduction of technical terms ("PAGs," "CRP," "survival rates," "dosage commitments"), the use of formulas and rules of thumb, and the technical language of "sectoral analysis" or "emergent norms" serve to distance the reader from a prospective experience of blast, firestorms, black rain, collapsed buildings, charred bodies. The very language of technical analysis tends to protect us from imagining the intensity and scale of a nuclear disaster and to reinforce the underlying assumption that such disasters may be analyzed, studied, planned for, and controlled.

The Selection of Best Case and Rejection of Worst Case

Each of the three authors chooses explicitly to focus on best case assumptions. Hanunian comments on the futility of analying attacks in which "everyone or no one" would survive. Hans and Sell deem it "unrealistic" to consider evacuation risks under the worst case, a "catastrophic initiating event." Perry simply adopts, without justification, the starting assumptions of the crisis relocation planners. In all cases, the choice of the best case and the rejection of the worst is held to be "realistic," "reasonable," or "logical," because it is the assumption that makes *analysis* possible.

Subsumption of Nuclear Disaster Under the General Category "Disaster"

It is crucial, both for the special arguments and for the global one, that nuclear disaster be assimilated to a generic *type* of collective experience called "disasters." Only through this move can the authors make nuclear disaster subject to an empirical analysis based on studies of past experience. Thus, the authors variously assimilate a prospective nuclear disaster to plagues, wars, nuclear power plant accidents, and natural hazards. (Only Perry considers the "like" case of Hiroshima, and he sees it through the eyes of a military analyst who is impressed with the persistence of the will to resist, as that will was presumably manifested by those outside the cataclysm.)

Simplification by Selective Inattention to Sources of Complexity and Uncertainty

Whatever is opaque to analysis is removed from analysis. Hanunian chooses to disregard such complexities as the disruption of social organization and the interacting effects of nuclear disaster on climate and ecology. Hans and Sell choose to use "average values of cost or losses" so as to circumvent in their analysis the "tremendous range of variables directly related to the production of goods and services and their impact on each other and the community."[57] Perry chooses to finesse the uncertainties associated with the enormous scope of nuclear disaster by considering a massive (prospective) disaster, and the massive evacuation associated with it, as a set of smaller disasters and evacuations distributed among communities across the country; he is thereby enabled to avoid the uncertainties attendant on disaster and evacuation at a very large scale.

Simplification by the Use of Selected Measures, Models, and Rules of Thumb

Hanunian's use of the Cobb-Douglas production function, which allows tradeoffs of capital and labor; Hans and Sell's use of NMVA death rates; and Perry's use of a decision calculus derived from Herbert Simon's model of "bounded rationality" all make analyzable phenomena that would otherwise pose insuperable obstacles to analysis. Moreover, these measures, models, and rules of thumb are justified because they permit analysis, or else they receive no justification at all. They are part and parcel of an underlying disposition to adhere to prevailing models of *rationality.* Just as the analysts employ the armamentarium of Technical Rationality in their estimation of risks, costs, and benefits of various courses of action, and in their construction of planning sequences, so they attribute rationality of the same sort to the anonymous actors who will play their parts in a future disaster—e.g., the enemy technicians who will select "rational" targets and the prospective evacuees who will make "rational" decisions about relocation.

Relegation of Uncertainties and Complexities to
Residual Categories

The phenomena removed from analysis through the various strategies of simplification are relegated to a residual or (in Clifford Geertz's terms) a "junk" category. They are set aside as imponderables; they are dismissed as unreasonable; they are derogated as myths. And where they are not so dismissed and derogated they are bound over to the future ministrations of continuing, progressive, cumulative scientific inquiry.

The ways in which these discrete moves make up an interconnected system of moves can best be understood by relating them to their underpinnings—that is, to assumed but unstated assumptions about knowing and the known. It is assumed, to begin with, that the objects of these studies—nuclear disaster and its impacts on society, collective behavior in response to warnings of disaster—represent a form of reality that is inherently lawful. The laws governing reality, including social reality, are taken to be there *in* the reality, binding past and future together in a coherent and potentially knowable whole. With respect to this coherence, the future is taken to be essentially like the past. There are, in principle, no lacunae in the fabric of the knowable—no overwhelming uncertainties, no unique cases that escape the categories of inquiry.

It is assumed, in the second place, that reality, including social reality, can be understood and made predictable by a process of collective scientific inquiry. Models of increasing scope and complexity can be constructed so as to "fold in," progressively over time, the elusive phenomena that specialists make into objects of study. The cumulative scientific study of the relevant phenomena is assumed to converge on a single "ultimate" understanding.

Finally, it is assumed that the collective behavior of human beings is inherently predictable—through the use of models drawn from cumulative social scientific research—and that, being predictable, it is also controllable. Plans, which are rational in the sense that they are based on analysis of risks and benefits and on empirically grounded descriptions of patterns of collective behavior, can be rationally constructed and executed. The economic (albeit bounded) rationality of the planners is mirrored in an analogous schema of rational decision attributed both to the enemies who launch attacks and to the populations who respond to warnings of disaster.

In the light of these assumptions, the systematic interconnectedness of the authors' moves becomes clearer. Nuclear disaster cannot be treated as a unique and therefore unknowable case. It must be assimilated to generic categories of events that span past and future and permit the extension to the unknown future of generalized descriptions of patterns of disaster-related behavior derived from studies of the past. For this reason, only best case scenarios are permissible; only limited, discrete attacks are consistent with the empirical treatment of disasters as a category. Only they, moreover, lend themselves to the sort of planning that depends upon an "outside" that remains a source of safe places and a base for rational execution of plans for evacuation, shelter, and recuperation.

The analytic imperative, grounded in the essential analyzability of social and physical reality, demands both a decomposition of global problems into manageable parts and a purging of unanalyzable phenomena. When uncertainty and unmanageable complexity cannot be dissolved by decomposition, they must be relegated to safe places beyond analysis—a procedure justified both by our obligation to analyze what we can and by our faith in the progressively greater capacity of scientifically based explanations to encompass phenomena that temporarily escape analysis.

Similarly, we are justified in quantifying what is quantifiable, adopting rules of thumb that promise access to predictive generalizations and implementable plans, and employing models—however questionable the evidence for them may be—if they provide a basis for prediction and planning.

The entire line of argument identifies "reasonableness" about nuclear disaster with a schema of "rationality" that is exercised by the analysts and attributed to the faceless individuals who are the subjects of analysis. The entire line of argument is also shot through with a distinctively moral perspective. A moral imperative—an imperative that commands us to be socially scientific about nuclear disaster and technically rational in planning for it—drives the inquiry at every stage and undergirds each of the moves described above. The analysts behave as though they are under a moral imperative to deflate the so-called myths and mysteries that surround the subject of nuclear disaster, to simplify the phenomena under investigation so as to accommodate it to their models, and finally, to analyze and plan for the best case attacks in which crisis relocation planning might conceivably lead to the saving of lives. But this moral imperative is just another facet of the imperative to be reasonable in the sense of Technical Rationality. In the last analysis, it is one and the same thing, under this perspective, to be reasonable and to be moral in the face of nuclear disaster. Yet, the entire edifice of analysis, prediction, and planning comes tumbling down as soon as we question the moves and the underlying assumptions that give the edifice a foundation.

Why assume that nuclear disaster will be in the form of best rather than worst case? And if it is worst, what becomes of the assumptions that lend plausibility to analysis of impacts, predictions of survival or economic recuperation, plans for "safe places," and effective execution of plans?

Why assume that the global problem of nuclear disaster is decomposable into separate, component estimates of selective impacts, risks of evacuation, probabilities of citizen compliance with warnings? Why assume that such imponderables as the disruption of social organization and of ecologies can legitimately be set aside? Why assume that simplifying measures, models, and rules of thumb are legitimately applicable? And if these strategies of simplification are abandoned, what becomes of analysis and prediction of the impacts of nuclear disaster and of plans for its mitigation?

Why assume that, under conditions of unimaginable disaster, our adversaries, our planners, our officials, and the population at large will behave in accordance with the canons of decision analysis or in conformity with descriptions of patterns of collective behavior derived from the study of the limited disasters of the past? Indeed, the very eagerness of the applied social researchers to puncture the "myths" of nuclear disaster suggests that they are at least marginally aware—and in Perry's case, the awareness is more than marginal—that collective perceptions of nuclear disaster, and collective attitudes toward plans for its mitigation, may refute the descriptive generalizations on which "rational" planning depends. What becomes of the underlying, lawful stability of social reality when it is seen as vulnerable, in this peculiar way, to a shift in awareness and attitude? And what becomes of the cumulative convergence of social scientific inquiry when analysts, who differ in their stance toward nuclear disaster, arrive at increasingly divergent estimates of impact and behavior?

From such a questioning of the mystique of Technical Rationality, there emerges a very different conception of "reasonableness" and "morality"—one in which reason begins by recognizing the uniqueness and radical uncertainty of the event about which we reason, and morality begins by accepting our inability to predict, plan, or control our responses to phenomena that lie beyond analysis.

3

Speaking the Unspeakable: The Language of Civil Defense Research

John Haj Ross

Seek unto them that have familiar spirits,
and unto wizards that peep,
and that mutter.

Isaiah 8:19

All of us are accustomed to making routine "translations from the English." For instance, when on the real estate page, we read: "cozy bungalow" or "starter home" or "snug as a bug in a rug in this dream 2 BR Cape," we know what the people who wrote these ads mean, if we have ever been in a house that realtors describe in those terms. They mean something that they cannot say: The house is small. They cannot speak this truth, for to do so would scare away clients. So the words that they permit themselves to say function as euphemisms—"nice" words for nasty things, as when Americans refer to toilets as "powder rooms," "comfort stations," and so on. Another instance where we are aware of the need for translation is when we are buying a used car. We soon learn to read between the lines when we see phrases like "good mechanical condition," "some body work necessary," or "parts car."

In both of these cases we are alerted to the need for translation because we are aware that we are reading advertisements, and we know that there are truths about houses and cars (their delapidation, cramped-ness, unreliability, etc.) that are unmentionable.

The translation problem does not become acute until we are reading an ad that is not clearly labeled as such. In such a case, we may make the mistake of taking statements at face value and not trying to ferret out the unspeakabilities that lie below the surface of what we read.

I will examine in this chapter some of the language that has emerged around the contingency plans for the aftermath of a nuclear attack on the United States. I propose to treat the words scrutinized as advertisements and to listen very closely for what is unspeakable, to try to identify the propositions that the authors of these words would have us believe. The document we will look at is neither the best nor the worst of the prose that has been generated around these plans. It is simply meant to be representative of a kind of writing that we often encounter from the Departments of Defense and State. The document in question is called *Survival of the Relocated Population of the U.S. after a Nuclear Attack,* by Carsten M. Haaland et al., prepared by the Oak Ridge National Laboratory for the Defense Civil Preparedness Agency. The abstract reads as follows:

The feasibility of continued survival after a hypothetical nuclear attack is evaluated for people relocated from high-risk areas during the crisis period before the attack. The attack consists of 6559 MT, of which 5951 MT are ground bursts, on military, industrial, and urban targets. Relocated people are assumed to be adequately protected from fallout radiation by shelters of various kinds. The major problems in the postattack situation will be the control of exposure to fallout radiation, and prevention of severe food shortages to several tens of millions of people. A reserve of several million additional dosimeters is recommended to provide control of radiation exposure. Written instructions should be provided with each on their use and the evaluation of the hazard. Adequate food reserve exists in the U.S. in the form of grain stocks, but a vigorous shipping program would have to be initiated within two or three weeks after the attack to avoid large scale starvation in some areas. If the attack occurred in June when crops on the average are the most vulnerable to fallout radiation, the crop yield could be reduced by about one-third to one-half, and the effects on crops of possible increased ultraviolet radiation resulting from ozone layer depletion by nuclear detonations may further increase the loss. About 80% of the U.S. crude refining capacity and nearly all oil pipelines would be either destroyed or inoperative during the first several weeks after an attack. However, a few billion gallons of diesel fuel and gasoline would survive in tank storage throughout the country, more than enough for trains and trucks to accomplish the grain shipments required for survival. Results of a computer program to minimize the ton-miles of shipments of grain between Business Economic Areas (BEAs) indicate that less than 2% of the 1970 rail shipping capacity, or less than 6% of the 1970 truck shipping capacity would be adequate to carry out the necessary grain shipments. The continuity of a strong federal government throughout the attack and postattack period is essential to coordinate the wide-scale interstate survival activities.

The procedure we shall adopt here is to compare what the authors of the report wrote with what they might have written, comparing the effects upon us of these variants. We will soon see that the choices the authors make all derive from a central set of unspeakable propositions, the truths of which are too unpalatable to survive being said. Like "this house is cramped," these propositions must be carefully avoided.

Let us start with a simple example:

The authors said:	They could have said:
"6559 MT."	"6,559 megatons,"
	"6,559 megatons of dynamite," or
	"6,559,000,000 tons of dynamite."

The difference between MT and megaton may seem too trivial to mention, but it is symptomatic here. Abbreviations like MT imply familiarity. Many of us have been exposed to "hospitalese"—the jargon spoken by the nurses and doctors whose profession is the quick action required to save lives. Here we encounter abbreviations like "IV" (intravenous) and "D and C" (dilation and curettage). Probably the space program has acquainted us with the largest number of abbreviations: EVA, LEM, STS, TDRS, OMS, VAG—on and on and on. Why, we may ask, are all these abbreviations necessary? What do they convey?

My impression is that they are designed to imply control—that is, that things are under control. The fear that might be engendered by a plain English term like "a walk in space outside the ship" is partially defused by describing it with a long Latinate phrase like extravehicular activity. It is then routinized by allowing it only the three letters, EVA.

This too is the message conveyed by MT. The shorter the phrase, the stronger the implication that things are under control. The change from "one million tons" to "one megaton" is the same change from the everyday word "million" to the Greek prefix *mega* that we see in "extravehicular" instead of "outside the ship."

Latin was once the language in which all scientific papers were published. As new concepts and terminology were created, Latin and Greek stems and prefixes were used to confer prestige upon the concepts. Thus, "megaton" sounds more scientific than "one million tons," and "MT" has the additional flavor of the control implied by routine interaction—the contempt that familiarity breeds.

In a word, the hidden suggestion in this abstract is that the authors are not worried by MTs of nuclear explosives. Everything is going exactly as planned; everything is under control. This is a theme that we will find again and again in many subtle ways.

Let us examine another phrase:

The authors said: They could have said:
"The postattack situation."   "The situation after the attack."

What is the difference here? After all, are not these two phrases synony-
mous? Loosely speaking, they may be, but which of the two accords the
attack more reality, more autonomy, more power, and more danger?

The answer, I think, is clear: the word "postattack" trivializes the
attack—pulls its fangs, so to speak, because of two things. First, the
replacement of the everyday English word "after" by the Latin prefix *post*
confers the blessing of Latinate scientific terminology, but above and
beyond, "attack" is no longer a full noun. It has been stripped of its article
(the) and, in fact, it is as if the event of the attack itself had been swallowed
up by being forced into one word with the prefix *post*. For instance, it is
hard to refer to the attack with a pronoun if "attack" has been forced with
post. The sentence "The postattack problems lasted much longer than it
did itself" is absurd; the parallel sentence, "The problems after the attack
lasted much longer than it did itself," is possible.

But we can take the argument one step further. While the authors
could have written "The situation after the attack," they could also have
written, "The situation after being attacked," or even, "The situation
after we have been attacked." What are the differences here? What is
implied?

It is clear that the authors have adopted the highly nominal style that
is characteristic of government prose. As we will all remember from
exhortations of our grammar and high-school English teachers, if we
want to write vividly, we must express ourselves with verbs. Compare
the difference in impact of:

1. I feel lonely;
2. I have a feeling of being lonely; and
3. There is a feeling of loneliness in me.

The difference between 1 and 2 is merely one of nominal style,
where the verb "feel" is replaced by the nominalization "feeling." In 3,
the same has happened with "loneliness," and in addition, the personal
has been suppressed by putting the first person pronoun in an oblique
case (me) instead of the nominative I.

The authors of our text have chosen *against* vividness. Instead of
"the way things are after someone has attacked us," we have "the
postattack situation." The implication is clear: the vividness of a scene
that we might picture if we allowed ourselves to imagine six billion tons of

explosives being dropped on us is too overpowering. It is to be down-played, contained, and controlled by being encased in nouns.

Possibly the peak of nominal style is attained in the last sentence of the abstract. Let us turn to examine this sentence with some care.

The authors say:	They could have said:
"The continuity of a strong federal government . . . is essential."	"It is essential that a strong federal government . . . continue."

What are the differences here? Why has the verb "continue" been given in nominal form?

Here the reason is somewhat different—it is not that "continue" is too vivid a verb and must be "tamed," or leeched by being nominalized. There is another reason. Here, what the authors want to avoid is our asking ourselves whether a government can continue in a country that has just had 6 billion tons of explosives dropped on it.

To my ear, when they say "the continuity . . . is essential," the presupposition that something will continue is much stronger, while if they were to say, "that a . . . government . . . continue is essential . . ." they would be giving the readers too much room to ask themselves the forbidden question.

A picture is beginning to emerge. We are beginning to sensitize our hearing to just what it is that they are not saying.

What They Are Saying:	What They Are Not Saying:
A routine amount of bombs will fall.	The explosive power of such an attack is inconceivable.
A strong federal government will continue.	There may in fact be no government of any kind.
Everything is under control.	Nothing is under control.

There is one other matter. We have all heard the difference between the optimist, who sees the bottle as half full, and the pessimist, who sees it as half empty. In the quoted monograph, and in other articles of its kind, all we hear about is survival and the survivors. There is one word that is as strictly forbidden in such a scenario; that word is death.

We have read of what it was like to "survive" the blasts at Hiroshima and Nagasaki. We have heard of the guilt that the living felt at not being dead with the rest of their families and neighbors. We have heard of the human reality of feeling dead inside as the slow poison of radiation felled people months or years into "the postattack situation" or as grotesquely deformed children were born to the survivors. If we have read such accounts, we should not be surprised that the authors of *Survival of the*

Relocated Population of the U.S. after a Nuclear Attack present only the other side of the story. For in order to make it possible, even briefly, to consider such a hypothetical "attack and postattack period," the authors must depersonalize their description as much as possible. One way of achieving this goal is to refer to huge numbers of people. They talk of "large scale starvation" and of "severe food shortages to several tens of millions of people." They do not let us see a small child grow weaker and weaker, with darkening eyes, as that small individual slowly crumples and dies of hunger.

The way to prevent the vividness of the picture of one solitary death is to focus on huge masses, to talk of "population," or of "personnel," or even of "people," but never to mention children, or women, or men. And what of "military, industrial, and urban targets?" What kinds of targets are these last? The real target in "urban" bombing is the women and men and children who live there—but let us not say those words; let us hide them under "urban."

I could go on, but I think that if my point has not been made already, further analyses of this text, or of similar ones, will be superfluous. I have likened such writing to a concealed, and therefore more dangerous, kind of advertising. Just as advertising tries to blind us to the defects of the sponsor's merchandise, so also such texts as the one we have looked at try to induce us to accept some assumptions and not to look for what dare not be said. The linguistic means that we find employed are not particularly subtle, and I claim no great originality in calling attention to some of them. Through such devices as using abbreviations, nominal style, and depersonalizing wherever possible, in addition to the use of large numbers of polysyllabic Latin or Greek stems, we are being sold a bill of goods. The proposition is, basically, that while a nuclear attack would cause us some inconvenience for a period of several weeks or months, it would be no more than that—that thereafter, life would go on almost as we enjoy it now.

But the unspeakable truth we hear in so many ways—no matter how much in the idiom of absolute prediction and control the words are said—the truth that life in the wake of a nuclear attack may be worse than death, no matter how few the number of weeks it takes trucks to start bringing some food to some areas. The fact is that no matter how much in control of a "postattack situation" we would like to see ourselves as being, the forces of nuclear war are vaster than any of us can get our minds around. The truth that these authors cannot say and must suppress is that *we must never fight a nuclear war*. Once this is seen to be the case, there are many concrete steps to be taken, the first of which being, perhaps, to cease to write prose that derives from the opposite assumption.

4

The Uncertain Trumpet: The Impact of Crisis Relocation on Military Strategy

Admiral Noel Gayler

For if the trumpet give an uncertain sound,
who shall prepare himself to the battle?

I Corinthians 14:8

Q. *Why are Crisis Relocation Plans being developed*

A. In principle it's simple. Only a small percentage of the total land area of the U.S. is included in the built-up parts of our larger cities, and in areas near key military installations. But something like two-thirds of our people live in these possible risk areas—places that could suffer the blast and heat effects of nuclear weapons, should there ever be a large-scale attack on the U.S.

Because there is nothing quite so helpful as being, say, ten miles or more away from a nuclear weapon when it goes off, it seems prudent to develop ways for helping people move away from the risk areas, should time and circumstances permit during a crisis. . . .

SOURCE: Defense Civil Preparedness Agency, *Questions and Answers on Crisis Relocation Planning*, Information Bulletin No. 305, U.S. Government Printing Office, Washington, D.C., April 20, 1978, p. 1.

... the critical decision to be made by the Soviet leaders in terms of sparing the population would be whether or not to evacuate cities. Only by evacuating the bulk of the urban population could they hope to achieve a marked reduction in the number of urban casualties.

Faced with these prospects, a reasonable Soviet decision-maker will in all likelihood evacuate his cities before striking U.S. cities. If he does this, our intelligence will see it and we will have time to use our greater number of cars and trucks to get out of our cities by the time they do.

Therefore, we are planning on the likelihood that we will receive the strategic warning needed to evacuate. Considering the large asymmetry in losses we would suffer if they evacuated and we did not, it is only prudent to assume strategic warning and proceed with crisis relocation planning.

SOURCE: FEMA, *U.S. Crisis Relocation Planning*, Washington, D.C., February, 1981, pp. 2, 4.

If the U.S.S.R. ever relocates its population in a crisis, the U.S. should rapidly respond by (1) placing its strategic forces on generated alert (if this has not already been done), and, if this does not clearly induce a cessation of the Soviet relocation within two or three hours, then (2) relocating the U.S. population. This would prevent a severe asymmetry in population vulnerability and reduce the chance that the U.S. would have to yield to Soviet demands. The Soviets would almost surely not be surprised if the U.S. responded to their relocation in this manner, and the chance that the U.S. action *per se* would produce serious instability would be relatively low. The U.S. should remain relocated as long as the U.S.S.R. does. "De-relocation" might later occur by mutual agreement, or spontaneously.

SOURCE: Roger J. Sullivan, et al., *The Potential Effect of Crisis Relocation on Crisis Stability*, prepared for the Defense Civil Preparedness Agency, System Planning Corporation, Arlington, Virginia, September, 1978, p. 5.

CONSIDERATIONS CONCERNING THE "SURGE" PERIOD

In defining and analyzing the CD postures and programs, it was assumed that a "bolt-from-the-blue" attack is unlikely (indeed, a program based on Postures 1, 2, 3, or 4 [postures range from no civil defense to extensive population relocation with some urban blast shelters] could not cope with such an attack) and that any attack would very probably be preceded by several days or weeks of intense crisis. Thus, a one to two week "surge" period would be available, during which preparedness could be enhanced .... Regarding the surge period, there are three times which must be distinguished:

t_1 = the time at which the President orders the beginning of the surge

t_2 = the time at which he orders the population to execute the CD posture (i.e., either to evacuate or to take shelter)

t_3 = the time at which the attack begins.

For all programs considered, it was assumed that at least one week occurs between t_1 and t_2. The time between t_2 and t_3 could be minutes, hours, or days; and the President's decision at t_2 would evidently be a strong function of his estimate of this time interval.

SOURCE: Roger J. Sullivan, et al., *Candidate U.S. Civil Defense Programs*, prepared for the Defense Civil Preparedness Agency, System Planning Corporation, Arlington, Virginia, March, 1978, p. 10.

President Reagan directs implementation of seven-year civil defense program [to]: . . .
—enhance deterrence and stability in conjunction with our strategic offensive and other strategic defensive forces. Civil defense as an element of the strategic balance should assist in maintaining perceptions that this balance is favorable to the U.S.;
—reduce the possibility that the U.S. could be coerced in time of crisis;
—provide for survival of a substantial portion of the U.S. population in the event of nuclear attack preceded by strategic warning, and for continuity of government should deterrence and escalation control fail.

SOURCE: FEMA, Office of Public Affairs, *News*, Release No. 82-26, Washington, D.C., March 30, 1982, p. 2.

INTRODUCTION

We should all understand the extraordinarily dangerous situation we are in. The political and ideological struggle between the United States and the Soviet Union has a still unlikely but intolerable potential outcome—nuclear war. With blithe insouciance, certain "strategists" and policymakers, ignorant alike of war and of nuclear weapons, suggest various nuclear threats, defenses, and even employments as legitimate components of a national strategy.

One most dangerous aspect is our capacity to entertain illusions—in this case the illusion that defenses against nuclear weapons can effectively protect populations. Civil defense has long been touted in some circles as having this capability, at least in some measure. Now it is also suggested that technology, in the form of space weapons and other exotic schemes, can protect us against mass destruction. Magic shields and magic bullets will keep us all from harm! But this is all illusion; neither civil defense nor space defenses can be effective in the real world.

An even more dangerous idea—in that it increases the likelihood of nuclear war—is that because of defense the risks are small enough to permit chess-playing strategies with nuclear forces. Nuclear coercion, bluff, threat, and menace are suggested as political and strategic instruments, to be feared coming from the Soviet Union, perhaps even to be employed by the United States. This is illusion raised to the point of self-destruction.

CIVIL DEFENSE

Let us look first at the "magic shield"—civil defense. No one disputes the incredible damage done to cities, industry, agriculture, public works, and the military by multiple nuclear blasts. All buildings, all homes, all hospitals, all facilities are destroyed. The complex web of transportation and communications is totally disrupted. The life-giving land, the air, and the water are poisoned. Livestock are killed, crops destroyed. Perhaps—no one can really know—more far-reaching effects threaten the earth itself. "But we can save the people" (all but a few tens of millions) is the claim made for civil defense:

- By moving everybody out of cities before an attack. (A week's notice required.)
- By providing blast shelters for those essential people not evacuated.
- By suggesting plans for the expedient construction of fallout shelters for those evacuated.
- By protecting essential communications, machinery, and facilities for reconstruction after attack.

The general idea is that with civil defense, nuclear war won't be so bad after all. The trouble with all this is that each and every one of these ideas is nonsense:

- We won't have a week's notice. There is not the slightest evidence that the Soviet Union is intent on attacking us, and they have ample reason to understand that such an attempt would subject their own country and people to the threat of overwhelming retaliation from the United States. But even if they were planning such an attack, they would certainly not give us that warning period.
- We can't evacuate and sustain the population of great cities in the countryside. Even if we attempt to do so, the opponent could easily track the movement and retarget to the evacuation areas.

• The tough fact is that the power and accuracy of nuclear weapons are sufficient to destroy any fixed target on earth. Deep shelters would become deep tombs. Notice, for example, that the United States plans to abandon deep shelters for senior officials in favor of mobile command posts.

• The notion that a family, with shovels, can improvise a fallout shelter and live in it for weeks is absurd. Food, water, disposal of waste, heat—all are required for survival and none are reasonably available. As for digging in the ground, try that in New York, Moscow, Minneapolis, or Leningrad in the middle of winter! Collective shelters may be even worse: They can be incubators of disease, are not conceivably adequate to accommodate the numbers involved, and are in any case themselves targetable.

• We can expect that, because of the multiple effects of nuclear weapons, essentially all transportation will be destroyed. Vehicles will be smashed, roads and bridges and rail lines destroyed, and ships sunk. No one has suggested even a remote possibility of preventing this. Industrial capacity for repair or reconstruction will be nil. All general-purpose communications will be gone—telephone, telegraph, radio, TV. With tremendous effort we may, or may not, be able to salvage specialized military nets, connecting an assistant secretary of agriculture (the surviving constitutional successor to the president) with the Strategic Air Command colonel who is the surviving senior military officer. As a contribution to the military aspects of assured deterrence, such a surviving communications net, if attainable, makes sense; as a contributor to the survival of populations, it makes none.

So we have here a string of logical and practical absurdities. The claim that substantial additional numbers of the population may be saved by civil defense measures is simply wrong. Under certain circumstances—attack during an attempted evacuation of cities, for example—it may even cost additional lives. None of this is to detract from the great potential usefulness of civil defense organizations in natural disasters such as fire, flood, earthquake, or industrial accident. Where help can be organized from the outside, civil defense can be invaluable. But in nuclear war, there is no surviving "outside."

But what about the Russians? Don't they have a massive civil defense, and doesn't it give them a big strategic advantage? The short and accurate answer to these questions is no. The Soviets indeed have spent a lot of money—not nearly so much as some suggest, but a lot. They appointed General Altunin, reputed to be a hotshot, to direct their program. They have put out a lot of civil defense manuals, reminiscent of our own in their innocent impracticability. They have built a number of strong shelters for their leadership, but they now know, as we do, that no strong point can sustain a direct nuclear hit. Evacuation of cities and expedient fallout shelters are even less practicable in the Soviet Union than they are in the United States. The Soviets don't have the transport and supporting infrastructure that we have, and they have far more severe winters. They don't even make much pretense of protecting their industry. The civil defense effort in the Soviet Union has lapsed into a characteristically bureaucratic show without substance. The Russians even have a word for it—*pokazuka*—meaning empty show of no material consequence. It is a pervasive element of Soviet life and of the relation of Soviet citizens to the pronouncements of their rulers. Industrial production, agricultural "success," scientific achievements, civil defense—all of these are regarded in the same way we regard TV advertisements. No one confuses them with truth or accuracy. Soviet civil defense cannot have strategic value in the eyes of Soviet planners because they know its emptiness even better than we.

SPACE TECHNOLOGY

Now let us talk to the "silver bullet"—the idea that science will somehow protect us from a rain of nuclear ballistic missiles. This is an idea President Reagan has entertained for some time. It had its principal public unveiling in his speech of March 30, 1983. Unfortunately, the president deserves more credit for the humanity of his vision than for the realism of his solution.

The basic idea is that ballistic missiles can be attacked during takeoff or in flight by energy beams generated in space or generated on earth and bounced off a mirror in space to the targets. The specifics of the schemes are difficult to evaluate, for none have been furnished. There is reason to believe that indeed no serious system design has taken place, probably because the technical difficulties are overwhelming. The general argument seems to be: "Science will find a way, given enough time and enough money." Not much to analyze, but we can take a look at some publicly mentioned ideas:

• Lasers. If earth based, they must penetrate cloud, but they cannot. There is insurmountable energy absorption and defocusing. If space based, lasers require many tons of fuel in orbit per shot. Also, the countermeasure is simple: make the missile reflective.

• Particle beams. These can only propagate in space. If they are charged particle beams, they can't hit anything, as their path will be deflected by the earth's magnetic field. We don't know how to make and accelerate neutral particle beams to the necessary massive total energy rates.

• Space based x-ray lasers pumped by nuclear explosives This untried scheme involves hundreds of nuclear bombs orbiting in space to drive a beam of hot x-rays toward a target. Each shot, of course, destroys its own device. As in all these other schemes, countermeasures are obvious and simple.

• Antiballistic missiles (ABMs). There is general agreement that while ABM systems can conceivably help to promote the survival of some out of many hard targets, they cannot defend populations.

• Non-nuclear space interceptors. These systems all run aground on the numbers problem; it is cheaper and easier to build additional warheads than effective interceptors.

The military problems are even more formidable than the technical ones. Tactical and physical countermeasures even to single-shot engagements are obvious and simple. The space platforms are more expensive and more easily attacked than the target missiles. But the command, control, and accuracy problems of simultaneous engagement of hundreds of missiles in the presence of deception and countermeasures, where none can be allowed to "leak" through, seem insuperable. In the end, even if, by some miracle, all ballistic missiles could be stopped, we would still have the bombers and the cruise missiles to contend with. They are perfectly capable of destroying either country by themselves.

When future advances in science, our modern god, are invoked as the source of potential alternatives, it is difficult to make a case, in some absolute sense, that a desired objective is impossible. But we can say with some confidence that ballistic missile defense sufficient to safeguard populations will not be available in this century and very probably will never be available.

STRATEGIC IMPLICATIONS

Let us now turn to the strategic implications of our analysis of the value of active and passive (civil) defenses of populations. In order to entertain the idea of a preemptive or disarming nuclear strike, the attacker must be assured of one of two conditions: (1) He must be able substantially to destroy any retaliatory force—a capability that cannot be achieved against current Soviet or American forces; or (2) he must be able to protect his control, his military, his industry, and his population against a counterstrike. This, too, is not achievable.

In sum, there is no strategic usefulness either in active or passive defense when applied to relations between the superpowers. The proper response of an American president to attempted nuclear blackmail is: "Don't be silly—you know I have you by the neck, just as you have me." No remotely likely force imbalance will change this situation.

There remains the problem of the nuclear terrorist. How can we protect against him or his blackmail? Here the threat is clandestine introduction of one or more devices. The delivery is by something as prosaic as an automobile or truck or fishing boat. There is no warning; the target city may not be disclosed; there is no target against which to retaliate. This is inherently a very tough problem, but it is clear that only such measures as safeguarding nuclear weapons and vigilant intelligence can have much efficacy.

We have now reached the estimate that both civil defenses and active defenses against nuclear attack have no usefulness with regard to interactions between the superpowers and little applicability to other nuclear threats. These ideas and programs, however, are in the following ways much worse than useless:

• The diversion of resources from more useful tasks, both civilian and military, is immense. A nuclear oriented civil defense program will cost many billions. Space oriented active defense is literally a bottomless sink for money.

• The diversion of resources and attention from real security and defense needs is serious.

• Most important, the impression conveyed that nuclear war is something that can be defended against, can be mitigated, or is in some way tolerable is irresponsible and dangerous.

Real war is not like these complicated tit-for-tat imaginings. There is little knowledge of what is going on, and less communication. There is blood and terror and agony, and these theorists propose to deal with a war a thousand times more terrible than any we have ever seen, in some bloodless, analytic fashion. I say that's nonsense. We deceive ourselves, and we deceive our opponent into believing we have aggressive intentions that we do not have. Nuclear strategists, bureaucrats, and public leaders must, as Einstein urged, change their way of thinking about nuclear weapons. The use of these weapons is not proportional to any sane objective, and they automatically recoil on the user. In these ways, nuclear weapons are not rational instruments of war, and the sooner we recognize that fact the safer we all will be. The only protection against a nuclear war is not to have one.

This is not a counsel of despair. Simple and practical ways exist to reduce the likelihood of nuclear war to the vanishing point and at the same time improve the security of all concerned. These means must not be clouded by futile attempts to make the unworkable work.

5

Alarms of Struggle and Flight: Citizen Response to Crisis Relocation

Philip Herr

Shall a trumpet be blown in the city,
and the people not be afraid?

Amos 3:6

After a thorough review of the empirical literature within the structure of the emergent-norm/bounded-rationality model, three critical variables in people's evacuation decision-making processes were isolated: (1) definition of the threat as real (that is, development of a belief in the warning); (2) perceived personal risk (the extent to which the individual believes he is in danger); and (3) possession of an adaptive plan (knowledge of safe routes of egress and safe destinations). In addition to these variables that form the primary components of the decision-making process, our review of empirical studies shows that nine additional factors should be included in a comprehensive model of warning-response behavior: (1) the family context in which the warning is received; (2) prior education and training for coping with crisis; (3) the content of the warning message; (4) the source of the warning message; (5) perceived credibility of the warning source; (6) the perceived locus of control; (7) extent of community involvement; (8) the individual's patterns of kinship relations; and (9) demographic characteristics, particularly race and ethnicity.

Based upon the critical review of the disaster literature, a series of statements (empirical conclusions of hypotheses) was defined that summarizes the relationships among all twelve variables described above. Nine primary propositions were presented as conditions that directly impinge upon the

likelihood of compliance with an evacuation warning. Ten secondary propositions were also generated that serve largely to describe interrelationships
among the network of variables. The nine primary propositions are
enumerated below.

1. The likelihood of compliance with a request to relocate is enhanced if the
   individual has an adaptive plan.
2. The likelihood of compliance with a request to relocate is increased if the
   individual believes that personal risk is high.
3. Compliance with a request to relocate requires that the individual perceive
   the threat as real.
4. Compliance with a request to relocate is more likely if family members are
   kept together during relocation.
5. The closer one's relationship to extended kin, the greater the number of
   potential credible sources of warning information.
6. The greater an individual's involvement in the community, the more
   likely he is to be exposed to information regarding response to
   emergencies.
7. The greater the level of community involvement, the greater the number
   of potential contacts for warning information.
8. The greater the community involvement, the greater the number of
   credible sources of warning information.
9. Individuals characterized by an external locus of control are less likely to
   comply with a request to relocate.

The preceding assertions, along with the ten secondary propositions
enumerated [earlier], form the basis of a model of human warning-response
behavior. Based upon the nature of the factors in the model, it was suggested
that several issues combine to indicate that citizen compliance with a warning
to evacuate under CRP or a technological emergency involving a nuclear
component might be higher than the observed levels of compliance with
natural-disaster warnings. Four reasons were offered to explain this likely
discrepancy. First, since U.S. citizens have little prior experience—except
vicariously—with nuclear threats, it is anticipated that the threat of nuclear
attack and consequent radiation would generate a high degree of reflexive fear
that is associated with attention to warning messages and compliance with
emergency measures. Second, the initial warning source—the president of
the United States—would be considered authoritative and credible by most
citizens. Third, assuming news media describe events leading up to the time of
a decision to relocate, the public would have an opportunity to develop a
perception of real threat before the warning to evacuate is issued. Finally,
because the actual destructive potential of a nuclear attack is objectively
great—and partly because this potential has been exaggerated in the popular
literature—citizens would tend to define personal risk as exceptionally high.

SOURCE: Ronald W. Perry, *The Social Psychology of Civil Defense*, Lexington Books,
Lexington, Mass., 1982, pp. 98, 99.

Based on the study of individual evacuations and consultation with persons having experience in managing and studying various aspects of evacuations, some general conclusions can be made:

1. Advanced planning is essential to identify potential problems that may occur in an evacuation.
2. The risk of injury or death to evacuees does not change as a function of the numbers of persons evacuated.
3. The risk of injury or death to evacuees can be approximated by the National Highway Safety Council statistics for motor vehicle accidents, although subjective information suggests that the risks will be lower.
4. Most of the evacuees utilize their own personal transportation during an evacuation.
5. Most of the evacuees assume the responsibility of acquiring food and shelter for themselves.
6. Evacuation costs are highly area-dependent and should be computed based on local demographic, economic, and geographic conditions.
7. No panic or hysteria has been observed in evacuations.

In summary, large or small population groups can be effectively evacuated from impact areas with minimal death and injury risks and, in most cases, they can take care of themselves provided adequate plans are developed and executed to minimize potential problems that may occur peculiar to the impact area. Costs would probably not be a deterrent in initiating an evacuation.

SOURCE: Joseph M. Hans, Jr. and Thomas C. Sell, *Evacuation Risks—An Evaluation,* U.S. Environmental Protection Agency, Las Vegas, June 1974, p. 54.

INTRODUCTION

How will people respond if a crisis relocation request is actually made by civil defense authorities? Clearly the design, reasonability, and utility of crisis relocation plans depend crucially on the answers to this question. With that in mind, FEMA commissioned Ronald W. Perry, Michael K. Lindell, and Marjorie R. Greene, all of the Battelle Memorial Institute in Seattle, to examine implications from the experience of natural hazard response for likely CRP response. Their 1980 report has been somewhat revised by Perry and published as *The Social Psychology of Civil Defense.* Those two publications, together with reports on recent attitude surveys on the same topic, are the preeminent sources in the literature on likely public response to CRP.

Perry specifically states the intent of his book, saying that "in particular, analytic concern has focused upon answering the question:

How would U.S. citizens respond to an official request to relocate in the context of crisis-relocation planning?"[1]

The answers given, though carefully conditional, are broadly supportive of the feasibility and desirability of CRP. Perry states that "after much review of social-science research, some examination of physical-science studies, and some speculation, it seems appropriate to conclude that crisis-relocation planning certainly *could* become effective public policy as one part of strategy for managing the threat of nuclear attack."[2] He also says that

> the two major difficulties (resulting from failure to develop CRP)—from which many other negative consequences would accrue—involve the very high cost (in terms of lost life) of the initial attack and the substantial time period which would be required for recovery. These problems are substantial enough in themselves that they could conceivably contribute to a serious failure in the nation's ability to resist an aggressor. It would seem that this conclusion alone, without any elaboration of "food riots" or related problems, is sufficient to justify the vigorous pursuit of Crisis Relocation Planning.[3]

Perry makes clear, however, that there are necessary preconditions to successful CRP that have not yet been met.

> Our review of emergent-norm theory indicated that if crisis relocation ever was to perform effectively as a standby mechanism, it must meet at least four criteria that at present appear to be largely lacking. First, CRP must have a well-defined and unambiguous structure that is widely disseminated to the public. Second, provisions must be made for role training and preparation of supporting cadre at all political levels and jurisdictions who will be responsible for implementing CRP. While at present many federal-level civil-defense personnel seem to understand the objectives and operations of CRP, there is a gap in both understanding and acceptance between federal and regional authorities on the one hand and state and local authorities on the other. Third, for CRP to function as a standby mechanism, the public must be trained to recognize and properly interpret the warning message that signals the implementation of the standby mechanism. Finally, CRP must become a highly visible program that is perceived by the public and authorities alike as the most effective means (coping mechanism) for dealing with a nuclear attack.[4]

That final point is a key one—one that this chapter will extensively explore. If people don't believe that participating in CRP will serve their self-interests better than would not participating, they aren't likely to cooperate, especially since the "price" of cooperation, as will be discussed, is not small.

CRP has two putative values: to reduce the human consequences of nuclear attack, should it occur, and to make such attack less likely by providing the nation's leaders with another strategic capability—that of emptying all target areas. That capability might enable leaders to be relatively firm in a confrontation, providing them with both reduced fear of the consequences, since the populace would be "safe," and with reduced expectation of attack, since the value of that attack to an aggressor would presumably be diminished. The balance of mutually assured destruction would be significantly tipped.

If half the population cooperates and half doesn't, the objective of reducing human consequence, given attack, is half achieved. However, if it appears likely that half the population will cooperate and half won't, with some uncertainty either upward or downward, the objective of gaining another strategic capability isn't achieved at all. Leaders will not be confident either that the population is safe or that the aggressor will view the expected value of his attack to be substantially diminished. The strategic value of CRP is achieved only if it is apparent that the vast majority of citizens will choose to cooperate and will be capable of relocating. If even a substantial minority clearly will not cooperate or if there are major uncertainties about willingness or ability to cooperate, the strategic value is lost.

Perry's work and the recent FEMA-sponsored survey research fail to be persuasive that the requisite degree of cooperation will be achieved, and that work fails to even attempt to address the more fundamental question of whether a demonstrable CRP capability would be stabilizing or destabilizing in world relations. Those failures will be explored through the remainder of this chapter. In the process of that exploration, two other major sources relied upon by CRP supporters will be examined: *Evacuation Risks—An Evaluation* by Hans and Sell[5] and a series of polls taken during 1982 on behalf of FEMA by the Gallup Organization.

A PROGRAM PERCEIVED AS THE MOST EFFECTIVE MEANS

Perry states, and it certainly is true, that for CRP to perform effectively there must be, among other things, a widely held perception by both the public and officials that CRP is the best possible coping mechanism for dealing with the threat of nuclear attack.

"The best possible coping mechanism" is evaluated in individual terms and in prospect. Selection of CRP as "best" means a positive answer to the question: Is cooperating with CRP the most advantageous way for me to deal with the risk of future nuclear threat, rather than doing nothing or doing something else, such as preparing a bomb shelter? "Cooperating" means not only relocating on order but also cooperating with the necessary planning and preparation steps years or decades in advance of their potential execution.

During World War II civil defense measures received nearly universal acceptance, in part because they weren't very demanding (a few buckets of sand, window coverings, and a flashlight), in part because their rationale was uncontested (for example, it was clear that keeping lights shielded in coastal areas would deprive submariners of navigational aids), in part because there was broad public support and respect for wartime authorities, and in part because cooperation was easily monitored and noncompliance brought both social and governmental sanctions. Crisis relocation enjoys none of those advantages. What is asked is enormously demanding. The rationale for CRP is labyrinthean, and examining it raises concern that compliance may actually make the dreaded attack more likely. Subsequent to Vietnam, near-universal reflexive support for authority seems unlikely to recur. Intent to cooperate won't be evident in advance, and by the time sanctions can be applied, it may be too late.

What Is Asked

For World War II the price of compliance with civil defense requests was that of obtaining and installing a few materials. For CRP, the price will vary from place to place but, if the alarm is ever sounded, will at best entail substantial hardship and sacrifice. The perceived cost of relocation is critical to the level of participation. That cost will be seen as certain if relocation is undertaken, but it is balanced against two uncertainties: whether an attack will in fact take place and whether beneficial survival is possible, even given relocation. If the perceived likelihood of actual attack is low and if the perceived degree of survival benefit resulting from relocation is small, a large and certain cost of relocation will prove decisive for many, if not most, and they will select other coping mechanisms.

Relocation cost in fact would be large. First, getting there *won't* be half the fun. Evacuation movement will be difficult, slow, and hazardous. The premise that evacuation movements are likely to be orderly and safe rests heavily on the research performed in 1974 by Hans and Sell, of the Environmental Protection Agency, in order to estimate the risks of death, major injury, and cost associated with evacuation prompted by a radiological emergency at a nuclear power plant. It also rests on the Three Mile Island nuclear plant experience—the only radiologically triggered evacuation in the nation's history.

Hans and Sell screened 500 events and investigated 70. The key empirical findings are succinctly summarized in a single paragraph:

> A state of "panic" does not exist during an evacuation which would result in reckless and high-speed driving. The evacuations were very orderly and vehicle traffic tends to move at relatively low speeds (35mph is the average). Nationally, 74% of traffic accident fatalities occur at speeds greater than 40mph. At least 50% of the National Motor Vehicle fatalities have been attributed to drinking, whereas drunk-driving has not been observed in evacuations. From published reports and observations of personnel familiar with evacuation, traffic moves at a much slower rate, and cannot even be compared to commuter traffic leaving a city. The slowdown is caused both by the fact that there is more traffic on the highways and feeder routes and that more personnel are involved in traffic control.[6]

Supportive arguments are appended—chiefly extensive quotations from Dynes and Quarantelli, of the Disaster Research Center at Ohio State University, whose work done in the early 1970s is widely cited in both civil defense and nuclear power station studies, chiefly in countering claims that people will panic, act irrationally, or become demoralized in a catastrophe.

An effort is made by Hans and Sell to identify the fundamental determinants of evacuation behavior. There is only one reported result: evacuation time appears to be an inverse function of population density. Lack of paramatization and total lack of direct evidence, such as attitudinal survey results, render inferences about CRP based on the events studied of dubious validity.

First, the largest evacuation examined, Hurricane Carla, involving approximately one-half million persons, was tiny compared with evacuating any one of the nation's major metropolitan areas, let alone evacuating all of them simultaneously, as CRP would involve. The scale of evacuation contemplated in CRP is wholly without precedent. The evacuation of London in World War II, cited by Perry as evidence of large-scale evacuation capability, involved 1.5 million persons,[7] less than 10 percent of the number purportedly to be evacuated under CRP from the New York metropolitan region alone, even without counting Long Island.

Second, no real effort has been made by Hans and Sell to establish whether human behavior would differ in response to radiological as opposed to other emergencies, and those who rely upon Hans and Sell have failed to establish that behavior in response to nuclear attack would parallel response to other disaster agents. In fact, there is substantial evidence that there *are* differences. At Three Mile Island, sixty times as many people evacuated as were directed to do so—a phenomenon unparalleled in response to other emergencies. Attitudinal research in Washington[8] and Long Island[9] make clear that fear of nuclear hazard is in a class apart from other hazard fears, sufficient to explain the Three Mile Island experience and sufficient to destroy any confidence in other disaster evidence as valid precedence for behavior in nuclear hazards. Kai Erikson, testifying regarding emergency planning at the Shoreham, Long Island nuclear station, made one of the distinctions vivid:

> Radiation cannot be seen, touched, heard, smelled, tasted, or sensed in any other direct way, so people have no way of knowing whether or not they are being exposed to it. And, to make matters a good deal worse, people who suspect that they have been in the presence of radiation cannot know for years—for generations, even—whether or not damage has been done, and if so, to whom.[10]

Susan Saegert, in materials prepared for that same emergency planning effort, notes that public fear is also heightened by sharp differences of opinion among experts and between experts and laymen and by the lasting impression created by vivid images like that of a "China syndrome." She adds the observation that education may actually increase fear and irrational behavior. The threat of nuclear *war* would carry each of those considerations even further from the levels associated with non-nuclear hazard.[11]

Traffic modeling for the Shoreham nuclear station's evacuation plan, an effort to provide a workable plan for protecting fewer than one-half million people, illustrates what can be expected under large-scale evacuation. Individual cars were projected to be stalled at critical intersections for up to nine hours, even before factoring in accidents, running out of gasoline, or aberrant behavior.[12] Behavior while so stalled with the threat of impending nuclear holocaust is unlikely to be calmly rational, and phased evacuation to avoid such occurrences is inconceivable.

Once arriving in the host communities, conditions will be found to be patchwork at best. The general relocation design is that host communities are to typically accept about five times their own population in evacuees and to host them for a few weeks if nuclear attack does not materialize and for months or even indefinitely (whatever that means in this context) if it does.

Capacity of host areas to support long-term fivefold expansion has not been documented in literature available to us, possibly because that capacity *can't* be documented. A study by Gilmer and Kennedy, of the Institute for Defense Analyses, prepared for the Defense Civil Preparedness Agency, examines two types of space adequacy: shelter space for presumably short-term occupancy and congregate space for longer term occupancy.[13] For sheltering, ten square feet per person was assumed adequate—half the area occupied by a cot; for longer term occupancy forty square feet was assumed adequate—equivalent to about twenty-five people occupying space equivalent to that in a typical single-family house.

Using the ADAGIO computer program and Texas and New York as test states, the researchers found that even at those extraordinarily high densities and accepting the validity of the Corps of Engineers input data on facilities,[14] there were deficits in both shelter and congregate space totaling more than a 25 percent shortfall in Texas and more than a 50 percent shortfall in New York.[15] The report offered no resolution for the shortfall, but rather simply pointed out that "fewer people can be sheltered than are currently being planned for unless extraordinary measures are undertaken" and then went on to clarify that the figures *already* reflect extraordinary measures assumed to have been taken.[16]

In short, *if* there is compliance with relocation requests it appears that the necessary space for accommodation simply won't be there, which means improvised or no shelter at all for many. The Anchorage, Alaska crisis relocation plan explicitly recognizes that this is an extremely cold proposition at best and thus provides the following instructions on construction of rudimentary shelters and personal insulation in the bush: "First, cover your cotton shirt and pants with 10 thicknesses of newspaper wrapped around your body and tied with strips of cloth. Then around each arm and leg, wrap and tie 8 sheets of newspaper, thus insulating your limbs with at least 16 thicknesses."[17]

Not only shelter will be short. Food and water will be severely limited, even in the short run while local capacity is supplemented by supplies stockpiled or brought by evacuees. Sanitation when a rural town of 2,000 is joined by 10,000 urbanites accustomed to sewerage will be difficult at best and could turn those host areas into "pits of disease," in the words of Beverlee Myers, director of California's Department of Health Services. "It is a hoax," she said, "to suggest that adequate medical care and supplies would be available to control outbreaks of those illnesses."[18]

Clearly, crisis relocation will be no picnic. It will entail substantial hardship, sacrifice, and even hazard, whether or not a nuclear attack materializes. With certainty, it exacts a high cost for participants, to be balanced, if at all, by uncertain benefits of relocation in the uncertain event that nuclear attack actually materializes. For many, the costs are likely to be judged as being too high to justify the uncertain benefits of participation.

The Complexity of the Rationale

In World War II the civil defense rationale was straightforward. If I blacken my windows, it contributes to making this area a more difficult target for the enemy to spot. It can't do any harm.

For CRP, the rationale is far more complex. First, many believe that cooperation with CRP planning *is* harmful in that it creates an illusion of safety possibly leading to increased national adventurism and at least marginally increased probability of devastation. The national purpose of CRP is apparently to make a small nuclear war sustainable and survivable. One can easily doubt that support for such a premise reduces risk.

Hurricanes clearly are not made more or less likely by planning response to them. Flooding, however, *may* be made more likely if reliance on hazard response, such as an evacuation plan, substitutes for developing hazard control, such as dams. Acceptance of unworkable paper plans for emergency response allows nuclear plants to be built and thereby increases the very risk the plans are designed to reduce. Similarly, community relocation planning plausibly could make nuclear attack likelier in either of two ways. First, popular acceptance of and reliance on CRP could reduce the political urgency of achieving *real* means of avoiding rather than ameliorating the consequences of nuclear conflict. Second, in a crisis situation, to the degree that relocation plans are credible to national leaders, their reluctance to risk nuclear escalation might be reduced.

Perry demonstrates recognition of this distinction between planning for natural hazards and CRP by stating that "some people feel that by discussing and preparing for a disaster we somehow risk predisposing it to happen. . . . Unfortunately, in the case of nuclear attack, unlike natural disasters, there is a political dimension to preparedness that may indeed lend some credibility to such arguments."[19]

Second, there is severe doubt about CRP feasibility. Attack must not come too quickly or we will be caught midevacuation, which would be worse than having stayed in place. It must not come too long after warning, for civil life in the host communities won't be sustainable indefinitely. There is doubt about participation levels and doubt about movement capability. There is also doubt about host area receptivity to hordes being moved for the purpose of gaining international negotiating advantage.

There are at least four alternatives to support for CRP. One can plan an independent relocation scheme, with timing and evacuation location selected to avoid the official CRP uncertainties; one can plan to shelter as an alternative survival tactic; one can fatalistically do nothing, not thinking about the unthinkables beyond trusting that the probability of nuclear war is low but that the probability of survival, given nuclear war, is miniscule; or one can actively oppose all survival planning on grounds that it is illusory and risk increasing. That the rationale for choice among these alternatives is complex is attested to by the reality that the populace is currently deeply split among them, as evidenced by FEMA's surveys, which will be discussed later.

Support for Authority

A third distinction between World War II civil defense and CRP is the changed level of support for authority. To be sure, a great deal of sacrifice is being asked in the name of CRP, and the logic of why it makes sense may be obscure at best, but won't people fall into line anyhow when the elected president of the United States requests it? On this question even Perry has doubts:

> It is argued that in a situation where the president of the United States announces the warning to relocate and newspapers publish full-page evacuation instructions . . . the source is unimpeachable and contributes positively to a definition of the threat as real. This result is not necessarily always the case. For example, during the nuclear-power-plant accident at Three Mile Island, Pennsylvania, warning messages or other communications that were often contradictory were issued by a variety of presumably authoritative officials and the result was general public confusion.[20]

The erosion of trust in presidential authority has been widely observed. In the case of support for CRP, that erosion is compounded by dissent from others in government. For example, the widely respected federal Office of Technology Assessment states that "although it is true that effective sheltering and/or evacuation could save lives, it is not clear that a civil defense program based on providing shelters or planning evacuation would necessarily be effective."[21]

Civil defense officials in communities in Colorado, Indiana, Iowa, and North Carolina, among others, are on record as not supporting CRP. Over thirty county and municipal governments in eight states were known in July 1982, to have acted to reject cooperation with CRP, and the number is growing.[22]

Widely Perceived as the Best Possible Mechanism?

In summary, the prospects for CRP ever being widely held to be the best possible coping mechanism are not good. The costs of compliance are large, the rationale is evasive, and reliance on authority figures produces little help.

FEMA has commissioned the Gallup Organization to conduct attitudinal surveys regarding CRP, using questions structured by FEMA.[23] The results of these surveys make clear that at present relocation is hardly in the running as the public's perception of the best mechanism. Surveyed between May and June of 1982, 35 percent of a sample of 1,000 adults said that in-place shelters was the "one most important thing the government should provide" as part of the civil defense program; only 3 percent selected "a relocation plan"—the lowest response for any of the six items listed. A later survey (October 8 to 25, 1982) shifted the question to the *three* most important things the government should provide. Fifty-four percent selected "shelters near home or work," while only 15 percent selected "a relocation plan"—again the lowest response of any of the six items listed.

FEMA's questionnaire design is easily assailed as prompting the responses the agency seeks. In this case, the finding is unequivocal despite that fact. Relocation planning is simply not widely perceived as the best possible mechanism for coping.

THE OTHER PRECONDITIONS

Perry's three remaining preconditions for effective crisis relocation—a well-defined, unambiguous structure, provisions for cadre role training, and public training for response—can now be briefly reviewed.

A Well Defined, Unambiguous Structure

To be effective, CRP must be clear to people. They must know who is in charge at each level, what roles people are expected to play, what each individual is to do, what resources will be available, and what logistic and psychic support will be provided.

If there truly were concurrence that CRP is the most effective possible coping mechanism for nuclear attack, there is no reason, in principle, that such a well defined and unambiguous structure could not be developed and disseminated. Lacking that concurrence, ambiguity and confusion are inevitable, with local officials and even some federal agencies making statements sharply divergent from FEMA's positions. A prominent characteristic of contemporary society is that no effort is likely to succeed if it requires near-universal acceptance. Proceeding with hardware-based strategies, such as the dense pack MX, requires mustering only a bare majority in Congress and can survive even popular majority opposition. Use of population relocation as a strategy is not that robust; if a large share of the people won't cooperate, the strategy fails.

Cadre Role Training

It certainly is true that role training and preparation for cadre at all levels is essential to CRP success. The issue is more serious than that. A civilian-based cadre that can be depended upon in unprecedented conditions must be developed. Evacuation planning depends upon many citizens to carry out crucial tasks—not just professional policement, firemen, and the National Guard, whose reliability is likely to be high, but also citizen volunteers such as schoolbus drivers to transport the autoless, highway workers to keep roads operating, gas station personnel to mete out remaining fuel supplies, and garage mechanics to repair or push out of the way the inevitable breakdowns and wrecks. All will have a classic role conflict of serving their family in the evacuation or serving the public by remaining on the job. Dynes, Quarantelli, and Kreps, in their widely cited 1972 study, *A Perspective on Disaster Planning*, essentially dismiss the concern, again drawing on experience gained in lesser and different kinds of emergencies.[24] Again, the transferability of that experience is dubious, even to nuclear plant core melt emergencies, let alone the far greater demands of CRP. Testifying on a nuclear plant emergency plan, Erikson noted that local surveys indicated that in the event of nuclear emergency two-thirds of the local vounteer firemen and schoolbus drivers would resolve their role conflict by serving their family needs first and their public role second, if at all. He went on to point out that he knew of "no situations, anywhere, in which emergency personnel reported to duty without knowing that their families had been safely evacuated from the danger zone."[25] In the case of CRP, safe evacuation for the family means a matter of days lost, not hours, but mass evacuation without those volunteers is impossible.

Circumstances for citizen volunteers will be vastly different under CRP than in any previous disaster. First, because family care will take days, not hours, and second, because the fear of nuclear hazard eclipses all others not by a narrow margin but by a huge gulf.[26] Third, there are no "outside" resources to be drawn upon, since virtually the entire populace will be either evacuating or preparing to be a host. Fourth, there unquestionably would be hesitation about the appropriateness of the effort. CRP is not a program for reaction to a disaster that has occurred, but rather an anticipation of one that *might* happen, and whose happening *may* depend upon the very relocation being contemplated, with successful relocation possibly *increasing* the risk rather than reducing it. There is no parallel to this set of circumstances in any other class of hazard, even in nuclear power stations. As Vietnam demonstrated, lack of credibility for the objectives of an effort can be crippling to support, even among the military, let alone among civilians.

Public Training

The public can be trained to understand CRP and interpret warning messages, but it isn't clear that that critical step, the fourth of Perry's necessary conditions, will be taken. Instead, a "surge" of preparedness training just prior to actual evacuation is said to be the intent, with no general involvement of the public prior to that.[27]

Last minute preparation diminishes public controversy, but whether surge education can do the job remains questionable. Certainly at this point the public is not only untrained but uninformed. The first FEMA-Gallup survey asked if people believed that the government had plans to relocate people from high-risk areas in the event of a crisis. Only 21 percent definitely felt that the government has such plans, while 34 percent believed the government does not have such plans.

SUMMARIZING: PERSONAL DECISIONMAKING

Perry diagrams a linear rational model of emergency decisionmaking, based on a general model of hazard response under development for many years.[28] In fact, personal decisionmaking is unlikely to use such a simple sequential "yes-no" format, but rather is likely to involve simultaneous weighing of all the considerations Perry lists. That model provides a convenient structure for summarizing consideration of how people are likely to respond to an official request to relocate. Given that people receive by radio or otherwise a message that attack is threatened and relocation is ordered, and given also that the rockets aren't yet launched (since in that case the issue is moot), there are various possible responses to Perry's steps:

1. *Does the threat really exist?*   There are no environmental cues, there is no way of confirming the threat independently, and the source, presumably the office of the president, lacks credibility because:

   a. it has been mistaken often before;

   b. no one can *really* know what the other side is intending, so no one can *really* know the level of the threat; and

   c. we've been manipulated before and may be being manipulated again.

Depending upon the nature of the buildup to the relocation request, the threat may be perceived as more or less real, but unless nuclear attacks are already underway elsewhere, there is likely to be large doubt about the reality of the risk. The scenario where such attacks are underway elsewhere and yet *we* have a week to relocate seems an unlikely combination of circumstances.

2. *How big is my risk?* Public understanding of the consequences of nuclear attack is being steadily improved, but ability to judge the probability of bombs actually falling, even after the president has spoken, remains poor. However, that ability is absolutely crucial in the relocation decision, since most persons will be weighing certain hardship if relocation is in fact undertaken (traumatic travel, no shelter, food and water and sanitation problems, and perhaps the dog must be left behind) versus some probability of quick death if evacuation is not undertaken.

3. *Is protection possible?* Surely many if not most will harbor doubts whether protection is possible—doubts about logistics, the extent of diffusion of radioactivity into "safe" areas, and survivability in a post-attack environment are likely to preclude an unequivocal affirmative answer to this question.

4. *Can protective action be undertaken?* Is there time? Can central Maine really accommodate Boston? Again, doubt rather than categorical answers seems likely.

5. *Will protective action significantly reduce the negative consequences?* Consequences of either relocating or refusing to relocate depend upon an uncertain event: the bombs actually falling. Some now believe, and in time more may believe, that the probability of the bombing is not only affected by emergency planning but is also affected by emergency response. If many people refuse to leave the cities, will nuclear attack be as likely as if it were an attack on empty shells, or will actions on both sides be more guarded as a result? A decision analyst can easily diagram such a case where the event probabilities are a function of individual choice. For most citizens, this simply yields more doubt. Relocation will certainly entail hardship and may possibly make attack marginally more likely. Remaining *could* entail quick death but may make attack less likely. Does that mean that relocating reduces negative consequences?

6. *Do alternative actions yield superior consequences?* Some may believe that sheltering is better. Some seem certain to undertake blind flight. Some seem certain to be frozen into inaction. Some will believe that the best action is to join with others in no action, in the hope that doing so makes less probable the atomic holocaust which they judge likely to be fatal, regardless of protective actions taken.

Three separate FEMA-Gallup polls probed people's present intentions regarding compliance with crisis relocation orders. In each case, a series of introductory questions prepared interviewees for a positive response (e.g., asking "do you agree or disagree that the United States should have a relocation plan?"). Despite that, in each survey a major share of those questioned indicated doubt about compliance. For example, in the third survey (October 1982) people were asked: "Suppose there was a tense international crisis that might lead to a nuclear attack, and you were told that the government had plans to try to take care of you and your family. How likely would you be to follow those plans if your local civil defense officials told you to go?" Only 42 percent said it was "very likely" that they would follow plans, even though "plans" aren't specified, so could be thought to consist of sheltering or other minor effort. An earlier poll (in May and June) specified relocation and drew a 47 percent "very likely to follow" response—still less than half, still nowhere near strong enough to give confidence that relocation can, without enhanced public support, be used as a strategic option.

*   *   *   *   *

Far from supporting the likelihood of strong public support for CRP, the available literature suggests that necessary support won't materialize. Available publications point out necessary preconditions for success but no evidence of ability to meet those preconditions. Enormous uncertainties are ignored or lightly dismissed. There is no direct behavior evidence adduced, only inferences from vastly different circumstances. FEMA's own survey research adds to rather than diminishes doubts. Clearly, the program lacks sufficient support to be counted on as a strategic element in the nation's array of capabilities.

6

Outward Bound: The Transportation Assumptions of Crisis Relocation Planning

Daniel Brand

And the shepherds shall have no way to flee,
nor the principal of the flock to escape.
                                        Jeremiah 25:35

The problems of crisis relocation and of daily commuting by essential workers were analyzed for the population at risk in the New York metropolitan area and for populations of outlying risk areas in New York State. The Defense Civil Preparedness Agency (DCPA) supplied the populations at risk and the areas suitable for hosting.

Objectives

The goals stated by DCPA were to relocate all risk populations within three days at distances no greater than 200 miles. Satisfaction of these goals was not an absolute requirement, however. If necessary, operations could continue for a longer time and people would travel greater distances.

Problem Definition: Base Case

The duration of relocation operations and the distances of travel are influenced strongly by policies and conditions that have not yet been officially established. When such inputs were not available, assumptions were adopted by the analysts, after consultation with DCPA personnel. These assumptions were used to define and to solve in detail a single "base case." Alternative policy assumptions and conditions were then described in qualitative terms and evaluated in relation to the base solution.

The most important policy assumptions for the base case were:

- Boundaries of the New York Crisis Relocation Planning Area were drawn to include all but 5 New York counties plus four Pennsylvania counties.
- Hosting capacity was assumed to be 5 relocatees for each host area resident.
- The entire risk population was assumed to relocate during the main operation.
- Essential workers, comprising 8% of the population, were assumed to commute daily to key jobs. Essential workers and dependents (comprising another 12% of the population) were assumed to relocate to host areas chosen to ease commuting burdens.
- Households having access to an auto were assumed to relocate by auto (except in one area where a small group was airlifted to shorten commute times).
- Certain transportation resources, not otherwise slated for use, were borrowed from New Jersey and Pennsylvania.

Relocation Times

In the base solution, 95% of the risk population started relocation journeys by the end of the third day. The remaining 5% relocated via auto and began their journeys by D + 3.3 days. The three-day goal was not achieved in the base case but could be achieved under several of the alternatives that were described. The alternatives were not analyzed in the detail needed to produce quantitative results.

Relocation Distances

The 200-mile goal for relocation distance was exceeded because of the lack of sufficient hosting capacity within that range. It is now clear that a more detailed goal statement for travel distances is needed because relocation burdens imposed by distance vary greatly among modes. For example, trips of 400 miles or more via air are easy on travelers, while 100-mile trips in trucks or freight cars will impose severe hardship on some. Trips of 150 miles in buses with small, hard seats (such as those used for urban transit and schools) will be exhausting for many travelers. Auto travel is relatively comfortable, however, the gasoline tanks of most autos limit the distances that can be traveled. Trips longer than 250 miles will require refueling some autos.

Average trips via autos were about 200 miles. However, 20% of the relocation trips were longer than 250 miles, and some were almost 400 miles. Shorter travel distances would be achieved under some alternatives, but the 200-mile goal cannot be achieved. Beneficial changes increased either road capacity to hosting areas in the south-central counties of New York or the hosting capacity in other areas east and south of the New York metropolitan area. Conversely, changes that reduced close-in hosting capacity increased travel distance via auto.

Average distances via air and rail were not estimated but would be tolerable except perhaps on one rail route where freight trains are used. Trucks were not used for long journeys. In the base case, bus trips averaged about 100 miles—a distance considered likely to be tolerable.

Transportation Resources

Transportation resources for crisis relocation are relatively abundant and afford planners some freedom of choice. Vehicles of all types but one—intercity rail passenger cars—were available in greater quantities than needed. Generally, capacities were limited by transportation facilities rather than vehicles. For example, the base solution used all highway route capacity, all railroad route capacity to host areas, and all commercial airport capacity in host areas.

Planning and Management

Planning and management are critically important to the successful conduct of crisis relocation operations. Some problems of planning and management were explored in this research. No unyielding obstacles to success were discovered, but many important and difficult problems remain to be worked out. Advanced preparation and small investments in facilities and equipment will be required. Transportation management is critically dependent on communications.

Public Response

The success of crisis relocation operations also depends on generally constructive and cooperative public responses. Travelers must follow instructions and schedules. Changes may occur hour by hour, and travelers must adjust their behavior accordingly.

Recommendations

Detailed analyses of alternative cases should be made using the move table transportation and allocation analysis techniques developed in this research. The qualitative treatment of the alternatives presented in this report is not adequate for evaluations and should be supplemented. Various alternatives of interest to policymakers, planners, and transportation analysts should be described, analyzed in detail, and evaluated as inputs to official plans.

Formal methods and procedures for crisis relocation analyses should be developed and documented. Computer programs and labor-saving techniques should be developed. Improved methods will benefit policymakers and planners and can be used by the DCPA to test the adequacy of local and state plans.

Surveys should be made of all risk areas in the United States having large risk populations of, say, 2 million or more. The surveys should assess relative difficulties and special problems of large areas. Those areas found to face especially difficult problems should be studied by teams of specialists as well as by local and state planners.

SOURCE: Clark O. Henderson and Walmer E. Strope, *Crisis Relocation of the Population at Risk in the New York Metropolitan Area*, prepared for the Defense Civil Preparedness Agency, Stanford Research Institute, Stanford, Calif., 1978, pp. xiv–xvii.

INTRODUCTION

The FEMA crisis relocation plan calls for the evacuation of 150 million Americans from about 400 high-risk areas to about 2,000 presumably lower risk, host areas—some, as in the case of New York City, up to 400 miles away. Most areas are primarily small rural towns. The two kinds of areas that constitute FEMA's high-risk list are: regions around sixty-three "counterforce" sites (important military installations), and 330 other military-industrial installations and urban areas with populations of 50,000 or more.[1]

Some of FEMA's most difficult and most studied relocation problems occur in the Washington to Boston "Northeast Corridor" of the United States. Within the Northeast Corridor, the most difficult relocation problems occur in the New York area: "The 11.33 million persons at risk in the New York metropolitan area reside in 3.8 million households with an average of 3.1 persons each. About 6.5 million persons reside in households having access to an automobile. . . . About 4.8 million persons live in households without autos and relocate by air, water, rail, and bus."[2]

> The capacity of the highway system in the vicinity of the very large cities determines the time scale of a crisis relocation in the Northeast Corridor. It does not appear possible to empty the large cities (Boston, New York, Philadelphia, Baltimore, and Washington) in a period of three days unless limited-access highways are made one-way outbound. Even so, over four days would be required to evacuate New York City.[3]

In an effort to lower the four-day time estimate for evacuating New York City, a separate study was undertaken. In this study, the Stanford Research Institute was contracted to "make an allocation permitting the movement out of the risk areas and into the host areas in a period not to exceed 72 hours while the maximum distance to be traveled by relocatees should not be more than 200 miles."[4] Despite the best efforts of the contractor, "the three-day evacuation target for the New York metropolitan area was not met—the last auto departs the risk area about 3.3 days after initiation of the movement."[5]

FEMA has used its Northeast Corridor and New York region crisis relocation studies as the basis for its statement that evacuation of the high-risk population in the urban areas of the United States can realistically be accomplished within 3.3 days. Even if the assumptions on which these studies rest were valid, FEMA now assumes that we would *have* three days lead time for a nuclear attack. This appears to stand the problem on its head. Three days warning of an attack seems reasonable to FEMA (although the warning time to notify the affected population and prepare the transportation system for the evacuation is not included in the three days). Thus, FEMA requires a solution to be devised employing a series of highly implausible assumptions to demonstrate the feasibility of planning for a nuclear attack by emptying our cities. One might ask why FEMA has made such a series of questionable assumptions in its analysis to conclude that our cities can be evacuated in so short a time. The answer may be because few would believe that the enemy would wait three weeks while we evacuated our urban areas. If the problem had to be remolded to fit this requirement, no one would take such a plan seriously.

The material presented in this chapter will demonstrate the lack of credibility of FEMA's crisis relocation planning. It will show (1) that uncertainty swamps the basis from which we can address the problem of estimating evacuation times for our cities under the kinds of crisis conditions that would lead ordinary citizens in a democracy to flee their homes and (2) that the actual evacuation time may be closer to three weeks than three days. Indeed, the period may be much longer than three weeks, in which case those stranded on the highways with no food or gas may envy those lucky enough to be anywhere else. In truth, an accurate estimate of relocation times for our urban population is impossible to make with high confidence. The only conclusion that can and will be drawn in this chapter is that FEMA's three- or 3.3-day estimate of evacuation time is based on an extraordinary confluence of assumed ideal transportation flow conditions and disciplined human behavior, the existence of which transportation engineering studies and past evacuations under emergency conditions do not support.

FEMA'S TRANSPORTATION CRP ASSUMPTIONS

The major assumptions on which FEMA's three- to 3.3-day time estimate to evacuate the major cities of the Northeast are based as follows:

1. Multilane divided highways with access control will carry 1,500 passenger vehicles per hour per lane at 40 miles per hour for twenty hours a day for the entire three-day evacuation period.[6]

2. Travel demand is controlled so that "traffic flows via all modes and on all routes can be regulated within about plus or minus 10% of planned flow rates."[7] This means that the capacity in the first assumption will be maintained because there will be no spontaneous evacuation surges *above* these amount that would congest transportation facilities and cause flow rates to drop

dramatically. It also means that traffic flows will not fall *below* the planned rate for any substantial period of time.

3. No flow interruptions will occur on the freeways caused by unplanned incidents (e.g., accidents, vehicle breakdowns, running out of gas, illegal entry onto roadways, etc.) that would lower the capacity in the first assumption.

4. Highly uniform roadway conditions are assumed along freeways used for evacuation. This means that the nonuniform road conditions associated with reversing all inbound lanes on freeways to make them one-way outbound do not lower the capacity in the first assumption.

5. Highway capacities are evaluated at cordon lines drawn near the cities being evacuated rather than in host areas, where highways are fewer.

6. At bottlenecks, which determine evacuation times from the New York region, the capacity assumed for *non*-access-controlled highways is the same as for access-controlled freeways in the first assumption.

7. Only one auto will be used for evacuation by households possessing more than one auto. All other autos will be left behind and not used by households not owning an auto, larger households, and households desiring to evacuate in stages.

8. The evacuation capacities of buses and trucks using highways are based on constant travel speeds of 40 mph on freeways, 35 mph on uncontrolled highways, 30 mph on local feeder and distribution routes, and 45 hours of operation during the three-day evacuation period. This means seven round trips are assumed to be made from New York for each bus with all seats taken, including doubling up in seats by children under twelve.[8]

9. Passenger trains are assumed to carry 1,500 passengers with baggage including 300 to 600 standees and their baggage, children doubling up in seats. Thirty box car freight trains are assumed also to carry 1,500 passengers (2,500 from New York). Trains are assumed to travel 40 to 50 mph on average, operate for twenty hours per day, and depart every half hour from the major northeastern cities other than New York.[9] From New York, passenger train service frequency increases by up to a factor of five on existing passenger lines and is begun from scratch on other lines.[10] Similar optimistic operating assumptions are employed for water and air transportation.

Each of these assumptions is discussed in the following sections. Most of the discussion is drawn from studies done directly for FEMA or its predecessor agency, the DCPA. It will be shown that those making the projections of evacuation times, and developing plans for accomplishing the evacuations, do not heed very well their own findings or those of their fellow researchers under contract to the same agencies for crisis relocation planning.

Hourly and Daily Highway Lane Capacities

According to the *Highway Capacity Manual*,[11] Level of Service D provides a speed of about 40 mph and sustained maximum service volumes in the range of 1,400 to 1,650 passenger automobiles per hour per lane depending upon conditions. The manual also states that "passenger vehicles stopped in line will rarely get under way at a faster rate, on the average, than 1,500 passenger cars per hour per lane."

FEMA researchers have written the following cautions regarding highway capacities for crisis relocation planning. These are useful to consider:

> Basic transportation planning guidance cautions that the capacity of most regional road networks will be severely taxed by the relocation effort. Bottlenecks are likely to develop on narrow rural roads outside city limits. If an initial rush to evacuate the city causes severe congestion to develop behind these bottlenecks, the success of the entire relocation plan will be threatened. Although many of the potential road capacity problems may be solved through careful advance planning, planners must recognize that rated road capacities are not likely to be attainable for twenty-four hours per day, and that severe peaks in travel patterns may be expected, particularly on the first day of relocation. Assumptions of smooth flow over a three day period will result in overly optimistic and potentially disastrous assessments of road network capacities."[12]

> The possibility of severe congestion on evacuation routes argues for the use of extremely conservative safety factors in crisis relocation planning.[13]

These sobering reminders of crisis relocation conditions are useful to keep in mind when considering the descriptions in the authoritative *Highway Capacity Manual* and its recent revisions of the Level of Service D flow conditions assumed in the CRPs.

> Level of Service D borders on unstable flow. Speeds in the range of 40 mph can be maintained on highways with AHS = 70 mph (the highest

average highway design speed for highways having the most gradual curves and grades) if no incidents *occur. . . . Minor incidents or breakdowns may cause extensive queueing."* (Italics added.)[14]

Fluctuations in volume and temporary restrictions to flow (at Level of Service D) may cause substantial drops in operating speeds. Drivers have little freedom to maneuver, and comfort and convenience are low, *but conditions can be tolerated for short periods of time."* (Italics added.)[15]

At Levels of Service D and E, speed is highly sensitive to flow changes. *Thus the range of service volumes over these levels is relatively small."* (Italics added.)[16]

The last quote means that if volumes attempting to use the road exceed the narrow range of volumes under which Levels of Service D and E can be provided by the roadway, the Level of Service will drop to F.

Level of Service F describes forced flow operation at low speeds. . . . Speeds are reduced substantially and stoppages may occur for short or long periods of time because of the downstream congestion. *In the extreme, both speed and volume can drop to zero."* (Italics added.)[17]

The *Highway Capacity Manual* gives many examples of maximum observed volumes on various types of roads in the United States. These volumes support the well-known observation that freeways and other access-controlled highways in California and, to a lesser extent, the Midwest carry more vehicles per hour per lane under ideal conditions than do those in the Northeast. Evidence to support the effect of different driving populations on roadway capacity is provided by the following quote:

Engineers in CALTRANS' [The California Department of Transportation] Sacramento office . . . compared weekend traffic flows on major freeways with flows on those same freeways during the daily commute period. They found that weekend traffic through highway bottlenecks leading to Northern California resort areas flows at a rate that is consistently 10 percent to 20 percent lower than the rate observed at those same bottlenecks during weekday commuting periods. . . . These findings provide quantitative support for the intuitive position that *Highway Capacity Manual* observations made during peak commuting periods should not be applied uncritically to crisis relocation planning.[18]

Indeed, in the latest revisions to the *Highway Capacity Manual*, "it is *recommended that the maximum service volume be reduced by 10 to 15 percent* where weekend traffic is being considered. There is some evidence, particularly from California, that reductions for weekend traffic may be even larger than this." (Italics in original!).[19]

Therefore, to account for differences in driving populations, whether between the East and West coasts or between drivers familiar and unfamiliar with the roads, volumes during evacuations under the same flow conditions (e.g., Level of Service D) should be reduced in the Northeast by at least 20 percent. This was not done by the authors of the Northeast and New York crisis relocation studies.

The calculation of 1,500 vehicles per lane per hour also assumes the presence of the following capacity-increasing roadway conditions along the entire length of the freeway:

- No peaking of flow;
- No flow interruptions caused by unplanned incidents on the freeway itself;
- Highly uniform roadway conditions along the evacuation route.

The wrong assumptions on any of these factors can cause unstable flow, severe congestion, and Level of Service F conditions of very low capacity. FEMA's own researchers discuss the effect of the factors as follows:

> Officially documented capacities represent the maximum attainable flows under ideal uninterrupted conditions; yet flow in emergency situations such as a crisis relocation is uncertain and confused with interruptions caused by accidents and breakdowns. It is extremely unlikely that evacuation flows can be organized to schedule their departures uniformly over a twenty-four hour day. Recognizing these problems, it is recommended that the road capacities be adjusted conservatively to allow for interruptions by incorporating a safety factor in the evacuation route capacities, and that a 16-hour "evacuation day" be used. This is not meant to suggest that no one will leave during the remaining eight hours of the day, but rather to reflect (1) the impossibility of maintaining maximum flow conditions for an uninterrupted 24-hour period, and (2) the likelihood that fewer people will leave their homes in search of lodging in the host area during these late night/early morning hours. This 16-hour day assumption alone is somewhat unsatisfactory, however, as it assumes departures will be spread evenly over 16 hours, and ignores the potential congestion resulting from an uneven distribution of flow.[20]

Note that the researcher recommends a sixteen-hour day rather than a twenty-hour day. This is a 20 percent lower capacity figure than that assumed in the Northeast Corridor and New York crisis relocation studies!

No Peaking of Flow

The assumption used in the CRPs about peaking of flow is stated best in the New York region study:

> It has been assumed that traffic flows via all modes and on all routes can be regulated within about > 10% of planned flow rates. This degree of control is necessary if production targets are to be achieved. If traffic flow exceeds the planned upper limit, there is a high risk that congestion will occur and flow will drop below standard. If traffic flows fall below the planned rate for any substantial period of time, some production will be lost beyond hope of recovery.[21]

The authors of this CRP recognize that the assumption of highly uniform flow is required to maintain the high capacities assumed in the crisis relocation plans. Other FEMA researchers also recognize the critical nature of the assumption. Billheimer and McNally, for example, note that "in addition to accident-related stoppages, *freeway flow can break down completely if entering vehicles cause the capacity of the roadway to be exceeded for significant periods of time.*" (Italics added.)[22]

Daily Traffic Flow at the Queens Midtown Tunnel, New York City. Photograph courtesy of Physicians for Social Responsibility.

In order to ensure no peaking of traffic flow, a complicated control system is required for evacuation of a city. In addition, considerable reliance is placed on being able to alter people's departure times to fit the available capacity. The assumption that no peaking of flows from a city can be achieved by the proposed scheduling methods founders on at least two counts. First, the methods proposed are not practical or feasible to carry out. Second, they will not stimulate the desired uniformly timed relocation response in the general population.

With regard to the impracticability of the proposed methods, crisis relocation planners themselves state:

> Direct attempts to partition the population into hour-by-hour departure times should be avoided. Use of many partitions of the traffic load, such as assigning a time to each terminal number in an automobile license plate number, is not recommended, even though this would further smooth out departures. Asking those destined for particular host counties to delay leaving in preference to others is unlikely to be perceived as reasonable and fair.[23]

Measures to enforce individual vehicle inspection are viewed by crisis relocation planners as "contraproductive." These would:

> Deny access to individuals with personal host area destinations which do not conform with public assignments. . . . Such schemes are personnel-intensive, put public safety officers in the untenable position of denying life-saving freeway access to some while admitting others, and create additional bottlenecks on the outbound routes.[24]

In addition:

> Traffic engineers and public safety personnel agreed that movable barricades (i.e., saw horses and plastic cones) are useless during today's rush-hour conditions and would certainly not deter traffic under life-threatening conditions. Even today, drivers typically move or ignore such barricades.[25]

Improvisation in real time in making changes hour by hour with travelers adjusting their behavior accordingly is also viewed dimly by the same authors of the New York plan in their Draft Guidelines document.

Crisis relocation planners acknowledge that "preparing off-again, on-again schedules with short time frames [i.e., hour-by-hour] . . . is a traffic control measure for crisis relocation [which should] *never* be applied."[26]

Even if the proposed methods of scheduling exiting flows from a city were feasible and practical, the assumption that they stimulate the highly uniform demand response needed to ensure the assumed highway capacities founders on the ability of *any* set of transportation actions to control the behavior of the population in the intended manner. For example, crisis relocation planners state that "it is likely that many citizens will leave large cities in the face of crisis in a 'spontaneous evacuation' whether or not they are advised to do so."[27]

> If the perceived danger to a city is real enough to warrant evacuation, then it is real enough to cause people to want to leave as soon as possible. No matter what movement controls are imposed to force a smooth, orderly evacuation, it is likely that the initial hours following the announcement of relocation will see a mass exodus in excess of any planning factors reflecting an assumption that departures will be spread uniformly over a two- or three-day period. Moreover, even after the initial rush has subsided, certain hours of the day will prove more desirable than others for travel, and these hours will further distort assumptions of uniform flow. If an initial rush to the exit routes causes protracted traffic tie-ups, the success of the entire relocation plan may be threatened. . . . Extreme tie-ups may lead to panic, abandoned vehicles and the total disruption of the relocation process.[28]

Conversely, it may be very difficult to get many people to move at all. This is a problem that transcends planning for the *transportation* of those who do move. In this regard, a comprehensive study of incidents requiring evacuations (floods, hurricanes, hazardous material spills, dam breaks, etc.) reviewed the literature on this subject and reported the following:

> People will often stay in a potentially threatening situation rather than move out of it. This really should be expected. Human beings have very strong tendencies to continue on-going lines of behavior in preference to initiating new courses of action. . . . There is no reason to believe that because the disaster agent is radiation rather than some other agent, that this, in itself, will provide sufficient motivation to leave. Rather, the opposite viewpoint should be taken—people will be hesitant to leave. Cognizance should be given in the planning stage to this problem and appropriate thought given to its remedy.[29]

In conclusion, the assumption that no peaking of flows from a city will occur founders both because the proposed traffic control methods are not feasible or practical and because they will not stimulate the desired uniform relocation response in the general population. The result is unstable flow and Level of Service F—conditions leading to very low capacities on evacuation routes.

No Flow Interruptions Caused by Unplanned Incidents on Freeways

This assumption is stated in the following manner:

> For uncontrolled-access highways, capacities have been computed according to the *Highway Capacity Manual* and then reduced 20 percent to allow for minor interruptions of flow, such as turning and crossing movement by police and supply vehicles, and for other frictional factors. This reduced capacity is defined as the effective capacity. *No capacity reduction was made for controlled-access highways; therefore, the effective capacity of controlled highways is the same as the capacity computed according to the manual.* (Italics added.)[30]

The fact that little caution has been observed in reducing capacities to account for unplanned flow interruptions under crisis conditions can be seen from the following quotes from documents produced by the crisis relocation planners themselves.

> Only a small fraction of the auto fleet should experience breakdowns—perhaps 1 percent to 2 percent."[31]

> Detailed procedures are needed for reaching disabled vehicles, for clearing them off the evacuation highways and for removing them for repair or disposal. Where two-way flow has been maintained along an evacuation route, access by tow trucks from "downstream" maintenance facilities and gasoline stations will be relatively straightforward. *However, vehicles disabled on one-way bridges, in tunnels or along stretches of one-way-only roads will be very difficult to reach as traffic piles up behind them.* (Italics added.)[32]

> One aspect of crisis relocation traffic which is often overlooked is the importance of adequate traffic control measures at host-area destinations. It is essential that ample off-highway parking be provided near reception and care centers. In addition to parking lots, nearby fields and other suitable spaces should be striped to accommodate the efficient parking of arriving vehicles. Under no circumstances should queues of arriving vehicles be allowed to extend backward onto main evacuation routes. *This possibility affords more of a threat to the limited highway capacity in most host areas than the possibility of stalled vehicles or accidents, and will be harder to correct if it does occur.* (Italics added.)[33]

Comprehensive studies of incidents (floods, hurricanes, hazardous material spills, dam breaks, etc.) that required the evacuation of large numbers of people recount many problems encountered in various evacuations and make clear that the optimistic assumptions of the FEMA planners with regard to flow interruption are unrelated to experience. "From published reports and observations of personnel familiar with evacuation, traffic moves at a much slower rate, and cannot even be compared to commuter traffic leaving a city. The slowdown is caused both by the fact that there is more traffic on the highways and feeder routes and that more personnel are involved in traffic control."[34]

Over and over again, the importance of sufficient trained personnel for traffic control to minimize unplanned interruptions of flow during the evacuation is stressed in crisis relocation planning documents:

> It is imperative that public safety officers keep traffic moving during crisis relocation. Slowdowns and stoppages require immediate police attention and control if a continuous flow of traffic is to be maintained. ... Critical segments of roadway should be kept under continuous aerial surveillance, and flows should be redirected as problems develop on some routes and unused capacity appears on others.[35]

> In the absence of effective planning and control, monumental traffic jams will develop, accidents will compound congestion, vehicles will be abandoned, relocation routes and destinations will be altered, panic is likely, and the relocation effort will be doomed to failure.[36]

> Road service vehicles will be required along all routes to remove stalled vehicles from traffic lanes as quickly as possible. Existing road service vehicles will have to be assigned to duty stations. Improvised road service vehicles, such as pick-up trucks and farm tractors, will have to be added to the fleet.[37]

On the other hand, there is some doubt that enough traffic control personnel will be available to keep traffic moving:

> The national availability of uniformed law enforcement personnel is 2.1 officers per thousand residents (3.3 officers per thousand residents in cities over 250,000). It seems clear ... that the need for experienced police officers during evacuation is certain to exceed the number of personnel available locally.[38]

In addition, "some defections may be expected among even the most dedicated public safety personnel under crisis relocation conditions."[39]

Even if sufficient personnel were available, their effectiveness may be in doubt for ensuring the uninterrupted flow conditions assumed in the crisis relocation plans:

> Some traffic engineers experienced in vehicle control around major sporting events were skeptical of the effectiveness of stationing personnel at freeway on-ramps to control traffic access during emergencies. Effective real-time metering of flow requires an ongoing knowledge of

traffic conditions upstream and downstream from the control point, as well as an ability to assimilate and act on this knowledge. Such metering can be accomplished effectively by traffic signals in the relatively predictable conditions accompanying rush hours. Experience in one-of-a-kind events, however, suggests that officers stationed at on-ramps tend to rely exclusively on flow conditions at that ramp in selecting a metering strategy. If traffic is moving well at their station, officers will allow more cars to enter the roadway.[40]

The need to meter flow in an orderly fashion onto highways to preserve their capacity when unrestrained demand exceeds capacity is well known. This need exists in many cities even under conditions where people have adapted their daily commuting routine to the available highway capacity. Several U.S. cities meter traffic now as it enters one or more critical bottleneck sections of their major expressways. Los Angeles, as might be expected, has the most sophisticated system. The freeways are equipped with detectors that identify congestion and automatically slow down the rate of entry of vehicles onto the freeways when congestion begins to occur.

Unfortunately, this very attractive system, operated by probably the most efficient, well-staffed, and well-paid transportation department in the country, also breaks down. Perhaps the most famous breakdown was associated with the first day of the now infamous Santa Monica Freeway "Diamond Lane" (a lane reserved for buses and carpools only) when one entry ramp signal was stuck on green for a time. The traffic inadvertently allowed on the general purpose traffic lanes congested the freeway for the entire morning rush period.

If this finely tuned automatic system is subject to breakdowns, even under the best of circumstances, with *only one* entry point uncontrolled for a limited period, metering flow in an orderly fashion onto many highways without electronic vehicle detectors under crisis relocation conditions to preserve their theoretical capacity does not hold much promise. Instead, CRP planners envision the following system for entry control on outbound routes (this may be contrasted with the L.A. system):

> The most effective and efficient means for regulating entry to evacuation routes is to block key intersections and freeway entrance ramps temporarily with large vehicles such as trucks or trailers. Public safety personnel may remove those barriers in response to changing traffic conditions or published departure schedules.[41]

The outlook for *preventing* traffic tieups with such a primitive system, receiving its first *real* test during its first use, appears bleak indeed. This would be the case, even if *every* officer reported for duty.

Finally, if traffic does come to a halt because of an unplanned interruption, how long would the blockage last, and how much capacity would be lost? "The California Highway Patrol estimates that for each minute (freeway) traffic is blocked completely, ten minutes are required to clear the resulting traffic jam."[42] This estimate is supported by some mathematical modeling of freeway incidents done by crisis relocation planners:

> In [an] example, [an] in-lane incident has reduced the capacity of a four-lane freeway from 7,400 vehicles per hour to 4,300 vehicles per hour. . . . The demand rate was set at 7,000 vehicles per hour. Under this set of circumstances, [a] 30-minute incident would have caused a total delay of 2,616 vehicle hours and congestion would have lasted for almost four hours (3.88 hours). At its peak, as much as 1,350 vehicles would have been held up by the incident. *For this simple blockage situation, the time it takes for normal traffic flow to resume is almost eight times that of the incident duration.* (Italics added).[43]

It is interesting that the demand rate in this example has been set at 7,000 vehicles per hour, or 400 vph less than the capacity of 7,400 vph. The difference between demand and capacity is extremely important in the calculation of total delay and incident duration. In fact, a difference of 200 vph would double total delay and incident duration, making the factor of eight in the quote equal to a factor of sixteen. A zero difference between demand and capacity raises both of these measures to infinity. In the situation of rush hour traffic on a California freeway, demand subsides after the peak and the freeway recovers after a time, consistent with the factor of ten estimated by the California Highway Patrol. However, given all the conditions of excessive demand states described in this chapter, there is no reason to believe that entire freeways will ever be given an opportunity to recover under crisis relocation conditions as a result of a demand rate that is lower than capacity. In fact, the only reasonable scenario for recovery on one section of freeway is if flow is blocked from entering that freeway section by break downs caused, at least in part, by the first stoppage—and so on in a series of stoppages and unstable flow conditions which characterize Level of Service F conditions of very low capacity. This makes highly implausible the assumption of highly uniform uninterrupted flow conditions that would allow maintenance of the assumed freeway capacity of 1,500 vph per lane.

Highly Uniform Roadway Conditions Along Freeways Used for Evacuation

The issue of uniformity includes the critical FEMA assumption that the nonuniform roadway conditions associated with reversing all inbound lanes on freeways to make them one-way outbound freeway do not lower the capacity used in the CRP of 1,500 vph per lane. In general, nonuniform roadway conditions of freeways are bottleneck sections containing grades, ramp merges, weaving sections, and sections with differing numbers of lanes. The *Highway Capacity Manual* warns that such conditions can affect freeway capacities:

> The procedures described so far, which apply to a single uniform roadway section, will suffice to establish the (capacity) characteristics of a long section of freeway, provided the section is free of any restrictive elements. However, in most situations there will be a variety of elements, such as grades, ramp junctions, weaving sections, or sections with differing numbers of lanes, along any freeway segment of significant length, which produce nonuniform characteristics. Balanced operation of the complete freeway section demands the relating of the operation of each of these separate elements, as previously determined, to the overall operation of the section. . . . Any highway section, including a freeway, can have only one capacity between a particular point of entrance and the next exit; *namely the capacity of the most restrictive subsection within that section.* (Italics added.)[44]

The *Highway Capacity Manual* gives many factors by which capacities should be reduced due to nonuniform roadway conditions. Depending on the presence and mix of these factors, the capacities of freeways can be reduced by as much as 25 to 50 percent or more.

Capacity factors are not, of course, provided for reversing freeways. This is an unorthodox treatment the capacity reduction of which is very dependent on such site-specific, nonuniform roadway conditions as entrance (exit) ramp configurations, median strip crossing roadways, and the presence and effectiveness of enforcement personnel to control traffic and restrict access to the freeways in the "wrong" direction. With regard to the effect of capacity on enforcement personnel, "the California Highway Patrol estimates that for . . . an enforcing officer present on the side of the roadway, flow rates may drop by as much as 25 percent."[45]

Reversing freeways is a critical assumption to the success of the crisis relocation plans to evacuate the major cities of the Northeast Corridor in less than three days. This single action is planned to reduce the relocation period of the New York region from over five days to about three days.[46] It also brings the relocation period for the Boston-Providence and Washington metropolitan areas from over three days to under three days. The justification for reversing freeways in crisis relocation planning is not provided in a very convincing manner:

> Most evacuation planning conducted in the 1950s was based on the option of making all highways one-way outbound. By this means, one can conceivably double the capacity of the route. The application of this

solution to CRP's appears to be rather controversial. All in all, the technique seems more difficult than it did two decades ago. For example, Hubenette et al. observe: The initiation of wrong-way flow would be difficult and time-consuming. Sequential phasing would have to be developed so that upstream on-ramps were closed and traffic on the freeway directed off at certain off-ramps. This ramp closure and freeway clearing would involve physical control to guarantee success. The reliability of signs to perform the task is doubtful, since 100 percent clearing of the freeway would be required. One car proceeding in the direction opposite to the heavy flow could completely block the freeway by causing one major head-on collision. . . .

The geometrics of existing off-ramps are such that they tend to make a wrong-way turn difficult. The paths traveled by vehicles attempting to use the off-ramps as on-ramps would be awkward. Also, since motorists would be proceeding in the wrong direction, they would have to use on-ramps as off-ramps. The terminals of most on-ramps at the street intersection are such that it would be difficult to turn onto the street in the proper direction.[47]

After reciting the above (and other) convincing arguments for why they and other authorities consider reversing freeways not to be practical, the authors of the Northeast Corridor crisis relocation plan suddenly reverse their opinion based solely on having six hours mobilization time for the reversal move. The authors go on to establish one or two other "convincing" arguments for the feasibility of the concept. These include the fact that "off-ramps at interchanges are protected by conspicuous WRONG WAY signs but the access is convenient enough that motorists enter the off-ramps on occasion."[48]

It is clear that reversing freeways will be a labor-intensive exercise. Any personnel left over from assuring uninterrupted flow on freeways going in the right direction will surely be heavily engaged in the system envisaged for reversing freeway flow:

Essential elements of a traffic management scheme, as we see it, include placement of control personnel at freeway ramps to control and meter access and at street and highway intersections to prevent or regulate cross traffic; deployment of highway patrol and other mobile units to deal with accidents and other stoppages and to provide minor supplies and repair services along the route; *employment of a surveillance subsystem of traffic counting devices, trained observers at fixed positions, in automobiles, and in aircraft, and suitable communication links; operation of a control center capable of digesting surveillance reports and other intelligence and issuing operating instructions; and development of effective means of communicating with the drivers of vehicles both by radio and by means of simple signs and signals.* (Italics added.)[49]

The prospects for successful operation of such a complicated traffic control system in the first few days of a crisis seem dim indeed for the same reasons given in the previous section on the difficulty of ensuring uninterrupted flow on freeways. Indeed, the problems of one-way flow may be worse since access to any point on the freeway by control personnel and tow trucks will not have the benefit of two-way roadway operation.

Perhaps the most damning indictment of reversing freeway lanes comes from the same authors of the Northeast Corridor CRP, who state in their guidance document for crisis relocation planning:

> Theoretically, converting the highways to one-way routes is possible and a convenient solution to the movement problem. The actual conduct of such an event may be another matter, however. Operational, logistic, and control requirements could very well be overwhelming. Also, effective utilization of highways converted for one-way movement might ultimately be more dependent on human behavior than a function of the extraordinary traffic mechanisms that would be in effect.[50]

In summary, the assumption seems heroic indeed that freeways can be operated entirely one-way outbound with no loss in hourly lane capacity relative to normally operated outbound lanes with no flow peaking or unplanned interruptions. First, the lack of uniformity of roadway geometry, and the presence of control personnel will reduce capacity. In addition, the probabiliy of flow peaking and unplanned interruptions occurring and causing unstable flow (Level of Service F) conditions and very low capacity are even higher on freeway roadways than on regular freeway lanes. For these reasons, the availability of a considerable portion of the highway capacity assigned to carry the fleeing population of our largest cities, particularly the New York region, must be considered in doubt.

Evaluating Highway Capacities Near the Cities Being Evacuated

The Northeast Corridor crisis relocation study describes the cordon method used to evaluate highway capacities as follows:

> In this approach, a complete transportation analysis is not attempted. Rather, a cordon line is established between each risk area and its allocated host counties at a location where the relationship of available lanes to traffic volumes appears to be most restricted. For this purpose, the general relocation flow was noted from the allocation data and the highway net in that direction evaluated. Casual observation indicated

that many routes were available within the large risk areas and that surplus routes were generally available in most host counties. Thus, the cordon lines were set up fairly near the major risk areas. . . . These cordons were established with an element of judgment and there is some possibility that they may not represent the limiting capacities.[51]

In addition, the transportation needs of populations coming from different medium as well as very large risk areas were not studied for their effect on reducing still further the available highway capacity away from the major cities.

Considering the amount of money that has been spent on crisis relocation planning, it is surprising that conventional computerized network analysis techniques have not been used. These techniques have been used for the last twenty years to plan transportation facilities in every major city in the country.[52] These techniques involve dividing a region (like the Northeast Corridor is divided) into zones consisting of risk areas and host areas.

The highway network (as well as other modes) is coded in terms of the location, capacity, and speed of each transportation link in the network. Trips between originating risk areas (zones) and destination host areas are then "assigned" to the shortest or most logical routes between the zones. These trips by origin-destination (O-D) zone pair are, in effect, laid across the network, and the resulting flows on each link or route section are accumulated. The speeds on each link that result from the accumulated flows assigned to that link are then calculated and the volumes are compared to capacities to determine where problems exist. Normally, this information is used in conventional transportation planning to find out where capacities should be increased and where new facilities are not needed. In crisis relocation planning, when there are capacity problems, travel itself between origins and destinations would have to be adjusted. This could mean selecting other destination host areas, *but not risk areas*. Most important, however, is that it means problems *rescheduling or assuming lower rates of flow over longer periods to evacuate the cities*.

Conventional network analysis can easily identify the traffic bottlenecks. These are most likely to be on the line haul (long distance) routes, or in the local distribution roads within the host areas. The earlier quoted comprehensive study of emergency evacuations in this country did a statistical analysis relating the time required to evacuate the affected area to the population density of the area. The evacuations in the data were not on the scale of a nuclear evacuation, but the results are revealing. "Road networks generally decrease as the population density decreases; therefore, more time may be required for evacuation because of limited choice and direction of roads."[53] What is surprising about this result is that since the total population of a region generally decreases with population density, the number of people to be moved is likely to be lower with lower population density. Nevertheless, more time was needed for evacuation as population density decreased. This indicates that the road capacity usable for evacuation falls off even faster than the local population to be evacuated. However, in the event of nuclear attack and the major regional migrations contemplated in the crisis relocation plans, it is proposed to superimpose metropolitan area populations on road networks in lower density areas that *already are slower in handling evacuations of local populations.* This strategy does not give much comfort.

A conventional network analysis is likely to show that the expressways and other highways within or near the major cities are not the bottlenecks in evacuating urban populations. These highway networks are built to carry large volumes of heavy commuter traffic between the cities and their suburbs and between suburbs. While these roads may realistically become congested as everyone tries to move at once during a crisis, the CRP assumption that flow will be regulated over three days or longer means that these urban highways are not likely to be the bottleneck. It follows that the closer the cordon line is drawn to the metropolitan area, where road capacity is high, the fewer bottlenecks will appear to limit capacity. In addition, few if any smaller risk areas will have their traffic added onto the roadways at these cordons.

In the Northeast Corridor study, the highway cordons are drawn quite close to the centers of the major large cities.[54] For New York, the cordon is an arc drawn north of New York about 35 to 40 miles from midtown Manhattan. For Philadelphia, the distance to the cordon is only 15 to 20 miles from the city center. For Baltimore the distance is 25 to 35 miles, and for Washington, D.C., the distance is 50 to 55 miles. For Boston, the arc is about 65 to 70 miles north of the city. These distances can be compared to the *average* relocation distances for the population in each of these cities.[55]

Boston	138 miles
New York	153 miles
Philadelphia	95 miles
Baltimore	88 miles
Washington	89 miles

These average relocation distances are long enough that there *will* be smaller urban areas with their own fleeing population competing for roadway space and prolonging evacuation times. The Northeast Corridor study did not consider the transportation loadings of these smaller areas on the highway network. However, the same authors of the Northeast Corridor study write in their Draft Guidelines document:

> Most large population centers are surrounded by smaller urbanized areas that are also risk areas—the outlying smaller risk areas located at varying distances from the major population center add substantially to the transportation problem by increasing the relocation distances for risk area populations in order to avoid excessively high hosting ratios.[56]
>
> Transportation problems associated with the several smaller risk areas that are in the pattern of relocation flow should also be examined to the level of detail necessary, to avoid having the smaller risk areas preempt transportation resources needed for the overall relocation movement.[57]

Perhaps to explain why the highway capacity requirements of the smaller risk areas were not specifically analyzed, the Northeast Corridor study states that "risk areas with populations of 1 million or less pose simple transportation problems in all stages of a crisis relocation in comparison with the very large metropolitan areas."[58] The study then goes on to quote the findings of an earlier study of three prototypical urban areas: X, with population 250,000; Y, with population 500,000; and Z, with population 1,000,000.

> Area X could be evacuated in three days or less by use of two two-lane undivided highways or a single multilane divided highway. Area Y would require three undivided rural highways or one multilane route. Area Z, the typical risk area of about 1 million persons, would require one Interstate or freeway route and one other divided highway or three undivided two-lane two-way highways. Thus, the [number of] lanes required for relocation by first auto are quite low in comparison with the highways that would ordinarily be found leading from cities of the sizes considered.[59]

While it is true again that the number of lanes ordinarily "found leading from [these] cities is not a problem," the study does not consider the number of lanes available for these cities at some distance away or in the host areas. For example, the central and northern portions of Maine, New Hampshire, and Vermont are each served by about the highway capacities being discussed for one or two smaller cities requiring evacuation (e.g., Worcester and Springfield, Mass., Hartford and New Haven, Conn., etc.). What is left over for the several million persons in the Boston metropolitan area?

FEMA planners continue to recommend cordon methods for finding the bottleneck sections that control evacuation times. These methods are incapable of accounting for all travel between all risk and host areas and logically assigning all traffic to all the relevant links in the network.

Cordons are to be drawn at progressively greater distances from the major risk area:

> [This] is a simple though inexact way of determining the available highway capacity. . . . [At each cordon] trace each highway toward the risk area and toward the host area for a reasonable distance to be sure that the characteristics of the highway and the number of lanes observed at the cordon are in fact *typical* of the route. (Italics added.)[60]

The use of "typical" highway cross sections is in fact wrong. As quoted previously from the *Highway Capacity Manual:* "Any highway section, including a freeway, can have only one capacity . . . namely, the capacity of the most restrictive subsection within that section."[61] The assumption of a uniform or typical number of lanes on freeways or other roadways crossing one or more cordons between the risk and host areas ignores the presence of the nonuniform roadway conditions affecting capacity discussed in the previous section. These nonuniformities will cause unstable flow (Level of Service F) conditions and reduce capacity over that calculated at the cordon, even in the absence of flow peaking or unplanned flow interruptions.

In this chapter we have concentrated on detailing the conditions in a crisis that are likely to affect flow conditions and capacities of single highway sections. Now we see that the analysis techniques used in crisis relocation planning are not capable of even finding the bottleneck sections that control capacity in the network and therefore control evacuation times. These bottlenecks are a function of both highway supply and demand. In turn, the demand for any single highway depends on how well it operates relative to other routes in the network *for all origin and destination areas for which it is the shortest or a logically feasible route.* Since the crisis relocation plans have not used appropriate network analysis techniques to account for all the demand, the availability of a considerable portion of the highway capacity assigned to carry the fleeing population of our largest cities must (again) be considered in doubt.

At Bottlenecks, Non-Access-Controlled Highway Capacities Equal Freeway Capacities

So far, we have restricted our discussion of factors influencing highway capacity to those factors affecting the 1,500 vehicles per lane per hour freeway capacity assumed in the crisis relocation plans. At the beginning of their New York region relocation study, the authors appear to assume lower capacities for non-access-controlled highways (900 per hour outbound for two lane undivided highways and 1,200 per hour per lane for multilane highways) in an attempt to account for flow interruptions along the route:

> For uncontrolled access highways, capacities have been computed according to the *Highway Capacity Manual* and then reduced 20 percent to allow for minor interruptions of flow, such as turning and crossing movement by police and supply vehicles, and for other frictional factors.[62]

The first criticism of these capacities is that if 1,200 vph per lane for multilane highways represents a 20 percent reduction, the original capacity "computed according to the *Highway Capacity Manual*" is 1,500 vph per lane. This is, of course, the same capacity as was assumed for limited-access freeways. This means that no capacity reductions are made to account for the fact that we are not dealing with limited-access highways but rather a completely different type of roadway. Therefore, in addition to the criticisms given previously of 1500 vph per lane as the capacity of a freeway, it appears that the CRP planners have now assumed away all the differences between freeways and other types of roadways with the sole exception of the occurrence of unplanned flow interruptions. These differences are critical in such areas as fixed traffic interruptions and nonuniform roadway conditions along the entire evacuation route. These differences are discussed in the *Highway Capacity Manual:*

> By definition, traffic on all highways except freeways is subject to interruption, although the degree varies widely. Fixed traffic interruptions obviously will influence both operating speeds and capacity adversely. These fixed traffic interruptions on the roadway include signalized intersections, stop signs, railroad grade crossings, and the like.[63]

The CRP analysts therefore assume there will be *no* fixed traffic interruptions or nonuniform roadway conditions during an evacuation. We can only hope they don't also assume their freeway speeds of 40 mph. For lower speeds, the manual states:

> If speed limits must be restricted to 35 mph or below, indicating substantial roadside interference, the characteristics of the traffic flow are changed too completely for uninterrupted-flow criteria to be applicable even in modified form. . . . Such highways should be analyzed as urban arterials.[64]

The manual goes on to describe the Level of Service D conditions (assumed in the CRPs) for urban and suburban arterials as having average travel speeds of "less than or equal to 15 mph" and "approaching unstable flow."[65] It says that "these conditions may be tolerable for short periods of time or at occasional bottlenecks, but create unacceptable delay when they exist for a considerable portion of the peak hour along an entire section of street."[66] This statement demonstrates that assuming freeway capacities for non-access-controlled roads is without merit.

Then, as if the analysis were not heroic enough already, the statement is made at the end of the relevant section of the New York region crisis relocation study that at the bottlenecks that control evacuation times, the capacities of the non-limited-access roadways were *not* reduced by 20 percent from freeway lane capacities (!):

> It has been assumed that bottlenecks will be identified in plans and that special efforts will be made to control traffic and to prevent turning and crossing movements within the bottlenecks. Consequently, the effective capacity at the bottleneck is the full capacity computed according to the *Highway Capacity Manual*—it is not reduced 20 percent as discussed above. . . . Several modifications of freeway interchange and rural at-grade intersections are assumed to have been made prior to the crisis to provide needed capacity. These modifications have not been studied in detail but it is expected that most would require relatively small investments. The modifications include widening interchange ramps, widening and channelizing at-grade intersections, and other short-length changes. Some ramp shoulders may be converted to traffic lanes for relocation traffic.[67]

The report goes on to give a list of bottleneck sections that need improvement. These include doubling the width of a bridge over the Hudson River and a new direct four-lane expressway connection between two existing expressways.

Considering all the factors present under crisis relocation conditions, the capacities assumed for non-access-controlled highways are not attainable. First, the conventional non-access-controlled highways are presumed to operate like freeways except for unplanned flow interruptions. Then, at the critical bottleneck sections controlling evacuation times, the non-access-controlled roadways are also presumed to be restored to freeways in terms of the effectiveness with which unplanned interruptions can be controlled. These assumptions are not tenable, particularly under crisis conditions. In addition, under such conditions, there would be even worse problems controlling the peaking of demand and flow interruptions for ordinary roads than for limited-access highways. Therefore, for all of these reasons, the potential for a complete breakdown of flow (Level of Service F) appears very likely.

Use of First Autos Only for Evacuation

The Northeast Corridor and New York region crisis relocation studies assume that only one auto will be used for evacuation by households possessing more than one auto. "Persons in housing units having access to one or more automobiles are expected to use the most suitable vehicle for relocation travel—up to limits imposed by highway capacity. . . . It is assumed that persons who reside together will relocate together."[68] The single auto used will be "loaded by the average household size in the various risk areas and not to capacity. Other automobiles in those households with more than one will be assumed to be unused."[69] The assumption that all other autos will be left behind and not used by autoless households, larger households, households desiring to evacuate in stages ("women and children first") is a major assumption (indeed, breathtaking). All the highway loading and evacuation times are based on this assumption.

A very large number of additional cars are available in the major risk areas that could be used by those seeking to relocate under crisis conditions. Many millions of more cars are available in the five major Northeast Corridor risk areas than households that are assumed to relocate in one auto. In percentage terms, there are 74 percent more cars available and unused than are assumed to be used for evacuation.[70] This ranges from 58 percent more in the New York area, to 93 percent more in the Boston-Providence area. There are also millions more persons needing to be relocated by nonauto modes than there are available unused autos. In fact, the ratio of persons not relocating by auto to autos not used is 1.85 in the five major risk areas combined.[71] The automobile capacity, if not the highway capacity, is clearly available to move the entire population at risk in the Northeast Corridor.

> It may be noted . . . that the number of unused autos exceeds the number of people requiring transportation in all cases. Since there are about as many drivers as there are automobiles, one might be tempted to explore how these second automobiles might be put to use. In this feasibility analysis, we did not assume any use of these vehicles.[72]

The reason for not assuming use of these vehicles is obvious. "It was found earlier. . . . that first automobiles dominated the problem of highway capacity."[73] The New York study calculated that "each loss of 0.1 persons per auto will lengthen the (evacuation) operation by 0.1 days."[74] This, of course, assumes that *no* congestion results from the additional cars, and that *traffic moves with no flow peaking and no flow interruptions at the capacities discussed in the previous sections.* In reality, of course, the additional second cars that are likely to be used will make it even more difficult to maintain orderly traffic flows equal to capacity for any length of time.

The way that auto occupancy levels are proposed to be enforced is descredited due to the individual policing of persons and autos that would be required.

> Because of the importance of maintaining planned levels of auto occupancy, planners will need to monitor traffic streams entering relocation routes and compute running averages of vehicle occupancy and take corrective action when necessary. For example, if the average is observed to fall below target, drivers of vehicles with one person (or perhaps two persons) would be denied access to the relocation route.[75]

Experience indicates that the percentage of available autos used in an evacuation will vary with the circumstances of the evacuation.

> In Mississauga (Ontario, Canada—hazardous materials spill), where there was no threat to autos left behind, the average number of vehicles used to evaluate was 1.24 vehicles per household . . . if this experience holds true during crisis relocation, the number of cars on the road will increase by 24 percent over planned levels, and available road capacity will be decreased accordingly.[76]

There are several reasons why this 24 percent is a very low estimate of the additional number of cars on the road during a nuclear evacuation. These reasons include:

- In Mississauga, an auto-oriented suburb of Toronto, nearly all households had autos. In the major Northeast Corridor cities, the pressures to use available cars on the part of the 30 percent of the population assumed not to use autos[77] will be enormous.
- The nonauto alternatives proposed to be used for evacuation are so unattractive (as discussed below) that persons without cars will not want to rely on these nonauto modes.
- Autos left behind in a nuclear evacuation are clearly at risk. Given the importance of autos in an evacuation, and the investment tied up in them, the pressures to take all of them along are very great.
- Given that personal effects and valuables left behind in a nuclear evacuation are also clearly at risk, and that the need for creature comforts in unknown host areas are great, a nuclear evacuation will involve much more baggage being carried than the short Mississauga evacuation. Indeed, the crisis relocation planners state that "emergency advice at the time will urge relocatees to take clothes, medicines, food, bedding, and other essentials with them."[78]

It is logical, therefore, to posit the actual use in an evacuation of a very high proportion of the 74 percent more cars available than are assumed to be used in the plans. There is no way to enforce only the use of first autos, only by those households owning autos. Indeed, leaving second autos at home is specifically described as "impossible to enforce"[79] by FEMA's own planners.

For all of these reasons, the assumption of first car use only by (only) car-owning households is unrealistic. It greatly underestimates the number of cars that would be on the roads. The traffic control and management problems would be much greater, and the reliability of the vehicle fleet itself would be less than that experienced in normal commuting hours when the capacities assumed in these studies have been measured. The great number of extra cars would add to all the problems of flow peaking, unplanned flow interruptions, marginal friction from non-uniform roadways, traffic control personnel, blocked ramps, and so on— problems that have been assumed away in the crisis relocation plans. For these reasons, eliminating the first-auto-only assumption would by itself add days to any reasonable estimate of relocation times for the major risk areas, even if the added traffic could be managed at the capacities assumed in the crisis relocation plans.

Bus and Truck Capacities

Buses and trucks are used to evacuate a portion of the population assumed not to use cars because they belong to non-car-owning households. The problem of relocating carless households is worst in the New York region, since about 43 percent of the population is carless.[80] In the other four major risk areas in the Northeast Corridor, the percentage is about 20 percent.[81]

The bus and truck assumptions used are as follows. Buses carrying fifty persons make seven round trips between New York and the host areas during the three-day evacuation period with all seats taken, including doubling up in seats by children under twelve. This large number of round trips per bus reduces the numbers of buses needed to accomplish the evacuation. It assumes fifteen hours per day of operation over the three-day evacuation period, traveling at the same uniform highway speeds as those assumed for auto. These speeds are 40 mph on freeways, 35 mph on non-access-controlled highways, and 30 mph on local feeder and distribution routes.[82] For the other four major Northeast Corridor risk areas, the number of passengers per bus is slightly less (40 per bus) and the speeds assumed are less important since only two round trips per bus are needed. Trucks are very important in carrying relocatees from the other risk areas. Each tractor-trailer truck is assumed to carry thirty passengers and baggage; smaller trucks carry ten persons.[83] Trucks were not required for use in New York, since that study sought to maximize the use of nonauto modes (rail, air, and water) as well as the more efficient bus highway mode (discussed below). However, trucks account for most of the nonauto highway travel in the other major Northeast Corridor risk areas.[84]

Making the most efficient use of highways by carrying large numbers of people in buses and trucks is an important element of the crisis relocation plans. In New York, almost 30 percent as many people are to be moved in buses as in first autos.[85] For the other four major risk areas in the Northeast Corridor this figure is about 10 percent for buses and trucks combined, except for Baltimore-Wilmington, where all nonauto persons are assumed to be able to be moved by the off-highway modes of freight rail and air.[86]

Rather than admit to their strategy of relocating the populations of the major risk areas by the more efficient buses and trucks, the authors of the plans profess ignorance of how to use the remaining available autos to relocate the population. They say that "although a vast resource of second automobiles will remain in the risk areas, a reliable—or even plausible—way to mobilize and use these vehicles is not apparent. Even if a ready means were available, these additional passenger cars are likely to strain the capacity of the highway system more than the comparable fleet of buses and trucks."[87]

The first criticism of the planned bus and truck use, therefore, is that it is unlikely that most of the assumed bus and truck users will wait around to be moved by these other highway modes when so many cars remain available to be borrowed, rented, or stolen. The pressures to use the available cars, in part by the carless, were discussed in the previous section. In addition, people don't even like to use transit modes in peacetime. In a time of crisis, the planned wait-and-use-transit response is simply not something that can be counted upon to happen. The resulting greater use of more capacity-consuming autos will further congest the highways and make it even more difficult to provide the bus and truck capacity in the first place.

The second problem with the bus and truck assumptions is the highway speeds. The 40 mph average freeway speed is critical to being able to use the same bus equipment from New York for the assumed seven round trips. Slower average speeds will not allow the same buses to be turned around; rather, they will be "lost" in the traffic jams and not available for their next outbound trip. From the discussion in all the previous sections of the assumed highway capacities, no flow peaking and uninterrupted flows, and so on, we can be profoundly skeptical of the assumed bus and truck speeds. The result of lower speeds will be that far more buses than planned on will be needed to carry the projected bus loads of people. Indeed, if only one round trip per day (three trips in the three days rather than seven) could be made by each bus, nearly 12,000 bus vehicles will be required to evacuate New Yorkers.[88] This is more full-size buses than now exist in the entire state of New York.[89]

Even more troublesome than the availability of buses is the availability of drivers for the buses. Bus operators have available only a fraction more drivers than vehicles. The required number of drivers normally increases faster than vehicles as the mileage and hours per day of operation increases. In addition, the plan assumes that bus drivers would be willing to leave their families to drive carless persons to the host areas. It assumes further that these same drivers will return to the risk areas to pick up more bus loads of people, while working many more hours per day than usual. Bus drivers may be willing to drive their buses out of a risk area with their families on board, but they are less likely to leave their families in the chaotic conditions presumed to exist in the host areas. This fact is recognized and assumed to be solvable in the crisis relocation plans, which state that "of course, drivers are likely to be torn between their occupational and family duties during a crisis, especially when a relocation is directed. Detailed planning will be needed to assure that drivers' dependents are relocated in a manner to maintain the family integrity."[90] The solution to the problem of ensuring the availability of bus drivers, as for so many other public safety and traffic control personnel, is not really attainable.

There are many other reasons to doubt the projected use of buses and trucks in these crisis relocation studies. These reasons include:

- Trucks are unheated. Counting on them to move large numbers of people in the winter for long distances, with much time spent standing still, is not an enjoyable prospect.

- Since most freeways are made one-way outbound, maintaining the assumed high average travel speeds on the inbound return trips using less direct smaller roads is unlikely.

- There are many segments of the urban population whose limited mobility problems transcend simply not owning a car. These are the elderly, the handicapped (physically and mentally), and institutionalized populations (hospitals, prisons, etc.) who will not be able to use the nonauto modes that are made available to them. This is a large group of people who are not likely to relocate using any transportation options provided in these plans.

- The majority of the buses available to move people are city transit buses. These are not known for their comfort and especially not for their reliability for long trips.

• The assumed occupancy of all buses at 100 percent plus doubling up in seats by children under twelve is certainly optimistic. Other FEMA researchers assume 75 percent occupancy in their *Planning Guidelines*.[91] The assumption of 100 percent occupancy leaves little space for baggage and assumes (again) a uniform scheduling of demand that is unlikely to occur.

In summary, the assumption that 30 percent as many persons can be moved from New York in buses and trucks as in cars founders on many points. These include (1) that the demand won't be there because the large number of available cars will be preferred to the buses and trucks, and (2) buses and drivers won't be available to supply the projected number of departures because of the high speeds assumed on the roadways. Both reasons operate together to result in a bus-truck system that at best operates to offer far fewer departures which are only partially filled by evacuees. The bus-truck strategy is therefore flawed for reasons that follow from the flaws in the automobile highway system assumptions discussed in earlier sections of this chapter.

Capacities of Nonhighway Modes

The crisis relocation planners recognize the importance of moving as many people as possible by nonhighway modes. They state that "to the extent that the remaining 40 percent [of the population in New York who don't own an automobile] are relocated by bus and truck, their movement would compete for highway capacity with the first autos, thus adding to the length of the movement phase,"[92] and that "since highway capacity is demonstrably strained by the number of first automobiles to be handled, rail and air modes of transport should be used to the greatest extent possible for carless relocatees."[93]

The numbers of people planned to be moved by off-highway modes is significant. In New York, over 25 percent of the total population is moved by air, rail, and water. This is about half the number of people moved in cars.[94] The capacity assumptions relating to each of the three nonhighway modes will be discussed briefly.

For rail, it is assumed that ten-car passenger trains carry 1,500 passengers with baggage, including 300 to 600 standees and children doubling up in seats, depending on the seat capacity in the trains. Thirty boxcar freight trains are assumed to carry 2,500 persons plus baggage from New York and 1,500 persons plus baggage from the other major risk areas. This allows six square feet of unheated floor space per traveller from New York. Trains are assumed to average 40 to 50 miles per hour, operate in most cases for twenty hours per day, and depart every half hour from the major Northeast cities other than New York. From New York, passenger train service frequency increases by up to a factor of five on existing passenger lines and is begun from scratch on other lines.[95] These rail services are assumed to move half the nonhighway evacuees from New York[96] and the great majority of nonhighway persons from the other four major Northeast Corridor risk areas.[97]

The discussion of these rail service and capacity assumptions parallels that for bus and trucks in the previous section, with some unique rail problems also identified. First and foremost is the demand side criticism that it is unlikely most of the anticipated rail users will want to use the services offered when so many automobiles remain available. The rail services offered are not attractive. Unheated freight cars are assumed to carry all or the great majority of rail users from three of the four major risk areas outside of New York.[98] Although it is not clear how many freight cars are used to carry New Yorkers, the passenger car equipment availability assumptions for New York are certainly optimistic. For example, only one of the six train routes used to evacuate New York is assumed to use over 25 percent of AMTRAK's national equipment inventory. For all these reasons, therefore, it must be concluded that the unattractiveness and likely unreliability of this nonauto mode will cause people to prefer to use the large number of available remaining cars.

The second major criticism of the rail assumptions in these plans is that three of the six routes that evacuate the majority of assumed New York rail users run only 24 miles to 45 miles to their suburban terminal stations. Users of these trains would either have to be bused in any event or, for the 33 or 45 mile routes, would be delivered "a short distance within the host area."[99] Given that the latter persons would have to be bused as well to their final destinations, this will simply increase the load on the highway system outside the normal suburban commuting area where highway capacity constraints are the greatest. Thus, for the New York region, where the nonauto movement problem is the greatest, the nonhighway mode becomes, once again, a highway mode.

The third major criticism of the rail assumptions are the travel speeds assumed. The 40 to 50 mile per hour average travel speeds are critical to being able to use the same equipment for the large number of round trips assumed to be made over the three-day period. The authors of the plans recognize that this assumes a doubling of freight train speeds:

> Although freight trains typically make average speeds of 20 m.p.h. for entire journeys, enroute delays in relocation service can be minimized

and speeds of 40 m.p.h. appear practicable. Indeed, a common average speed will be essential on lines where mixed passenger and freight trains are to be employed.[100]

Indeed, a 50 mph speed is assumed for the AMTRAK route to Buffalo. These speeds are comparable to average passenger train speeds now in the Northeast Corridor (e.g., between Boston and New York). However, train crews will be unfamiliar with the equipment and with daily operating conditions on the route since passenger train departures increase by up to five times on some lines from New York and start from scratch on many other lines. It is doubtful that these unfamiliar train crews can double freight train speeds and maintain normal passenger train operating speeds for large numbers of additional trains under crisis conditions. This also assumes that the crews will show up (as discussed previously), that there will be no accidents or derailments, and that all freight tracks are upgraded, if necessary, to the track class that permits such high trainspeeds.

The result of slower speeds is that far more rolling stock will be needed than planned for to carry the projected train loads of people. This will strain the already highly optimistic assumptions on the availability of equipment, to say nothing about the availability of train crews. As is the case for bus and truck drivers, the availability of train personnel is more likely to be a problem than the availability of rolling stock. This is probably true, even considering the problems of getting enough locomotives and cars in position on only six hours notice to begin the stream of first departures.

There are several other problems with the rail capacity and service assumptions that make it quite unreasonable to assume that rail can be counted upon to carry as many evacuees as planned. These include the fact that many carless people have mobility problems that transcend simply not owning a car and that assuming uniform 100 percent occupancy of the trains leaves little space for baggage. For these reasons and more, it is not likely that rail will play the projected major role in relieving the highway loadings and shortening evacuation times.

The use of aircraft for crisis relocation of the population involves assumptions that are equally difficult to believe. Eighty percent as many people are projected to be moved by air as by rail from New York. This is one-fifth the number of people moved by autos, or nearly half the people moved by nonhighway modes from New York.[101] The air movement projected from the other four major Northeast Corridor risk areas is smaller but not insignificant. It ranges from 72,000 people moved in three days from Baltimore-Wilmington to 288,000 people moved from Boston-Providence.[102] The capacity assumptions involved in moving this many people by air are impressive. The small host airports are assumed to handle one arrival and one departure every ten minutes throughout a twenty-hour day. This is 240 operations per day. The smaller aircraft able to use these small airports are assumed to carry 100 passengers plus baggage,[103] while the New York study assumed up to 440 passengers per plane, plus baggage.[104] The latter figures assume that 20 percent of the passengers are under twelve and can double up in their seats and that an additional 20 percent of the seated passengers would sit on the floor without seat belts. The possibility that "this practice would have to be discontinued in periods of rough air"[105] was noted in the plan, but the practice was assumed anyway.

In considering these numbers of aircraft operations per day, it should be noted that 240 operations per day at the small host area airports equals the activity at many major hub airports in the country. It is also over half as many current daily operations as at John F. Kennedy International Airport itself[106]—one of the three major departure airports from the New York area. These three airports (including La Guardia and Newark) are planned to increase their combined ordinary number of daily departures from 735 to 1,810 flights—an increase of two and a half times. Thus, it is expected that in six hours about two dozen host airports in the Northeast Corridor will be turned into the equivalent of major hub airports and at least seven existing hub airports now at or close to their normal daily capacity will double or triple their flights handled.

These planned increases in capacity under crisis conditions with six hours preparation time are impressive indeed. Even if the equipment exists in the national inventory, it has to be doubted that the key air traffic control personnel and pilots will show up to operate the system. The former, particularly, are in short supply, and even if there were some multiple of extra controllers available, their job requirements do not lend themselves to switching locations quickly. It takes considerable familiarity to operate a crowded air traffic network, and the Northeast Corridor airspace will be crowded indeed. In addition, the probability of defections of even the most dedicated personnel under crisis relocation conditions has already been discussed. The pilots that do report for duty will be both unfamiliar with the routes and quickly fatigued from long hours of dangerous duty. The chances of accidents are certainly greater under the proposed plan, if only because the flights are so short and involve a much higher number of takeoffs and landings than normal aircraft operations. One runway crash can disable a host airport for many hours.

In addition to the seemingly insurmountable problems of ensuring that pilots and controllers are available, there are major uncertainties that are ignored in these air system plans. The first is the presence of bad weather which would reduce airport capacities. The second is that military flight operations may close all or part of the air space to civilian relocation traffic. At a minimum, military flights may endanger civilian flights to some level not considered acceptable in peacetime. In addition, there are the same criticisms of this nonauto mode as those discussed above. These are that most people will prefer to use cars, and those that do show up at the departure airports won't schedule themselves perfectly to fill every plane. Indeed, most major airports are jammed with ground traffic now. Think of the problems in getting two to three times as many people to the airports as now, while all the other modes are jammed with evacuation traffic.

Despite all these problems, there is one relatively unassailable assumption in the air travel plan: the line haul travel speed assumed. Since the aircraft must stay airborne, we can assume they will maintain their high cruising speed. However, they may have to take indirect flight paths and hold for a long time above saturated host and risk area airports. These probable increases in turnaround times will increase equipment, pilot, flight attendant, and controller requirements.

In summary, the assumption that nearly half the persons on non-highway modes can be evacuated by air from New York, with lesser numbers from other cities, founders at least as much on human scale problems as on technology. That is, people will prefer using the available autos for relocation, and there are not enough pilots and air traffic controllers available to operate the proposed greatly expanded air system. These problems, as well as the uncertainties of bad weather and the possible military preemption or endangering of airspace make it unreasonable to assume that air travel can play the role envisioned in relieving highway congestion and shortening evacuation times from our major cities.

Finally, water transportation is assumed to play a role in crisis relocation only in New York. Three hundred thousand persons, or 10 percent of nonhighway persons, are planned to use ocean freighters and liners, ferries, cruise boats, tugs, and barges.[107] Ocean-going ships operate as far north as Albany, although "a detailed study of host ports was not made. Generally, it will be desirable to move people as far north as possible because this gives maximum relief to overloaded highways."[108] It was assumed that thirty of the seventy to eighty partly loaded ocean freighters in port in New York on a typical day would be loaded with four to six thousand persons and carried to Albany. Several thousand more persons are assumed to be carried on three to six ocean liners, even though "on the average, two liners would be in port and three more would arrive during the [three-day] relocation exercise if not diverted while at sea."[109] Also, "It is common practice for vessels to come in on Thursday and leave Saturday morning. There is no assurance that any given number of liners will be in port at the outset of an emergency."[110]

The Staten Island ferries are all assumed to be pressed into service and to make two to four round trips to Troy, New York, north of Albany. They account for about one-third of the waterborne capacity. Unfortunately, this eliminates their use as a nonhighway mode in shuttling around New York the 40 percent of the population without cars and without direct subway connections to the major train, and air terminals.

The entire fleet of cruise boats and tugs are programmed to be used for relocation, even though the former are seasonal and thus unavailable for four months of the year. In addition, half of all the barges are assumed empty at any given time, and these are also used, allowing six square feet of bottom space per person (regardless of the just previously carried cargo). Two and a half round trips per tug and barge are assumed during the relocation period.

These waterborne passenger loadings assume maximum utilization of the existing fleet (and sometimes the nonexisting fleet). As such, they can be seriously faulted for many of the same reasons as can the other nonauto modes. The principal criticisms are that people will prefer to use the available cars for relocation and that serious defections will occur among the crews and captains of these ships. In addition to not showing up for duty, one can easily assume that the crews of the smaller vessels will use their own ships to escape with their families. Other problems with the water transportation system assumptions are the assumed presence of the ships which are often not in the harbor; the need for the ferries for intraurban service in a crisis; and the fate of passengers in unheated freighter and barge holds and on freighter decks and (possibly) uncovered barges.

It must be concluded that the water transportation scheme in New York crisis relocation study is seriously flawed. It is also not to be believed that people would use the system even if it were able to be put in place. This is because people would prefer to use cars, and would not schedule their departures to match the available capacity. For these reasons, this nonhighway mode also will not play its intended role in relieving highway congestion and shortening evacuation times.

SUMMARY AND CONCLUSION

As stated at the beginning of this chapter, there is uncertainty in estimating evacuation times for our cities under the kinds of crisis conditions that would lead ordinary citizens in a democracy to flee their homes. The most important causes of uncertainty are the assumptions that: (1) people will regulate their evacuation times so as not to cause flow peaking; (2) vehicles will rarely break down or have accidents in heavy traffic; and (3) all required personnel will report to their assumed duties as traffic control officers and operators of the complicated networks of bus, truck, rail, air, and water systems that are intended to make the highway system operate smoothly. About the most certain thing that can be said of these three assumptions is that they are certain to be wrong. As one FEMA research team states, "massive rearrangements of normal traffic patterns seldom work smoothly on the first few days of installation. Yet in the case of crisis relocation, the first days are the only days available."[111]

Seven of the assumptions discussed in this chapter are quantitatively evaluated here for the errors they cause in estimating evacuation times for our cities:

1.   FEMA's assumption of six hours evacuation preparation time is not included in the three-day evacuation time estimate. A longer estimate of twelve hours was quoted earlier from other FEMA planners. A more reasonable minimum estimate would be a day (24 hours), since this is the time needed to change people's work routines and allow as many persons as possible to get themselves into place to operate the evacuation system. Indeed, some moving of train rolling stock (cars), air traffic controllers, and other needed logistics will take longer. Also, to satisfy the plans' stated prerequisite for needed personnel to show up for duty, it would take at least a day to relocate their dependents "in a manner to maintain the family integrity." For these reasons, twenty-four hours is the more realistic minimum estimate of system preparation time.

2.   The basic freeway capacity assumption of 1,500 vehicles per hour per lane should be reduced by 20 percent to account for differences in driving populations between rush hour observed capacities in the West and drivers in the East who are unfamiliar with the roads (and with many of the vehicles).

3.   The assumption that the highways will operate at their maximum capacities for twenty hours a day should be dropped to (at least) a sixteen-hour evacuation day. As quoted in this chapter, the FEMA planners state that even this sixteen-hour day assumption "is somewhat-unsatisfactory as it assumes departures will be spread evenly over 16 hours, and ignores the potential congestion resulting from an uneven distribution of flow."

4.   The assumption that all roads can be operated one-way outbound with no loss in capacity due to nonuniform roadway geometry accounts in the New York plan for about a 25 percent overestimate of highway capacity. (Other risk areas have comparable capacity reductions but their operating plans are less well documented.) This reduction

assumes half the normal capacity for reversed lanes to account for such problems as capacity bottlenecks at entrance ramps, crossing median strips, and the added marginal friction of controlling access to regular two-lane roads made entirely one way. Since the New York plan has all roads operating one way from the city itself with only two identifiable minor roads as exceptions,[112] halving the capacity of half the roadway lanes results in a 25 percent capacity reduction.

5. A conservative and minimal 10 percent reduction in capacity from that assumed in the plans accounts for the crudity of the cordon method used to find the bottlenecks at which roadway capacities should be evaluated.

6. The capacity of the highways used to evacuate New York should be reduced by 10 percent to account for the fact that the capacity of non-access-controlled highways is actually not reduced by 20 percent (as stated in the plans) to account for traffic interruptions at the bottlenecks. Rather, the highways are assumed to operate like freeways in this regard. The 10 percent reduction results from over half the roadway lanes from New York being two-lane non-access-controlled roads.[13]

7. In addition to first autos, essentially all of the approximately 75 percent available other autos in the risk area of the Northeast Corridor will use the highways for evacuation. This allows us to ignore the effects of the many assumptions made for nonauto modes in carrying so many of the people presumed to be evacuated in the allotted three days. That is, to the extent these other modes fail to fulfill their scheduled numbers of departures because of personnel and equipment shortages, the population will use the remaining cars. Ignoring the errors in the nonauto mode assumptions is conservative in that these errors increase evacuation times. In addition, the use of the 75 percent remaining less reliable second and third cars by unfamiliar drivers not well able to prepare the cars for long trips will greatly increase the uncertain effect of assuming no reduction in roadway capacities due to unplanned flow interruptions (running out of gas, other vehicle breakdowns, accidents, etc.).

The above capacity reductions are multiplicative in their impact since they result from independent effects. The resulting multiplier can be applied to the three-day Northeast Corridor time estimate, rather than the 3.3 day New York estimate, to be conservative.

The net result of these various factors is to reduce the capacity of the roadway system to less than 40 percent of the amount estimated in the plans [(0.8 × 0.8 × 0.75 × 0.9 × 0.9)] while handling 75 percent more cars. This increases the relocation time by 4.5 times [1.75 ÷ 0.39)] plus one day for system preparation, or a total of over fourteen days. The result is over two weeks to evacuate the population rather than the three days estimated in the plans.

As discussed earlier, this two-week estimate is also based only on the effects of those assumptions that may be quantified with some degree of certainiy. The estimate does not include the evacuation time extending effects of errors in three of the most uncertain assumptions in the crisis relocation plans: (1) no flow peaking, (2) flows uninterrupted by vehicle breakdowns or accidents, and (3) all required traffic control officers and nonauto mode operators reporting for duty.

As the inevitable initial surge of traffic comes and the congestion and traffic jam sets in, the California Highway Patrol's estimate of ten minutes to clear each one minute of traffic jam may be a reasonable factor to use to measure the error in these last three assumptions. This means multiplying the length of time needed to evacuate our cities by an additional factor of ten. The California factor of ten is even based on traffic subsiding after one or two peak commuting hours, allowing highways to recover except possibly once each twenty-four hour period in the middle envisioned in these plans, traffic will not ease up to allow the highways to recover except possibly once each twenty-four hour perod in the middle of the night.

In summary, the true evacuation time estimated on the basis of those assumptions whose errors can be quantified with some degree of certainty lies closer to three weeks rather than three days. The true evacuation time may be far longer than three weeks if the factor of ten is a reasonable estimate of the time required to clear up the inevitable enormous traffic jams. As cars run out of gas and break down and people run out of food and water, there will be no spare highway capacity anywhere with which to distribute life-promoting food and equipment. There will be no empty roads on which to flee or to service the population attempting to flee. In fact, most of the civilian population will be out in the open on clogged highways without their familiar life support systems during the very period when the threat of nuclear attack is greatest. Therefore, rather than consider these to be crisis relocation plans, they should more properly be called chaos relocation plans. Such "evacuations" will only increase human suffering and increase the threat of nuclear reprisals.

7

Knowing the Worst Too Young: Children and Crisis Relocation

Irwin Redlener

The tongue of the sucking child
cleaveth to the roof of his mouth for thirst;
the young children ask bread,
and no man breaketh it unto them.

Lamentations 4:4

... Other patients who may be classified as "hard-core" or "hard-care" patients, but are not necessarily aged, include persons receiving the following therapies: respirator, kidney dialysis (as of January 1, 1974, 46.9 persons per one million population were receiving kidney dialysis therapy), oxygen tent, stryker frame, and traction. Serious burn patients, immature and premature babies (in 1970, 7.9 percent and 9.3 percent of all live births occurring in 38 states and the District of Columbia were immature and premature, respectively), and babies delivered by Caesarian section are also included in the "hard-core" general hospital population.

SOURCE: M.N. Laney, et al., *Management of Medical Problems Resulting from Population Relocation*, prepared for the Defense Civil Preparedness Agency, Research Triangle Institute, Research Triangle Park, North Carolina, May 1976, pp. I-4–I-7.

The most dramatic single general requirement for social organization in this period is meeting the conditions of the race for economic viability . . . [and] . . . one central social issue is whether depletions in the labor force can be met from other sources. Assuming attack conditions under which there were unexpected, excessive losses of males, it would be reasonable to expect entry of large numbers of women into the labor force. But the factors governing the entrance of women or dependent minors into the labor force are imperfectly understood for many conceivable situations. At what point does the entry of women into the labor force depress the population growth rate to unacceptable levels—particularly when in the short term, labor-force requirements may appear more critical than restoring population growth rates? The parallel issue for dependent minors is to determine at what point the removal of youth from the educational process, in order to meet needs of the labor force or military service, will critically deplete the long-term educational base required for a technical-industrial society.

Here, also, the problem of orphans can be seen in larger perspective. The orphan problem is illustrative of the kinds of needs for restoring basic social relationships that will exist in the reorganization period. During the adaptations imposed by warning, impact, attack, and shelter, short-term adjustments to broken social ties must be made. As the society moves toward restoring its preattack institutional forms, however, short-term adaptations to meet purposes of immediate survival must be replaced by restoration of social relationships which can meet functional needs of individuals and groups. . . .

SOURCE: S.D. Vestermark, Jr., "Social Indicators of Social Effects and the Social Inventory after Attack," in *Postattack Recovery from Nuclear War*, Office of Civil Defense, Washington, D.C., 1967, pp. 350–51.

IMPLICATIONS OF THE FINDINGS

All the implications of the findings contained in this report cannot be examined because the state of demography does not allow for the relating of social processes to demographic processes in every instance. The results do, however, allow us to place certain parameters on community processes that are of interest to the designers of countermeasure systems. If the population of communities changes as much as the extreme cases in this analysis, postattack migration policies will have to be drawn or spontaneous migration in response to a variety of pressures will relocate the postattack population. The changes in composition documented in this report would not be allowed to persist uncorrected by the community. Unfortunately, we cannot assess the "natural" pressures that might be acting on such communities.

The problem of caring for the dependent population has been often raised. These results underscore that problem without offering any means of solving it. Simply because evacuation increases the dependency ratio is no reason to abandon that defensive posture. The saving in lives may be more important than the additional problems. However, some planning for those problems should be undertaken.

The most practical implication of this analysis is that postattack surveys of the population will be necessary if resources are to be well used for the benefit of future generations. . . .

SOURCE: William W. Pendleton, *A Second Study of the Demography of Nuclear War*, prepared for the Office of Civil Defense, Human Sciences Research, Inc., McLean, Virginia, August 1967, p. 58.

PREMATURE BABY

If the baby is born before it is due and is very small, he will sleep most of the time. He may look bluer than other babies.

The most important thing is to keep him warm. If the shelter is cold, it may be wise to wrap the baby and place him inside the mother's clothing or bed for her body heat. If this is done, precautionary measures should be taken to prevent suffocation.

It may be possible to keep him warm with hot water bottles in a large box into which a smaller box may be placed for his bed. Be careful not to burn the baby.

The premature baby needs very little food—nothing at all for 2 or 3 days. If he seems strong enough to suck at the mother's breast, that should be tried. Otherwise, use a spoon or a medicine dropper in the manner described in the section "Making a Formula."

The very small baby may need to be fed every 2 or 3 hours. He may be able to take only one or two teaspoons of the evaporated milk and water mixture at a time. If he spits up, he is probably getting too much.

Bed may be made from drawer, box, basket, etc. It should be heated with warm bricks, bottles, stones, or similar items. Be very careful not to use next to baby and run risk of burning him. A small box may be put inside a larger box with heated articles between. Pad and line with newspapers and cloth or blankets, and cover the structure with a blanket to keep heat in.

SOURCE: Defense Civil Preparedness Agency and the U.S. Public Health Service, *Family Guide Emergency Health Care: A Reference Guide for Students of Medical Self-Help Training Course*, Department of Health, Education, and Welfare, Maryland, September 1972, p. 76.

A number of health and medical problems are bound to be associated with plans for rapid evacuation of large populations over substantial distances. While these problems among the general population would pose difficulties, for special population subgroups such as the institutionalized, the handicapped, and the elderly, they might represent insurmountable obstacles. Children constitute one such population subgroup and in this chapter we focus on the health and medical problems involved in plans for their evacuation in the event of nuclear war.

Inattention to the special concerns of children is crucial to FEMA's claim that CRP ensures survivability, because the duration and quality of societal survival is inexorably linked to the fate of children. A society without children is experiencing its final generation. A survival plan designed without substantial priority given to the youngest generation is unlikely to be based on assumptions that reflect true understanding of the notion of human survival.

Confronting the effects of using weapons of mass destruction forces us to exercise precision in defining the term "survival." In addition to the immediate human toll they exact, nuclear weapons carry the potential to destroy the support systems necessary for all aspects of human existence. Industry, economy, food production, government, transportation, communications, and energy production are vital contributors to the complex megasystem of modern society.

Confusion over the working definition of survival is central to current civil defense planning for nuclear war. Webster's *New Collegiate Dictionary* defines survival as "living or continuing longer than another person or thing" or, "the continuation of life or existence. . . ."

The concept of continuity is key to this definition. When applied to a society or nation subjected to the extensive devastation wrought by nuclear war, the definition of survival becomes most complex and problematic. In FEMA's usage, however, the meaning of survival could be more appropriately defined as limited to the concept of "aliveness." Here we have no sense of continuity, of existence through time. Under the entry for *alive*, Webster's gives: "having life, not dead or inanimate." The design of crisis relocation planning, to maximize short-term "aliveness," fails to incorporate any understanding of what is involved in securing real survival over time for individuals or for society as a whole.

The greater the extent of nuclear destruction, the closer we approach the limits of the most rudimentary definition—simple biological survival. Such an outcome does not support long-term societal continuity and fails to embrace the intricate fabric of human existence. Each of us lives within overlapping perimeters of basic social units: the family, the community, and society as a whole. Ensuring continuity of these units must be viewed as required elements in programs that are proclaimed as securing our survival in the event of nuclear war. Children, our messengers to the future, provide that living connection to the years ahead, mitigating the limits and mortality of the elders.

Seen from this broader perspective, in addition to attending to the need for immediate, biological aliveness, our survival as a nation may well be linked to our ability to preserve continuity of social values and social systems. Western attitudes have evolved over centuries to the relatively recent recognition of the value of children as a collective resource, preserving, modifying, and embellishing the accomplishments of society during passage from one generation to the next. In the last 200 years, paralleling and contributing to a decline in infant mortality in industrialized societies, adults have come to view children as offering a key to understanding our own humanity.[1] Children express essential emotions unencumbered by complicated adult overlays. Each generation of children is mankind starting anew; a rebirth and chance to take the best of parental and social values and move civilization one more step forward. Children present the world with hope and adults with a running vision of past, present, and future. Without children, we do not know ourselves and, as a society, lose meaning as surely as we lose being.

Sound investment in programs and facilities to assure maximum opportunity for all children to enjoy health, emotional contentment, and full development of potential has expanded enormously in the decades since World War II. Part of the system to provide these opportunities includes an extensive national program of child health maintenance and thousands of pediatric hospital in-patient units, intensive care units, and special therapeutic and custodial centers. These latter include psychiatric units and residential environments for intellectually impaired or developmentally disadvantaged children.

As a society we have also committed our energy to the search for increasingly effective ways of caring for marginally viable infants and children. Progress has been particularly great in the field of neonatology, to the extent of changing our basic concepts of viability. A generation ago, the tiny premature was left to establish his or her own prognosis. Little was available for general life support, not to mention therapeutic intervention. Today in virtually every medium-sized and large city neonatal intensive care units are capable of providing well controlled environments and a wide variety of therapies for a host of problems that twenty years ago would have meant certain death for an infant. Children's intensive care wards offer the hope of life to thousands of children with life-threatening illness or trauma.

In view of this investment, it is reasonable to examine the nature and feasibility of FEMA's concept of *child* protection in the nuclear age. If we cannot protect our children, we truly cannot promise survival to ourselves and our society. Failure to deal with the special concerns of children during the evacuation phase—the first element in FEMA's population protection plan—offers an important yardstick with which to evaluate the survival potential the plan creates. Whatever hardships are

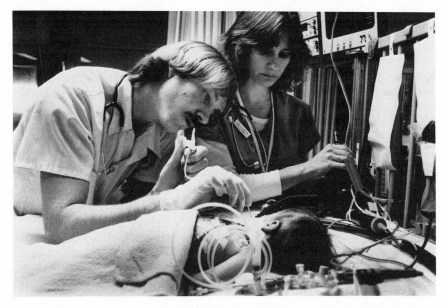

Intensive Care Unit in University Hospital Setting. Photograph by Ken Bernstein. From the film, Code Gray: Ethical Dilemmas in Nursing. *Reproduced by permission of Fanlight Productions, Boston, Ma.*

imposed by evacuation will be compounded by the shelter period and immeasurably intensified in the event of nuclear war.

Despite the existence of much literature on children in war and disaster, children receive only incidental or oblique attention in FEMA policy statements and civil defense research reports.[2] Studies dating from the 1960s, using more limited attack scenarios on nonrelocated populations, discuss disproportionate infant and child mortality and increased numbers of orphans in terms of their effects on subsequent demographic profiles.[3] An article on radiation post-attack notes that at given exposure levels children are more prone than adults to develop later malignancies. The article also suggests a post-shelter work strategy that relies on an outdoor older labor force.[4] Reports on medical plans for crisis relocation assign hospitalized children to the "hard-core" category that might not be relocatable, but do not further discuss the issues involved.[5]

As we assess the problems specific to childen inherent in the CRP model of evacuation, it is important to note that the burden of establishing feasibility rests with FEMA, since it is they who are promoting their plan as ensuring survival from the ravages of nuclear war. Were their claims less extravagant, our scrutiny might be less severe.

THE IMPACT OF POPULATION EVACUATION ON NEEDS OF CHILDREN

A pre-attack evacuation plan is fraught with hazards for children. Even if no attack came, the process of relocation would devastate the health care delivery system to such a degree that a substantial danger would be created for children sick at the time of CRP activation. Children who became sick or who were born with special problems during the evacuation phase would confront a decimated, disorganized system incapable of providing sophisticated, potentially life-saving care. Of necessity, the morbidity and mortality rates for the pediatric patient would increase dramatically. At least for the child population, evacuation would exact its own death and disability toll. No attempt to address this issue has been advanced by FEMA.

From the child advocacy perspective, numerous questions arise pertaining to the health needs of children and other issues relating to their general well-being. We can formulate the questions; FEMA remains responsible for the answers.

Which Hospitalized Children Can Be Safely Discharged?

In contrast to the adult hospitalized population, very few children are admitted for diagnostic or elective workups. Most pediatric patients, excluding those receiving routine newborn care, are maintained in hospitals for the treatment of acute and often life-threatening infections, acute trauma, or necessary surgical procedures. A substantial portion of pediatric in-patients are assigned to intensive care facilities—especially premature and sick newborn units. In the newborn intensive care unit, the hold on life is often very precarious. The withdrawal of even few elements of the complex care system will, for many infants, significantly reduce the chances for survival.

It would be unrealistic to expect that more than 20 percent of all hospitalized children could be safely discharged to their families, themselves in the midst of crisis evacuation. Those children who were discharged would still need some form of ongoing medical care and observation. How this would be provided during evacuation and during the host area preparation phase is never established by FEMA.

Children with physical handicaps manifested by impaired mobility would be proportionately less able to move freely and participate in the strenuous and stressful relocation process. Patients awaiting surgery for critical illness, or those who are chronically ill and dependent on such resources as renal dialysis, will have a substantial increase in mortality rate. At least 85 percent of children's dialysis beds are located in risk areas. Host areas would generally not be able to duplicate these services; thus, patients removed from their primary resource center would be subject to unacceptable risk.

How Will Appropriate Care Be Provided for Those Children Who Cannot Be Discharged from the Acute Hospital Setting?

The provision of adequate care to acute hospital patients who are unable to be discharged is a complex task. A disproportionate number of physicians and support workers will be required to remain behind for these children. Most will be needed on-site and cannot reasonably be expected to commute into the hospital for the delivery of care.

Additionally, many parents would be reluctant to leave areas where their children are hospitalized. Would FEMA provide vital services during and beyond the initial evacuation phase for families who chose to stay with their babies? The questions are haunting and not addressed. Separation of children from families has been found in other war or disaster settings to be a major factor in exacerbating social distress.

Who Will Provide Care for Institutionalized Children During and After Evacuation?

Thousands of children in target area residential settings must be adequately accounted for in crisis relocation planning. They include children with severe developmental and intellectual handicaps as well as children and adolescents in residential psychiatric facilities. The burden of establishing feasible plans for dealing with such children during relocation again falls upon FEMA planners, who do not address the issue.

How Can Care Be Provided in the Host Areas to Those Hospitalized Children Who Have Been Evacuated?

Assuming that a significant proportion of specialized health care providers must remain behind in order to care for the majority of children who cannot be evacuated, it is clear that inadequate resources will exist for assignment to the host communities. Many of the health care providers will likely opt for remaining with their families. It is impossible to know how many physicians, nurses, respiratory therapists, and others will be willing to remain in an urban population center designated as a prime target risk while their families flee to some distant relocation center.

What Mechanism Could Be Established to Cope with the Usual and Expected Incidence of New Medical Problems in the Evacuated Population?

Again, if one assumes that a substantial number of the critical health care providers remain behind to manage the nondischargable patients in the target areas, a deficit remains in the health care system available to the host areas. Furthermore, the host areas would undoubtedly experience deficiencies of specialized facilities, equipment, and supplies necessary to care for anticipated ongoing health care needs. The incidence of serious perinatal problems would be at least as great in the evacuated population as in the pre-evacuation general population. Given the absence of adequate facilities and the deficiency of specialized personnel, a substantial rise in perinatal mortality and morbidity would be expected.

What happens to the two-year-old who develops acute bacterial epiglottitis in the host community? What happens to the six-month-old with meningitis or the seven-year-old with acute appendicitis? A long list of unanswered questions begins to emerge as the analysis of crisis relocation proceeds.

What About Special Nutritional and Hydration Needs of Children?

The younger the infant, the more critical is the need for an adequate nutritional base. Those children under one year of age who are not breast feeding (at least 50 percent of all infants) will require special formulas and feeding regimens. There is no evidence that FEMA has made or plans to make provisions for these special requirements either during evacuation or in case of actual attack.

A related secondary problem is the hydration status of children. It is safe to assume that the incidence of viral and bacterial infections as well as gastrointestinal derangements secondary to stress or other factors would be substantially increased during the shelter period. Young infants would be particularly susceptible to dehydration. A few large watery stools in a four-week-old infant, for example, can result in significant clinical dehydration. Discontinuation of all feedings and provision of intravascular fluid replacement would be required. No provision has been made to manage this situation in the host areas.

What Are the Plans to Deal with Behavioral, Social, and Psychiatric Problems of Children?

With the collapse of the customary care-taking network, adults and children alike would experience acute anxiety, if not panic, in the face of the sudden, forced exodus from major population centers and normal life patterns to unknown and distant host areas. Uncertainty over the fate of homes, communities, and relatives, and fear of the unknown stress of relocation and of the harsh realities that might follow, may not be assuaged by assurances from evacuation officials. Anger may develop as doubts grow about provision of needs and protection from harm. The residents of the host areas will be unable and perhaps unwilling to comfort and nurture the evacuating millions. The extent to which anxiety and possible panic might dominate the collective psyche of the evacuees will have particular impact on the young.

Parents, themselves stressed to their limits, may not be able to provide for the physical, let alone emotional, needs of their children. Many children will inevitably be separated from their parents or primary caretakers. Who then will look after them? Each evacuee will be struggling to make those adaptations required for survival. Few may be willing to assume the additional responsibilities of children who have been separated from their own parents. Studies of wartime evacuation during World War II observe that the social disruption created by separation of families and billeting of strangers with strangers eroded cooperative spirit, intensified antagonisms among individuals, and exerted a significantly adverse impact on group morale.[6]

In an extreme scenario, one might contemplate regional collapse of social control during evacuation and impending attack. Groups of children might band together and, on a comparatively inadequate scale, enter the struggle for sustenance and shelter on their own terms, contributing to migrancy and delinquency that may attend the massive social disintegration caused by the evacuation. Widespread violence spurred by fear and dissolution of social order would place children in extraordinary danger.

Nothing in FEMA's plans for evacuation and shelter reveal any comprehension of the potential magnitude and severity of the psychological problems both adults and children might encounter. No recognition is given to the fact that in situations of extreme stress the children, as the most vulnerable members of society, are the first to suffer.

CONCLUSION

Over the last several years an abundance of information has become available to the general public, so that few among us have been able to escape the conclusion that nuclear war would be a tragic catastrophe for all nations of the Northern Hemisphere, and perhaps for the world. Yet, many people still prefer to deny any notion of finality or irreversibility. They cling to the concept of ultimate survival, precious to the human need for continuity. Civil defense plans for nuclear war prey on this innate hopefulness that persists in human beings no matter how grim the present may seem. People want to believe that there is a way out, that FEMA has a plan that will ensure survival.

Survival for our society, however, is inextricably bound to the survival of our children. Without the sense and substance of generational continuity, survival beyond short-term aliveness is impossible. The failure of CRP to provide for the care and nurturance of children as the highest possible priority represents a wholly insufficient understanding of the meaning of survival.

The plan is not only conceptually marred but, if carried into effect, would pose a significant threat to the health and well-being of the young. The dangers are inherent in the basic nature of the plan and would become manifest because of the evacuation itself, even if a nuclear war were never to occur. The activation of crisis relocation would without doubt markedly increase mortality and morbidity among the child population, with the youngest at greatest risk. It would probably disrupt child-adult relationships profoundly and extensively, and it might very well cause an increased incidence of psychological casualties. *All these effects can be realistically entertained as consequences of the plan itself.*

For these reasons, CRP can be seen as offering a promise of survival it cannot possibly deliver. Far from granting us a chance for life, it serves to foster a dangerous illusion that could cause great harm, especially to our young.

PART II

The Flood: During and After

8

A Home in That Rock: Sheltering the Relocated Population

Lawrence E. Susskind

And the kings of the earth
and the great men
and the rich men
and the chief captains
and the mighty men
and every bondman
and every free man
hid themselves in the dens
and in the rocks of the mountains.
                          Revelation 6:15

The Federal Emergency Management Agency has determined that a protection factor of 40 will provide adequate protection for public fallout shelters. For PF 40 protection, only 2½ percent of the open-field radiation will reach the shelter location for which the PF was calculated.

FALLOUT SHELTERS

There are a variety of situations for which fallout shelters are needed. One such situation is the protection of the general population during that time period when the fallout radiation is hazardous to life. In general, public fallout shelters have the function only of providing protection from nuclear fallout radiation. However, there are some activities in our society which must be accommodated even during periods of extreme hazards. Health-care service is one such activity. . . .

Higher protection factor levels and shelter environments of higher quality are established for Emergency Operating Centers and hospitals than for public fallout shelters, in order to give added assurance that the emergency staffs can perform their work effectively and efficiently. The Federal Emergency Management Agency recommends that these types of emergency service facilities have a protection level of PF 100 or better.

PUBLIC FALLOUT SHELTERS

Public fallout shelters are facilities providing protection from fallout radiation which are intended for use by the general public during emergency periods. These do not include private fallout shelters in residences and other buildings which are not intended to be available to the general public, although the standards are the same for both.

Basic Considerations

Public fallout shelters have but one purpose—to provide the minimum necessary protection from fallout radiation in a minimum life-sustaining environment. The minimum protection level for public fallout shelters is PF 40. The minimum life-sustaining environment consists of a supply of drinking water, tolerable temperature and humidity (these are combined in a human comfort factor called *effective temperature*), sanitary facilities, adequate fresh air, and low-level lighting if natural light is not available in the shelter. These are the basic elements covered in the standard for public fallout shelters. . . .

Identifying The Shelter

Since it often is the case that only part of a building will provide protection of PF 40 or better, the suitable shelter space must be identified for users, including its boundaries and limits. Diagrams of floor plans are one way to do this; trained shelter managers offer another way.

A Minimum Standard

As is the case with most building standards, minimum criteria which meet the intended objectives are given in the standard for public fallout shelters. The principal reason is to keep the cost for meeting the standard to the lowest possible level and yet meet the desired objectives. Accordingly, there should be no hesitation to exceed the standard for public fallout shelters, provided that the particular building situation and economics permit.

Radiation Shielding

As indicated in the description of the radiation hazard above, the fundamental objective of a fallout shelter is that it provide protection from fallout radiation for occupants. Suitable radiation shielding is the most important feature that any shelter offers and should be given priority attention in establishing any fallout shelter.

Higher protection factor values, if they can be achieved with little or no extra effort, are especially worthy of consideration. The advantages of minimizing the amount of radiation that a person receives are indicated in the preceding discussion of radiation effects upon living tissue. The ultimate measure of the amount of radiation received, of course, is the protection factor. If protection factors greater than PF 40 can be achieved, they certainly should be provided.

Temperature

The maximum effective temperature value for public fallout shelters is higher than would be permitted in spaces used daily. The effective temperature value of 82°F (28°C) for public fallout shelters is an upper limit of tolerance for sedentary people, and should not be exceeded. Fully occupied fallout shelters in warm, humid climates are especially likely to produce effective temperatures in excess of the upper limit value unless large air-flow volumes are provided.

Because heat buildup occurs in a relatively closed fallout shelter at full or nearly full occupancy, a minimum dry-bulb temperature of 50°F (10°C) normally can be maintained without adding heat to the space. Dry-bulb temperatures that are too high will be the usual situation rather than temperatures that are too low for comfort.

Ventilation

Proper ventilation of fallout shelters is, perhaps, the second most important consideration. Fresh air—that is, oxygen—is essential to sustain life. Ordinarily, this is not a great concern for buildings which are designed for daily use. We take for granted that a fresh air supply is introduced into building spaces through normal ventilation, which may be either natural air flow or mechanically driven air flow.

Fallout shelters present new ventilation problems. First, the very purpose of a fallout shelter usually results in it being a relatively closed space, possibly a basement or an interior space. Natural ventilation is restricted in such circumstances, and mechanical (forced) ventilation cannot be relied upon, because electric power cannot be assured to remain available during and after a period of nuclear attack. Second, when a fallout shelter is fully occupied up to its limit, which is one person in every 10 square feet of floor area, the consumption of oxygen, discharge of carbon dioxide, buildup of unpleasant odors, and heat and moisture buildup from occupants combine to create nearly intolerable conditions in spaces which have poor or no ventilation.

For these reasons, the ventilation system of a fallout shelter must be carefully checked. If natural ventilation is to be used, then the air-flow volume must be sufficient to meet [adequate] health and comfort conditions. . . . If deficiencies are found, then either the shelter occupancy must be reduced, or forced ventilation must be provided. If forced ventilation is to be used, then a reliable power supply to the fans must be assured to maintain the required air-flow volume.

Potable Water

A supply of drinking water is the only other feature of public fallout shelters which is essential to sustain life for periods longer than just a few days. Accordingly, provision must be made for the needed water. 3.5 gallons of potable water per shelter occupant are to be provided. This amount is based upon a 14-day shelter stay-time, or one quart per day, and is for drinking purposes only. No other uses are included in the base amount. If other uses of water are expected in the fallout shelter, such as for sanitary purposes, then the storage capacity must be increased.

There are several ways in which the required drinking water can be provided in a fallout shelter. The one way not to be counted upon is the public water main. Public water supply systems are likely to be disrupted during a period of nuclear attack—either due to power failure which could render pumping stations inoperative or due to breakage of the water lines at some remote point. This means that the emergency water supply must be at or near the fallout shelter—either storage tank(s) or a well at the site. Water can be stored either in permanently installed tanks or in individual containers. Occasionally, it will be possible to obtain the required water from that trapped in building lines. In such cases, a suitably located outlet valve will be needed to withdraw the water. . . .

SOURCE: FEMA, *Standards for Fallout Shelters*, Washington, D.C., 1979, pp. 21–24.

Prediction of the aftermath of a nuclear conflict—a war that has never occurred—is an enormously difficult task. Nevertheless, the areas of uncertainty gradually are being reduced.

A close look at the facts shows with fair certainty that with reasonable protective measures, the United States could survive nuclear attack and go on to recover within a relatively few years. . . .

The problems Americans would face and what they would have to do about those problems to return the Nation to "normal" have been fairly well defined.

Priority needs of people—beginning while in shelter and continuing when they leave shelter—would be for leadership, reassurance, and information and instructions. . . .

All communities should plan to be self-reliant in the event of nuclear attack. Many communities may be isolated by the attack—cut off from outside help, supplies, or information. Within a given area, it may be impossible to reach certain towns, villages, or even isolated houses. Surviving communities may be on their own for several weeks after an attack. . . .

Within 24 hours after the end of an attack, nearly all the hazardous local fallout would be down on the ground, and radiological monitors would have determined how much fallout had occurred in each local area. It would then be possible for radiological defense officers and monitors to make sufficiently accurate predictions of fallout radiation intensities to permit planning for emergence from shelter.

The first persons to be allowed out of public shelters, for short periods of time, would be emergency workers. They could spend increasingly longer periods of time outside shelter to replenish food and other supplies, to make repairs, and to restore public utilities and other essential facilities.

As radiation levels continued to decrease, nonemergency workers could be allowed to leave public shelter, and persons in home shelters could be told that it would be safe to go outside.

SOURCE: FEMA, *Camera-Ready News Columns*, No. 15, Washington, D.C., December 1980.

America's civil defense planning effort begins with the assumption that somehow, in the face of an impending nuclear attack, roughly 145 million Americans will have adequate warning and will be persuaded to abandon their homes and workplaces and move, in an orderly fashion, to predesignated shelters in outlying areas.[1] This is an assumption with which most civil defense planning in the United States currently begins.[2] Note that even under the best of circumstances more than 80 million Americans would be relegated to makeshift home basement shelters with less than desirable radiological defenses.[3]

In this chapter I will examine the kinds of commitments we, as a nation, appear to be making to civil defense. I will review the questions we should be asking ourselves about the system of shelters currently proposed, the cost implications of the civil defense program currently in effect, and the logic of a crisis relocation planning program that may add to rather than diminish the chances of nuclear war.

SHELTER PREPARATION

What would it take to have adequate shelter ready and waiting should that awful day come? First, the U.S. government (or some private organization) would have to commit billions of dollars to cover the cost of identifying, building, and equipping public shelters. These shelters would have to be adequate to protect and provide for evacuees for a period of at least two to four weeks, and perhaps much longer. A management system would have to be devised to allocate evacuees from large cities and other targeted areas to public shelters or private residences (shored up at the last minute). This management system would also have to handle the rapid importation and allocation of food, water, and other crucial supplies not stocked in shelters beforehand. Communications, medical assistance, food preparation, sanitation, radiological detection, and other minimal conditions would have to be met amid an atmosphere of terror and disorder. While current civil defense planning in the United States has not yet come to grips with the problem of maintaining America's basic industrial, economic, and political infrastructure, it also would have to be "sheltered" and brought under the umbrella of crisis relocation management.[4] These would seem to be minimally acceptable conditions for adequate civil defense.

How does one begin to think about the logistics of providing public shelters for 145 million relocatees which will adequately protect those individuals from radiation and enable them to survive when cut off from the outside world for a minimum of two weeks? How many such shelters already exist? How many will have to be built from scratch? To what extent do existing buildings lend themselves to conversion to shelters? What is the true magnitude of cost involved in building, equipping, and managing these buildings so that they can be called on if needed?

One gets a sense of the huge numbers involved here when one realizes that if 1,000 people could be accommodated in each public shelter (and that is more than the maximum size of existing designated shelters), the country would require 145,000 such structures. The buildings could not be distributed randomly across the landscape but would be needed in the nation's small towns—the places least likely to contain existing structures that might lend themselves to protecting large numbers of people.

The true cost involved in developing a shelter system that meets the government's own specifications of adequacy are far in excess of what FEMA is currently proposing, as the following analysis indicates. It is important to underline that the cost estimation presented here is an extremely conservative one as it includes figures *only* for the 145 million relocatees. The analysis says nothing about the billions of dollars that are surely involved in protecting the remaining third of the nation's population that has not had to move but is assumed to hunker down, fortify its shelters and wait out the nuclear attack in its existing locale.

In 1968 the Department of Defense completed its National Shelter System. It is important to note that this system only identified "potential" shelter spaces. That is, with certain modifications, the spaces identified could provide some type of reliable fallout protection for citizens.[5] At the time this inventory of potential shelters was completed, though, the government had not yet developed detailed relocation plans. Thus, the National Shelter System did not provide an inventory of buildings suited to the needs of the evacuees most likely to arrive in each nonmetropolitan area.

In a 1979 report entitled *Instrumentation Requirements for Radiological Defense Crisis Relocation Planning*, the Oak Ridge National Laboratory summarizes the most recent relocation estimates generated by the Defense Civil Preparedness Agency (DCPA). Relocation is presumed in only 515 counties. Public shelters adequate to house all relocates are not presumed to exist. The order of preference among available shelters is assumed to be (1) National Shelter Survey (NSS) shelters (most desirable), (2) CRP facilities, (3) home basements, and (4) expedient shelters. Estimated distributions of these shelters for the lower forty-eight states are as follows: 34 percent of the population in NSS shelters, 17 percent in CRP facilities, 42 percent in home basements, and 7 percent in expedient shelters. The computer simulation used by the DCPA indicated that three-fourths of the people requiring expedient shelters would be in "only" four states: California, Florida, Louisiana, and Texas.[6]

What is painfully obvious is that the federal government is currently assuming a system of civil defense that will guarantee adequate shelter to only 50 percent of the population under the best of circumstances. Even that estimate, to come true, would require the expenditure of billions of dollars annually. Yet, for the next seven years, the president has requested (and the key committees in Congress have agreed to) an expenditure of only $300 million a year. And of this, only 5 percent will be passed through to local governments for actual improvements in shelters.[7]

In 1968, the Department of Defense contracted for survival supplies to be placed in fallout shelters, and these were delivered to cities throughout the United States. These supplies consisted of food, medicines, and sanitation equipment.[8] The food that was distributed had a shelf life of five years.[9] In many communities, the supplies distributed fifteen years ago have not been replaced. We have no system in the United States for monitoring and replenishing these stores. Just the cost of maintaining the food, water, and medical supplies needed to stock each shelter is enormous. When one realizes that most of these foodstuffs would have to be held off the market and then discarded, it is not hard to realize the likely public reaction to government proposals to keep a system of shelters adequately stocked. Thus, it is not surprising that current civil defense planning efforts in the United States assume that most evacuees from urban areas will bring the supplies they need with them.[10] While this assumption may not appear reasonable, given the speed with which evacuation would have to occur and the difficulties of ensuring that the necessary commodities were available and that citizens would know what to do, it may be a more reasonable assumption than the alternative—i.e., continually restocking thousands of public shelters with food, water, and medical supplies.

But suppose we could find a way to acquire surplus food at well below market rates. At best, we might be able to put aside $5 per person per day worth of food for fifteen days. (We do not know exactly how long people would be forced to remain in shelters following a nuclear blast; indeed, the time will vary by location depending on the pattern of attack, prevailing winds, and a variety of other factors. I am assuming a minimum of fifteen days.) For 145 million people to find the food they need on the day they arrive in the shelters, it would require an expenditure of approximately $9 billion. That makes no allowance for the cost of shipping, unloading, and storing everything, especially if it were done beforehand. A substantial portion of that expenditure would have to be repeated every five years.

The task of building new shelters or upgrading potential shelters would also be expensive. FEMA, in its manual, *Standards for Fallout Shelters*, specifies that the inside temperature must be no higher than 82°F nor lower than 50°F during a given day.[11] To meet these temperature specifications—given the climate range of the continental United States—and to allow for an adequate oxygen and carbon dioxide exchange within the shelters, FEMA has estimated that the shelter ventilating systems must provide from 7.5 to 50 cubic feet of fresh air per minute per shelter occupant. At this mechanical ventilation rate, public shelters with minimum head room of 6.5 feet will be required to support population densities of one person per 10 square feet.[12] Were these ventilating systems to fail, however, this space allocation (65 cubic feet per person) would not long support life. It constitutes approximately one-tenth the 500 cubic feet per person required for shelters planned without mechanical ventilation.[13]

In addition to ventilation, potential or new shelters would have to be designed to ensure adequate lighting. FEMA suggests a minimum power-driven lighting level of two footcandles at the floor. To rely on "natural illumination"—an alternative proposed by FEMA—would restrict light in the shelter to daytime hours and, since glass provides poor shielding against radiation, would erode protection factors.[14] Battery operated equipment would certainly be needed to provide twenty-five footcandles of light for special activities such as first aid and food handling.[15] The October 1977 issue of *International Civil Defense* stressed the need for two-way communications systems in fallout shelters.[16] Most existing shelter spaces do not have communications systems that are readily accessible to shelter occupants. Telephone lines and normal radio systems can be knocked out by weapons blasts, power outages, and electromagnetic pulse (EMP).[17] "Radios carried to shelters will have to be protected against EMP as well as dampness."[18] All of these requirements suggest dramatic cost increases over currently projected levels of spending.

Space, lighting, and communication requirements, if not met, will aggravate what are sure to be crowded and stressful conditions. One summary of the relevant social-psychological literature on the stresses likely to be experienced by shelterees says:

> Living in an atomic fallout shelter for two weeks may involve many physiological deprivations and adverse environmental conditions. Many of these stresses have significant effects on behavior. These include decreased efficiency in performance, difficulties in concentration, irritability, depression, and personality disturbances. Special groups such as children, pregnant women, and the ill would be particularly affected. A common element in the various environmental stresses is frustration. Common reactions to frustration include aggression, depression, regression, and withdrawal. If we assume that a great many people who make it to shelters will be suffering the effects of radiation

poisoning and that a great many shelter occupants will die during the
two to four weeks they are in the shelter, any failure to meet minimally
acceptable conditions will only aggravate what are sure to be hellish
conditions.[19]

The construction costs for shelter space will surely run to a
minimum of $10 per square foot. If we assume that two-thirds of the 145
million relocatees are sheltered in modified existing structures, the remaining 48 million will have to have structures built for them. Assuming
then that each person represents $100 in construction costs (ten square
feet per person × $10 per square foot), the bill for new shelters will run to
$4.8 billion. Again, remember that at ten square feet per person we would
be creating almost intolerable conditions, especially if evacuees were
forced to remain in the shelters for more than two weeks.

To convert existing buildings to shelters, it is necessary to install or
modify ventilation systems, to seal all windows and doors, to provide
adequate communications with the outside for shelter occupants, to
ensure some type of power system for lighting, and to organize the
buildings in such a way that they can accommodate a large number of
people, many of whom may be seriously injured. In addition to these
design specifications, millions of dosimeters and survey meters would be
required and would have to be checked and replaced on a regular basis.[20]
Assuming conversion costs at one-third that of new construction (a
conservative estimate), the bill for the 96 million people in converted
quarters comes to approximately $3.2 billion.

One county in North Carolina has done a detailed analysis of the
costs involved in developing an operational system of shelters. In addition to the costs outlined above, the county also looked at the cost of
maintaining a siren warning system and adequate radiological defenses.
The Radiological Defense System was designed

> to provide our citizens with accurate and timely information on the
> threats posed by radioactive fallout in the event of a nuclear war. The
> system was composed of Radiation Monitors in Fallout Shelters and
> Weapons Effects Reporting Stations (WERS) who would collect data on
> radiation levels and report to a Radiological Defense Officer (RDO)
> located in an Emergency Operations Center (EOC). The RDO would take
> the information collected from Monitors throughout [the area] and
> provide advice and guidance as to the extent of the threat and steps to be
> taken for protection. The RDO would also be responsible for informing
> persons when it was safe to emerge from their fallout shelters as well as
> reporting to the State the local conditions in our area. This type of system
> was in operation in [the area] for many years. The system was mostly
> abandoned in the mid-1970s. . . .[21]

The cost of reestablishing an adequate radiological defense system and a working siren system (including the training of local personnel to operate and repair these systems) would surely run into the thousands of dollars for each shelter or set of shelters, thus adding additional millions of dollars to the national tally.

Adding together the figures for new construction, conversion, meters, food, and radiological defense systems gives a bottom line of roughly $20 billion of capital costs to build and stock sufficient public shelters for the 145 million people that FEMA anticipates relocating. If we assume that planning and management represents approximately 10 percent of capital cost, the total bill for preparing an adequate system of public shelters runs to over $22 billion.

Are we, as a nation, prepared to spend millions of dollars every year to maintain a system of operating shelters? Are we willing to spend more than $22 billion to develop such a system? In the authorization hearings on the Department of Defense's request for appropriations for fiscal year 1983, the staunchest supporters of America's civil defense program were quite pleased with the prospect of a $250 million allocation and a seven year allocation "plan" that would funnel a total of $2 billion into civil defense planning, almost 10 percent of which would be set aside for research. One of the arguments used repeatedly in congressional hearings in favor of the CRP evacuation-shelter program is its relatively low cost.

Although America's civil defense planning establishment continues to assert that an adequate system of shelters could ensure the survival of a substantial portion of the population following an all-out nuclear attack, they are not, in fact, ensuring that such a system will actually be built. Therefore, we are setting ourselves up, as a nation, for the day when some small proportion of our country's leadership will have to decide which part of our population will have even a chance of surviving and which will not. For even the most optimistic civil defense planners assume that one third of the population will have to be relegated to makeshift home basement shelters or totally expedient shelters. I do not believe, in practice, that such a choice—who should live and who should die—can or will be implemented on such a massive scale. One can only hope that no citizen will ever be put in the position of having to make such a horrific choice.

SHELTER MANAGEMENT

In 1980, FEMA distributed a package of camera-ready newspaper columns designed for release to the public as emergency information. One column in particular deserves review. It was entitled, "Would

Survivors of Nuclear Attack Envy the Dead? . . . Experts Say 'No'."[22] The column reveals a number of important assumptions being made by national civil defense planners about life in the post-attack period:

> Other pressing needs that would develop quickly in the post-shelter environment include rescue, treatment of the injured and ill, disposal of the dead, preparation of casualty lists, reestablishment of public health procedures, formation of work groups, decontamination, restoration of water and food supplies, debris clearance, expansion and deployment of public safety forces, preservation and salvage of assets, emergency repairs, emergency housing, and restoration of industrial and agricultural production.[23]

Those managing the shelters would, in effect, have to worry about the restoration of community life in the post-attack period. This would, of course, include the management of life in the shelters immediately following an attack. Shelter managers (how would they be selected?) would have to make and enforce a great many crucial decisions: (1) How long would evacuees be expected to remain in the shelters? (2) How would scarce resources and medical care be rationed? (3) How would the bodies of those who died be handled? (4) What support would the shelterees need from the shelters even after it was safe for emergency workers to return above ground? Somehow, each shelter would have to be assured of the necessary medical and technical personnel. Each shelter, for example, would need people skilled in radiological monitoring.

The FEMA newspaper article suggests that

> within 24 hours after the end of an attack, nearly all the hazardous local fallout would be down on the ground, and radiological monitors would have determined how much fallout had occurred in each local area. It would then be possible for radiological defense officers and monitors to make sufficiently accurate predictions of fallout radiation intensities to permit planning for emergence from shelter.[24]

Again, according to FEMA,

> Some communities would experience blast damage to buildings, utilities, or transportation. Fires could add to the problem. In such circumstances, the community must determine how it can most effectively undertake emergency repairs when fallout radiation levels permit. Limited decontamination of essential facilities and areas may be necessary.[25]

In light of recent studies, this confident tone is unwarranted. Indeed, the entire problem of radiation assessment seems much more serious than federal civil defense planners have envisioned. (See Chapter 11.)

Setting aside the enormous uncertainties involved in assessing external and internal radiation doses, the key problems facing shelter managers will be (1) maintaining control in the shelter until such time as it is safe to go out, (2) beginning the process of emergency repairs and replenishment of supplies before the entire shelter population emerges, (3) reestablishing a system of local government and restoring some semblance of economic activity following an attack, particularly after emergence from temporary shelters.

How will shelter managers maintain control? If foodstuffs and shelter space have to be rationed, some sort of police system will have to be installed. How will shelter managers keep order? Who will determine the hierarchy of political or organizational control within each shelter? How will decisions be enforced? Will full equality of shares and power be the rule or will certain individuals, because of their prior status or importance to the shelter community, be accorded special privileges?

How will shelter managers go about repairing the physical damage in the outside community? How will they be assured of the skilled manpower they need? Will there be adequate electricity to power repair operations? Is it reasonable to assume that decontamination of food and water is a possibility? Is it reasonable to assume that anyone will be motivated to work at all?

How will the restoration of economic and political life outside the shelters be managed? Will shelter managers become temporary officials during the post-attack transition? Will the pre-attack government have sufficient credibility to mobilize the necessary activity? Will everyone assume the roles (e.g., status, class, power) they had before the attack? If vast segments of the population are wiped out during the attack, will we have the necessary skilled personnel to revitalize the economy, or will we revert to a kind of self-sufficient rural lifestyle in which each community seeks to provide food, water, and other necessities for itself? The asking of these questions, let alone any serious effort to answer them, is not a part of the research agenda dealing with shelter.

My assumption is that temporary shelters will become post-attack dwelling places for quite some time. Evacuees from urban areas are not likely to return to that home base for many months, if at all. Materials needed to construct new (above ground) shelters will not be readily available. Fallout shelters may provide the only possible living quarters for most of the survivors of a nuclear attack, regardless of how quickly the radiation dissipates. I wonder most about the difficulty of restoring any semblance of pre-attack economic and political life given the vast losses we are likely to suffer and the destruction of basic communication, transportation, industrial, and agricultural systems we are likely to experience. If I were beginning the task of training shelter managers, I would put as much emphasis on the problem of managing the post-attack transition to a new form of community life as I would on managing life underground.

ETHICAL AND STRATEGIC CONSIDERATIONS

I do not believe that the national government has been honest with the people of America regarding the cost of building and maintaining an adequate system of public shelters. I doubt whether there would be public support for the massive expenditures required to ensure equal protection to all Americans. If more people understood what the probable loss of life would be with the system of shelters that the government presently contemplates, even under the best of circumstances, there would surely be greater skepticism about the prospect of "winning" or "surviving" a nuclear attack. I am afraid that America's effort to provide a system of civil defense has lulled the population into a greater willingness to contemplate the prospect of nuclear war while, in fact, the civil defense system currently contemplated would probably result in the destruction of at least one-half the population.

If the public understood that current plans call for a system under which self-appointed crisis managers will have to decide who will live and who will die they would be outraged. If the general public understood what life in a ten-square-foot area for two to four weeks were like—with family, friends, and neighbors dying painfully at close quarters from the effects of radiation, without adequate medical care or space to minister to those unable to care for themselves—I doubt there would be a public willingness to contemplate a shelter system that, if successful, only encourages the construction of more weapons by the Soviet Union.

9

Things Fall Apart: Problems of Governance and Social Control

Michael Lipsky

Destruction cometh;
and they shall seek peace,
and there shall be none.
Mischief shall come upon mischief,
and rumor shall be upon rumor;
then shall they seek a vision of the prophet;
but the law shall perish from the priest,
and counsel from the ancients.

Ezekial 7: 25, 26

This report assumes that we may fail to exploit to the fullest our economic potential for recovery following a nuclear attack because of failures in post-attack management in both the political and the economic sectors. It also presumes that very large-scale changes in such arrangements will not win acceptance, so that the best hope for improvement is to look for more marginal adjustments in our continually evolving management systems, adjustments which might contribute substantially to post-attack recovery at little peacetime cost.

The report is optimistic, in that it believes that a number of such adjustments deserve to be explored. The post-attack considerations addressed include making government more effective in bringing about economic recovery and, very importantly, making sure that government continues as government, i.e., that we do not sink into anarchy. . . .

The holding of elections after a nuclear attack will certainly be a very difficult process. While many might thus conclude that it will not be worth the bother, as other needs are more pressing, the impact on the legitimacy of the government and on the public's willingness to follow it should not be overlooked. Any authority will have a great number of difficult and unpopular decisions to make, and the stamp of voter approval counts for quite a bit here.

Again, there are developments in the trends of technology and peacetime attitudes that may help us. We have all along been balancing a desire to make it possible for as many adult Americans as possible to vote, against the need to prevent vote fraud (i.e., to prevent anyone from voting more than once). Extensive and complicated registration requirements were often found necessary for the latter purpose in the past, with proponents of easier systems charging that this was merely an excuse to discourage poorer and less educated people from voting. Defenders of these requirements countercharge that proponents of liberalization were scheming to return to the vicious days of big-city machine politics, where many people were bribed to vote more than once, or where long-dead voters fictitiously cast their ballots for the machine candidate.

The breakthroughs in computer data storage and related communications should soon offer some important ways out of the dilemma here, allowing voters to escape all but a tiny amount of bother with registration (even when they move from residence to residence), while at the same time guarding against voter fraud. It is not easy to predict the pace of these changes, except to guess that the situation will be better by both yardsticks in 1990 than it is in 1980. . . .

One has to make a bet in one direction or another, and the following might be proposed. Rather than assuming that martial law will ever be necessary in its fuller sense, the emphasis might rather be placed on full-fledged reliance on the normal channels of legal authority—i.e., governors, mayors, sheriffs, judges—as the National Guard and the federal Army serve as they do now in natural disasters, entirely at the behest of civilian officials.

The pitch of legal tone would thus be very comparable to what has been applied to urban rioting in the United States, for we have every reason to believe that the degree of public lawlessness and riotousness in the post-attack situation would be lower than in a power failure on a hot and humid evening. . . .

In summary, it is clear that we will need some participation by military policy, and perhaps threat of military force, in the post-war political governance of the country if economic recovery is to be achieved. It is less clear, however, that any extensive reliance on formal martial law or suspensions of normal constitutional processes must be contemplated, since the past experiences of urban rioting and civil war probably exceed the degree of disunion we would encounter after a Soviet attack. Rather than thinking in terms of *replacing* proper civilian authority, we might instead plan for *augmenting* it with the technical and manpower help the military services can offer; even in the extreme case of stubborn opposition to national purposes by state and local officials, the most effective avenue for the President may be entirely parallel to what he uses now in the exercise of federal authority: the deployment of resources and incentives which can be withheld as the price of non-cooperation. . . .

SOURCE: George W. Quester, *Options for Accelerating Economic Recovery After Nuclear Attack*, prepared for FEMA, Analytical Assessments Corporation, Martina Del Rey, Calif., July 1979, pp. ix, 39, 43, and 46.

- *The reception and care of evacuees* in host areas may be viewed as fundamentally a problem of *maintaining and/or creating organized patterns of behavior—in fact, organizations themselves—which can both:*

  a. deliver essential services, including governmental and police services, and essential goods to a greatly expanded population; and

  b. simultaneously, incorporate the relocated population in the new distribution of work which reflects at least the following priorities:

     (1) the need to provide goods and services to the total population in its new posture;
     (2) the need to maintain a degree of normal economic production through the evacuation period;
     (3) the need to maximize concerted economic effort following a disruptive attack.

- One implication of the above points is that evacuation or reception-and-care planning should not view the hosting problem as one in which a relatively small host population is providing organizational mechanisms, social control or police services, and essential goods to a relatively large population of evacuees. To conceptualize the problem solely in those terms could produce efforts which would, in effect, overburden the organizational capacity of host areas at a time when the organization of evacuated populations is necessarily disrupted. *Preparedness agencies will need to plan for maximizing the country's organizational capacity at all stages of a crisis,* and to be on guard against the possibility that their countermeasures might serve to disrupt that part of the organizational structure not already disrupted by the crisis, the evacuation, or the attack itself.

Whether or not it proves feasible to maintain organizational ties, a massive relocation problem cannot be addressed apart from the question of *organization in host areas during the crisis period.* If organizational continuity is not stressed— for example, if the problem is viewed solely in logistical and policing terms— this leaves to chance or "natural processes" the development of social organizational patterns in respose to the crisis. At a minimum, contingency planning should then provide for dealing with a wide range of emergent situations which may not be consistent with carrying out the desired reception-and-care policies—or consistent with re-establishing a complex economy in the postattack period. . . .

Other Characteristics of Relocated and Host Populations. This report has focussed on population characteristics of an economic nature, suggesting that they must be reflected in any effective and efficient approach to organizing the population and maintaining stability through a relocation period. Clearly, there are other social characteristics—most notably, race and individual or family status—which would dramatically affect the viability of a relocation effort and posture. The principal effect of such variables would be to diminish the acceptability of the relocation and impose additional problems of managing the effort. These effects should of course be considered, but the present report has been restricted to a set of fundamental characteristics which must be reflected in the organization of the population for productive roles. To the extent that the organizational base is provided, it would be easier to cope with social or other problems arising from any source.

SOURCE: William G. Gay, et al., *Crisis Relocation: Disrupting Relocated Populations and Maintaining Organizational Viability,* prepared for the Defense Civil Preparedness Agency, Human Sciences Research, Inc., McLean, Virginia, April 1974, pp. ix, x, and 98–99.

INTRODUCTION

Crisis relocation planning (CRP) as envisaged by FEMA posits a number of fundamental assumptions about the nature of governance, legitimate public authority, and leadership. Any evaluation of the CRP approach must explicitly surface these assumptions and examine them from the perspective of one concerned with governance and authority.

The CRP scenario has four stages: (1) the relocation of 150 million Americans; (2) their reception and stay in the host community prior to any nuclear war; (3) the "holding period" in the shelters during and following a nuclear attack; and (4) the "post-shelter" world. At each of these stages, questions arise about authority and leadership; these must be answered if one is to have confidence that the scenario can work. Based on review of available relevant research material, it is my conclusion that the proposed CRP process raises many issues about governance that have either not been addressed at all or, if addressed, have not been adequately answered.

The following pages lay out the basis for such a conclusion focusing on: (1) the nature of legitimate authority; (2) the role of authority in the stages of CRP; and (3) the foundations of FEMA's assumptions about authority and legitimacy.

THE NATURE OF LEGITIMATE AUTHORITY

All political systems depend for their operation and maintenance upon the cooperation of their members. In this connection most analysts concentrate attention on systems of laws to explain popular acquiescence to regimes because laws mobilize the coercive powers of states in efforts to achieve collective objectives. However, upon a moment's reflection it is obvious that law cannot achieve what the society will not freely agree to. The classic illustration of this observation was Prohibition. The law's widespread unpopularity, the people's unwillingness to obey it, and the subsequent high cost of maintaining such a law—including costs of law enforcement and the development of an underground economy in liquor—largely account for its repeal. More to the point, we may generalize that when the majority of the members of a political system will not freely cooperate with its central objectives, the cost of pursuing collective ends may become excessive. Even prisons—coercive institutions to be sure—are able to function only so long as the inmates go along with their procedures, regulations, and restrictions.

The essence of political authority is general popular acceptance of the rightfulness of leaders' orders and preferences. This does not mean that citizens cannot contest the views of leaders. It does mean, however, that there are orderly procedures for contesting those views and that once those procedures have been pursued the results of those processes are generally accepted and the rightfulness of the leaders' views is established. Democratic societies also provide for the likelihood that claims to political authority will be contested. As a result, they elaborate constitutions, develop procedures for the recruitment and elevation of public officials, and establish systems of courts in order to secure widely accepted mechanisms to settle disputes and grievances.

It is obvious that the more disruptive civil defense plans are to the general population, the greater is their dependence on political authority and its maintenance. Interestingly, the old civil defense plans, which relied upon supplying existing public buildings and other large structures within target cities with food and water and designating them as fallout shelters, raised no similar issues of political authority because the demands of such plans on the population were much less severe.

Political authority can never be wholly divorced from considerations of its counterpart: political legitimacy. Legitimacy refers to a quality of institutions and leaders such that people generally accept the correctness or rightness of a particular idea, institution, or relationship. Political legitimacy cannot be proclaimed or pronounced. It exists in the social constructions of the population and the attitudinal structures that endow phenomena with political character.

Why is political legitimacy necessary to the civil defense plans as projected by FEMA? It is necessary because so many people would be required to engage in such extraordinary behaviors and endure such extraordinary hardships that the extent to which they would cooperate with the plans is a critical part of the planning process. However, the plausibility of the political legitimacy of current civil defense planning is lacking in the planning documents that I have been able to address. Five characteristics of legitimacy bear particularly on the plausibility of the FEMA civil defense plans.

First, people must accept the origins of civil defense orders. Those orders must arise or be communicated by people selected by some process that is broadly acceptable to most of the population. These processes can range from the formal mechanisms of governmental succession to the informal acclaim that "natural" leaders are accorded when they display qualities of courage or resourcefulness under fire. It follows that the more that formal, traditionally acceptable procedures can remain intact, the more that central direction of the society can be sustained.

Second, political legitimacy and authority are not the only values that account for the behavior of civilians in times of crisis. Other important values compete for primacy—loyalties to family and to friends, sense of social responsibility, and so on. In short, behavior is motivated by a wide range of considerations of which political legitimacy is only one.

Third, political legitimacy is not inexhaustible and may be challenged by competing ideas and notions of legitimacy and may be influenced by the content of political messages. Social scientists have explored the extent to which people will obey authority even if the commands given by that authority seem antagonistic to other values (as in the famous Milgram experiments).[1] Although it often seems astonishing how far people will go in following authority and how much leaders can influence the political agenda, it is obvious that political authority cannot sustain popular acquiescence if there is too great a conflict between their messages and other values.

Fourth, from a systemic perspective, political legitimacy only exists to the extent that people remain in the system, not only physically but also psychologically. The messages of political authorities cannot be transmitted if people do not perceive themselves to be in the system to receive them.

A last consideration regarding civil defense and political legitimacy is that legitimacy requires maintenance of the political community. During times of revolution, civil war, and domestic insurrection the issue of which government is the "right" government—which government speaks for the people—is often a central point of conflict. Nuclear wars would undoubtedly pose similar challenges.

THE ROLE OF AUTHORITY IN THE FOUR STAGES OF CRP

The central domestic political problem of the president's civil defense plans is whether or not citizens would consent to the massive evacuation, relocation, and subsequent hardship involved in the plans. The problem, as correctly stated by one study commissioned by FEMA, is that "at least 95 percent of a society's 'social control' or 'orderliness' is contributed by the people themselves."[2] But this warning alone cannot transform the extraordinarily disruptive activities of evacuation into the normal routines and interactions called for by this analysis. Evacuation involves massive migration of people from their homes to unfamiliar rural and small-city outposts in a short period of time with little notice, extraordinary dislocations in the economy and in the lives of the people who undertake evacuation, fantastic self-help projects based upon heroic assumptions concerning the physical capabilities of evacuees and the resources they are likely to have at their disposal, and severe communications and resource distribution problems to maintain the dislocated populations for an indefinite period of time.

Evacuation

Let us briefly consider the problem of obtaining compliance with evacuation. While each city and each neighborhood in large cities is assigned a rural location to which to evacuate, the coordination problems surrounding this aspiration are immense. Aside from the severe logistical issues treated elsewhere in this volume, there are powerful reasons to believe that people would not follow the evacuation plan. Some would linger in the city, doubtful whether the threat were real or if they could evacuate expeditiously. There would also be great uncertainty among the critical workers who are supposed to remain on their jobs in the cities (albeit at risk) whether they should indeed man those posts or follow their families to remote locations. Plans for the Boston evacuation call for critical workers to be relocated in Natick with their families and to commute to their essential jobs in Boston during the day. Meanwhile, communities farther away from the center of Boston (ground zero) than Natick are scheduled for total evacuation.[3] The turmoil would be stupendous as people made last-minute arrangements to secure their houses, acquire cash, sell valuables, obtain supplies, and perhaps leave a two-week supply of food and water for the pets they are instructed to leave behind.

Other disruptions of the plan would arise from the fact that many city dwellers would seek—indeed would be encouraged to seek—refuge in areas other than those to which they were designated because of family ties or friendships and a preference under circumstances of great uncertainty for some familiarity with members of the host population.[4] Evacuation would be further complicated by the problem that privileged individuals who were part of the civil defense effort would be in a position to seek their own safety or shelter rather than comply with their official assignments (for example, a bus driver might seek to protect his family rather than report for hazardous transport duties).

A critical and much neglected aspect of the problem, moreover, is that there must remain vast uncertainty over the likelihood of the ultimate catastrophe actually occurring. Citizens would privately hold different perceptions of the risks of noncompliance and would weigh differently these consequences against the high, and in some ways more certain, risks of compliance.

Another threat to political authority arises from the likelihood that authoritative orders would conflict with other significant personal values. In particular, the likelihood that people would seek to secure the safety of family and friends through ad hoc arrangements born of panic instead of accepting relocation in the evacuation areas would substantially raise the costs of evacuation plans. It is evident that planning officials recognize this concern but, perhaps because there is little that they can think to do about it, this concern has been ignored except in injunctions to city dwellers to leave all weapons behind and in the anticipation that martial law may be required.

Reception in the Host Community: The Possibility of a "Phony" War

The deficits in the evacuation plan contribute to the likelihood that the fabric of the social units that would seek sustenance and safety in the host communities for weeks or months would be less cohesive and more subject to tensions based on perceived inequities.[4] The confusion and uncertainties surrounding the exodus would also undermine the emergence of leadership based upon home community cohesion. Emphasizing the need for leadership development represents the sole way in which official evacuation documents address this key issue.[5]

Other concerns for the legitimacy of local officials, on whom so much responsibility would fall, arise from the recognition that a post-evacuation "community" would comprise a large number of outsiders—that is, people from the city—who would be the "guests" of a population and its leadership with which previous contact and thus understanding were nonexistent. The FEMA city instructions, predictably and understandably, read as if they were composed by travel agents anxious to instruct tourists in proper behavior abroad while simultaneously trying to reassure them that the natives are tractable. "If you are invited into a private home, be considerate and do your share to help your host. Remember that you are a guest. . . ."[6] Yet, if one tries to imagine the reality behind the FEMA evacuation plans, the mind conjures up an image of desperate and isolated families and parts of families from large cities seeking shelter and having to accept the authority of public officials with whom they have had no previous contact and have no claims of accountability. Thus, a plan already so heavily dependent upon decentralized leadership and initiative would be confounded by a population from the city orphaned of leadership.

The relationship between the host community and the evacuees will shift to a radically new phase when and if the bombs begin to fall. But what if the "phony war" drags on? The urban newcomers and the rural hosts will find their interaction increasingly strained. During the phony war phase the tensions would mount to unprecedented heights, for, unlike refugees from a flood or even from a nuclear plant catastrophe, the disaster is not yet a real event, but remains hypothetical and therefore subject to nightmarish speculation until nuclear war actually breaks out.

And what if the bombs never come? What if the evacuated population watches the sky each day, and nothing happens?

In some ways, the most intriguing problem of political authority arises in the reasonable chance that the country might be cast into the limbo of a post-evacuation age in which the holocaust is avoided. As others have observed, under FEMA's plans, the bomb, if it were to come, can come neither too soon nor too late. If it comes too soon it will catch the people on the road. If it comes too late, people will get anxious and drift home to a world that has lost wealth, suffered disruption, and spent substantial resources to avoid an eventuality that never took place. Undoubtedly, tensions would continue to be high and international and domestic problems would be no closer to resolution then they had been in the past. In the meantime the urban population will have spent an uncomfortable, possibly traumatic time in communities in which they were not welcome, with growing skepticism over the ability of government to forecast events accurately or provide for their welfare. My point is not to fault a government that would evacuate the population if it thought it necessary. Given all of this, rather, I question whether, since the actual likelihood of nuclear attack is not certain, political leaders might be reluctant to incur the high social and economic costs of evacuation, the extent of which costs no one has fully assessed.

Nor, to my knowledge, has anyone attempted to identify the costs of economic and social disruption and weighed these against the less than certain probability that there would actually be an attack. One can imagine many situations in which the political and economic costs of proceeding with evacuation would be so extensive, and the uncertainty regarding the threat of a nuclear exchange so high, that large-scale evacuation could not reasonably be ordered. This is the case aside from the belief of opponents of current civil defense planning that evacuation would increase the likelihood of a nuclear attack because it appears to anticipate Soviet retaliation for the first strike by the United States.

The legitimacy of political command is not endlessly elastic. Proposals have to meet the test of plausibility and efficacy if they are to maintain their potency. In this connection it is conceivable that one could persuade millions of people to relocate on short notice in strange areas and build underground shelters according to the necessary rigorous technical requirements. What seems particularly questionable from the perspective of the continuing legitimacy of the evacuation plans, however, is the scenario that unfolds in the event of an evacuation and a continuing international stalemate at high levels of tension. Once people have left their homes and no holocaust has occurred, initial relief would likely give way to increasing skepticism and irritation as weeks go by, hardships increase as rural communities deplete their resources, and the welcome extended by hosts to their urban visitors wears thin. I suspect that under such circumstances evacuees would begin to return to their homes as the fear of looting and other losses increases, economic resources are exhausted family by family, people begin to seek ways to restore their previous life patterns, and the fate of hapless pets becomes more and more worrisome.

The population would exert great pressure to return to a pre-crisis footing. Eventually, an order for normalization would be issued. If international tension persisted, would political leaders call for another evacuation directly on the heels of the first one? Surely international crises are not so predictable that periods of high tension are dramatically different from periods of lower tension that last only several weeks. Nor do the highs and lows come in intervals separated comfortably enough so that the citizenry would tolerate periodic evacuations.

Full-scale civil defense mobilization and evacuation would be a demand one could make on the American population only once. What does that mean for evacuation as a strategy? Does it mean that the putative enemy simply waits for the "all clear" before engaging in aggression? Does it mean that American political leaders would be under pressure to take perhaps overly bold initiatives in order to justify the alarm under which it put the entire country? If civil defense is a weapon, it, like a nuclear attack, can only be deployed once. It is appropriate to mention this here because it involves issues not only of military strategy but also of political legitimacy.

On the issue of what to do if nothing happens and the cost benefit of when and how to announce that CRP is in effect, FEMA is ominously quiet—for good reason. There is no relevant experience or literature from which to draw a precedent to this situation. The likelihood of survival is high, partly by definition and partly because there has been no destruction of basic facilities. However, the political costs of prolonged evacuation experiences cannot be estimated by any known experience and, I would submit, would represent a severe constraint on the ordering of evacuation in the first place.

Public Authority and the "Holding" Period

The issue of legitimacy of leadership during the evacuation period and pre-attack phony war that we have described is relatively clear-cut compared to the questions that emerge once the nuclear attack has begun. Even under the most optimistic of FEMA scenarios, planners assume that among the many lives in jeopardy will be those of key leaders—hence the

FEMA concern for "magic mountain" plans that will whisk national leaders to safety from whence they can continue to direct the affairs of the battered nation. The severity of this concern led one analyst to propose that a system of substitute or vice officials be developed to shadow important public offices and thereby provide for continuity in the event of a civil defense mobilization.[7] There are elaborate plans to protect the president and all presidential successors and to remove several thousand top-level bureaucrats from the primary executive agencies and departments to a series of relocation centers scattered through a region surrounding Washington, D.C. in a 350-mile radius. The plans seek to secure the health and safety of these officials as well as their ability to communicate with each other and with the military. At least in theory, these plans ensure that designated public officials will be available and able to carry on command and control functions while under siege.[8] To this end these officials presumably currently engage in war games designed to prepare themselves for these roles.

This emphasis on leadership is neither misplaced nor suprising, if one accepts the assumptions guiding current civil defense planning.It is not misplaced because it is obvious that securing leadership roles and governmental continuity should be a first objective of wartime preparedness. It is not surprising because, to the extent that the problems of evacuation and mass dispersal are perceived as managerial issues, it is appropriate to concern oneself with the questions of who will give orders and make decisions. Furthermore, an emphasis on top-level management is understandable since, of all the parts of society affected by civil defense, FEMA would be most able to influence and guarantee the deployment of federal officials. However, for those millions of Americans waiting out the hours, days, and weeks following the opening of nuclear hostilities, the real issue will be questions of control and authority within the shelters. FEMA research has provided few answers to some of the most basic questions about those issues of authority and control. To quote from Lawrence Susskind (see Chapter 8):

> How will shelter managers maintain control? If foodstuffs and shelter space have to be rationed, some sort of police system will have to be installed. How will shelter managers keep order? Who will determine the hierarchy of political or organizational control within each shelter? How will decisions be enforced?

Of equal interest is who will decide which people will have gone into which shelters. The shelters in a given host community are dissimilar in one fundamental way. They offer different protection factors against radiation. Who decides and on what basis do they decide who goes into which type of shelter? The power to make that decision is, one can argue, the power to decide who will live and who will die (see Chapter 11). The government issues at the local level get even more demanding when one branches out beyond the individual shelter to consider relationships among the shelters. Who decides where food, water, and medical supplies go? Whose dosimeter gets fixed?

There is much talk in the FEMA literature about Emergency Operating Centers and veiled references to the role of the military and martial law to deal with these tough issues of control and authority during the holding period. Fear of the breakdown of order and competition among shelter communities for scarce resources is of great concern to the planners who recognize that martial law and a very different kind of political authority might well have to be introduced in such a society of despair. The severity of this problem led at least one consultant to suggest that the government might do its own food hoarding in order to have some means with which to maintain the allegiance of the population.[9]

Additional leadership support might be provided by the military if the population were placed under martial law. This eventually has extremely high consequences not only in the restriction of liberties and self-direction that the U.S. population values so highly but also for the high costs of social control that are implicit in the resort to military rule. Nor do we have any reason to think that military personnel are particularly trained to work in areas of community justice and resource allocation, which would be at the heart of the political legitimacy problem in the holding period after the nuclear attack had occurred.

Political Legitimacy and the Post-Shelter World

At some point people will start to come out of their shelters— perhaps after two to four weeks, as FEMA optimistically estimates the safe duration of stay, or over a more extended, intermittent period, regardless of safety, as Jennifer Leaning (see Chapter 11) indicates may more accurately reflect population behavior. They and their colleagues from all the other shelters must face the issues of political authority and control presented by the post-nuclear attack world. The intensity of political disintegration cannot be evaluated in any meaningful way.

Whether martial law or anarchy will dominate is impossible to predict. There are no FEMA studies that portray an accurate picture of the post-attack world because none is possible. Jonathan Schell tells us how bad it can be. In his post-attack world there is no need for political authority, legitimate or otherwise, because there is neither anyone to exercise it nor anyone to exercise it on.[10] Between Schell's dead world and FEMA's view that 80 percent of the relocated population can survive a nuclear attack lies a wide range of possibilities. Each point along the spectrum has its own demand for control and authority. We cannot say much more than this. Nor can FEMA. The degree to which social and political bonds have been shattered, political authority broken, and community scattered is a function of decisions made outside the domestic political arena and within the world of international military and diplomatic strategy.

THE FOUNDATIONS OF FEMA'S ASSUMPTIONS ABOUT LEGITIMATE AUTHORITY

FEMA bases many of its assumptions about the nature of political authority and control on research that has focused on the political and institutional response to natural crises and other wars. The assumptions about legitimate authority are derived from precedent where possible. In the absence of precedent the logic is based on analogy or partial analogy. And over all, research is produced and used to provide "scientific legitimacy" to the process.

Perhaps the boldest stroke of the overall FEMA scheme, and one that deserves closest attention, is the assumption that the rural communities would accept "cityfolk," would share scarce resources and skills, and would tolerate the invasion of outsiders for any length of time. The unexamined corollary is that cityfolk would not have doubts about this assumption or would trustingly put their doubts aside for the duration of their bivouac.

At best, the civil defense assumptions draw upon the sense of community spirit and general cooperation that attends the early stages of natural disasters such as snowstorms and hurricanes, where members of communities gather together to help one another. But there is no comparison between the experience of a natural disaster and the protracted agony and uncertainty of life after evacuation. At the very least, this is because after natural disasters relief may be forthcoming from other parts of the country, the National Guard is available without competing claims on its time, and the catastrophe is believed to have a foreseeable end. None of these conditions would be likely to prevail in evacuation for nuclear disaster.

It is interesting to consider, in the light of the impossibility of drawing lessons from direct previous experience, how FEMA has attempted to rationalize its program with respect to the issues of political authority. Studies I have reviewed ignore the problem of making inferences with confidence from past experiences. One study, for example, sought to develop the best guesses of people who were considered familiar with issues relevant to civil defense in order to develop a consensus on the likely problems and the potential of evacuation.[11] The study employed a delphi technique—a research approach designed to force consensus among people with disparate views. The study does not indicate whether the respondents were selected randomly or could be considered biased toward survivability. It proceeds by asking what are the likely problems that would be encountered and whether they could be overcome. This study could conceivably be useful to planners in identifying possible problem areas. It could not, however, be utilized to provide confidence that evacuation plans would succeed since there is no relevant experience that the respondents could draw on and, in any event, the notion of survivability is not well defined. Moreover, the critical question of whether or not evacuation plans ought to be put into effect in light of the possibility that they would not be needed (a point I stressed earlier) is not part of this study's concern.

Another study—this one of black opinion leaders—inquires about the impact of evacuation planning on minority communities. It suffers from the same defects at a lower level of effort and seems to be a low-cost attempt to "touch base" with minority sentiment in anticipation of criticism focusing on possible neglect of this important aspect of relocation planning.[12]

Another study takes for granted the application and implementation of FEMA planning and attempts to identify areas in which current policy innovations could better prepare the society to undertake relocation efforts.[13] It does not ask whether relocation would succeed, but instead says: if relocation had to proceed, what could be done today that would prepare the society better tomorrow for successfully undertaking such plans. Thus, it offers such incrementalist proposals as selecting alternates for public office so that, if public officials were unavailable to assume roles during a crisis, there would be legitimate successors already in place. Likewise, it recommends that developing a computer-aided capability to know where food stocks are currently located would greatly assist the central government to command continuing citizen loyalties through food allocations—an innovation that if currently developed might cost very little but be valuable in the event of a crisis. This study is pixyish in the sense that it offers sensible small-level thinking about an extraordinarily complicated and controversial idea whose premises are by no means self-evidently sensible.

These studies, and the individual city relocation plans that have been produced (complete with impressive highway route maps for each neighborhood) represent the most significant attempt to influence the political legitimacy of relocation planning. They are designed to provide the impression that relocation planning is based upon studious reflection—to secure, in other words, the appearance of "scientific legitimacy."

To be sure, FEMA is not the first governmental agency to concern itself with scientific legitimacy for political purposes. But because FEMA is manifestly concerned with achieving the specific objective of protecting the population from attack, it is organizationally incapable of raising fundamental questions about the premises of its mandate or commissioning studies that challenge its calculation of probable costs and benefits. It has produced a body of work that may provide "symbolic reassurance" that leadership has carefully prepared for the unthinkable, but the material basis on which that reassurance rests, at least in the area of post-evacuation governance, remains to be provided.[14]

10

Dulce et Decorum Est: Medical and Public Health Problems of Crisis Relocation

H. Jack Geiger

The harvest is past,
the summer is ended,
and we are not saved.
Is there no balm in Gilead;
is there no physician there?
Why then is not the health of my people recovered?

Jeremiah 8: 20, 22

A portion of the typical general hospital patient census is in the hospital for elective procedures, or procedures that can be postponed. In the event of crisis relocation, these patients could be discharged from risk-area hospitals immediately, or over the 3-day evacuation period, and relocated along with the general population. Approximately 75 percent of general hospital patients falls into this category. Another portion, about 15 percent of general hospital. patients, can be discharged and relocated to host areas, but will require continued medical attention once they arrive in the host area. This continued medical attention may be provided on either an inpatient basis (with the use of host-area hospitals) or on an outpatient basis. . . .

Among the facilities in a community that have a potential h/m [health and medical] application during crisis relocation are colleges and universities, which offer beds, infirmaries, and laboratories. . . . Conflicts in the use or uses of college and university facilities would be resolved in the early planning stages. . . . During crisis relocation, the establishment of outpatient clinics in the host areas can help cope with the increased demand for health services that accompanies the influx of relocatees into the host areas . . .

[This report] provides the planner with a method of using the crude death rate to estimate the number of deaths that could be expected for a 2-week relocation period. This method takes into account only those deaths that would occur under normal preattack conditions and does not account either for the increased number of deaths that could result from the stress of crisis relocation or for those that could result following a nuclear attack.

SOURCE: M.N. Laney, et al., *Detailed Health and Medical Annexes to Crisis Relocation Plans*, prepared for the Defense Civil Preparedness Agency, Research Triangle Institute, Research Triangle Park, North Carolina, April 1979, pp. 5-3–5-5.

Capabilities of Allied Medical Facilities and Application in Crisis Relocation

... this research examined the capabilities of selected allied medical facilities with a view to their use as supplemental primary care facilties during crisis relocation. The allied medical facilities considered were chiropractors', dentists', and osteophaths' offices; nursing homes; and veterinary clinics and hospitals.

Since dentists and osteopaths are primary care providers, it is reasonable to expect that they will continue to serve as such during crisis relocation, the only real change in their activities being in the volume of patients that they see. Accordingly, their offices will not be available as supplemental primary care facilities. Similarly, it is expected that chiropractors will continue to provide primary care. Indeed, with individuals unaccustomed to strenuous physical labor engaged in the development of expedient shelter, a number of strained backs requiring the assistance of a chiropractor may be expected. . . .

By foregoing or, at least, restricting the treatment of animals, veterinary clinics and hospitals can be used as outpatient facilities for the treatment of human patients. In addition, the mobile dispensaries used by veterinarians engaged in large animal practices would seem applicable as mobile outpatient care units. . . .

SOURCE: D.R. Johnston, et al., *Study of Crisis Administration of Hospital Patients and Study of Management of Medical Problems Resulting from Crisis Relocation*, prepared for the Defense Civil Preparedness Agency, Research Triangle Institute, Research Triangle Park, North Carolina, September 1978, pp. 1-6–1-7.

CONCLUSIONS

This research study has shown that the health and medical (h/m) problems likely to be encountered in a crisis relocation situation will be those that are normally present in a population plus a set of problems due to relocation itself. Thus, the h/m aspect of relocation is largely a matter of continuing to provide primary care to both the hospitalized and the nonhospitalized populations. In addition, it is believed that relocation will cause an increase in the number of stress-induced problems such as premature births, emotional crises, and exacerbations of metabolic disorders and outbreaks of communicable diseases should congregate care facilities become overcrowded and unsanitary. An additional problem is that of the "hard-core" patient too ill or severely injured to be moved to a host area. "Hard-core" illnesses include both organic and psychiatric disorders. . . .

Therefore, the challenge confronting the h/m planner is to provide acceptable substitute consumer-provider relationships in health services in host and risk areas, but especially in host areas. . . .

In the assignment of personnel, the h/m services differ from the other emergency services in that much of the medical work force (e.g., physicians and dentists) is self-employed and therefore could not be assigned to a host area on a organizational basis, e.g., as a hospital might be. Also, many nurses, if married to key workers, are likely to go with their husbands instead of following the hospital organization to its relocation assignment. . . .

While this study was concerned with providing h/m services, including medical care, public health, and mortuary services, for a relocated population, it identified primary medical care as the major task of crisis relocation health and medical services.

SOURCE: M.N. Laney, et al., *Management of Medical Problems Resulting from Crisis Relocation*, prepared for the Defense Civil Preparedness Agency, Research Triangle Institute, Research Triangle Park, North Carolina, May 1976, pp. 1-148–1-149.

The promise of life—life for the individual, for the population, for the nation—is at the very core of all the claims made by FEMA and its predecessors on behalf of civil defense. For the individual, FEMA insists, life will be protected and preserved (though with less than complete certainty), and risks will be substantially reduced during a nuclear war and its aftermath. In the aggregate, FEMA spokesmen repeat over and over again, the Crisis Relocation Program "could result in total survival of over 80 per cent of the population."[1] And on the national level, they add, the United States would not only survive as a national entity but would recover. Any medical analyst aware of the massive, almost incomprehensible, burden of trauma, burns and radiation injury that nuclear war would bring, and concerned about such secondary consequences as epidemic disease and starvation, must ask at once whether these assertions have a basis in reasoned study, analysis, and research.

Yes, says FEMA. In "years of research," one FEMA witness assured a recent congressional hearing, "no insuperable barrier to recovery has been found" in some 370 research reports addressing such problems as "radiological phenomena and countermeasures, availability of food and water, health and medical problems, economic impacts, social and psychological impacts, late radiation and genetic effects, and ecological problems."[2]

Yet these confident assurances are offered in the face of a formidable problem—one that is shared, curiously, by nuclear war strategists and civil defense planners. Neither those who plan nuclear wars nor those who propose to defend against them can call upon precedents, for there are none. As there is no empirical model for predicting all the effects of a 6,000-megaton attack on a modern industrial nation, so there is none for testing the separate parts of any national civil defense scenario. There is no data base; civil defense, like nuclear war itself, must invent its own reality.

Every civil defense "reality," therefore, must be a construct of hypotheses and assumptions—that is, guesses. Civil defense "research" cannot, by and large, subject this guesswork to empirical test—there is no laboratory of nuclear warfare—to distinguish it from wishes, dreams, or lies. Computer "simulations" and computer "models" can neither simulate nor model nuclear war; they are simply ways of manipulating the same basic hypotheses and assumptions, more or less arbitrarily assigning quantitative dimensions to them and calculating the consequences of changing one guess or another.

These general principles must apply to that fraction of civil defense research that specifically addresses the medical and health care problems of nuclear war, crisis relocation, and its aftermath. Most of this research consists of studies performed on contract by organizations outside the formal medical and public health academic and scientific communities. It is all the more important, therefore, that these studies be subjected to the same kind of rigorous scrutiny and analysis they would have received had they been submitted to reputable scientific journals (as few have) for publication. In assessing the medical and health care aspects of civil defense planning, it is useful to identify four phases within the overall crisis relocation plan, to select a few major problems in each phase, and then to examine FEMA's research on these problems.

MEDICAL AND PUBLIC HEALTH PROBLEMS OF THE EVACUATION PHASE

The proposed journey of approximately 145 million people to host areas—a total migration of some 15 billion person-miles in three to five days—would be an event without precedent in human history. Some idea of its magnitude and complexity can be derived from the projections for a single state. The director of the Nuclear Civil Protection Division of the Massachusetts state government has testified that:

> In Massachusetts . . . 4.8 million people reside in the risk areas and will require relocation. Of this total, about 1.2 million will be hosted in New

Hampshire and 0.8 million hosted in Maine. It is expected that about 0.5 million will relocate spontaneously during the expected buildup of international tensions, leaving the state the responsibility of hosting 2.3 million of its own citizens as well as 400,000 from Connecticut, and 150,000 from Rhode Island for a total of over 2.8 million people. . . . In addition, Massachusetts must provide transportation planning with appropriate controls for about two million people from Connecticut and Rhode Island who will be traveling through Massachusetts enroute to host areas of New Hampshire, Vermont and New York.[3]

Whatever the other logistical problems of this enormous flow of people (one FEMA presentation suggests that it be portrayed to an anxious public as a "weekend-like activity"),[4] we may be certain that disease and death will not take a holiday. The National Center for Health Statistics (NCHS) estimates that Americans make 4.3 million visits to hospital emergency rooms for life-threatening emergencies every 6 months;[5] that is 165,385 every week. Among 145 million people in a five-day period there would be 77,500 such life-threatening emergencies—acute myocardial infarctions, gastrointestinal hemorrhages, seizures, acute pneumonias, and the like—all occurring while people are in cars, buses, trucks, trains, boats, and planes, dispersed and headed *away* from sources of medical care. There would, in addition, be some 38,360 births during this period, unless all women in the last weeks of pregnancy are to be left behind in the high-risk target areas. Further, most medical personnel—the physicians, nurses, technicians, and others from host areas—would themselves be in mid-migration, according to FEMA plans, together with truckloads of medical equipment, drugs, and supplies. How are the acutely ill to be identified, separated out from the vast moving tide of humanity, and brought to care? Who would the driver of an automobile notify that a passenger was having an apparent heart attack, and how would he do it? Where would care be obtained?

A major study entitled *Management of Medical Problems Resulting From Population Relocation* prepared for the Defense Civil Preparedness Agency (DCPA—a FEMA predecessor) by the Research Triangle Institute, (RTI) in 1976, addresses this problem only briefly but in a way that is characteristic. It offers simple assertions, or hopeful imperatives, without reference to a research base. Thus,

Ambulance vehicles, if not being used to transport patients to the host area, will continue to operate in emergency situations as they normally do. In the event of severe injury or acute illness, the ambulance team will provide rapid-response, on-site medical care, continued care enroute to a definitive care facility, and care during the patient's transfer from the ambulance to the hospital emergency department. . . . Air ambulance

services . . . offer rapid long distance emergency medical services. Also . . . helicopters are able to go into areas that ground ambulances
cannot reach due to rough terrain.[6]

The report goes on to suggest the designation of some hospitals as
"emergency medical service system regional hospitals" and that two-way
radio be used "to coordinate quick response of emergency medical
personnel to the emergency scene by ambulance." Then, on-site
emergency medical care will be given to the victim by ambulance atten-
dants "often with the support of a physician via radio communication"
and "the ambulance attendant can determine the closest hospital that has
the required facilities for continued care."[7]

The study concedes that physicians in the host areas "may not have
the requisite expertise to deal with certain specialized medical problems,
such as intracranial hemorrhage, crushing chest wound, bleeding gastric
ulcer, etc.," but it suggests that "a specialist in another location could
direct the medical or surgical treatment of such conditions, if some form
of communication link existed."[8] The next five pages of the study are
devoted to a listing of two-way radio, telephone, and telegraph communication systems, and the next seven pages to a description of two-
way medical television. In any case, the study urges, from the very onset
of relocation, radio and television stations should broadcast programs "to
educate the public in simple first-aid measures as well as to inform them
concerning medical supplies that they should take with them during
relocation."

Of course, the migrant tide may not be so huge, and the possibility
of monumental traffic jams may not be so great, because in FEMA's
estimation not everyone may choose to leave the risk areas. Also, "spontaneous evacuation is more likely to characterize the more well to do
segments of our society. . . . [t]o the extent to which key workers are in
the middle or upper income brackets, chances are rather good that many
will be among the early evacuees."[9] Those who choose not to migrate, the
same report says, "might include disproportionate numbers of the sick,
the disabled and handicapped, people with mental problems, alcoholics,
drug addicts, and some of the lonely elderly."[10] A scenario prepared by
William M. Brown of the Hudson Institute describing a hypothetical
nuclear crisis (and sent to all crisis relocation planners as a document of
"great benefit") speculates that the stay-behinds will also include antiwar
idealists, pet lovers, and members of "minority communities who might
not be willing to tolerate the culture shock of a relocation to a 'strange
environment' in which they believe they would feel lonely and un-
wanted."[11] No matter, argues Brown. "There would be plenty to do
without having to drag along perhaps 10%-20% of the population many

of whom are screaming or foot-dragging protestors, and who may possibly include some potential saboteurs of the CRP."[12]

For one substantial population, however—the hospitalized and those in nursing homes and other institutions—there will be no choice; more precisely, choices will be made for them. The overwhelming majority of the nation's general hospitals, speciality hospitals, nursing homes, psychiatric hospitals, and facilities for the handicapped and mentally retarded are in the risk areas. At any given moment, according to NCHS research, there are likely to be 1.2 million patients in nursing homes, 795,000 in general hospitals, 226,000 in specialty hospitals and hundreds of thousands more in other facilities.[13] What will happen to them?

A major research study in this problem area concedes that some of them are too ill or injured to be moved. These would include severe burn patients, those requiring continuous cardiac monitoring, those with serious infections requiring isolation, patients on respirators or in traction, and premature infants. In addition,

> consideration will have to be given to those who are nonambulant, chronically or severely ill, or injured. Many are not able to walk or move around unassisted and cannot therefore care for themselves. Others are incontinent, making it undesirable to place them in a shelter with evacuees. Many . . . have serious hearing or visual problems and others are not always aware of their surroundings [and] cannot be released unattended.[14]

In 1963, Brown made an early attempt to solve this problem. In the event of a crisis, he estimated, 90 percent of all general hospital patients could simply be discharged in less than a week—sent home to (presumed) family or friends who would provide all necessary care during the 50- to 200-mile relocation to host areas. Only the remaining 10 percent—called "hard-core" patients—would have to stay. They include patients like those described above, and particularly the aged suffering from such conditions as malignant neoplasms, diabetes, vascular lesions of the central nervous system, and heart disease.

No empirical studies of real patients in real institutions were offered to support this estimate. Thirteen years later, a study by the RTI reassessed the problem. For general hospital patients, RTI staffers prepared a list of 128 diagnoses, weighted for average length of stay, and gave it to three medical consultants—described as "a surgeon and an internist, both experienced in emergency medicine, and a pediatrician with a background in research." The report continued: "Following a face-to-face briefing on crisis relocation and the consolidation problem by an RTI staff member, each consultant was asked to estimate, on the basis of his experience, the per cent of patients that could be discharged outright and the percent that could be relocated to a host area for each of the 128 diagnoses."[15]

Using this technique, they found that only 9.5 percent of all hospital patients would be nonrelocatable. "This research," the RTI report concluded, "provides an independent confirmation of Brown's 1963 estimate that 10 per cent of hospital patients were nonrelocatable, or, as he put it, 'hardcore.'"[16]

In fact, the RTI study made one major and one minor modification of Brown's assertions. Without comment or supporting documentation, it cut the time required for these massive discharges from hospitals from six days to three days. And among the 90 percent of patients who are not "hardcore," it made some distinctions: 75 percent would be "dischargeable," meaning they could be discharged immediately, or over the three-day evacuation period, and relocated to the host area with the general population; but fifteen percent would be "relocatable," meaning that they could be relocated to the host area but would be "in need of continued medical care, which may be provided in the host areas on either an inpatient or an outpatient basis."

What is so startling about this so-called research and independent confirmation is that it is not empirical research at all—even in one of the few areas in which empirical research is possible. It would have been feasible to have teams of physicians in a sample of hundreds of general hospitals review all of the hospitalized patients, according to specified criteria, to determine their suitability for discharge or relocation. That, of course, would have required medical specification of the rules and conditions for safe discharge. It would also have required the teams to determine, on a case-by-case basis, whether each patient had family or friends competent to provide care, whether the patient was able to withstand an immediate long trip, and what his or her continuing care requirements would be. One danger in such empirical research is that physicians across the country would have been made aware of the implications of crisis relocation for their patients. In any case, no real patient was ever studied; instead, abstract diagnostic categories were reviewed and three consultants' opinions were obtained.

When the RTI research was subsequently "tested" in three cities— Colorado Springs, Colorado; Macon, Georgia; and Utica-Rome, New York—no real hospital populations were reviewed and no real patients were ever studied. Instead, the total number of general hospital beds in each of these cities was determined, 9.5 percent was subtracted, and all the rest were labeled "dischargeable" or "relocatable."

In the case of psychiatric hospitals and nursing homes, the same study noted, there are some problems. In psychiatric hospitals, "90 percent of residents are ambulatory but only 47 percent are aware of their surroundings at all times." And "forty-three percent of nursing home residents are nonambulant; 50 percent are not mentally aware of their surroundings at all times; about 17 percent have hearing or vision problems; and 25 percent are incontinent." Nevertheless, this time without benefit of diagnostic categories or consultant opinions, the report asserted that "most of the hospitalized *or institutionalized population* can be discharged and relocated.[17] (Italics added).

For the patients who are to be relocated—a nationwide total that may approach 250,000—the move from risk areas to host areas "would not necessarily require sophisticated emergency medical service vehicles." In the RTI staff's judgment,

> buses or vans would probably be suitable for most relocatable patients. They are spacious enough to allow the transport of relocatable patients that need to be lying down or that are attached to simple support equipment, such as an IV bottle. These patients should be accompanied to the host area by medical personnel. Other relocatable patients, such as circulatory, respiratory or accident patients, may require continuous monitoring, oxygen, or other services in transport that are available only in ambulances or rescue vehicles.[18]

Back home in the cities and target areas, those patients deemed hardcore might also be consolidated in a single hospital. There, they would be cared for by a skeleton staff of physicians, nurses, technicians, and others—all part of the mass of 30 million key workers who would remain in risk areas or commute daily from nearby suburbs in twelve-hour shifts. For these patients and healthcare personnel there would be some attempt to increase fallout protection, although blast and fire would be the major threats to survival.

Although it is identified as a task of health and medical care planners in civil defense risk areas, few details have been made public concerning the assignment of some health workers to remain in risk areas while the majority travel to host areas. One report notes there may be problems because married nurses may prefer to leave with their families—a problem that is apparently not foreseen in the case of married physicians, laboratory and x-ray technicians, or hospital laundry and other health workers.

More detailed planning has been carried out on some problems. More than twenty pages of one research report are devoted to a checklist of "legal questions to be considered in planning for the management of medical problems during crisis relocation," covering license laws, liability, hospital privileges, drug laws, and reimbursement. The report concludes that "lacking precedents, the medico-legal implications of emergency medical services and crisis relocation planning interfaces are largely unpredictable."[19]

MEDICAL AND PUBLIC HEALTH PROBLEMS OF
THE EARLY RELOCATION PHASE

Most of the tasks of the early relocation phase, to judge from the civil defense literature, are organizational. Host area hospitals—in those host areas that do contain them—must discharge most of their patients to make room for the anticipated burden of area populations that have suddenly tripled or quadrupled, as well as to care for the relocated hospital patients from risk areas. Medical staffs and support personnel arriving from risk areas must be distributed throughout host areas in some rational fashion, presumably related both to the distribution of shelters and the existence of medical facilities. "Packaged Disaster Hospitals," if they are available, must be unpacked and set up and staffed.

In addition, systems for the distribution of food and water must be established and—of particular concern to medical and public health planners—systems of sanitation, waste disposal, and garbage collection must be established since existing resources cannot possibly handle the increased population load. Finally, CRP manuals call for the appropriate establishment of mortuary services and plans for the registration of the dead.

Literally thousands of pages of FEMA research reports are devoted, therefore, to lists associated with these tasks; there are lists of personnel, lists of drug supplies for different types of cases and in the aggregate, lists of operating room and other hospital supplies, lists of radio communication systems and frequencies, lists of medical equipment, and lists of existing facilities.

In terms of actual medical care for relocated populations just arriving in the host areas, the judgment has been reached that the major need will be for primary ambulatory care—not inpatient services. (Whether or not this is a realistic approach to the ongoing burdens of illness and death in the relocated and host area populations will be considered in the next section of this chapter). In any case, this approach represents an attempt to concentrate on what might conceivably be done, regardless of urgency, whether or not it is most appropriate to needs.

Civil defense medical planners in host areas are therefore urged to convert every available resource into sites of primary care delivery—not only existing medical care resources (hospitals and physicians' offices) but also veterinary clinics, college infirmaries and dormitories, dentists' offices, and suitable spaces in public buildings.

The general population, meanwhile, will be engaged in shelter construction and improving fallout protection. Several models of expedient shelters have been proposed; a typical example has dimensions of 12 feet by 3.5 feet by 6.8 feet and includes a small foyer and entryway. One independent calculation suggests that this would require excavation of more than twenty tons of earth, proper emplacement of more than 200 pieces of lumber, including heavy roof supports, weighing a total of about 1,000 pounds, and a three-foot-thick cover of earth weighing eight tons. For this task, FEMA claims results from empirical tests:

> Experiments were conducted in 1977–78 that involved asking four dozen average American families to construct expedient shelters of various designs. (These designs required moving four to six cubic yards of earth per person. ...) These families were given only simple written instructions and diagrams on how to construct the shelter. To provide an incentive, they were paid a base price of several hundred dollars, plus a bonus if they constructed the shelters more rapidly than the standard time. The officials conducting the tests were impressed that not a single family dropped out of the experiment. In fact, almost all of the families earned the bonus.[20]

Since the report does not add that a cubic yard of earth (in conditions that exclude frost and mud) weighs 2,700 pounds, this account does not make it clear that the requirement per person is to move from 5.4 to 8.1 *tons* of earth. The findings conflict with those of equivalent "research" conducted by Dr. Vergil Fairbanks of the Mayo Clinic. With diagrams of the expedient shelters and their specifications in hand, he consulted morticians in his own community, who told him that "an experienced gravedigger in very good physical condition can excavate about 6 tons of earth in 6 hours, when conditions are very favorable, and using very sharp and long-handled shovels and picks; the work is extremely hazardous (from cave-ins, often fatal) and it can only be done where there is at least seven feet of soil above rock" when the ground is not frozen.[21] For residents of the city of Rochester, Minnesota alone, Dr. Fairbanks calculated, the construction of expedient shelters would require about 100 acres of land and more than 10 million pounds of lumber.

FEMA research planners have anticipated at least some of the problems. They have included chiropractors in the manpower pool to provide primary care in the host areas, noting that "indeed, with individuals unaccustomed to strenuous physical labor engaged in the development of expedient shelter, a number of strained backs requiring the assistance of a chiropractor may be expected."[22]

MEDICAL AND PUBLIC HEALTH PROBLEMS OF THE SHELTER PHASE

If we assume that everything has proceeded smoothly to this point, the host areas now contain 195 million people who, according to FEMA plans, will remain indoors, underground, or in expedient shelters for at least one to two weeks until radiation levels have dropped sufficiently to permit at least brief trips outside. This FEMA estimate contrasts sharply with the findings of one of the few detailed and quantitative studies by FEMA contract researchers to be published in a scientific journal. In *Health Physics*, Drs. K.S. Gant and C.V. Chester of the Oak Ridge National Laboratory hypothesize a 5,000-megaton attack, assume that 80 percent of the population is safely in shelters with protection factors of 200 (so shielded that the inside shelter radiation level is one two-hundredth of the level outside the shelter). They conclude that in many areas with the worst fallout, "continuous shelter could be required as long as 41.4 days . . . with as much as 267.3 days expiring before the full 16 hours could be spent outside the shelter each day.[23]

Assuming that the continuous shelter requirement is only two weeks—and not the six weeks estimated above, even though in many shelters the protection factor will not be near 200—what will be the burden of illness in a population of 195 million people during this period? If we assume that the 195 million is a representative sample of the noninstitutionalized population of 220 million residents in the United States, approximate answers to this question can be derived from data compiled regularly by the NCHS on hospitalizations, the incidence of life-threatening emergencies, the prevalence of chronic conditions, the incidence of acute conditions, and the number of ambulatory office visits, by diagnosis, under ordinary condition. Since fallout shelters cannot be construed as ordinary conditions, and since stress and crowding will sharply increase the incidence of many diseases, the estimates given in Table 10-1 are, if anything, extraordinarily low.

TABLE 10-1.   Estimated Prevalence of Selected Diseases in Host Area Populations In Shelters.

Disease	Prevalence Rate/1,000 in General Population	Number in 195 Million	Number on Medications in 195 Million
Thyroid	13.9/1000	2,710,500	2,008,481
All anemias	14.5/1000	2,827,500	NA[a]
Diabetes	20.4/1000	3,978,000	3,273,894
Epilepsy	3.1/1000	604,500	453,375
Urinary system, all diseases	28.0/1000	5,460,000	1,665,300
Calculus of kidney/ureter	3.3/1000	843,500	174,388
Prostate[b]	13.1/1000	2,554,500	715,260
Uterus/Ovary[c]	13.1/1000	NA	NA

a. Data no available.
b. Males only.
c. Females only.
SOURCE: *Vital and Health Statistics*, Series 10, no. 109 (Washington, D.C.: National Center for Health Statistics, March 1977), tables A and B.

In a host area population of 50,000 persons—not an unusual concentration—there would, therefore, be approximately 695 individuals with thyroid disease, 770 with anemias, 1,020 with diabetes, 150 with epilepsy, 1,400 with genito-urinary tract disease, and so on. To these must be added all those with chronic heart conditions, hypertension, asthma, ulcers, emphysema, and other frequent and serious conditions.

Using somewhat older data, FEMA researchers have estimated the prevalence of chronic conditions in host area populations of various sizes and in a 500-person shelter, using a mathematical correction to obtain figures with a 90 percent probability. Their figures are given in Table 10–2.

These are the figures for people *entering* the shelter period. As all prevalence figures do, they speak to the heavy burden of illness, the requirements for medication, and the implied requirements for continuing medical treatment in any representative population. It is important to remember that these figures are based on the noninstitutionalized population of the United States, so they do not include those initially so ill that they required hospital or other institutional care.

But what will happen *during* the shelter period? What will be the expected incidence of episodes requiring medical care while the shelter populations are confined? Table 10–3 offers some estimates to answer this question.

More information on acute episodes during the shelter period can be abstracted from NCHS figures on ambulatory office visits of the general

TABLE 10–2.   Expected Number of Individuals with Chronic Conditions in Host Area Populations of Varying Size.

Condition	Expected Number in a Population of		
	500	25,000	100,000
Chronic sinusitis	61	2,640	10,300
Arthritis & rheumatism	59	2,539	9,900
Asthma and hayfever	51	2,159	8,400
Hypertension	38	1,550	6,000
Heart conditions	32	1,296	5,000
Chronic bronchitis	22	862	3,300
Ulcer of stomach, duodenum	12	452	1,700
Paralysis, complete/partial	6	192	700
Emphysema	5	166	600
Diabetes	14	500	2,000

SOURCE: Adapted from M.N. Laney, et al., *Management of Medical Problems Resulting from Population Relocation* (Research Triangle Park, N.C.: Research Triangle Institute, May 1976), table XXI; original prevalence data drawn from *Vital and Health Statistics,* Series 10, nos. 83 and 84 (Washington, D.C.: National Center for Health Statistics, September 1973).

TABLE 10–3.   Calculated Incidence of Acute Conditions for a Population of 195 Million Persons in a Two-Week Period.

Condition	Rate/100 Persons per Year	Expected Number of Episodes, 195 Million Persons, Each Two-week Period
Common childhood diseases	1.6	125,250
Pneumonia	1.49	111,750
Bronchitis	2.91	218,250
Influenza	48.2	3,615,000
Upper gastrointestinal	5.1	382,500
Genito-urinary	5.97	447,750
Fractures/dislocations	3.77	282,750
Open wounds/lacerations	8.6	645,000

SOURCE: *Vital and Health Statistics*, Series 10, no. 141 (Washington, D.C.: National Center for Health Statistics, 1981), table 1.

population, by diagnosis. Assuming that each visit represents an illness episode, one can construct Table 10–4.

How many of these episodes would be serious or life threatening? Reference has already been made to the fact that, in a six-month period in 1980, the U.S. population made 4.3 million visits to emergency rooms for life-threatening conditions. Assuming that the same rates apply, the total of life-threatening episodes for 195 million people in a two-week period would be 294,385.

Similar but disease-specific information can be calculated from the NCHS's data on hospital discharges, expressed as rate per 10,000 persons per year, in the general noninstitutionalized population in 1980. If one assumes that, in any average period or for the year as a whole, discharges equal admissions, one can use these data to estimate the episodes of serious and/or life-threatening conditions (the NCHS rubric) in a population of 195 million in a two-week period. See Table 10–5.

TABLE 10–4.   Calculated Episodes of Selected Illness for a Population of 195 Million Persons in a Two-Week Period.

Illness	Office Visits/Year, U.S. Population	Episodes in Two Weeks, 195 Million Persons
Otitis media	11,166,000	429,462[a]
Diabetes	8,947,000	306,263
Asthma	6,786,000	232,290
Contact dermatitis/ eczema	5,683,000	194,533

a. This calculation assumes that *all* noninstitutionalized children are included in the shelter population.
SOURCE: *Vital and Health Statistics*, no. 77 (Washington, D.C.: National Center for Health Statistics, 1982).

TABLE 10–5.   Calculated Number of Serious or Life-Threatening Episodes of Illness Ordinarily Requiring Hospitalization, for a Population of 195 Million Persons in a Two-Week Period, for Selected Illnesses.

Condition	Rate/10,000 General Pop- ulation	$\bar{X}$ Length of Stay, Days	Number in Population of 195 Million in Two Weeks
Acute bronchitis and bronchiolitis	10.7	5.5	8,026
Pneumonia	35.1	8.3	26,324
Asthma	18.3	6.0	13,726
Ulcers	16.3	8.6	12,226
Appendicitis	11.9	5.5	8,926
Inguinal hernia	27.3	5.5	20,476
Cholelithiasis	20.5	9.3	15,376
Renal calculus	13.9	5.0	10,426
Disc disorders	17.2	9.9	12,900
Diabetes mellitus	28.9	10.5	21,676
Blood and blood-forming organs	15.0	7.2	11,250
Acute myocardial infarction	19.3	17.2	14,476
Congestive heart failure	18.0	7.1	13,500
Cerebrovascular disease	35.7	12.7	26,766

SOURCE: *Vital and Health Statistics*, Series 13, no. 64 (Washington, D.C.: National Center for Health Statistics, March 1982), table 13.

What would be lost to the sheltered population, in terms of urgently needed in-hospital care, if it were confined to shelters by dangerous radiation for two weeks? An estimate may be made simply by multiplying the last two columns of Table 10–5—that is, multiplying the anticipated episodes of each illness by the average length of stay. The total for the 195 million shelter population 1,928,170 hospital days. In reality, of course, the effect would be measured in terms of in-shelter deaths rather than days of hospitalization lost.

A special problem is represented by deliveries and births. If it is assumed that all women in the late weeks of pregnancy are left in high-risk areas, and a nuclear attack occurs, few would survive. If it is assumed that all women in the last weeks of pregnancy are moved to host areas and confined to shelters, then—again using NCHS data on the general population—the events listed in Table 10–6 will occur in the shelters during a two-week period.

Since there are substantial seasonal variations in births, actual figures would depend on the time of year, year-to-year changes in the birth rate, and so on. But in any case, the figures in Table 10–6 are probably substantially lower than the anticipated reality in at least two key respects. The stress of relocation and sheltering is likely to increase

TABLE 10–6. Deliveries, Live Births, Complications of Delivery, and Birth Defects; Two-Week Period.[a]

Episode	Total/Year, 1980, U.S. Population[b]	Expected Number in Two-Week Period
Hospitalizations for delivery	3,762,000	144,692
Live births	3,598,000	138,384
Complications of delivery	1,010,000	38,846
Birth defects	25,624	1,840

a. Since it is assumed that all woman at risk are sheltered, in this table the general U.S. population and the sheltered population are identical.
b. 220 million; numbers are rounded to the nearest thousand.
SOURCE: *Vital and Health Statistics,* Series 13, no. 64; and "Annual Summary of Births, Deaths, Marriages, and Divorces: United States, 1980," *Monthly Statistics Report* 29, no. 13 (September 1981).

the complications of delivery and, in particular, to increase the number of premature infants. Infants with birth defects are likely to fare even more poorly under shelter conditions without medical care.

To the appalling burden of disease in the shelters must be added the anticipated episodes of mental illness. Again, relevant NCHS figures on psychiatric hospital discharges, ambulatory office visits for mental disorders, and discharge diagnoses of psychosis and alcoholism can be used to estimate what will happen among 195 million people in the shelter period. See Table 10–7.

Some, but not all, of this staggering total of in-shelter emergencies, life-threatening illness, psychiatric disorders, and problems of delivery and the newborn is reflected in a calculation, using older data, by FEMA contract researchers at the RTI. These data appear in Table 10–8. Again (see also Table 10–2), they have used a mathematical correction to obtain figures for the expected number of acute conditions in host area populations of various sizes, and in a 500-person shelter, with a 90 percent probability, during a two-week period.

The difficulty with all of these calculations of incidence is that they are based on the occurrence of illness and injury under everyday conditions, not shelter life. Since FEMA researchers have never published any data indicating that an actual shelter experiment has been conducted— packing 100 or 500 people of all ages and states of health into the cramped conditions of a model expedient shelter for two weeks, for example— there is no empirical basis for estimating what might happen.

Common sense and ordinary medical judgment dictate that illness and death in shelters will occur at levels far above those calculated in the preceding pages. While for a few conditions such as trauma, fractures, and dislocations the estimates are probably overstatements of the experi-

TABLE 10–7.   Calculated Number of Episodes of Psychiatric Disorder for a Shelter Population of 195 Million Persons.

Condition	Number/Year, U.S. Population	Number Expected in Shelter Population, in Two Weeks
Acute psychiatric disorders ordinarily requiring hospitalization	1.5 million[a]	51,346
Mental disorders ordinarily requiring office visit	24,343,000[b]	833,280
Diagnoses of psychosis ordinarily requiring hospitalization	507,000[b]	17,026
Alcoholism requiring hospitalization	439,000[b]	14,776

a. Average/year, 1974–1978.
b. 1980 data.
SOURCE: Vital and Health Statistics (Washington, D.C.: National Center for Health Statistics, 1982).

ence of an almost immobile shelter population, virtually every other likely factor will push the totals upward. The profound stress of a prolonged shelter stay under conditions of nuclear war and radioactive fallout is, in itself, sufficient to trigger acute episodes of many diseases. Alcoholics and drug addicts will undergo enforced withdrawal. Some number of patients whose health or survival depends on regular doses of steroids, insulin, seizure medications, antihypertensive drugs, cardiovascular drugs, and other medicines will inevitably forget or exhaust their own supplies. Strokes, heart attacks, respiratory arrests, and acute gastrointestinal hemorrhages will all exceed normal rates.

By far the greatest threat in shelters, and the one most likely to double or even triple episodes of illness, is that of epidemic infectious disease—particularly influenza, gastroenteritis, diarrhea, and dysentery due to shigella, salmonella, and other bacteria. All of them will be intensified by, and may themselves intensify, the likely conditions of life in many shelters: inadequate sanitary facilities, steadily increasing environmental filth and contamination, darkness, contaminated food and water supplies, extremes of heat, cold, or humidity, dehydration, and emotional reactions to death and the continuing presence of dead bodies. The elderly and chronically ill, pregnant women, and infants and children will be especially vulnerable. One can only speculate as to the fate of those "dischargeable" patients who have been ejected from their risk area hospital beds, taken on a 50- to 200-mile trip under difficult conditions, and brought into the shelters.

TABLE 10–8.   Expected Number of Cases by Acute Condition in Host Area
Populations of Varying Size in Two Weeks

Condition	Expected Number (90% probability) in a Population of		
	500	25,000	100,000
All acute conditions	51	2,177	8,587
Infectious and parasitic diseases	7	244	935
Respiratory conditions	30	1,205	4,730
Influenza	13	485	1,882
Other respiratory conditions (pneumonia, bronchitis, etc.)	2	61	223
Upper gastrointestinal disorders	2	51	186
Fractures/dislocations	2	42	150
All other acute conditions	9	332	1,280

SOURCE: M.N. Laney, et al., table XX.

These epidemics, in turn, are likely to be worsened by another
possibility: radiation injury. Some indeterminate number of the shelters
will prove to have protection factors inadequate to ambient radiation
levels. In other cases—to throw out the dead, seek water, or because of
panic—shelters may be opened briefly despite continuing dangerous
radiation levels. Individuals may move outside and then return, inevitably increasing radioactive contamination of the shelter environment. To
the problems already described must be added the probability of radiation sickness and its consequences: lowered immunity and increased
susceptibility to infection, as discussed further in Chapter 11.

Obviously, for bioethical reasons, there can be no experiments
exposing human beings to such conditions in order to confirm and
quantify these expectations. Existing knowledge in experimental epidemiology is only partially relevant. Animal studies would be difficult and of
uncertain value. But none of these are needed to buttress the view that the
medical and public health experience of sheltered populations would be a
disaster without precedent. Concentration camp and prisoner-of-war
experience in this and earlier centuries offer some parallels, but none of
them involved 195 million people.

Under the best of circumstances, with an intact medical care system,
no radiation threat, and unimpeded communications and mobility, illness on this scale would be difficult to deal with. How do FEMA's contract

researchers plan to provide medical care during the shelter period after a nuclear attack? In the main, they don't.

What is perhaps, most startling about the majority of available civil defense studies of crisis relocation medical care is that when they reach this point—with all of the risk area populations relocated, the expedient shelters built, the people huddled inside, and the continuing burden of illness and death to confront—*they assume no nuclear war and no radiation.* There is no other explanation for their scenarios of patients moving from shelters to primary care centers and back, or to the occasional regional or packaged disaster hospital, or for their endless calculations of medical personnel and hospital supplies, none of which would be applicable during prolonged periods of dangerous or lethal radiation.

At best, this "research" seems to assume that, if war and fallout do occur, radioactivity will be delayed in arriving, of brief duration, or of such low intensity as to constitute a tolerable risk. One such study, for example, suggests that if shelter occupants discover that their shelter is deficient in radiation protection, ventilation, food, or water, it may be necessary for one or more occupants to leave the shelter in search of help or supplies. "Such forays," the study continues, "may not be necessarily hazardous if the people leaving the shelter know where to go or what to do."[24] The same report goes on to suggest a kind of nuclear war fast-food take-out service for shelter populations:

> If there is inadequate water or food in the shelter, radio or telephone contact may be used to arrange for an emergency delivery, or to determine the closest point of supply to which volunteers from the shelter will run or drive to get the necessary supplies. The level of radiation intensity in the vicinity of the shelter should be monitored so that a fairly accurate prediction can be made of the dose to which the emergency crew will be exposed.[25]

A few published studies are more responsible, particularly those that deal with the possibilities of shelter epidemics and a number that attempt to calculate the consequences of radiation levels, shelter effectiveness, and the behavior of sheltered populations in terms of likely rates of radiation sickness or later cancer incidence.

The most honest FEMA materials are those designed for the general public to inform it about in-shelter first-aid procedures. The DCPA's pamphlet entitled *Protection in the Nuclear Age* devotes twelve pages, with diagrams, to general rules for any medical emergency, cardiopulmonary resuscitation, serious bleeding, fractures, the treatment of shock, and the like. For radiation sickness, for example, the pamphlet advises: "If the patient has headache or general discomfort, give him one or two aspirin tablets every 3 or 4 hours . . . if he is nauseous, give him motion sickness tablets, if available. If his mouth is sore or his gums are bleeding, have him use a mouthwash . . . if available, a mixture of kaolin and pectin should be given for diarrhea."[26] There is no explicit promise of effectiveness.

Even these documents, however, occasionally slip smoothly into an implied promise that there will be a functioning medical care capacity for sick or injured people in shelters. After noting that "fractured bones in the neck or back are very serious" because they may cause paralysis or death, the same pamphlet says such patients "should not be moved *until a doctor comes*."[27] (Italics added.)

MEDICAL AND PUBLIC HEALTH PROBLEMS OF THE POST-ATTACK PHASE

Little has been written about the reconstitution of medical care in the aftermath of nuclear war. Most attention has been given to the potential problems of famine and malnutrition and to the likelihood of infection and the spread of communicable disease. Abrams and Von Kanael,[28] Geiger,[29] Leaning,[30] and others have written extensively on the problems of survivors—with or without trauma, burns, and radiation sickness—in a world of malnutrition, dehydration, exposure and hardship, lowered natural resistance to disease, nonexistent sanitation, decaying human and animal corpses, and lack of drugs, laboratories, or medical care.

FEMA contract researchers, while paying particular attention to the potential for epidemics of tuberculosis[31] and plague,[32] have also attempted to estimate the probabilities of a wide range of infectious and communicable diseases—incuding hepatitis, shigellosis, salmonellosis, typhus, typhoid, rabies, tetanus, and diptheria—and to speculate on the kinds of controls that might be attempted.[33] A number of studies have attempted to calculate the post-attack incidence of radiation-induced leukemias, solid tumors, birth defects, and genetic changes.

Studies of the post-attack period must operate in the realm of assumption and speculation even more than do studies of earlier periods. What is not known—about the spread of disease under these circumstances and the possibilities of ozone layer depletion, massive forest fires, impairment of photosynthesis, disruption of the food chain, and lowering of ambient temperatures—far outweighs what is known, for, once again, fortunately, there are no precedents. Hiroshima and Nagasaki, miniscule events by today's nuclear standards, do not serve as precedents, for they were isolated and limited events in otherwise intact societies and, ultimately, help could arrive from an unaffected outside.

One conclusion does seem clear. Uncertain as they must be, *none* of the studies is consistent with the FEMA promise of "total survival of 80 percent of the population." At best, increased early escape from blast, heat, and radiation will simply swell the numbers doomed to die within a year or two of infection and starvation.

SOME BIOETHICAL CONSIDERATIONS IN CIVIL DEFENSE

There is a paradox at the very heart of civil defense efforts in nuclear war. It is little noted by the public and only grudgingly acknowledged, if not concealed, by civil defense planners. Yet it has the most profound consequences for physicians and other health workers and, indeed, for all human beings during and after a major nuclear attack.

The paradox is as follows: the more survivors there are, in relation to the depleted resources and devastated economic and social structure of a nation after nuclear war, the less likely is national recovery. Any extra survivors created by civil defense, M.I.T. physicist Henry Way Kendall noted in congressional testimony, would grossly overburden the nation's depleted agriculture and industry. He added that "the consequence of having a large civil defense program that provided effective urban evacuation and thus was a short-term success would be to *enhance* the subsequent level of death and injury, and make even a vestigial recovery of an industrial nation a more remote possibility."[34]

A review entitled *Candidate Civil Defense Programs*, prepared for DCPA in 1976, specifically raised this question under the heading, "Some Likely Questions and Criticisms." The ensuing comments first denied the problem, then suggested that it should never be raised publicly, and then reluctantly acknowledged its truth. The entire comment merits quotation:

> CRP (as well as other Civil Defense Programs) may not be desirable because we might, in the event of a war, end up with too many survivors (relative to remaining resource base and reconstruction possibilities). This is not an argument likely to be made public but it *has* been made within the government, if only by *very few* people.
>
> a. We would prefer to save the *maximum* number of our people, insure the *maximum* continuity of our organizations, institutions, culture and of our way of life. Unless we would want to protect *our people, our institutions, our cultures and our lifestyles* (that is, the quality of American life), we would be unlikely to go to war in the first place.
>
> b. The argument is contrary to the letter and intent of the Congressional (and of course, Administration) mandate to "protect life and property" against the hazards of nuclear war.

   c. It is the kind of "in-house" argument that, if publicized, would
      raise the wrath of our people against *any* government, or its
      employees and technicians who have such a low valuation of the
      importance of the dignity and worthwhileness of lives of Ameri-
      cans, their families, their institutions, and their culture.
   d. Yet, we recognize the dilemma: maximization of survival in attack
      environment may well be at partial odds, or at odds over some
      definable ranges of magnitudes, with maximization of long-range
      survival and/or with maximization of the nation's recovery poten-
      tial. The nation's traditional value system, however, favors the
      emphasis on maximum population survival as the highest
      priority.[35]

   It takes no great insight to understand that, if maximum short-range
survival is at odds with maximum long-range survival, the last sentence,
favoring "maximum population survival," says nothing and simply
denies the admitted paradox.
   But the contradiction between short-term human survival and
whatever is defined as "national survival" has been noted and discussed
by civil defense researchers, including those who address the problems of
caring for the ill and wounded. For physicians and other health workers
trained in a bioethical commitment to individual human beings, some of
the research comments suggest an ominous change.
   One study observes that "it is important to remember that the
Emergency Medical Care System [in a nuclear war] is a resource allocation
system, not a treatment system" and that "the optimum Emergency
Medical Care System is the optimum resource allocation strategy that
tends to fulfill the goals of the recovery program."[36]
   It goes on to suggest that "any formula for converting available
resources into an estimate of the number of patients who could be treated
implies the (tacit) agreement among medical practitioners as to an acceptable treatment level and prognosis prediction *consistent with the austere
post-attack environment.*"[37] (Italics added.) Finally, it is explicit: "If treatment demands exceed capability, then certain injury or *personnel categories*
may be refused treatment." (Italics added.)
   How might this be done? The author lists a set of possible triage
strategies in rank order:

   One strategy is to commit resources such that the speed of return to duty
   of key injured personnel is maximized. The definition of key personnel
   would be those people whose function is such that they would eventually be instrumental in guiding total national recovery. The functions
   would be weighted so that the immediately needed people, such as
   doctors and nurses, would be most important, while those who would
   not be needed until later, such as masons, carpenters, would be least
   important.

This would result in "a table of manhours potentially gained by providing treatment. This table can be weighted according to personnel functions. The method of providing treatment would be to treat the injured who would provide the most additional manhours at the most important time periods."[38]

The basis of this approach to triage is not the medical condition, needs, or treatment requirements of the individual patient. It is, rather, the needs of the fatherland, and the determination to achieve the highest possible productivity and the lowest possible dependency ratio. This is a new moral prescription for physicians. And aside from the rather obvious pandering to medical workers (in reality, masons and carpenters may be far more useful in the devastated post-attack world than physicians without drugs, equipment, or facilities) there is a curious omission. What priority is to be assigned to ill or injured children? Their "weighted personnel function "must be low; they can contribute few manhours. Yet, without children, what is the definition of "national survival"? This question is explored in Chapter 7.

A second triage strategy, the research report suggests, is "to minimize post-treatment care demands. In this case, each injury would be related to an estimate of personnel and material resources needed for continuing supportive care. The strategy . . . would be to assign treatment priorities to patients with small continuing care requirements."[39] This is, in effect, a new cost-benfit formula—in which the benefit of survival for the individual must be weighed against the cost in national medical resources.

A third strategy is "to minimize average treatment time. . . . The priority system involved would entail treating the least serious injuries first. It seems to be a valid procedure when the demand exceeds the supply, since the largest amount of people will be treated."[40] Again, this would require the physician to reject considerations of individual need and substitute the collective needs of an undifferentiated mass.

Only later in the list of strategies do we come to more familiar percepts. The fourth-ranked strategy is "the matching of treatment with demand," and the fifth is "to maximize the rate of resource commitment." But even then, it all may stop. "Superseding national priorities may also dictate the cessation of emergency medical care treatment."[41]

Another study is equally explicit. "Other measures of effectiveness than survivors/deaths should be investigated. For example: to what extent would surviving casualties, from case studies thus far, be limited in their contribution to post attack recovery?"[42]

These weighted judgments are not suggested for physicians alone. The Oak Ridge study of radiogenic cancer deaths, cited previously, confronts a situation in which continuing radiation levels may be so high that outside exposure would result in radiation sickness or carcino-genesis. Yet shelter populations, required by radiation dangers to remain sheltered for nine months, two years, or longer, must nevertheless send people out to secure food and water, "restore utility services," and decontaminate essential areas. In that situation, the report suggests quite logically, it makes most sense to send the older people (defined variously as over forty, over fifty, or over sixty) out first, for "older people will come to the end of their natural life spans before reaching the end of the risk plateau," and both cancer incidence and loss of life expectancy will be reduced. By the same token, "it appears that giving the younger members of the population the least contaminated food" (and the older members the most contaminated food) "would effectively reduce the number of cancer deaths from the ingestion of radio-isotopes."[43] The immediate aim here is, clearly, to protect children and younger people. The report concludes with the observation that this will "speed the recovery process."

What is the moral distance, one must wonder, between this "reasoned" (if distasteful) proposal and those nuclear war survivalist handbooks that prescribe high-powered rifles as part of the equipment for family shelters and include diagrams showing how family members can command maximum fields of fire? What is proposed in each is a strategy to ensure the "survival of the fittest." But more important, who will decide whether the survival of any individual serves the purposes of national recovery? And what, under these circumstances, does national recovery mean? What will the nation "recover"? Twenty years ago a critic of civil defense plans warned that "the social cost of going underground would not fall short of the total transformation of our way of life, the suspension of our civil institutions, the habituation of our people to violence and the ultimate militarization of our society."[44]

Nuclear war itself, of course, may do all that and more. But the implication of the paradox at the heart of civil defense is that the very process of planning for national survival may begin the process of destruction, in a kind of anticipatory anomie.

11

An Ill Wind: The Radiation Consequences of Nuclear War

Jennifer Leaning

And it shall come to pass,
that instead of sweet smell,
there shall be stink;
and instead of a girdle, a rent;
and instead of well-set hair, baldness;
and instead of a stomacher,
a girding of sackcloth;
and burning instead of beauty.

Isaiah 3:24

Q. *Have government studies been made relating to civil defense?*

A. Yes, several high-level studies were made in 1976–1978, on civil defense issues.

Q. *What was the result of the Department of Defense study?*

A. The study suggested that in a heavy, mid–1980's attack on both military and urban-industrial targets, having no civil defense could result in total national survival of perhaps 20 percent while the current program could result in total survival of some 30 percent. By contrast, reasonably effective (but not perfect) crisis relocation could result in total survival of over 80 percent. . . .

Q. *What about protection from radioactive fallout—wouldn't evacuees be facing death from fallout even if they made it out of town?*

A. If a crisis escalated to nuclear attack on the United States, the fallout radiation hazard would depend on how many weapons were detonated near the surface of the ground (rather than up in the air). Where fallout was deposited would depend on the direction the winds were blowing.

Thus, any given place in the United States could experience fallout—with varying degrees of radiation hazard (maybe severe, maybe not so severe). Some places, of course, might not receive any fallout at all.

Just being out of town can be a great lifesaver. In fact, a current study suggests that a substantial fraction of the survivors added through crisis relocation would survive simply by not being near nuclear detonations. Just being away from the blast and heat effects of the weapons could add many survivors.

However, to realize all of the potential for added survivors would require protection from radioactive fallout. Obviously, therefore, *all* evacuees and all residents of "Host Areas" as well should have fallout protection available. This is because no one can predict just which areas would experience severe levels of fallout, and which ones wouldn't.

Q.   *How would fallout protection be provided for evacuees and others in the so-called "host areas"?*

A.   There is some existing fallout protection now in the host areas—in college and commercial buildings, for example. Also, where people's homes have basements, many provide a pretty fair level of protection against fallout for those people.

But overall, the amount of fallout protection now existing in host areas is something less than would be needed by the residents, the people who live there right now. So if we are talking of maybe 110 million evacuees arriving in host areas, it is obvious that additional fallout protection would have to be developed during the crisis period.

This can be done by adding earth alongside and on top of existing structures. (It could be said that "protection from fallout is cheap as dirt.")

The Government's "Host Area Shelter Survey" is identifying buildings such as schools, churches, and commercial structures which offer the potential for improving their existing fallout protection by "crisis upgrading" actions—that is, by adding earth.

SOURCE: Defense Civil Preparedness Agency, *Questions and Answers on Crisis Relocation Planning*, Information Bulletin No. 305, U.S. Government Printing Office, Washington, D.C., April 20, 1979, pp. 2, 11.

What do Survivors Face? . . . [B]efore recovery can start, individuals must survive the blast and thermal effects, fallout and the prospect of being trapped without rescue or medical help. Once through the immediate postattack period (roughly the first week), there would still be many obstacles to overcome beginning with the possibility of insufficient life support requisites such as food, water and shelter.

The major elements in this "obstacle course to recovery" and the times during which they will be most important are outlined below:

Time After Attack	Attack Effect
1–2 days	Blast and thermal
3–4 days	Fallout
2–7 days	Trapped; no medical treatment
5–50 days	Life support inadequacies
2 weeks — 1 year	Epidemics and diseases

1–2 years	Economic breakdown
5–20 years	Late radiation effects
10–50 years	Ecological effects
2–several generations	Genetic

SOURCE: Defense Civil Preparedness Agency, *Research Report on Recovery from Nuclear Attack*, Information Bulletin No. 307, U.S. Government Printing Office, Washington, D.C., May 10, 1979, pp. 10–11.

TREATMENT OF RADIATION SICKNESS

Emergency treatment deals with the symptoms of the illness.

Headache.—Give an adult 1 to 2 aspirin tablets every 3 or 4 hours. For children, ½ aspirin every 3 or 4 hours.

Nausea.—Motion sickness tablets may be given in dosage previously prescribed by your doctor.

Vomiting and Diarrhea.—Encourage the patient to take liquid as soon as possible to make up for the fluid he loses through vomiting and diarrhea. Fluids should be started even though attacks of vomiting continue to occur. A salt and soda solution is valuable for this fluid replacement. It is prepared by adding 1 teaspoonful of table salt and ½ teaspoonful baking soda to 1 quart of cool water. *The patient should drink this solution slowly.* When vomiting has ceased the patient should be taking at least 6 to 8 cups of liquid a day. The salt and soda solution can be alternated with bouillon and fruit juices. Children will require less liquid.

Weakness.—Weakness is frequently associated with vomiting and diarrhea. Put the patient to bed and keep him warm and quiet.

Sore Mouth.—Use a mild salt solution mouthwash (½ teaspoonful to a quart of water). Give aspirin for pain and discomfort.

SOURCE: Defense Civil Preparedenss Agency and the U.S. Public Health Service, *Family Guide Emergency Health Care: A Reference Guide for Students of Medical Self-Help Training Course*, Department of Health, Education, and Welfare, Rockville, Maryland, September 1972, pp. 70–71.

In this chapter we focus on the consequences of exposing the U.S. population to the radiation released by nuclear war. Radiation, for the vast majority of people, is a total unknown. We cannot see it, smell it, taste it, hear it, or feel it. We only dimly understand how it causes damage. Virtually none of us have seen someone be sick from it, let alone die from its effects. In its invisibility and unfamiliarity it creates a sense of menace among us that is unrelated to any understanding on our part of what its actual effects might be. FEMA seeks to reduce that perception of menace because, as we discussed in Chapter 1, it is critical to the success of CRP that people think nuclear war is survivable, and central to that confidence is a sanguine attitude toward radiation.

Consequently, official discussion of this issue has taken the following form:

1. We live with radiation all the time and people should not be so afraid of it.

2. The actual consequences of radiation after a nuclear war are less sweeping than those who are uninformed perceive them to be:

   a. If evacuation proceeded according to plan, and 80 percent of those at risk in urban areas were evacuated to host areas, and if all those in the host areas were housed in adequate shelters for a two- to four-week period, there would be very few deaths from radiation;

   b. Because of radiation decay rates, after the requisite two- to four-week shelter period, there would be very few areas of the United States that would pose a significant radiation hazard;

   c. The only morbid consequence of radiation to consider after the two- to four-week shelter period is the possible increase in malignancies that would not be reflected in the population for many years and would not significantly affect survival prospects;

   d. Given a successful CRP, 80 percent of the total U.S. population would survive a full-scale nuclear war.

Stepping back from FEMA's particular interest in persuading people to cooperate with CRP, the relevant question, in terms of actual survival after a nuclear war, is not what people perceive radiation consequences to be, but what levels of morbidity and mortality this radiation exposure will actually impose. The debate over this question revolves around the following issues:

1. How much radiation will there be after a full-scale nuclear war?
2. How long will it last?
3. At what levels is it dangerous to human health?
4. What will be its short-, intermediate-, and long-term consequences on human health?
5. How do we protect ourselves from it?

These issues arouse debate because there are uncertainties over what the data base will actually be, controversy over the data we now have, and official distortion of both data projections and data interpretation.

Uncertainty about the data base directly affects discussion of the first two issues: how much radiation will there be and how long will it last. The data base uncertainties arise from (1) trying to generalize about the amount of radiation released from thousands of different weapons exploded at varying heights according to a scenario based on educated guess; (2) attempting to go beyond that initial estimate to predict fallout patterns, incorporating a vast number of variables about wind, weather, and terrain conditions; and (3) using the general, obscurely packaged information available in the public record.

Uncertainty about the data we now have bears on the last three issues: what levels are dangerous, how do we protect ourselves, and what are the health consequences over time. To begin with, the available data on human response to radiation is sparse and incomplete; careful scientists are therefore reluctant to generalize from it. Second, the answers on intermediate- and long-term responses are still coming in, and our understanding of the exposure doses is also in the process of re-evaluation. Third, the effects of radiation are most complex, with human response dependent upon radiation variables—its dose level, the rate at which it is administered, the kind of radiation it is—and upon human host factors—individual susceptibilities we cannot predict, age, intercurrent stress, and the time frame in which we look for consequences. Jumping off from these uncertainties, the controversy over the data we now have focuses on three major questions relevant to a discussion of consequences after a nuclear war:

1. What are the predictive relationships between what we know at high-dose and what we can extrapolate for moderate- and low-dose human responses?
2. What is the radiation dose required to kill human beings?
3. What are the radiation doses required to cause illness, acute or chronic?

In the discussion that follows, we review the controversies surrounding these issues of radiation exposure and human health consequences. Based on what we can discern from available data and from data projections on radiation released from a nuclear war, we argue that there is ample reason to question official predictions of outcome. Using realistic estimates of shelter strategies suggested by the Arms Control and Disarmament Agency (ACDA) and predictions of post-attack fallout levels derived from data of the Defense Civil Preparedness Agency (DCPA), we develop a model of radiation exposure for the U.S. population. These projections of radiation exposure during the shelter and immediate post-shelter period indicate much greater levels of morbidity and mortality than FEMA now predicts, and suggest that radiation consequences alone, without reference to other intercurrent stress (e.g., disease and malnutrition), may have a far more severe impact on post-attack survival than is officially claimed.

1.   HOW MUCH RADIATION WILL THERE BE AND HOW LONG WILL IT LAST?

The attack scenario used throughout this book is the one described by FEMA as the CRP-2B model, comprising a 6,559–megaton single attack on the major military and industrial centers of the United States and targeting as well all urban areas of populations over 50,000.[1] In this attack 1,444 un-MIRVed weapons (one missile, one warhead) would be detonated; of the 6,559 total megatons delivered, 5,051, or 77 percent, would be ground burst, conforming to a strategy designed to destroy hardened military targets such as intercontinental ballistic missile (ICBM) installations and strategic air command (SAC) bases.[2] Kiloton densities per square mile would in some areas be intense; large sections of the Northeast would experience an attack equivalent to 9 kilotons per square mile. Virtually all areas in the East would be within fifty miles of a weapons detonation. Figure 11–1 shows a computer map of megatons assigned to specific U.S. targets.

Attempting to estimate the radiation produced by such an attack involves myriad uncertainties. From the standpoint of population risk, there are three important periods of radiation exposure to consider: initial radiation release, early fallout, and delayed fallout. Uncertainties attach to estimates of dose in each category.

Initial Radiaton

Nuclear weapons of the fission-fusion-fission type assumed in this attack release most of their energy as blast, heat, and initial radiation within the first minute after detonation. Initial radiation, in the form of neutron and gamma radiation, can inflict serious injury. Because of the physics of these weapons, however, most people who might be within the radius of lethality from this radiation would also be killed by the intense blast and thermal effects. This relationship is especially pronounced with larger weapon yields. At lower yields, around 10 kilotons, as can be seen in Table 11–1, the lethal areas for blast effects (4.9 km^2)

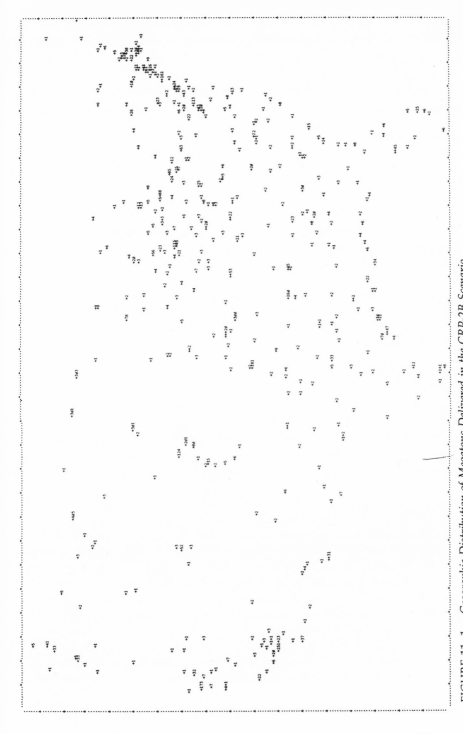

FIGURE 11–1. *Geographic Distribution of Megatons Delivered in the CRP-2B Scenario.*

SOURCE: Leo A. Schmidt, *A Study of Twenty-four Nationwide Fallout Patterns for Twelve Winds,* (Arlington, Va.: Institute for Defense Analyses, September 1981) [Prepared for FEMA], pp. 159–160.

TABLE 11–1.   Areas of Lethal Damage from Various Effects (in km^2).

Type of damage	Explosive yield 1 kt	10 kt	100 kt	1 Mt	10 Mt
Blast	1.5	4.9	17.7	71	313
Heat	1.3	11.2	74.2	391	1583
Radiation	2.9	5.7	11.5	22	54

SOURCE: Joseph Rotblat, *Nuclear Radiation in Warfare*, (Cambridge, Mass.: Oelgeschlager, Gunn & Hain, 1981), p. 70. Reproduced by permission of SIPRI and Taylor & Francis, Ltd.

and for radiation effects (5.7 km^2) become essentially the same, and for weapons in the kiloton range, the lethal radius for initial radiation effects exceeds that for blast and thermal injury. Since the airbursts over Hiroshima and Nagasaki produced virtually no local fallout, much of the radiation illness seen among the survivors and those who entered the cities as members of relief teams is thought to result from this neutron-induced gamma radiation.[3]

For populations evacuated from areas subjected to the direct effects of multiple large-yield weapons, (as would accord with the FEMA crisis relocation plan), initial radiation would have mortality consequences only in this regard: gamma radiation, induced in the urban rubble from intense neutron activity, could pose a substantial radiation hazard for several days to weeks and would prohibit re-entry to most major American cities for this time period.

Only about 5 percent of the total energy released from these weapons results in what is called residual radiation, defined as that portion of the radiation energy released after the first minute. It is this residual radiation that constitutes the components of early and late fallout.

Early Fallout

Weapons detonated at ground level, as the majority would be in the FEMA scenario, excavate millions of tons of earth from the earth's surface and scoop this material into the expanding radioactive gases created by the explosions. These particles of dust, covered with intense radioactivity, remain in the lower atmosphere and are carried by the winds to produce local early fallout. An estimate of early fallout levels commands major attention in this chapter.

Fallout maps for hypothetical war scenarios over the continental United States are available in the public record but in forms that make detailed projections of dose over time difficult to accomplish. These maps are derived from summing up the radiation releases from the dispersed megatonnage delivered and fitting these releases to a computer program that distributes the radioactivity according to a composite wind and weather pattern. The resulting fallout maps for the FEMA scenario and for other very similar ones express the radiation exposure over the continental United States in cigar-shaped elipses shaded according to intensity of dose. See Figure 11–2.

These fallout maps do not usually express radiation dose in a rate per hour form but instead use a cumulative expression which sums up the total fallout radiation dose, carried out to infinite time. (See Section 6 for a discussion of the assumptions used in these calculations of cumulative dose.) The relevant point here is that an expression of cumulative dose gives no information on the time it takes to reach that cumulative dose and, therefore, no information on requirements for duration of shelter stay. These maps are also drawn to very large scale; thus, only within a general regional area can one estimate fallout dose delivered. With the fallout data presented in this way, it is not immediately evident what the radioactive dose at a specific place might be at a certain point in time after the attack. Conversion tables are available that allow calculations back to the form of dose rate per hour or to estimates of dose at a certain point of entry into the radioactive field; but there is no way, given the current specificity of public information, to compensate for the absence of geographic detail. Whether or not access to the more detailed classified Defense Department scenarios would improve predictive accuracy is open to question. The scenarios are themselves hypothetical (based on estimates of Soviet strategic thinking), and local fallout patterns, dependent as they are on specific terrain, wind, and weather conditions, vary tremendously between what is predicted for even one small weapon detonation and what actually is seen to occur. See Figures 11–3 and 11–4 for a comparison of theoretical and actual fallout contours from a single weapon explosion.

The Weapons System Evaluation Group (WSEG) model for distribution of local fallout, expressed in a program called WSEG-10, forms the basis for most of the fallout maps available to the public.[4] In the most recent and detailed application of this program, Schmidt has taken the 6,559-megaton scenario, calculated mean prevailing fallout wind patterns, and produced cumulative dose fallout maps over the continental United States for a pattern conforming to each of the twelve months and for a hypothetical monthly pattern representing an average of the twelve months.[5]

From the standpoint of estimating the risk that fallout poses to the population, it is necessary to understand the uncertainties embedded in this average fallout map. First of all, in this model, as in all adaptations of the WSEG-10 that are publicly available, no attempt is made to incorporate effects of terrain and weather that might tend to concentrate areas of

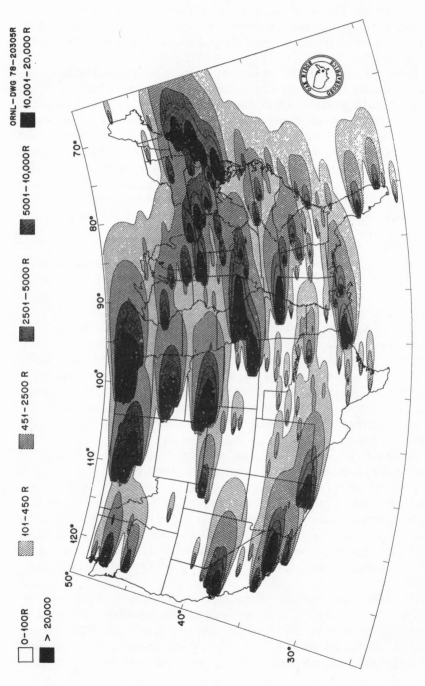

FIGURE 11–2. *Contours Showing Maximum Biological Doses (in rems)*.

SOURCE: Oak Ridge National Laboratory, DWG 78–20305R, in Cresson H. Kearney, *Nuclear War Survival Skills*, ORNL, September 1979, reproduced by American Security Council Education Foundation, Boston, Va.; 1979, p. 22.

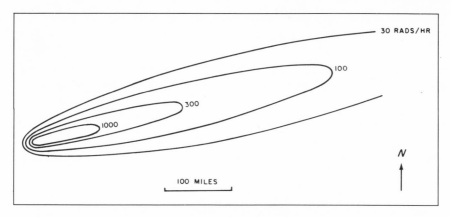

FIGURE 11–3.   *Idealized Fallout Contour (for 10-megaton, 50 percent fission, surface burst, 30 mph effective wind speed)*

SOURCE: Samuel Glasstone and Philip J. Dolan, eds., *The Effects of Nuclear Weapons*, (Washington, D.C.: U.S. Government Printing Office, 1977) p. 434.

fallout into what are called "hot spots."[6] Hot spots would pose unpredictable hazards to the population during the post-shelter period, since extreme variations in radioactivity over small distances could lead to morbid inadvertent exposures for months or years thereafter.

Second, the concept of an average wind direction obscures the population fallout risk posed by departures from the average. Schmidt's average fallout wind is derived by averaging monthly winds in the three atmospheric mixing layers that carry local fallout and then by averaging

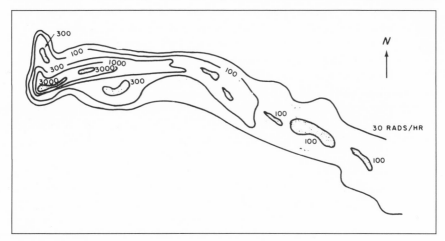

FIGURE 11–4.   *Corresponding Actual Dose Rate Contours (hypothetical).*
SOURCE: Glasstone and Dolan, p. 434.

that result over a twelve-month period. The mean wind velocity of 40 mph differs from the 25 mph velocity set by Haaland, who, using a fallout pattern based on a Defense Department adaptation of the WSEG-10 model, did not take into account the fact that winds carry fallout at several atmospheric levels.[7] The average prevailing continental fallout wind is from the northwest to southeast, heading, as it reaches the southeast, in a northeasterly direction before sweeping out to sea.[8] In 68 percent of the cases used to arrive at this fallout wind pattern, Schmidt found that the winds blew in this general direction. In 7.5 percent of the cases, however, the winds blew in a directly opposite direction (from east to west), with most variability occurring in the months of May, June, and August.[9] Erratic wind patterns, especially over areas of intense fallout, are most relevant to discussions of fallout shelter protection, where one must decide between (1) playing the odds and building a shelter that will shield against the fallout dose most likely to arrive and (2) building in protection factors that are designed to shield against much less likely, but much more intense, radiation fields.

Third, neither the FEMA scenario nor the WSEG-10 model accounts for the possibility that nuclear power plants might be targets of an attack on military and industrial installations. Because of the different half-lives of the radioisotopes contained in power plants and nuclear weapons, fallout from a nuclear reactor release remains at very high intensity much longer than fallout from a nuclear bomb. As can be seen from Figure 11–5, were a one-megaton bomb to explode on a 1,000-megawatt power plant, the resulting one-year cumulative 100-rad (radiation absorbed dose) fallout contour would cover an area seventeen times greater than the fallout for a one-megaton explosion. All these uncertainties (hot spots, wing variability, targeting scenarios) complicate attempts to arrive at estimates of fallout dose and, hence, of effective shelter strategies.

To account for the uncertainties involved in estimating fallout dose, Schmidt has presented the fallout data as a map of dose contours, in terms of mean cumulative dose.[10] (See Section 6.) Due to the variability of these doses, the standard deviation of the mean is very large, "almost always greater than the value of the mean dose."[11] Within this very wide range, as can be seen in Figure 11–6, this contour map shows most of the Northeast and West Coast receiving mean cumulative doses of 2,500 to 10,000 rads, with similarly intense doses in the Southwest and Midwest.

Since these dose contours express only the mean cumulative dose, however, they do not indicate the variability around the mean. Schmidt presents more detailed expression, in histogram form, of the variability of dose for the Northeast. This histogram reveals that, for example, residents in the Buffalo area would have a 30 percent probability of receiving a dose under 500 rads, a 1 to 2 percent probability of a dose between 500

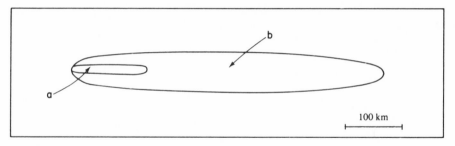

FIGURE 11–5.   *Contours of 100-Rad Fallout Dose in One Year, Starting One Month after the Detonation of (a) a 1-Megaton Bomb and (b) a 1-Megaton Bomb on a 1,000-Megawatt Nuclear Reactor.*

Area (km²)

Dose (rads)	1-Megaton Bomb	1-Megaton Bomb on 1,000 Megawatt Reactor
100	2,000	34,000
50	4,000	46,000
10	25,000	122,000

SOURCE: Rotblat, p. 129. Reproduced by permission of SIPRI and Taylor & Francis, Ltd.

and 1,000 rads, a 10 percent probability of a dose between 1,000 and 2,000 rads, a 20 to 30 percent probability of a dose between 2,500 and 5,000 rads, a 20 to 30 percent probability of a dose between 5,000 and 10,000 rads, and a 15 percent probability of a dose between 10,000 and 30,000 rads.[12] On the contour map, Buffalo straddles the contour line between the 1,000 and 5,000 mean cumulative dose.

What is clear from Schmidt's fallout maps and histograms is that throughout the continental United States, an unsheltered population would have a significant probability of receiving lethal radiation exposure from the CRP-2B attack. From the standpoint of estimating population exposures and shelter strategies, however, the difficulties posed by such wide variability in expected dose cannot be overestimated. There is a tremendous difference in health risk defined by this range of exposures. Shelters sufficient to protect against the lower range of dose would do very little to shield residents from an exposure in the higher range.

These initial uncertainties in fallout dose and consequent population risk are only compounded with time. For the first six months, intensity of radiation decays as a function of $t^{-1.2}$, or, as a rough approximation, by a factor of ten for every seven hours of elapsed time. After six months have elapsed, the decay rate changes slightly to reflect a transition from the intense, short-lived isotopes that determine the slope of the curve in the first six months to the less intense but more long-lived

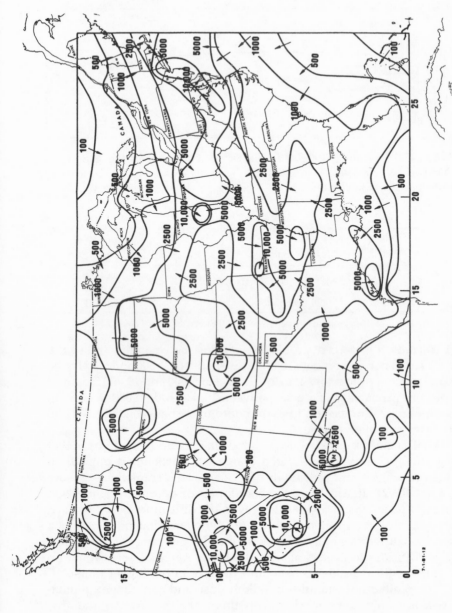

FIGURE 11–6.   *Mean Biological Dose Contours for CRP-2B Scenario.*

SOURCE: Schmidt, pp. 205–206.

isotopes that become the major contributors to the residual radioactivity thereafter. Referring to tables that express dose rates over time shows that these initially lethal levels of radioactivity that will blanket the continental United States in the form of early fallout from a nuclear war will continue to deliver significant levels of radiation for several years post-attack.

During the first year, as people emerge from shelters and begin to forage for food and water, construct places to live, and search for news of friends and relatives, their chronic exposure to persistent levels of radiation will continue to constitute a risk to life and health. Areas that experienced levels of fallout in the range of 200 to 10,000 rads per hour at H + 1 (one hour after weapons detonation) would, three months later, still be radioactive at levels ranging from 0.02 to 1 rad per hour. One week's exposure at these rates would result in doses of 3.4 to 168 rads.

At one year post-attack, these areas would still reflect dose rates ranging from 0.0016 to 0.08 rads per hour, or for full two-week exposures without shelter a two-week cumulative dose ranging from 0.5 rads to 27 rads. Two years out, for the same parameters, two-week exposures would result in two-week cumulative doses of 0.4 to 20 rads.[13] Hidden within these regions would be the hot spots, which could still, at two years post-attack, deliver much greater doses. These two-week doses must be added to the radiation burden people had already accumulated since the attack.

Late Fallout

None of these estimates of radiation dose rates over time incorporate measures of exposure delivered by the contribution of late or delayed fallout. Late fallout is created by the explosion of nuclear weapons at altitudes of 1,000 meters or greater. The resulting radioactivity mixes with upper atmospheric levels, decays in intensity during its transit through the stratosphere and troposphere, and eventually gets deposited, depending on wind and weather conditions, throughout the world's water and soil systems. Radionuclides constituting this late fallout are concentrated in biological systems and ultimately become part of the human food chain. This food chain contamination, in terms of health risk to the population, might additively or synergistically increase total radiation risk.[14]

To summarize our concerns with the official picture of the amount, extent, and duration of radioactive fallout from a full-scale nuclear attack on the United States:

1. The uncertainties in the scenario and the fallout patterns are numerous and complex;

2. The averages hide enormous variability in possible dose exposure;

3. Current shelter postures do not take this variability into account;

4. Even the average values expose most of the area of the continental United States to lethal cumulative levels of fallout;

5. A two- to four-week shelter posture will not protect the population from significant exposure for at least one to two years thereafter;

6. Nor will such a posture do anything to mitigate possibly serious radiation exposure through the food chain, contaminated by the contribution of late fallout.

2. AT WHAT LEVELS IS RADIATION DANGEROUS TO HUMAN HEALTH?

To evaluate FEMA's assertions about the health consequences of radiation exposure after a full-scale nuclear war on the United States, it is necessary to understand the biological effects of radiation on humans.

It is not controversial that subjecting cells to radiation produces changes that can be described in structural, morphological, and functional terms. Different cell and organ systems have very different thresholds of susceptibility to a given dose of radiation, although in general those cells that divide most rapidly are more radiosensitive. Allowing for these variabilities, the observed changes, when they do occur, are as follows:[15]

1. Structural: The energy delivered by radiation destroys or damages the DNA in cell chromosomes.

2. Morphological: Radiation injury to cells looks much like toxic injury from lack of oxygen or exposure to high temperatures.

3. Functional: In a pattern that appears to depend upon cell threshold and intensity of dose, the functional consequences are, in decreasing order of injury: death of that particular cell, destruction of its capacity to replicate, or damage to subcellular structures (DNA, organelles) that may spell either reduction in function or alteration in genetic material.

It is also generally accepted that residents of the United States are currently exposed to a range of approximately 0.05 to 0.3 rads per year from natural background and man-made sources. Although the health consequences of this level of exposure are not well understood, they are assumed to be relatively low. As guidelines for radiation protection, the National Council on Radiation Protection and Measurements has established the permissible limit of additional exposure for a member of the general public at 0.5 rems (for our purposes, 1 rad equals 1 rem) per year, and 5 rems per year for a worker in conditions of peacetime industry.[16]

Controversy within the scientific community intrudes when discussing consequences of exposure in higher dose ranges. Part of the controversy rests on the fact that our data on human response at these higher dose ranges are very inadequate. Our main source for data on the range of human response to high-dose radiation comes from the populations of Hiroshima and Nagasaki, exposed, in 1945, to air bursts of fission weapons. Two other populations still undergoing intensive prospective study, in addition to the Japanese, are the residents of the Marshall Islands, inadvertently exposed to fallout from the Bikini Atoll thermonuclear test in 1954, and a Utah population who were exposed at school age to fallout from tests conducted in the years 1951 to 1958. Other data sources include exposures from occupational experience (uranium miners), medical therapeutic protocols, and research and industrial accidents. The problems with this data base are numerous and uncorrectable since past circumstances, most of them tragic and incompletely observed, created the study designs. Working within the limitations of these data, however, it is possible to make some generalizations about the effects of radiation on human populations. These generalizations must be framed most cautiously, beginning and ending with the warning that since we are certain of very little we should proceed to act from the generalizations as conservatively as possible.

The factors affecting human response to radiation are:

1. Radiation dose;
2. Radiation quality;
3. Radiation dose rate; and
4. Age of exposed population.

Radiation Dose

It is generally accepted that the dose that will prove lethal to 50 percent of exposed humans is in the 360 to 450 rad range, depending on whether the dose is measured directly at the organ target level (the midline dose) or at the body surface. The term $LD_{50/60}$ means the lethal dose for 50 percent of the people exposed, followed for sixty days from time of exposure. Deaths after that point are assumed to result from other causes.[17] Much controversy surrounds the question of short- and long-term effects on humans at doses below LD_{50}. (See Sections 3 and 4.)

Radiation Quality

High linear energy transfer (LET) radiation, like neutron and alpha particles, which ionizes more densely per unit distance traveled than low LET radiation, like gamma and beta, has been shown per rad dose to be more efficient in cell killing. For assessing the biological effects of different forms of radiation in different tissues, it has proved important to specify this efficiency, labeled relative biological effectiveness, or RBE. Since radiation in nuclear warfare contains all forms of high and low LET radiation, and since the scale of detail used in this discussion is so general, distinguishing among the different forms of radiation delivered in fallout, although it might appreciably affect overall casualty estimates, is beyond the scope of this discussion. Assigning an RBE value of one to all radiation doses, as is done here, will tend to underestimate the biological effects of the radiation dose.

Dose Rate

This variable has great applicability in this discussion. It has been repeatedly observed that a given dose of radiation will inflict more severe damage if delivered all at once, in a single dose, than if fractionated and given in multiple, smaller doses over time. This dose fractionation effect pertains only to the immediate effects of radiation, however. For long-term effects like cancer induction there seems to be no difference between the incidence produced from several small doses and the incidence from a single large dose exposure. FEMA does not discuss the intermediate-term consequences of moderate doses, implying that fractionation of moderate doses (such as those that on the average will apply in the first few months after the shelter period) eliminates the health risk of these doses. Data available in the literature does not substantiate this implication, however. The reported effects of moderate dose fractionation suggest that they be evaluated on a cumulative basis.[18]

The reason that fractionating a given dose reduces prompt effects is thought to be that biological systems have repair mechanisms that, if not overwhelmed, will repair cellular damage and compensate for some degree of radiation injury. Estimates of this biological repair rate vary. The more optimistic estimates, from the standpoint of reducing cumulative radiation effects, are incorporated in the cumulative dose expressions found in the public literature on fallout exposures from hypothetical war scenarios. (See Section 6 for a more detailed discussion.)

Age of Exposed Population

Developing humans—those still in the uterus, infants, and young children—are particularly sensitive to radiation in terms of both acute response and long-term susceptibility to malignancy. It has also been suggested that older people are less resistant to acute doses.[19] Although the data are too limited to assign a quantitative value to the LD_{50} for people on either side of the age spectrum, it is known to be lower than that for healthy middle-aged adults.

FEMA consultants note that radiation exerts different effects on different age groups and suggest that early recovery and reconstruction work post-attack, which might result in significant radiation exposure, be performed by older people, who, it is·argued, will die of other causes before their induced cancers are experienced.[20] Among the problems with this suggestion is that older people, perhaps more sensitive to the acute effects of radiation, may be more susceptible in the short run to doses accumulated in early outdoor relief work.

3.   THE SHORT-TERM CONSEQUENCES OF RADIATION EXPOSURE

There are three main ways in which radiation can injure people: (1) whole body irradiation, (2) external contamination, and (3) internal contamination. Depending on the type and severity of injury, people experience a range of acute, intermediate-, and long-term effects. Early radioactive fallout primarily exposes people to risk from whole body irradiation and from external contamination. Internal contamination results from inhalation or ingestion of radioactivity either in its early fallout form or as it enters the body through contamination of the food chain. The principle short-term consequences of high-dose radiation exposure after nuclear war result from whole body irradiation. These effects have been traced in some detail through observation of the population subjected to the bombings at Hiroshima and Nagasaki, participants in medical therapies, and victims of radiation accidents in industrial and research situations. As will be discussed in Section 7, in the immediate post-attack setting there may well be millions of the sheltered U.S. population experiencing these high levels. Their symptoms, and fate, can be surmised from reviewing what has been observed in past experiences.

Whole Body Irradiation

Acute effects of whole body irradiation occur when the whole body, or most of it, is subjected to external radiation doses in excess of 20 rads.[21]

The initial, prodromal stage produced by radiation exposure indicates with some certainty the intensity of dose received and helps predict whether or not the course will progress to one of the three recognized radiation syndromes. This prodromal state is characterized by the onset, within a matter of minutes or hours, of anorexia, the symptom of mildest exposure. With larger doses, nausea, vomiting, and diarrhea may be seen. Fatigue is also considered one of the symptoms in this complex. The individual variability in response to a given radiation dose is wide and, given the state of our knowledge about susceptibility factors, unpredictable. For these reasons, the symptom complex is best described in terms of statistical probability. Table 11–2 shows the percentage of people who will experience one or more of the prodromal symptoms at a given level of radiation exposure. Assuming acute exposures were in the lower range of these dose levels, and that no further disease or severe stress were introduced, the prodromal syndrome would persist for several weeks, after which short-term recovery would be uneventful. The symptoms of people exposed to doses in the higher range might progress to conform to one of the three acute radiation syndromes described below. These syndromes, as defined by clinical experience and observed and treated by modern medicine, have usually resulted in death. In the post-attack setting, where medical care will be virtually unobtainable, death will be inevitable.

Hematopoetic

Hematologic abnormalities predominate at doses between 450 and 1,000 rads. The hematologic picture gives important information bearing on prognosis and therapy. Lymphocytes plummet almost immediately. Patients are at serious risk of infection if their total lymphocyte count drops to 1,000 within forty-eight hours of exposure and have experienced a lethal dose if the count drops to 100 within that time period. Changes in other white blood cells, in platelets (necessary for blood clotting), and in capacity to make new red blood cells will also occur. From a hematologic

TABLE 11–2.   Radiation Doses Producing Early Radiation Sickness (in rads).

Symptom	Percentage of Exposed Population		
	10%	*50%*	*90%*
Anorexia	40	100	240
Nausea	50	170	320
Vomiting	60	210	380
Diarrhea	90	240	390

SOURCE: W.N. Langham, ed., *Radiobiological Factors in Manned Space Flight* (Washington, D.C.: National Academy of Sciences, 1967), p. 248; cited in Rotblat, p. 33. Reproduced by permission of SIPRI and Taylor & Francis, Ltd.

standpoint, the peak risk of death from infection and hemorrhage occurs about three weeks from time of exposure, when the worst declines in platelets and white blood cells converge. What recovery has been observed in an intensive care setting will begin, if at all, from that point on.

Gastrointestinal (GI)

At doses of 1,000 to 3,000 rads, GI symptoms predominate, with the abrupt onset of nausea, vomiting, and bloody diarrhea progressing to severe hemorrhage from all mucosal surfaces. This intense fluid loss leads to electrolyte imbalances and dehydration. Death from infection or hemorrhage ensues within two weeks if the patient is untreated. Patients with this level of exposure are also subject to severe bone marrow depression and consequently are most susceptible to infection regardless of the fluid resuscitation they might receive.

Neurovascular

Neurovascular symptoms arise from exposures of over 3,000 rads and occur within the first hour to first two days. Victims present initially with confusion, stupor, or delirium and progress to sustained seizure activity and severe shock. All die from cerebral edema (brain swelling) and protracted hypotension (low blood pressure) within four days of exposure. People presenting with acute central nervous system changes or with symptoms of an acute mental status change always constitute a diagnostic and triage difficulty, and in the period immediately after a nuclear war alternate traumatic and psychological etiologies for these symptoms would be especially plausible.

According to modern medical practice in times of peace, assessing severity of radiation injury requires specifying time of onset of symptoms after exposure, baseline complete blood count, and chromosomal tests. Such assessment is helpful in the setting of a limited accident, where determining the level of exposure experienced by a small number of victims would help define treatment protocols and timing of follow-up studies.

For an individual exposed to 400 to 700 rads (without traumatic injury), intensive care therapy with reverse isolation techniques, bone marrow transplant, fluid resuscitation, antibiotics, white cell and platelet transfusions—performed in a setting with skilled hematology-oncology and burn unit capabilities—might result in a 50 percent chance of recovery requiring a protracted convalescence of two to six months. For exposures over 1,000 rads, in patients who present with GI hemorrhage within the first to fourth day, there would be, even in individual cases treated most aggressively and appropriately, little chance of survival. For exposures under 400 rads, intravenous fluid and electrolyte therapy with parenteral antibiotics might be able to support the patient through the initial stages of fluid loss, and, if bone marrow depression were not too severe, recovery would be possible.

A suggested protocol for treatment of someone exposed to a potentially lethal radiation dose follows:[22]

Immediately after diagnosis of exposure to 100 rad or more:

Avoid hospitalizing patient except in sterile environment facility. Look for preexisting infections and obtain cultures of suspicious areas— consider especially carious teeth, gingivae, skin, and vagina. Culture a clean-caught urine specimen. Culture stool specimen for identification of all organisms; run appropriate sensitivity tests for *Staph. aureus* and Gram-negative rods. Treat any infection that is discovered. Start oral nystatin to reduce *Candida* organisms. Do HLA typing of patient's family, especially siblings, to select HLA-matched leukocyte and platelet donors for later need.

If granulocyte count falls to less than 1500/mm³:

Start oral antibiotics—vancomycin 500 mg liquid P.O. q. 4 hr, gentamycin 200 mg liquid P.O. q. 4 hr, nystatin 1×10^6 units liquid P.O. q. 4 hr, 4 $\times 10^6$ units as tablets P.O. q. 4 hr. Isolate patient in laminar flow room or life island. Daily antiseptic bath and shampoo with chlorhexidine gluconate. Trim finger and toenails carefully and scrub area daily. For female patients, daily Betadine douche and insert one nystatin vaginal tablet b.i.d. Culture nares, oropharynx, urine, stool, and skin of groins and axillae twice weekly. Culture blood if fever over 101 degrees F.

If granulocyte count falls to less than 750/mm³:

In the presence of fever (101°F) or other signs of infection give antibiotics while waiting results of new cultures (especially blood cultures). The regimen suggested is ticarcillin 5 gm q. 6 hr I.V., gentamycin 1.25 mgm/kg q. 6 hr I.V. For severe infection not responding within 24 hrs, give supplemental white cells, and if platelet count is low give platelets from preselected matched donors. When cultures are reported, modify antibiotic regime appropriately. Watch for toxicity from antibiotics, and reduce medications as soon as practicable.

When granulocyte count rises to over 1000/mm³ and is clearly improving:

Discontinue isolation and antiseptic baths, antibiotics; continue nystatin for 3 additional days.

Medical therapy of this complexity requires a resource and supply network extending from laboratories through factories to hospitals, all of which will have been destroyed in the nuclear attack; a cadre of trained personnel, who, if not among the casualties, will be dispersed and ill equipped; and a ratio of providers to sick patients that the nuclear war will decimate. The remaining millions will need the care of the remaining few, and this care will be meager indeed. Faced with overwhelming numbers of people exhibiting all forms of symptoms (nausea, vomiting, diarrhea, gastrointestinal bleeding, altered mental states), the physician will have difficulty ascertaining whether or not the symptoms were caused by radiation exposure. Questions of exposure dose will be secondary and largely irrelevant because, regardless of cause, no treatment would be available, save perhaps the solace of a kind word, a held hand, a wet washcloth on the forehead, and, while stores lasted, the nonspecific aid of a penicillin injection and the suppressive mercy of a shot of morphine. In this catastrophic setting, the capacity to be humane, let alone effective, would be sorely stressed.

External Contamination

External contamination results from deposition on skin or clothing of radioactive material from either an accident or as fallout after a nuclear explosion. The risk of such contamination varies with the kind of contaminating particle and the duration of exposure. Individuals externally contaminated pose a risk to others if they directly transfer particulate material or if they are in such close proximity that from the standpoint of others they constitute an external radiation source.[23]

A perspective on what could be involved in applying decontamination procedures to people in large numbers can be gleaned from considering the current medical protocol necessary for skin decontamination of *one* person. That protocol involves:

1. *Decontamination site requirements*
   - Separate entrance and isolated air and water systems;
   - Drainage sluicing table;
   - Personnel dressed in water-repellent disposable total garb, including masks and gloves;
   - Labels for radioactive areas;
   - Beta and gamma Geiger counters, hand-held, battery-operated (alpha very difficult to get and maintain).

2. *Procedure on site*
   - Remove victim from contaminated area;
   - Remove all clothing;
   - Cotton swab samples of nares, ear canals, and mouth to test dose level at lab;

- Rinse out mouth and nose with water;
- Survey with Geiger counter;
- Wash with soap and water—especially orifices and hair;
- Survey with Geiger counter again;
- Repeat wash if necessary and shave all body hair areas if necessary;
- Avoid abrading skin—enhances absorption;
- Use occlusive dressings (to be removed every six to twelve hours) for persistent contamination (sweating will flush out much of the contamination from superficial horny skin layers).

In a situation prevailing after full-scale nuclear attack, producing intense radioactive fallout over millions of square miles, millions of people might require surface decontamination. These would include those who did not reach shelters before the arrival of early fallout; those who ventured out of shelters, even if momentarily, and found themselves coated by radioactive debris carried in a passing breeze, or splashed as they stepped in a contaminated puddle; and those who, remaining in shelters, were showered with radioactive dust that entered an inadequate shelter ventilation system. Most of these people should be considered to have suffered some amount of inhalation and ingestion contamination as well.

FEMA, assuming the bulk of the population will find shelter prior to the arrival of fallout and not leave until the danger is over, does not address the question of decontamination in much detail.

Internal Contamination

Internal contamination will occur whenever radioactive material is inhaled or ingested.[24] Inhalation of aerosolized radioactive particles, consumption of particles dusting food or water, and absorption of particles through mucus membranes or wound surfaces may all contribute to the internal body burden of radioactivity. Food chain contamination, incorporating radioactivity in concentrated forms, supplies the major, and more long-term source of internal contamination after a nuclear war. In early fallout settings, where people may also be at risk of whole body irradiation and external contamination, the possible synergism with internal contamination could seriously intensify exposure consequences.

The internal dose a person receives is dependent on complex interactions between the physical and chemical properties of the isotope and the biological system that metabolizes it; in general, alpha emitters, which deliver intense ionization in very focal areas, are most hazardous, followed by beta and then gamma. The chief health risks from internal contamination are expressed over years, as induction of malignancy in affected sites. A more acute toxic effect on the lung has been observed with high-dose inhalation injury, especially when combined with some component of external contamination and whole body irradiation. In this setting, over a several month period, a patient can experience progressive hemorrhagic pulmonary edema (blood and fluid in the lungs) resulting in death from infection and hypoxia (low level of oxygen).[25]

Assessment of dose received involves a series of calculations that are often very difficult to make even in isolated laboratory accidents where many of the parameters are well defined. In catastrophic situations—involving more than a few people in comparatively uncontrolled conditions—arriving at anything but a broad estimate may prove impossible. The suggested first aid treatment protocol focuses on procedures that prevent absorption or uptake into the systemic circulation. More experimental measures such as chelation, suggested for systemic therapy of internal contamination once it has occurred, are impractical for use on a population scale.[26]

First aid for internal contamination must be administered as soon as possible after exposure. In settings where populations are fleeing radioactive fallout, are sheltered for an obligatory period, or are emerging into a radioactive environment, it will be very difficult to assess what kind of internal contamination may have occurred and whether internal contamination continues to pose a substantial hazard. Since many of the procedures or antidotes are of uncertain efficacy and carry some risk of side effects, only one, potassium iodide, is recommended for use on a population scale. This antidote, taken as prescribed, will protect populations from one of the major contributors to early fallout—radioactive iodine. Administering potassium iodide saturates the iodine receptors in the thyroid and inhibits uptake of the radioactive forms. If administered within two hours of exposure, more than 90 percent of the radioactive dose will be blocked. The recommended dose is 100 milligrams of potassium iodide taken orally within two hours and then daily for ten days. At this dose, levels of thyroid stimulating hormone (TSH) may rise slightly, transient and clinically insignificant hypothyroidism may be induced in borderline thyroids, and a percentage of the population may develop a rash.[27]

In summary, the health consequences of radiation exposure are myriad. Our capacity to treat the acute exposures is limited. We cannot affect intermediate- or long-term consequences. What can we do requires a complex, sophisticated base of resources and skills that a nuclear war will destroy. FEMA underestimates both the demand that nuclear war will impose and the shortages it will create.

4. THE INTERMEDIATE-TERM CONSEQUENCES OF RADIATION EXPOSURE

Previous medical and scientific discussions of radiation injury have not focused on the consequences of chronic, intermediate-term, moderate-dose exposure. Rather, those discussions have concentrated either on problems of acute high-dose injury or long-term consequences of low-dose exposures. FEMA ignores the issue of moderate-dose exposure over time, yet from the perspective of both morbidity and mortality in the post-attack world such exposure may prove significant. The survivors will emerge from their shelters to face continuously, for the first few months and years, radiation exposures in the 0.1 to 10 rads per day range. These exposures will be additive to the burden the survivors had accumulated in their shelters.

What follows culls from the existing literature what is known about the health consequences of exposure at moderate levels, experienced with some chronicity. The information gleaned indicates that this level of radiation exposure may exert significantly negative effects on the capacity of the survivors to perform physical work, withstand infection, and conceive and produce viable offspring.

Much of this discussion is based on fragmentary data and inference because best estimates of threshold doses for humans subjected to chronic exposures of this intensity are very uncertain. The National Council on Radiation Protection and Measurements suggests a minimum threshold dose for acute symptoms of 0.14 rads per day, or 1 rad per week: "So far as is known at present, fractionated or protracted exposures at the overall rate of 1 R/ week for six years (about 300 R total) have little chance of causing any acute symptoms, although it is possible that some signs of significant radiation effect can be demonstrated by means of laboratory methods."[28] Whether protracted doses above this level, in the range of 0.1 to 10 rads per day, can produce clinically significant morbidity and mortality remains an unsettled issue.

The data on human response to chronic radiation exposure in the 0.1 to 10 rad per day range come primarily from radiation accidents and medical therapies involving whole body irradiation. Extrapolation from animal data introduces the factor of wide interspecies variation and can only be suggestive. Data from Hiroshima and Nagasaki do not speak directly to this question since, in the absence of local fallout, all exposures were relatively acute, and it is the chronicity, as well as the level of dose, that is important in determining health consequences. Fractionating large doses, compared to delivering a total dose all at once, reduces acute effects but appears to have little bearing on incidence of long-term effects. Chronic exposures in the dose range of 0.1 to 10 rads per day, equivalent to fractionating a sublethal total dose, appear to exert important, deleterious effects in settings where exposure could be determined. These effects are expressed in terms of accelerated mortality (in both diseased and nondiseased states), impaired fertility, altered immune response, fatigability, and increased incidence of congenital abnormalities. By ignoring this category of exposure, FEMA dismisses its potential for harm. This exploration of health consequences at these doses suggests, on the contrary, that many in the post-attack world will experience some of these effects.

Accelerated Mortality

The effects of chronic intermediate doses on mortality are suggested by Figure 11–7, which presents in composite form data on medical and accidental chronic exposures to intermediate levels of radiation. Over the course of one year, it is estimated that exposures to an average dose of 1.5 rads per day will produce a 10 percent probability of death; exposure at the rate of 3.5 rads per day, a 50 percent probability; and exposures of 6 rads per day, 90 percent probability of death in one year. Much of the data were obtained retrospectively in patients with other diseases; it is recom-

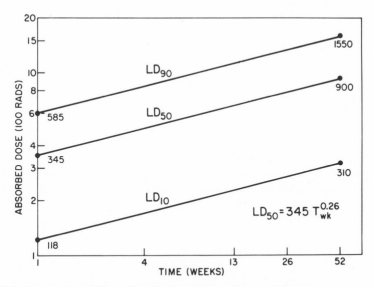

FIGURE 11–7.   Probability of Death According to Dose and Duration of Exposure.

SOURCE: Clarence C. Lushbaugh, "Human Radiation Tolerance," in Cornelius A. Tobias and Paul Todd, eds., *Space Radiation Biology and Related Topics* (New York: Academic Press, 1974), p. 501. Reprinted with permission from the U.S. Atomic Energy Commission and Academic Press, New York, NY.

mended that extrapolation to healthy populations should perhaps raise the threshold daily exposures by a factor of three.[29] However, since a significant proportion of those who survive the shelter period into the post-attack world may suffer from the effects of malnutrition, infectious disease, and other nontreated illness, their mortality curves might approximate the ones drawn here.

Animal data suggest that at comparable dose levels (accounting for interspecies variation in radiation sensitivies) capacity to respond to injury and intercurrent infection may be dramatically reduced. Researchers have found a markedly diminished burn rate survival for laboratory animals exposed to prior irradiation.[30] There is a known synergy in humans between burns and radiation injury.[31] Less is known about accelerated morbidity and mortality in mixed trauma and radiation cases. Animal data indicate that prior irradiation potentiates blunt trauma injury and reduces probability of recovery, but there is insufficient human evidence to quantify this interaction.[32]

Impaired Fertility

Fertility in both men and women exposed to doses in these ranges may be significantly impaired. Permanent sterility requires exposures to higher doses, estimated at over 600 rads acutely in men, 300 to 400 rads in women, older women being more susceptible at the lower dose range.[33] The sex difference is thought to be due to the fact that the ovary, unlike the testis, lacks the capacity to form new germ cells.[34] Since these sterility doses, if delivered acutely in whole body irradiation, would equal or exceed lethal whole body doses, few of the people in this category would survive. However, data from many sources clearly indicate that temporary azospermia, lasting one to three years, can result from acute exposures of 20 to 50 rads,[35] and persistent azospermia can be produced by doses as low as 0.2 rads per day if sustained over a two- to five-year period.[36] Women who received acute doses of 20 to 30 rads at Hiroshima and Nagasaki experienced persistent menstrual irregularities up to seven months after exposure.[37]

Altered Immune Response

The clinical use of radiation as an immunosuppressant in humans is well documented.[38] In therapeutic regimens (localized, high-dose, intermittent exposures), radiation may cause a variety of dose-related systemic and local side effects that could contribute to serious infection. These effects include a decrease in number and function of circulating white blood cells, decreased function of tissue-based scavenger cells, and damage to mucosal surfaces that form the barrier between the human blood stream and the bacterial environment of the gastrointestinal system. Patients who have received therapeutic doses of radiation are considered immunocompromised hosts, more susceptible to infection than healthy subjects.[39]

The extent to which radiation at much lower doses suppresses immune function and predisposes to infection is much less clear. Radiation in the ranges of 0.1 to 10 rads per day can damage intestinal mucosal lining, facilitating the entry of bacteria to the systemic blood stream and potentially fostering spread of infection.[40] Infection resulting from this breakdown in gut barriers is thought to be one of the main factors defining the synergism between burn injury and radiation.[41] Whether this radiation-induced intestinal injury would prove significant in the absence of burn trauma is not known for humans. We also do not know the clinical significance of the fact that fractionated radiation doses in this range can depress immune cell number and function.[42] These data are presented as indicating that, although not established, there may be a positive interaction between chronic intermediate doses of radiation and predisposition to infection, which, in the post-attack world, deprived of medical resources, could adversely affect population morbidity and mortality.

Fatigability

Fatigue has been described as one of the prodromal symptoms of acute radiation exposure and has also been observed to persist for months in those suffering severe but nonfatal instances of the hematopoetic syndrome.[43] In animal experiments, chronic intermediate radiation exposure results in a reduction in intensity and duration of general activity. This reduction extends through periods of food deprivation, which normally stimulate increased performance.[44] In other animal studies, enforced exercise delays recovery from radiation injury and increases risk of mortality.[45]

Effects on Fetal Development

Human sensitivity to radiation during intrauterine and early postnatal life is well known. Defects in fetal central nervous systems and in oocyte populations are discernible at levels of maternal exposure to an acute dose of 10 rads.[46] Table 11–3, drawing on data from Hiroshima and Nagasaki, gives the percent incidence of microcephaly (marked decrease in head circumference associated with serious or profound mental retardation) in infants exposed in utero during the most sensitive period for

TABLE 11-3.　Incidence of Microcephaly by Dose among Those Exposed at Gestational Age Six to Eleven Weeks.

Air Dose	Incidence	
(rads)	Number	Percent
0	31/764	4
1-9	2/19	11
10-19	4/24	17
20-29	3/10	30
30-49	4/10	40
50-99	7/10	50
100	7/7	100

SOURCE:　Committee on the Biological Effects of Ionizing Radiations, *The Effects on Populations of Exposure to Low Levels of Ionizing Radiation: 1980* (Washington, D.C.: National Academy Press, 1980), p. 483.

central nervous system damage—six to eleven weeks gestational age. Fetal wastage in Hiroshima is difficult to quantitate since most pregnant women had been evacuated prior to the bombing. In Nagasaki, however, of the 177 pregnancies investigated, 18.6 percent ended in miscarriage, 6.8 percent in premature delivery.[47]

The implications of this data are that fetal development may be significantly impaired if pregnant women are forced to persist in chronically radioactive environments of relatively low dose intensity.

5.　THE LONG-TERM CONSEQUENCES OF RADIATION EXPOSURE

Animal and human data confirm that radiation exerts important long-term effects on cancer incidence and genetic mutation rate. What is at issue in the scientific community is the relationship between the dose delivered and the population response.[48] Because there is not yet a clear relationship between the amount of radiation to which a population is exposed and the subsequent numbers of malignancies that it will develop, we cannot make a firm prediction about the incidence of cancer among survivors in the post-attack world. A variable peculiar to this context is that the high early mortality rates that will characterize post-attack demography for several years—from the independent and combined effects of infectious disease, radiation illness, and malnutrition—may reduce the number of exposed people who would otherwise survive to develop cancer in later years. Here we briefly review what is known from wartime experience about radiation-induced cancer and genetic mutations and present the most accepted estimates of incidence rates for these effects as they might be reflected among survivors after a full-scale nuclear war on the United States. These long-term effects may be much more pervasive and significant than FEMA, taking the optimistic view in the scientific debate, now predicts.

Cancer

In extensive study of populations exposed to relatively high dose radiation (the survivors of Hiroshima and Nagasaki, Marshall Islanders, uranium miners, and others), the carcinogenic effect of radiation—its capacity to induce cancers after a five- to 40-year lag period—has been repeatedly demonstrated. It appears that the incidence of only certain cancers is increased by radiation, and their time of peak occurrence varies with type. According to the Radiation Effects Research Foundation (formerly the Atomic Bomb Casualty Commission), follow-up studies on Hiroshima and Nagasaki survivors through 1978 reveal increased radiogenic cancer risks for leukemia, cancer of the breast, lung, stomach, and thyroid, and suggestively increased risks for multiple myeloma and cancer of the colon and urinary tract.[49] Only in the case of leukemia, which in years of peak incidence occurred at a rate ten times that in the nonexposed population, can a dose response curve be drawn.[50] Even that curve is now somewhat in dispute since the gamma and neutron dosimetry data for Hiroshima are under intense review.[51]

The most authoritative estimates of cancer risks on a population scale come from the International Commission on Radiological Protection (ICRP), whose probabilities are based on extrapolations from a broad range of data, employing a linear dose-response curve. Critics of the linear hypothesis maintain that it either over or underestimates incidence at lower doses. Recognizing that given our current understanding, the best assessment probably incorporates a large margin of error, the ICRP predictions are presented in Table 11–4 as gross indicators of risk.

The total risk of death from all cancers for both sexes comes to 12.5×10^{-3} per 100 rems, which means that if a million people were exposed to 100 rems, 12,500 would subsequently die of cancer. The numbers of nonlethal cancers induced by this radiation exposure might be double this figure and, in the absence of adequate medical care, might contribute to mortality from other causes.

Genetic Effects

Ionizing radiation can damage chromosomes, containing many genes, or alter the structure of just one gene. Genetic or chromosomal alterations in germ cells may be transmitted to the offspring of the

TABLE 11–4.   Risk Factors for Cancer Deaths.

Cancer Type[a]	Death Rate per 100 Rems
Leukemia	2.0×10^{-3}
Breast cancer	2.5×10^{-3}
Lung cancer	2.0×10^{-3}
Bone cancer	0.5×10^{-3}
Thyroid	0.5×10^{-3}
Other (stomach, colon, liver, salivary glands)	5.0×10^{-3}
Total	12.5×10^{-3}

a. No allowance made for age or sex of person exposed; since breast cancer occurs almost exclusively in females, the risk for them is double what is given here as an average for both sexes.
SOURCE: International Commission on Radiological Protection Recommendations, ICRP No. 26; cited in Rotblat, p. 47. Reproduced by permission of SIPRI and Taylor & Francis, Ltd.

exposed person. These defects may take several generations to reveal themselves in populations. Since it is assumed that radiation-induced genetic defects will be similar to the significant spontaneous mutations that currently occur at the rate of 10 percent of all live births, scientists employ the concept of doubling dose, or the radiation dose required to double the normal background incidence of significant mutation from all causes. The doubling dose concept assumes that the dose response curve is linear. It represents an average of known variations in sensitivities of gene type. From the data available, the value of the doubling dose in humans has been estimated to range between 50 and 250 rads.[52] This range is so wide as to have little predictive value. Recent studies of the F_1 generation (children of exposed population) in Hiroshima and Nagasaki show that although there is still no statistically significant evidence of genetic damage from radiation exposure, the various indicators suggest a trend in that direction.[53] Scientists caution that statistically negative evidence in this setting should not form the basis for asserting that radiation exposure results in no human genetic damage, because there is ample evidence from other sources that it does.[54] Incorporating this other evidence while also accounting for the negative findings in the Japanese data, the Committee on the Biological Effects of Ionizing Radiation of the National Academy of Sciences (BEIR III) has suggested that exposing a population to one rem will induce in the first generation five to sixty-five significant genetic mutations per million live births.[55] This figure may reflect a wide margin of error, but it serves as our best indicator to date. As is discussed in Section 7, the incidence of both these effects may, in absolute terms, markedly increase among those in the post-attack world who live to experience them.

6. POPULATION PROTECTION FROM RADIATION EXPOSURE

The CRP-2B attack would expose an unsheltered population located virtually anywhere on the continental United States to a lethal cumulative radiation dose. FEMA's relocation strategy would, on the average, move urban residents only 250 to 300 miles to more rural sites and thus would do more to reduce their exposure to the direct blast and thermal effects of the weapons than to the radioactive fallout.[56]

For protection from radiation exposure, FEMA plans to provide fallout shelters to both relocated and host populations for a two- to four-week period following the attack. With this strategy, FEMA predicts, most acute effects can be averted. This plan oversimplifies shelter protection by (1) underestimating the intensity and duration of radiation exposure, (2) minimizing the problem of achieving critical protection factors, and (3) ignoring the question of consistency in shelter use.

Radiation Exposure

It is important in the discussion that follows to understand the three different factors that interact to create health risks to humans from radiation exposure: cumulative exposure, biological repair rate, and exposure per unit time, or dose rate. Unless cumulative exposure, the sum of all radiation received up to a given point in time, has reached the lethal threshold, it is being continually reduced, although never erased, by the biological repair rate. This repair rate, based on DNA repair mechanisms, must continuously work against ongoing radiation exposure—the dose rate delivered by the radioactive environment. From what is understood, the acute effects of radiation exposure can be reduced by fractionating the dose over time and giving the biological repair rate an opportunity to heal some of the radiation-induced damage. At any given exposure level, however, it appears that some damage will never be repaired. The biological repair rate affects only that fraction of the damage that is considered repairable. Too much exposure at any given time will overwhelm the repair mechanisms and the person will die. The way in which the biological repair rate alters intermediate- and long-term consequences is not understood.

The health consequences that result from the dynamic interaction of these three variables are not sufficiently considered in FEMA's plans, which propose a protection strategy that will not protect. Underestimating the complexities involved in assessing radiation exposure reduces perceptions of risk, both on the part of the planners and on the part of the general public.

Cumulative Exposure and Dose Rate

In claiming, as FEMA does, that four weeks post-attack there will be few areas of the country posing a serious fallout risk, the problem of cumulative exposure is minimized. After two to four weeks from the time of peak radioactivity, the hourly dose rate may appear relatively low, but the accumulating dose over time still creates a substantial hazard. A reliance on dose rate rather than cumulative exposure will seriously underestimate risk. If in a given area the fallout dose rate at $H + 1$ is 10,000 rads per hour (as it may well be for significant areas of the country), a person entering the area after one month, assumed not to have been previously exposed, will from that point on, if unsheltered, accumulate a total dose of about 5,000 rads within the next year. Entering that area after one year has elapsed will still expose an unsheltered person to a cumulative dose of 300 rads by the end of that second year.[57]

Biological Repair Rate

Reliance on high biological repair rates is another factor in official expressions of radiation exposure that tend to understate risk. Of the two processes that contribute to the concept of cumulative dose—the radiation decay curve and the human biological repair rate—only the first is uncontroversial. The fact that biological repair takes place after injury of any kind, including radiation, is not in dispute. The dispute arises over rate of repair and whether this rate remains constant over a range of exposure.

One official assumption is that 20 percent of the radiation damage is unrepairable and the remaining 80 percent is repaired at an exponential rate of 10 percent per day.[58] Another official assumption, incorporated in Schmidt's data and used in the WSEG-10 computer fallout model, is that 10 percent of the radiation damage is unrepairable and 90 percent repaired at a rate of 3.33 percent per day.[59]

Others who have considered this question think both of these repair rate estimates may be too high, even for exposures occurring to healthy people who have had no previous history of radiation exposure, who do not have to persist in a chronically radioactive environment like the post-attack world, and who in other respects can claim good health. They also question whether this rate will remain constant and whether the DNA repair mechanisms, like many cellular systems, are affected by stress and disease.[60] The fact that there is a threshold dose that overwhelms the repair rate can be argued to imply that the repair rate has a continuum of response. If someone has been previousy irradiated in a medical or occupational setting, or exposed to 200 rads and then forced to continue in an environment delivering 10 rads per day, or is suffering from malnutrition, dehydration, disease, or traumatic injury, then it is unrealistic to assume the same repair rate will apply. In an official example of how a biological repair rate of 10 percent per day may reduce cumulative exposure, a person receives 200 rads on day four, 200 rads on day twelve, and 200 rads on day twenty. Delivered at once, as an acute dose, the person would have received a lethal dose of 600 rads. In this example, it is claimed, assuming a biological repair rate of 10 percent per day, the person's cumulative dose is effectively reduced to 384 rads—a dose still carrying significant risk of mortality but much below that for 600 rads.[61] No consideration is given to the possibility that a person's biological repair rate eight days after receiving an acute dose of 200 rads, and then after receiving, eight days later, another acute dose of 200 rads, may not persist at the vigorous level of 10 percent per day. There is no experimental evidence that directly addresses this issue. From clinical experience, it has been seen that a dose of 10 rads per day given to radiotherapy patients will in one week severely deplete the supply of growing cells in their bone marrow.[62] If doses of 70 rads given over the course of a week will kill young cells, it can at least be suggested that a dose of 400 rads, delivered in two pulses of 200 rads each separated by an interval of eight days will have adverse effects on human cell systems.

Protection Factors

In cooperation with the National Shelter Survey Team, FEMA plans to identify over the next ten to fifteen years (the time course dependent on funding levels), private and public sites that can be designated appropriate shelters or that could, with minimal construction, be upgraded to that category. FEMA estimates that by the late 1980s a sufficient number of shelters in rural areas will be so identified as to provide adequate shelter for both host and relocated populations.[63]

The protection principle of fallout shelters is based on the fact that the intensity of radioactivity decays with time and is reduced by shielding. The protection factor is a ratio of the radiation level outside the shelter to that inside and reflects the mass (density and thickness) of the materials with which the shelter is constructed. The higher the protection factor, the greater the reduction in dose the shelter affords. See Table 11–5 for examples of protection factors provided by different structures. FEMA defines a shelter as adequate if it affords a protection factor (PF) of forty or above, meaning that the shelter construction will reduce the

TABLE 11–5.   Radiation Protection Factors.

Structure	Neutrons	Initial gamma rays	Fallout gamma rays
Frame house	1.2 – 3	1.2 – 1	15 – 30
Basement	1.2 – 10	1.7 – 10	10 – 20
Multi-story building			
Upper stories	1.0 – 1.1	1.1 – 1.2	100
Lower stories	1.2 – 3	1.5 – 3	10
Shelter partly above ground			
with 60-cm earth cover	12 – 50	15 – 30	50 – 200
with 90-cm earth cover	20 – 100	50 – 150	200 – 1,000
Concrete blockhouse shelter			
with 20-cm walls	2 – 3	5 – 10	10 – 150
with 30-cm walls	2.5 – 5	10 – 20	30 – 1,000
with 60-cm walls	5 – 10	50 – 150	500 – 10,000

SOURCE: Rotblat, p. 120. Reproduced by permission of SIPRI and Taylor & Francis, Ltd.

internal radiation dose to one-fortieth of the dose in the external environment. This factor is a ratio in that it reduces the external dose by a certain amount; the safety it affords is relative to the intensity of the external dose. A home basement, shielded by an overlying roofed structure, would afford a PF of forty provided its above ground walls were covered with a foot of earth on all sides. A cubic yard of earth weighs approximately one and a half tons. Because the concept of PFs assumes a uniform radiation field, the shelter has to be sound in all directions. An unshielded window or poorly constructed wall may significantly reduce the PF from its theoretical value and expose shelter residents to radiation levels much higher than expected.[64]

Since FEMA plans that about one-third of the necessary shelters will have to be built or upgraded during the five- to seven-day crisis and evacuation period, the Agency has prepared extensive public instructions on shelter construction. See Figure 11–8 for examples.[65] Few of the suggested designs would provide PFs of forty.

As it is, a PF of forty offers little margin for construction error. In ambient radiation fields delivering 1,000 rads cumulative dose—levels characterizing much of the continental United States—a PF of forty, assuming the actual value accords with the theoretical, will reduce dose received to 25 rads, the lower limit of the threshold dose for prodromal symptoms of acute radiation illness. Reduction of this PF by half, which could easily occur in shelters constructed in haste or ignorance, would expose residents to cumulative doses of 50 rads. People sheltered in areas experiencing cumulative external doses of 5,000 rads (a large area of the

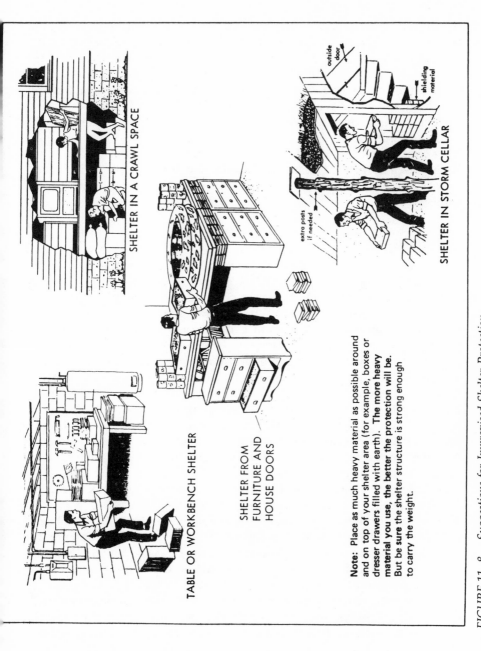

SHELTER IN A CRAWL SPACE

TABLE OR WORKBENCH SHELTER

SHELTER FROM FURNITURE AND HOUSE DOORS

SHELTER IN STORM CELLAR

outside door

shielding material

extra posts if needed

Note: Place as much heavy material as possible around and on top of your shelter area (for example, boxes or dresser drawers filled with earth). The more heavy material you use, the better the protection will be. But be **sure** the shelter structure is strong enough to carry the weight.

FIGURE 11–8.   *Suggestions for Improvised Shelter Protection.*

SOURCE: FEMA, *Camera-Ready News Columns,* No. 6 (Washington, D.C.: U.S. Government Printing Office, December 1980).

Northeast, Midwest, and West)[66] would, even with shelters providing an actual PF of forty, receive doses of 125 rads; degradation of protection by one-half would expose these residents to 250 rads cumulative dose. Nor does the PF of forty offer much margin of protection if the winds intermittently vary and levels greater than the mean expected fallout are delivered to shelter residents. A PF of forty cannot in the Northeast protect against possible fallout intensity level of 10,000 rads per hour. If the winds shift, as they occasionally do, levels as high as 30,000 rads per hour would strike sheltered populations usually upwind from SAC and ICBM bases in the Midwest.[67] A PF of forty will reduce that hourly rate only to 750 rads per hour. One hour at that rate will almost certainly kill all exposed.

Shelter Use

In addition to the margin of safety offered by PFs, the other main variable affecting shelter protection is consistency of shelter use. After the nuclear attack, it is intended that the population remain in shelters for a period of two to four weeks, until ambient radiation has decayed to levels considered low enough to permit exit for unspecified periods of time thereafter. In settings where radiation levels are decaying from initially high doses, the consistency of shelter use will be critical. Throughout this time period, the pressures to exit briefly will be pronounced: lack of food or water, accumulated wastes or dead bodies, poor air, deprivation of light, claustrophobia, inability to live with ongoing uncertainty. Yet each foray out of the shelter into relatively high radiation fields may substantially increase the cumulative dose each person receives. Crisis relocation planners intend to reduce some of these exit pressures by maintaining supply and communication networks.[68] The extent to which such systems will function during the first few months of the post-attack world are problematic and discussed elsewhere in this book.

By furnishing shelter areas with radiological defense (RADEF) sets containing instruments for reading radiation levels, FEMA intends to give shelter residents an independent means of assessing whether it is safe to leave the shelter, in terms of radiation exposure, regardless of other contingencies pressing them to do so.

Assessing radiation dose inside or outside the shelter, however, will be complex. Instruments like Geiger counters, called survey meters, measure dose rate in rads or millirads per second, depending on calibration; another instrument, the dosimeter, measures cumulative dose. These dosimeters and survey meters will measure the major contributors to early fallout—gamma and some high-dose beta radiation—but they may not register any alpha or much beta. As such, they will underestimate risks from external and internal contamination.

Consultants to FEMA recommend that the minimum acceptable distribution of dosimeters be one for every 10 people, one survey meter per 200 people, and one charger (power source) per eight dosimeters. Total costs for a minimum supply of 10.6 million RADEF sets comprising 2 dosimeters, 1 charger, and 1 survey meter was estimated in 1979 to be $453 million.[69] FEMA currently has approximately 237,000 of these sets in operational order and by 1989 intends to have secured a total of 7 million.[70]

Setting aside the planning and logistical questions in procuring and distributing these RADEF sets to the sheltered population, which FEMA has not yet worked out, one must address the issue of how useful these instruments would be if distributed.

First, since these instruments, designed for less expensive mass production, are different from the ones currently in stock, their calibration and error history is unknown.[71] Even well calibrated, the margin of error for current instruments is about 25 percent.[72] That error compounds the uncertainties in estimating human dose response; thus, the information from these meters will serve only as very general guides to the risk incurred.

Second, with one dosimeter per ten people, an individual will have difficulty knowing how much radiation he or she personally has received and thus how much more exposure can be safely sustained. This difficulty will be compounded if radiation rates vary significantly within the shelter. Formed unpredictably by the interactions of terrain and weather conditions, external hot spots, such as evaporating puddles of contaminated water, may create wide fluctuations of fields within the shelters. If the one dosimeter fails, occupants will lose even that very general indicator of their radiation history. If for any reason a person exits from the shelter briefly and leaves the dosimeter with the other occupants, that person will not have a record for that period of relatively more intense exposure.

Third, the survey meter will also measure only radiation fields within the shelter. Assessing external dose will be impossible unless the shelter is equipped with an external survey meter visible to shelter occupants in such a way as not to erode protection factors, or unless radio message units are transmitting such information. Dose rate readings either from an external meter or from outside communications will afford only the most rough approximation, however, since radiation fields can vary tremendously over several hundred yards, depending on changes in terrain and local concentration of hot spots.

Given these problems with assessment of dose, we cannot assume, as FEMA does, that people will be making informed and reasonable choices about when to leave their shelters. A realistic prediction of shelter use is that people will probably begin to make brief sorties from their shelters after the first two weeks, responding either to inaccurate dosimetry or, in defiance of that information, responding to more intensely felt priorities.

We suggest here a pattern of shelter use that more closely accords with how people might actually behave (see Table 11–6). This pattern has been adapted from one employed by ACDA.[73] It assumes that after the first two weeks, shelter occupants will begin to spend time outside on essential activities like foraging for food; by the second month, people will begin to reconstruct living areas and spend time in them; and by the end of two months, people will have returned to usual, pre-attack patterns of indoor-outdoor activity.

This pattern of shelter behavior is used to modify the theoretical PF by applying a fractional multiplier that reflects the actual duration of stay in the shelters. This fractional multiplier reduces the theoretical PF (in this case, forty) to what ACDA terms the Effective Protection Factor (EPF). In ACDA's assessment, the EPF is more likely to apply in the post-attack setting. Table 11–7 presents the method of calculating the EPF, assuming the shelter use pattern described in Table 11–6.[74] Under these conditions, a theoretical PF of forty is reduced to an EPF of 17.5.

7. ASSESSMENT OF RADIATION-INDUCED MORBIDITY AND MORTALITY IN THE POST-ATTACK POPULATION

In the preceding discussion we have described some of the uncertainties pertaining to estimates of radiation dose and assessment of health consequences in order to provide perspective on FEMA's assertions that the radiation from a full-scale nuclear war will pose little hazard to a population sheltered at a PF of forty for two weeks. In this section, for the sake of presenting an instructive example, we pursue a very different

TABLE 11–6.   Realistic Pattern of Shelter Use.

	Percentage of Time Spent in Each Environment		
Time From Attack	Shelter (PF = 40)	Frame House (PF = 3)	Outside (PF = 1.5)
First 2 weeks	100	0	0
2 to 4 weeks	75	0	25
4 to 8 weeks	40	40	20
8 weeks to infinity	0	60	40

TABLE 11–7. Calculation of Effective Protection Factor (EPF).

1) Definitions:

RN = residual number expressing fractional radiation exposure for a given shelter posture with a given PF

$$= \frac{1}{PF}$$

ERN = equivalent residual number expressing the weighted sum of residual numbers

$$EPF = \frac{1}{ERN}$$

2) Calculation of RN:

RN   *Percent of Time*

	Time	*PF = 40;* *RN = 0.025*	*PF = 3;* *RN = 0.33*	*PF = 1.5;* *RN = 0.66*
RN_1	0–2 weeks	100	0	0
RN_2	2 to 4 weeks	75	0	25
RN_3	4 to 8 weeks	40	40	20
RN_4	8 weeks to infinity	0	60	40

$RN_1 = (1.0 \times .025) = .025$
$RN_2 = (.75 \times .025) + (.25 \times .66) = .184$
$RN_3 = (.40 \times .025) + (.40 \times .33) + (.20 \times .66) = .274$
$RN_4 = (.60 \times .33) + (.40 \times .66) = .462$

3) Calculation of ERN:

Time after Detonation	Weighting Factor[a] $\times$	RN $=$	Contribution to ERN
0.5h–3.0h	.000	.025	.000
3.0h–24h	.606	.025	.015
24h–48h	.118	.025	.003
2d–7d	.138	.025	.004
7d–14d	.038	.025	.001
14d–30d	.028	.184	.005
1 mo–2 mo	.022	.274	.006
2 mo–6 mo	.027	.462	.012
6 mo–infinity	.023	.462	.011
			.057

ERN = .057

$$EPF = \frac{1}{ERN} = 17.5$$

a. Weighting factor reflects radioactive decay curve over time with fallout arriving at sheltered population 3 hours after detonation. See G.E. Pugh, et al., *Estimating the Behavioral Degradation of Fallout Protection Factors for Use in Damage Assessment Calculations* (Arlington, Va.: Decision-Science Applications, Inc., June, 1980) [Prepared for the U.S. Arms Control and Disarmament Agency], p. 15.

tack. While acknowledging all the uncertainties involved, we take the data FEMA provides and construct a specific model of population radiation exposure after nuclear war. This model generates numerical results, approximating in a most general way the potential death and illness we could expect from radiation alone after such an event. Juxtaposing these results with FEMA's claim that successful CRP will ensure the survival of 80 percent of the U.S. population casts further light on the extent to which this claim departs from what actually might happen.

Estimate of the Cumulative Radiation Exposure in the Post-Attack Population

An estimate of cumulative exposure, in the setting of the more realistic pattern of shelter use suggested by ACDA, is evolved in the series of calculations described in Table 11–8. Based on the percentage of population of each exposure cohort described by Haaland for the 1970 population, we have updated the number to accord with 1980 census data.[75] We take FEMA's assumptions that two-thirds of the population resides in high-risk areas (150 million, by 1980 figures) and that 80 percent of this population at risk had successfully relocated to the shelter areas. For each cohort of exposure, we have expressed radiation dose as total cumulative dose, in an unsheltered environment, for fallout arriving three hours after detonation. Column 3 converts this whole body surface dose to its equivalent midline tissue dose (70% of the surface dose) to

TABLE 11–8.   Acute Radiation Mortality

Exposure Cohort	Total Cumulative Dose (Rads)			Mortality	
Relocated U.S. Population 1980 (millions) (1)	Unsheltered Surface (2)	Midline (3)	Sheltered EPF = 17.5 (4)	(Percent) Probability of Acute Death (5)	(Millions) Numbers of Acute Deaths (6)
8.46	31,500	22,050	1,260	100	8.46
29.61	20,475	14,333	819	100	29.61
49.78	6,300	4,410	252	50	24.89
49.00	2,048	1,433	82	8	3.92
24.68	630	441	25	2	.49
15.02	205	143	8	—	
3.68	63	44	3	—	
15.50	16	11	1	—	
195.73[a]					67.37

a. Differs from 195 million due to rounding error.

accord with the form in which the mortality tables are expressed. We then calculating the actual cumulative exposure for each cohort by dividing the unsheltered midline tissue dose by the EPF. This step results in the data in Column 4, specifying the cumulative doses for the sheltered populations at different exposure levels. Column 5 assigns to these cumulative doses the predicted probability of death, as found in the mortality tables. Multiplying these probabilities, expressed as percentages, by the number of people in each exposure category, results in the data in Column 6—the predicted number of deaths, from radiation exposure alone, among the relocated and sheltered U.S. population. To understand the very limited way in which this exercise yields useful information, it is necessary to recognize the assumptions and estimating errors behind it.

1. In employing the CRP-2B model used by Haaland and FEMA, we have accepted the same imprecisions in the initial attack scenario and fallout predictions.

2. The assignment of population cohorts to these given exposure categories is based on the ADAGIO computer model used by both the Defense Department and FEMA for modeling CRP.[76] In accepting these population assignments as given, we are assuming that crisis relocation has proceeded according to plan.

3. Several adjustments in the population data were required to make them comparable with Haaland's 1970 figures. In his table, Haaland evidently assumed a virtual 100 percent successful relocation, since his relocated total population is 204.12 milion—approximately the same as the 1970 census total of 203.21 million.[77] Yet, since in his discussion he describes a 90 percent successful evacuation, and since FEMA assumes an 80 percent evacuation, the following adjustments were made:

- Since 150 million people in 1980 are judged to be at risk of direct targeting and thus compelled to evacuate, the evacuation fraction is 150/225; and since 80 percent of the 150 million are assumed to complete the process, the total shelter population in the host areas will be $(150 \times 0.8) + (225 - 150) = 195$ million people. On a proportional basis, the total shelter population in the host areas for 1970 would be 195/225 or 87 percent of 203, or 176 million people. Applying this factor (0.87) to each of Haaland's 1970 cohorts corrects for the fraction of the population that did not successfully relocate.
- The 1980 figures for each cohort were computed by applying the percentage each population cohort represented of the

1970 relocated total (176 million) to the 1980 relocated total of 195 million.

4. No biological repair rate was assumed in calculating cumulative doses, which tends to express the dose in the high range of estimate. This tendency is to some extent compensated for by the fact that the effective protection factor incorporates an assumed biological repair rate of 10 percent per day, which may tend to underestimate cumulative exposures.[78] Since these two tendencies act in opposite directions, and since either one alone works within the same order of magnitude, the presumption that their effects will effectively cancel is probably justifiable.

5. Assigning all cohorts of the population to the same pattern of shelter use clearly involves averaging what would in actuality evolve into very different patterns. The pattern of use assigned here can be viewed only as indicating the extent to which the theoretical PF may be eroded by population behavior.

6. The mortality probabilities assigned to these midline tissue doses are based on a standard mortality curve cited frequently in the literature.[79] (See Figure 11-9). This curve, although representing an accepted composite of known data, is derived from relatively few actual observations in humans, and for this reason must be used with some caution.

7. These probabilities also involve errors in the range of 50 percent in measuring dose received, which, combined with uncertainties about individual human response, make mortality predictions subject to wide margins of error.[80]

8. These probabilities also presume some minimal level of medical care and the absence of concurrent stress from disease, injury, or malnutrition.[81] Whether any care will be available in the post-attack environment on the scale necessary to exert any appreciable effect on need is highly unlikely. A more realistic assumption—that no medical care would be available—increases the mortality estimates to an extent difficult to quantify.

9. Finally, these figures underestimate mortality by ignoring the additive or synergistic effects of intercurrent or accompanying illness and stress. Many among the relocated, sheltered population will be suffering from gastrointestinal and repiratory illness, untreated chronic medical disease, injuries sustained by the attack or evacuation, and progressive malnutrition. What might not be a lethal dose of radiation to a healthy adult supported in a sanitary medical environment could, in the post-attack setting, spell certain death.

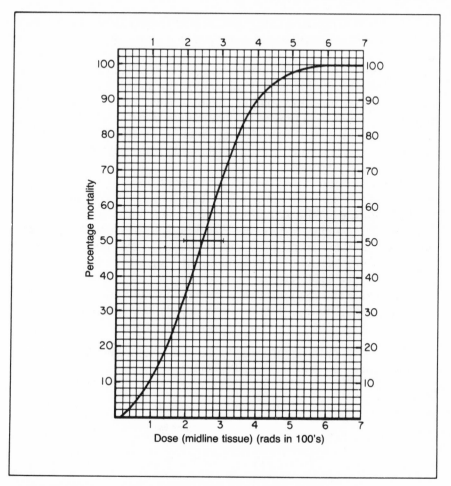

FIGURE 11–9.   Probability of Death from Acute Radiation Effects.

SOURCE: Rotblat, p. 35. Reproduced by permission of SIPRI and Taylor & Francis, Ltd.

Approximate Estimates of Radiation-Induced Morbidity and Mortality

Approximately 67 million people, among the 195 million sheltered, will, according to these estimates, die of acute radiation illness within days or months. Among those who survive acute effects, another 94 million will have been exposed to cumulative radiation doses ranging from 20 to 250 rads—an amount sufficient to cause significant changes in fertility, fatigability, capacity to withstand infection, and fetal development. Since the consequences of this level of chronic radiation exposure are least understood, quantitative estimates are impossible. The qualitative weight to give this potentially pervasive morbidity is indicated by reflecting on the stress that the post-attack world will impose upon these survivors. In these stressed circumstances, the survival edge will go to those who can work hard and fight infection. There will be less margin for those who cannot. At a time of peak mortality, those of reproductive age may be least effective at reproducing. In all parameters, at a time when conditions are worst and the need to respond greatest, the survivors may not be in shape to do so.

Both this population exposed to moderate doses and the 33 million in the low-dose exposure range will be at risk of developing malignancy and transmitting genetic mutations. According to the best, although still controversial, estimates of the ICRP and BEIR III discussed earlier, and assuming mortality from other causes (e.g., famine, disease) did not intervene first, the following numbers of long-term effects might be anticipated. (See Table 11–9)

We arrive at a total number of 5.95 million additional deaths from cancer for the lifetime of this exposed population, or a lifetime cancer

TABLE 11–9.   Long-Term Effects of Radiation Exposure Among Survivors of Acute Radiation Effects in Sheltered Population.

Relocated Population (in millions)	Exposure in Shelters (rads)	At Risk for Developing Lethal Cancer in Lifetime	
		Percent	Number (in millions)
49.78	252	50	24.89
49.00	82	92	45.08
24.68	25	98	24.19
15.02	8	100	15.02
3.68	3	100	3.68
15.50	1	100	15.50
Total	371		128.36

1) *Risk of Developing Lethal Cancer* $= 12.5 \times 10^{-3}$ per 100 rems.[a]
   $(12.5 \times 10^{-3}) (371 \times 10^{-2}) (128.36 \times 10^{6}) = 5.95 \times 10^{6}$
   Rate per 100,000 population
   5.95×10^{6} deaths among $128.36 \times 10^{6} = 4,635/100,000$
2) *Incidence of Serious Genetic Defects* $= 5$–65 per million live births per rem[a] in F_1 generation
   $(371) (5) = 1,855$
   $(371) (65) = 24,115$

a. 1 rem = 1 rad for these calculations

death rate, induced by wartime radiation exposure, of 4,635 per 100,000. The numbers of nonlethal cancers induced by this radiation exposure might be double this figure, and in the absence of adequate medical care, might contribute to mortality from other causes. This cancer mortality rate is twenty-seven times that of the 1978 U.S. death rate from cancer of all sites, 169.9 per 100,000.[82] The genetic mutations induced by parental wartime exposure would, in the F_1 generation, be 1,855 to 24,115 per million live births. These significant mutations should be added to the current incidence of approximately 100,000 per million live births. Since estimating the birth rate among the survivors involves much speculation, no attempt is made here to arrive at an absolute number of radiation-induced genetic defects among the first generation born to the exposed population.

The impact of this increased incidence will not be felt solely, however, among those who ultimately contract the malignancy or manifest the genetic defect. In his studies of the Hiroshima survivors, Lifton found that all who were exposed spent the remainder of their lives haunted by the fear that they carried genetic contamination and by the premonition of premature, grotesque death.[83] Those who try to survive in the post-attack world will all have shared similar horrors. Surrounded by remnants of loss, crippled by incessant uncertainty, and fearing always what time will bring—this will not be a vigorous population. Commonly held notions of health and longevity may have to change.

We devoted much of this chapter to explicating the controversies and unknowns involved in defining the war scenario, estimating radiation levels, and describing the state of our ignorance about human response. We present these casualty estimates only to point out how little we can say with certainty and to provide a context in which to evaluate FEMA's assertions of survivability. The claim that 80 percent of the population will survive a nuclear war on the United States can be substantiated only within a very bounded reality: deaths defined as only those deaths occurring within the first few post-attack days, arising only from direct blast and thermal effects. To arrive at an 80 percent survival figure, FEMA has chosen not to examine mortality, immediate and longer term, from radiation exposure.

8. CONCLUSION

There are other factors, such as infectious disease and malnutrition, that will contribute to cumulative mortality in the post-attack world. In the past, epidemics of disease and famine have produced steep peaks in death rates—what demographers call mortality crises.[84] Radiation introduces a new factor. There is much we do not know about it, even after years of experimental and therapeutic observation. Our experience with its effects on populations in wartime is very limited. By applying what we do know to scales of exposure that might very arguably pertain in the setting of nuclear war, this discussion suggests that, despite protective measures, casualty consequences might be staggering.

The fear that people have about radiation after nuclear war stems partly from a general fear of the unknown and partly from a specific fear of what radiation has been seen to do. We argue that both sources of fear are well founded. It is reasonable to be cautious when dealing with forces we do not understand and cannot control. Changing perceptions about radiation, as Perry has suggested, makes sense only if those perceptions are wrong.[85] In this context, facile reassurance, without basis in fact, serves the long-term interests of no one.

ACKNOWLEDGMENTS

The author would like to thank Herbert L. Abrams and Frank von Hippel for their very helpful suggestions and perceptive critical review.

12

The Good Earth: Agricultural Potential after Nuclear War

Howard Hjort

Therefore as the fire devoureth the stubble
and the flame consumeth the chaff,
so their root shall be rottenness,
and their blossom shall go up as dust.

Isaiah 5:24

POSTATTACK OPTIONS

During the postattack period, the resumption of transportation and communications is necessary to support the flow of food supplies, and this flow will be redirected in response to estimates and requests from the state food organizations in a manner that alleviates shortages and provides for a continuing supply of food throughout the United States. In the framework of CRP, however, the number of surviving citizens would be much greater than under in-place protection planning. Citizens will out-survive distribution facilities in a manner that will create severe supply/demand imbalances in a number of localities, and careful planning will be required to match supply with demand in the critical emergency period.

SOURCE: John W. Billheimer and Arthur W. Simpson, *Effects of Attack on Food Distribution to the Relocated Population*, vol. 1, prepared for the Defense Civil Preparedness Agency, Systan, Inc., Los Altos, California, September 1978, p. 5–1.

For planning purposes, we will assume that grain stocks on farms and in rural elevators will be the major source of food required for survival in the postattack period. As we have seen from the data presented, this source is adequate to supply the relocated population until the following harvest, under most circumstances readily foreseen. We also assume that these grain stocks are located primarily in the counties in which they were produced. . . .

We have assumed that the privately owned stocks of grains by farmers can be obtained by the government for relief of potential starvation of large fractions of the U.S. population in a postattack situation. Some form of guarantee should be given by the government to assure the farmer of just compensation for his labor and to allay his feelings of anxiety for his own future. Such a guarantee may be difficult to produce in a postattack situation unless it is evident to the farmer that the federal structure of government remains firmly in power. AM radio broadcasts of news and information, with frequent reassuring messages from the President would be necessary to convey this information. . . .

In 1972, trucks consumed about 8.1 billion gallons of fuel in transporting 470 billion ton-miles of intercity freight, about 8% of the total motor fuel (105 billion gallons) consumed for all highway traffic (Transportation Association of America, 1974) at an average rate of 22.2 million gallons and 1290 million ton-miles per day for trucks. The average quantity of distillate fuel oil, including diesel fuel, stored in tanks in 1973 was about 5.67 billion gallons, and the average quantity of gasoline was about 7.39 billion gallons (National Petroleum Council, 1974). We estimate that about 60% of these fuels will be destroyed in the CRP-2B attack, which would leave about 2.27 billion gallons of distillate fuel oil and diesel and 2.96 billion gallons of gasoline surviving, if these numbers were representative of the fuels in storage at the time of the attack. If this total of 5.23 billion gallons were to be used only by trucks in the postattack situation at the same average rate as before the attack, i.e., at 22.2 million gallons per day, this supply would last for 236 days, which is probably adequate to carry the nation through the survival state into the recovery stage.

SOURCE: Carsten M. Haaland, et al., *Survival of the Relocated Population of the U.S. after a Nuclear Attack*, prepared for the Defense Civil Preparedness Agency, Oak Ridge National Laboratory, Oak Ridge, Tennessee, March 1976, pp. 120, 129, 145.

In summary: there is no intrinsic reason why life support requirements for the survivors of a nuclear attack should not be met. The basic problem is one of getting the more than adequate surviving supplies of food and water together with the people who need them.

Prototype studies have been made and sample plans developed for selected localities. What is needed is the development of individual plans tailored to meet the needs of individual localities and situations throughout the country. A very modest investment in planning and perhaps some stockpiling is all that is required to assure that this obstacle to recovery is quickly overcome. . . .

Common sense supports the idea that this country could continue to grow the food and fiber necessary to sustain its citizens after nuclear attack. The United States has a highly efficient agricultural industry. Less than 4 percent of the total population is all that is required not only to meet the needs of the nation but also to provide huge surpluses for export. This industry is almost immune to significant damage in a nuclear attack. Farm machinery would be scarcely affected at all and the farmworkers themselves are not very vulnerable providing they take simple precautions against fallout. Priority allocations of fuel for the farm machinery and of fertilizers and other farm inputs is all that is necessary to bring the agricultural industry substantially back to its pre-attack rate.

SOURCE: Defense Civil Preparedness Agency, *Research Report on Recovery from Nuclear Attack,* Information Bulletin No. 307, U.S. Government Printing Office, Washington, D.C., May 10, 1979, pp. 13–14, 23.

The primary focus of this chapter is on the ability of the food system to provide food for those who survive the initial direct effects of the CRP-2B nuclear attack on the United States. Special attention is given to the critical situation confronting those who have been relocated. Since it is understood that the food support system in the host areas would be totally inadequate, the relocated people must continue to rely mainly on food that would be trucked from the risk area warehouses before the attack and on unprocessd agricultural products in rural areas after the attack. A large proportion of the relocated population would be in temporary shelters and would be fed en masse.

The short-term problem of food distribution after nuclear war involves the interaction of three imponderables: availability of crops in the field and grain and potatoes in storage, surviving transport and fuel capacity, and amount of time before the next harvest. The long-term problem involves that critical question of the next harvest: When can people plant the crops, how will they care for the crops and animals, and how productive will agriculture be? Current civil defense research examines the short-term problem as a function of what factors, viewed as independent variables, will survive, when in actuality these factors are parts of an interdependent system. On the long-term problem—return to agricultural productivity—the research offers little substantive comment, revealing in what is asserted a focus only on immediate weapons effects and an underestimation of the extensive ecological and economic perturbations wrought by nuclear war.

THE FOOD WE CONSUME

The American people consume, on the average, about 1,400 pounds of food per capita per year, amounting to an average of 3,420 calories per day. Per capita food consumption has been quite stable recently, but over the years there has been a slight upward trend. Animal products provide about 41 percent of the poundage consumed and contribute about 21 percent of our daily caloric intake. About one-fifth of our current caloric intake is provided by grain (see Tables 12–1 and 12–2).

Animal products are the major source of calcium, phosphorus, riboflavin, vitamin B6, and vitamin B12 and are important sources of iron, magnesium, vitamin A, and thiamin. Grain products are an important source of thiamin, iron, niacin, riboflavin, magnesium, phosphorus, and vitamin B6, in large part because these nutrients are added to the grain products during processing. Fruits, vegetables, and potatoes are important sources of ascorbic acid, vitamin A, iron, and vitamin B6 (see Table 12–3).

The National Emergency Food Consumption Standards, devised as recommendations for post-attack diets, differ substantially from current consumption patterns. Forty percent reductions in meat, fat, fruit, and vegetables would be compensated in part by increases in cereal, eggs, and milk.[1] In the post-attack radioactive environment, milk may not be an acceptable substitute, assuming it were available. Despite attempts to compensate, the caloric intake provided by this diet would be substantially lower with these standards in place. These standards are appreciably at odds with the tastes and preferences of the people, but they are even more at odds with the situation facing those who would try to survive after a nuclear war. As will be discussed, few would have a diet in accordance with the National Emergency Food Consumption Standards.

TABLE 12–1.   All Food: Per Capita Consumption, Retail Weight Equivalent, Selected Years from 1960 to 1981.

Years	Animal Products	All Foods Crop Products[a]	Total
1960	614.2	785.9	1400.1
1965	609.1	759.7	1368.8
1970	614.2	782.8	1397.0
1975	588.0	789.7	1377.7
1980	587.4	819.5	1406.9
1981	582.2	817.6	1399.8

a. Includes spices and herbs, estimates of fruits and vegetables used in soups and baby foods, and, since 1971, dehydrated onions.
SOURCE: U.S. Department of Agriculture, Economic Research Service, Food Consumption, Prices, and Expenditures 1960–81 (Washington, D.C.: U.S. Government Printing Office, November 1982).

TABLE 12–2   Nutrients Available for Consumption Per Capita Per Day.[a]

Year	Food Energy (Calories)	Protein	Fat	Carbohydrate (Grams)	Calcium	Phosphorus	Iron	Magnesium (Milligrams)	Vitamin A Value (Int'l Units)	Thiamin	Riboflavin	Niacin	Vitamin B6 (Milligrams)	Vitamin B12 (Microgram)	Ascorbic Acid (Milligrams)
1960	3,190	96	148	376	0.96	1.52	16.0	344	8,100	1.92	2.29	21.8	1.86	9.0	106
1965	3,200	97	150	373	.94	1.51	16.0	388	7,700	1.86	2.25	22.5	1.83	9.0	98
1970	3,340	101	160	382	.93	1.54	17.1	341	8,200	1.96	2.31	24.1	1.98	9.7	112
1975	3,260	99	152	381	.90	1.51	17.0	341	8,100	1.98	2.32	24.8	1.97	9.2	120
1980	3,400	100	162	393	.88	1.48	16.9	331	8,000	2.16	2.32	25.8	1.98	9.0	123
1981	3,420	100	163	395	.88	1.48	17.0	322	8,100	2.13	2.32	26.0	1.98	9.2	121

a. Quantities of nutrients computed by Human Nutrition Information Service, Consumer Nutrition Center, on the basis of estimates of per capita food consumption (retail weight), including estimates of produce of home gardens, prepared by the Economic Research Service. No deduction is made in nutrient estimates for loss or waste of food in the home, use for pet food or for destruction or loss of nutrients during the preparation of food. Data include iron, thiamin, riboflavin, niacin, vitamin A, vitamin B6, vitamin B12, and ascorbic acid added in fortification and enrichment.
SOURCE: U.S. Department of Agriculture, Economic Research Service, *Food Consumption, Prices, and Expenditures 1960–81.*

TABLE 12–3. Contribution of Major Food Groups to Nutrient Levels, 1981 (percentages).

Food group	Food Energy	Protein	Fat	Carbohydrate	Calcium	Phosphorus	Iron	Magnesium	Vitamin A value	Thiamin	Riboflavin	Niacin	Vitamin B6	Vitamin B12	Ascorbic Acid
Meat, poultry, and fish	20.8	43.0	35.8	0.1	4.2	28.6	31.0	14.1	22.0	27.3	22.9	45.5	40.8	71.7	2.0
Eggs	1.8	4.8	2.6	0.1	2.3	5.1	5.0	1.2	5.4	1.9	4.8	0.1	2.0	8.1	0.0
Dairy products, excluding butter	10.0	20.7	11.4	5.6	71.6	33.1	2.5	20.0	12.3	7.2	36.5	1.2	10.8	18.6	3.2
Fats and oils, including butter	18.4	0.1	43.3	–a	0.4	0.2	0.0	0.4	7.9	0.0	0.0	0.0	0.1	0.0	0.0
Citrus fruits	1.0	0.5	0.1	2.0	1.0	0.8	0.8	2.4	1.6	2.7	0.5	0.8	1.4	0.0	26.9
Noncitrus fruits	2.3	0.7	0.4	4.9	1.4	1.3	3.9	4.6	5.9	1.9	1.8	1.8	7.4	0.0	12.3
Potatoes and sweetpotatoes	2.7	2.3	0.1	5.2	1.0	3.6	4.6	7.1	4.6	4.6	1.4	6.0	9.4	0.0	13.3
Dark-green, deep-yellow vegetables	0.3	0.5	–a	0.5	1.8	0.8	1.8	2.3	20.6	0.9	1.3	0.6	2.3	0.0	10.7
Other vegetables, including tomatoes	2.5	3.3	0.4	4.7	5.2	5.1	9.9	10.8	17.0	6.3	4.7	5.7	10.7	0.0	28.1
Dry beans and peas, nuts, soy products	2.7	4.8	3.5	1.7	2.6	5.5	5.8	10.8	–a	4.4	1.7	5.9	4.2	0.0	–a
Grain products	20.1	19.0	1.3	36.5	3.8	13.4	31.6	19.3	0.4	42.7	23.7	28.8	10.8	1.6	0.0
Sugar and other sweeteners	17.1	–a	0.0	38.2	3.7	0.8	0.7	0.2	0.0	–a	–a	–a	–a	0.0	–a
Miscellaneous b	0.6	0.4	1.2	0.5	0.9	1.6	2.3	6.8	2.3	0.1	0.6	3.4	0.1	0.0	3.4

a. Less than 0.05 percent.
b. Includes coffee, chocolate liquor equivalent of cocoa beans, and fortification of products not assigned to a food group.
SOURCE: Ruth M. Marston and Susan O. Walsh, "Nutrient Content of the National Food Supply, 1981," *Nutritional Food Review* 21, U.S. Department of Agriculture, Economic Research Service (Washington, D.C.: U.S. Government Printing Office, 1983).

THE FOOD SYSTEM

The principal elements of the food distribution system are identified in the FEMA materials as producers, processors, wholesalers, retailers, and consumers. The entire food system depends on the national transportation network, and the producers are dependent on those who produce and provide them with the supplies and services they need to produce raw agricultural products.

The agroclimatic factors—land, rivers, temperature, rainfall—permitted the inherent productivity of American agriculture to be relatively high by world standards, and the stream of new technology applied by producers has pushed it higher and higher. While the aggregate land base is essentially fixed, there has been a massive increase in the use of capital and a massive decrease in the number of farmers and farm workers.

The United States produces more raw agricultural products than are used at home. We are the dominant exporter of animal feeds and oilseeds and a large exporter of vegetable oils, wheat, and rice. Trade in animal products and most other foods is small relative to domestic consumption. We are a net exporter of poultry meat and eggs, but imports of dairy products, fish, and red meat (beef, veal, pork, lamb, and mutton) are usually in excess of exports. We also are a net exporter of peanuts, tree nuts, dry beans, and dry peas. Canned vegetable, melon, and fruit imports exceed exports, except in the case of dried fruits. Fresh vegetable imports and exports are about in balance.

As the American farmer has become increasingly specialized, he has become more productive, and more dependent on others. The growth in the size of the average farm has been associated with the use of larger and more sophisticated machines and equipment that require servicing by specialists. Many farmers produce only one product (e.g., broilers or milk) and rely on others for supplies and services they need to produce the product.

The farmer depends on the farm supply and service industries for most of the items that are essential to the production process—credit, insurance, machinery, equipment, parts, repairs, seeds, chemicals, fertilizer, fuel, electricity, prepared animal feeds, and other supplies and services.

The farm supply industry, in turn, must depend on a steady stream of raw materials from other industries and power to produce the inputs for farmers. It is also dependent on the national transportation system for the raw materials and for moving their products to the local supplier before the farmer needs them.

The production of agricultural products is concentrated in certain geographic areas, and those who consume the food are concentrated elsewhere. The Northeast is heavily dependent on food production west of the Mississippi, in the Southeast, and in the middle Atlantic states. The Pacific Northwest produces five times more food than its population requirements and the Northeast produces only two-thirteenths of its food needs.[2]

Raw agricultural products begin their journey to the consumer with a trip from the farm to the first market. In some cases the initial trip is the only one; in others it is followed by many more. The initial trip may be very short or very long. Lettuce, for example, frequently is shipped from California to New York and delivered to the final consumer essentially in the condition it left the field. But the wheat in a loaf of bread has been processed beyond recognition and loaded and unloaded many times between the producer and the consumer. If often goes from the field to a bin on the farm, from the bin to a local elevator, from a local elevator to a terminal elevator, from the terminal elevator to a flour miller, from the flour miller to a baker, from the baker to the grocery store, and from the grocery store to the consumer. Each step requires energy and a transportation capability.

Most agricultural products are processed before being consumed. About 1.5 million employees are involved in processing agricultural products, which, in the case of meat, dairy products, and frozen foods, requires refrigeration.[3] Processing has become more energy intensive, and the equipment more sophisticated. Although some processing facilities are located near sites of production, often raw agricultural commodities must be moved great distances. Once processed, agricultural products are shipped directly to retail grocery stores and eating establishments or to warehouses that are in reasonable proximity to the retail outlets.

Retail food stores employed 2.6 percent of all nonagricultural industry employees in 1978; eating places employed another 4.5 percent.[4] The distribution of the retail food stores and eating places is essentially the same as the population, but the wholesale food distribution places are concentrated in the larger cities. The number of employees in the retail and wholesale food distribution system has been rising, primarily due to the growth in the fast food outlets. Some foods must be transported to the retail establishments on a daily basis, and the stocks of nonperishable goods only last a few days.

The supplies that are needed to produce raw agricultural products require materials, manpower, and energy to be produced, as well as a transportation system to move the materials and the farm supplies. The raw agricultural products are produced by farmers who require supplies and services according to a rigid schedule and who depend on tractor power and trucks that must have energy to function. The raw agricultural products are transported to the processors, wholesalers, and retailers on trucks, trains, and barges that must have energy to operate over roads, rails, and on rivers. The processors, due to their location, are more vulnerable to the direct effects of an attack than are producers, and retailers are more vulnerable than processors. But the wholesalers are vulnerable to the extreme. About 95 percent of the nation's agricultural wholesale capacity, 60 percent of the processing capacity, and 20 percent of the production capacity are located in the FEMA high-risk areas—targets for destruction from direct blast and thermal effects.[5]

The following description of current agricultural production factors frames the discussion of what impact a nuclear war might have on short- and long-term supplies in the United States.

The U.S. food system is energy and capital intensive. It is a highly specialized, mechanized, and fragile system. It is operated by humans, but the work is increasingly performed by ever more sophisticated machines and equipment that must have energy to operate and that must be maintained by specialists according to schedule. Each component of the food system depends on another component for essential inputs. Even minor disruptions within the system create chaos. Every aspect of its development that makes U.S. agriculture so wondrously productive and efficient makes it particularly vulnerable to the ravages of nuclear war.

Planting and harvesting of each crop (grain, fruit, vegetable) depend closely on meeting precise times in seasonal fluctuations; thus, accelerating or delaying schedules by as little as one to two weeks can drastically reduce harvest yields.

The nation's supply of livestock (115 million cattle and calves, including 11 million dairy cows, 379 million poultry, 53 million swine) are tightly bound to human support for shelter, food, water, and medical care.[6] Range cattle depend on man for supplemental feeding and scheduled migrations from summer to winter pastures and watering sites. Dairy cattle are fed carefully regulated diets and must be milked daily to avoid development of mastitis, which, if untreated, will frequently result in death or, even if treated, may permanently curtail milk production. Poultry, swine, and cattle in feedlots require frequent feedings of high-energy, carefully regulated diets.

High yields characterizing U.S. agriculture depend heavily on intensive uses of fertilizer, pesticides, and inbred strains of seed. Mechanized production techniques require complex machinery and extensive supplies of fuel and electricity.

A marked imbalance between consumer and producer concentrations in the United States defines total dependency on transportation systems to permit food to reach consumers on a continuous schedule. A similarly marked imbalance in skills highlights the specialized nature of U.S. agriculture: less than 2.5 percent of the population produces food for the rest of the country.

Crisis relocation will exacerbate the imbalances between supply and demand areas and will not appreciably affect the disparities in skills. The 150 million in risk areas will be moved an average of 250 to 300 miles from host areas—sufficiently far from main distributing and processing areas to disperse even further the necessary transportation network, and yet not close enough to sources of food production or storage to improve the geographical demand-supply imbalance.[7] Farmers reside in areas at high risk of fallout from ground bursts over midwestern military installations. With a crisis relocation strategy their mortality from an attack will not substantially differ from that of the rest of the population; therefore, the pre-attack ratio of farmer to consumer will persist unaltered.

IMPACT OF ATTACK

From an agricultural standpoint, the direct blast, thermal, and fallout effects of a CRP-2B attack on the United States will destroy industrial sites and transportation networks and will expose crops and animals to variable levels of potentially lethal radiation.

Destruction of major industrial areas will significantly reduce production of key agricultural factors: the loss of 80 to 90 percent of the petrochemical industry will destroy fertilizer and pesticide production; and direct blast and thermal effects will result in a 60 percent loss of food-processing capacity, a 95 percent destruction of wholesale sites, and extensive disruption of the transportation network.[8]

The exposure of livestock to potentially lethal levels of fallout, when combined with consumption of contaminated fodder, could threaten the survival of a large proportion of the animal population. Fallout, depending on the time of year, could kill young growing plants in the field or coat the more mature crop with radioactivity, which, if consumed, would pose a threat to humans and animals. Local fallout would also cover with intense radioactivity many of the grain storage sites not directly targeted.

POST-ATTACK POTENTIALS

An evaluation of food and agricultural potentials requires both a short- and a long-term focus.

Short Term

In the short term, defined as the first six months, the main problem will be one of distribution: moving whatever food stocks survive the attack to the relocated, sheltered population. With successful crisis relocation, approximately 195 million will survive the direct effects and persist into the shelter period. At least another 15 million of these people are expected to die of indirect effects (e.g., radiation, intercurrent disease) to bring the total number of survivors to approximately 180 million, or the 80 percent survival fraction FEMA predicts. This number places a significant burden on food transportation and distribution networks in a post-attack period. A less successful evacuation and shelter posture would reduce demands on the post-attack food system. Crisis relocation, by forestalling deaths in the cities, challenges the food system to support the lives of people who would otherwise have been killed. This challenge, although raised implicitly in the civil defense research literature[9] has not been clearly met.

The estimates of crop and livestock losses due to the direct effects of the nuclear attack are based on experimental studies and reflect serious gaps in knowledge, even with this limited focus. A comprehensive review of the status of research on the direct and indirect effects has been provided by Brown et al.[10] The highlights of their report are covered in the following paragraphs.

The primary factors affecting livestock survival and production after an attack are radiation exposure and environmental stresses. Research on the latter is extremely limited. Data on the effects of environmental stresses that are required include the possible impacts of temperature, insects, and parasites, and the effects of secondary infections. There also are inadequate data on the edibility of livestock products from animals subjected to fallout radiation exposures and from animals that have ingested fallout contaminated feed. Sufficient data exist only with respect to milk and eggs from cows and hens given radioactive feed.

Most of the livestock data are based on experiments that simulated fallout exposures to animals in sheds or barns, although some have been conducted to simulate fallout exposures to sheep and cattle in open pens and pasture. Experiments of the latter type on swine and poultry have not been conducted. Radiation sensitivities—showing cattle with thresholds similar to humans, and poultry and swine somewhat more resistant—are speculative because of insufficient data.[11] There have been no experiments to determine livestock lethality doses for external exposures simulating fallout radioactive decay combined with internal exposures from eating contaminated feed.[12]

With respect to crop survival, our knowledge is also based on isolated experiments. The interspecies variation has been observed to be wide: wheat, our major food grain, is more sensitive to radiation than corn or soybeans (our major sources of animal feeds and vegetable oils) and potatoes and rice.[13] The age and stage of development of a species is also important, most crops being more sensitive when they are young or at specific times in the development process. Survivability is a function of the dose rate, so the impact from one region to another can be very great. During the early stages of plant development the dominant source of radiation damage is beta radiation, but prior to plant emergence, and later in the plant growth stages, gamma radiation proves more harmful.[14]

Assessment of Food Stocks Post-Attack

Livestock

Ambiguity surrounds the question of what to do with the nation's supply of livestock in the event of a nuclear attack. Range cattle, unsheltered from lethal levels of gamma radiation, burned by beta fallout and thus more susceptible to infection, and subsisting on fields covered with radioactive fallout will be devastated by the attack.[15] Wholesale slaughter of these animals within the one to two weeks it might take them to die of radiation effects and before their systems were contaminated with bacteremias from infection might provide safe meat for human consumption.[16] The problems with this approach are: there would be no one to do the slaughtering during this time period, (all humans needing to be completely and constantly sheltered); and it would be virtually impossible to get this meat processed, refrigerated, and transported to the sheltered populations distant from where the animals are located. Dairy cattle, although more likely to receive some, albeit insufficient, shelter from barns during and after the attack, are much more dependent than range cattle on daily human attention for food, water, and milking. Again, humans will need to be sheltered and will have to subject themselves to substantial exposure risks if they try to provide these services to their animals during the first two- to four-week period post-attack. Dairy cows, denied nourishment and milking for several days, will become sick and die, regardless of whatever radiation exposure they may suffer. Poultry and swine, both species likely to be in shelters and relatively less dependent than dairy cows on human intervention, still require frequent feeding and, to a greater extent than cattle, consume a diet that in the post-attack world will directly compete with human supplies.[17] Their survival will create a rationing dilemma of uncertain magnitude.

These problems with livestock may prove quite recalcitrant to solution. Strategies to deal with them have not yet evolved in the civil defense research literature. It appears quite probable that most of the nation's livestock will succumb to the attack and that only marginal use could be made of the meat resource they represent.

Grain Supplies

Because less than one-half the crop under production is expected to survive a nuclear attack on the scale of the CRP-2B model, and because the destruction of the harvesting, processing, and distribution systems makes getting the crop fraction that does survive to the sheltered population most problematic, immediate nutritional support of the post-attack population will most likely have to be supplied solely by the grain stored in local warehouses and elevators, near production sites, and in regional wholesale centers.[18] In general, annual grain stores in the United States since 1945 have been sufficient to meet the basic annual needs of the population, defined as 3,000 calories per day, or two pounds per person of raw grain per day for the several months between harvests. There have been several years and six-month periods, however, when such stores have not been adequate.[19] Assuming that the attack occurs during a time when the United States has sufficient stores on hand, there are still three main problems in relying on stored grain for support of the population.

First, an exclusive diet of two pounds of grain per day for months will subject the population to serious deficiencies in vitamin C and reduce energy levels to an extent that may significantly retard work capacity. No processing will be available, and the raw grain will have to be boiled to be edible. Infants and young children, whose protein needs are high and whose digestive systems may not tolerate this diet, will be at particular risk of malnutrition. No grain is reserved for animal use—another reason why livestock survival will be problematic.

Second, it is not clear from the studies of food supplies in this setting what percentage of the grain stores will survive a nuclear war. Most of the stocks in the East and South are stored off-farm, in urban warehouses that are located in high-risk areas and so may well be destroyed in the attack. A disproportionate share of the food grain stocks are located in the Great Plains and in the Pacific Northwest. Much of the Midwest storage area may be contaminated for weeks or months by high levels of fallout. According to a study of a counterforce attack alone, only on midwestern military facilities, early fallout will contaminate 400,000 square miles of farm land and storage sites at levels making unsheltered activity (including unloading and handling grain stores) unsafe for four weeks to several months and denying access to agricultural land for at least one year thereafter.[20]

Third, the problem posed by distribution is enormous. Local area studies by Billheimer and Simpson confirm extreme supply-demand imbalances following a nuclear attack. The near-total destruction of the local distribution system in their area of study in Colorado would severely restrict the flow of foodstuffs during the immediate post-attack period. These authors concluded that there would be severe shortages of every commodity except potatoes and raw grain in this area during the first month after an attack.[21]

On a national level, according to a study by Haaland, approximately 60 percent of the stored grain would remain for use post-attack.[22] The effects of fallout, restricting access to these storage sites, is not considered in this assessment. Since, in Haaland's study, about 55 million in the post-attack population would be relocated and sheltered in areas with zero to ten days of food supply on hand, within two to three weeks post-attack grain would have to be transported from the remaining (and potentially radioactive) grain stocks in rural areas to the areas of need.[23]

Transportation Post-Attack

Conditions in the post-attack world will pose a tremendous obstacle to this transport task. Most railroad lines, bridges, and roads will have been destroyed. At least 60 percent of all fuel stocks will have been consumed in the attack.[24] Haaland, addressing the question of supplying the post-attack population with enough grain for six weeks after the attack, concentrates only on the question of fuel availability, assuming that a sufficient fraction of the trucking and rail transport system will survive to carry on this transport function. He estimates that fuel supplies "would last for 236 days, which is probably adequate to carry the nation through the survival stage into the recovery stage."[25]

The problems with this analysis include the fact that disruption of transport networks cannot be assigned fractional values because of bottleneck disjunctions. What fuel exists in storage may not be near the trucks that may have survived the attack. The rate and volume of grain shipped does not match need, and the apparent destinations for this transported grain are listed as Boston, Hartford, New York City, Albany—all high-risk areas and theoretically evacuated. Getting this grain supply to the people sheltered in the host areas is the relevant, and more difficult, task. Transport to these areas of need within the first two weeks may require transit through or on the periphery of intense radiation, and trying to engage workers for this task may prove futile. Food hoarding or consumption of fuel supplies for any other task but transport of food is not considered. Finally, nothing supports the assumption that after 236 days, or 7.8 months into the post-attack period, the agricultural economy would have reached a "recovery stage." Many considerations suggest that, in fact, the food situation after the first six months post-attack will have become more severe.

Long Term

After six months, all stored grain would have been consumed. The need to conserve seed supplies is not discussed in the government literature. The surviving population would have to produce the food they needed and would have to migrate to more productive agricultural areas than the site of most relocation depots. Production and harvest of crops would require enormous human labor, since few of the essential production factors applying in the pre-attack setting would be available. Fertilizer, pesticides, heavy machinery, and irrigation all depend on the existence of functioning refinery and petrochemical industries, which would have been destroyed in the attack. Without fertilizer, major crop yields are estimated to decrease by 50 percent. Yields can also be expected to drop in the absence of pesticides, especially in the setting of the post-attack world where insect vectors will have increased disproportionately because of their relative radiation resistance. Loss of fuel for farm machinery and irrigation pumps will also reduce agricultural yields; it is estimated that reduction of petroleum use to 20 percent of pre-attack levels would cut farm production to 30 percent of normal.[26]

Regardless of the extent to which a remnant of skilled farmers may survive the attack, the majority of the population will have had little experience with farming. People will be disoriented, hungry, and perhaps ill from radiation and disease. The act of turning topsoil contaminated with fallout will expose those who farm to increased exposure burdens, and the work required to prepare and plant fields may be beyond the capability of many. Questions about soil and seed contamination, when people are very hungry, will most probably be dismissed, however, and crops may well be planted with little regard to radioactivity.

For all these reasons, the yield cannot be expected to compare with the pre-attack world. Other, more indirect effects of the attack may have even greater impact on potential agricultural productivity. These have received inadequate attention in the civil defense literature. These indirect effects include losses due to mass fires, insects, erosion, inadequate sunlight, changes in rainfall patterns, and lowered temperature; these conditions, when combined, may exceed the reduction in productivity due to blast, thermal effects, and fallout (see Chapter 13).

Quantitative estimates of production in the first several years after the attack are beyond the scope of this discussion, but it is clear from the variables mentioned that problems with food production and distribution may create serious, widespread hunger and malnutrition, if not famine. In times of hunger, conserving seed from one growth's crop to use for the next season can prove socially and physically impossible. Areas that plan better and have better luck will become targets of attack from groups in need. In settings where food supplies are limited, human beings may have difficulty remaining human.

CONCLUSIONS

The FEMA assessment of the ability of the United States to provide food for those who survive a nuclear attack is based primarily on estimating the direct effects of blast, heat, and early fallout on crops already planted or stored. Research on indirect effects and on subsequent harvest potentials is totally inadequate. A limited effort has been made to estimate the losses due to destruction of the food system, but this work also is almost entirely devoted to immediate effects. The implicit and dubious assumption is that the components of the food system that survive the initial attack and the consequences of radiation will soon be available for use by the surviving population. But the food system depends on supports that are exceedingly complex and interconnected. Even a minor disruption in any one component of this support network—a severe storm, a strike, a fuel embargo—sends shock waves throughout the system. The disruptions associated with a nuclear attack would certainly reduce potential to produce food to a much greater extent than FEMA predicts and would cast in much greater doubt than we are led to believe the possibility of feeding the survivors.

13

When Light Is Put Away: Ecological Effects of Nuclear War

Paul Ehrlich

And I brought you into a plentiful country,
to eat the fruit thereof and the goodness thereof;
but when ye entered, ye defiled my land,
and made my heritage an abomination.

Jeremiah 2:7

[In 1945] . . . the Special Committee on Atomic Energy of the U.S. Senate was concerned that an atomic explosion might "ignite" the earth's atmosphere or start some sort of chain reaction in the air or in the ocean.

Although these extreme types of fears are no longer taken seriously, others almost equally catastrophic have arisen to take their place. They include:

—the triggering of a new ice age;

—upsetting the delicate balance of nature, leading to disastrous changes in the ecology;

—creation of vast radioactive wastelands that would be uninhabitable for generations; . . .

—depletion of the ozone layer in the stratosphere, thus decreasing the protection from ultraviolet radiation and causing proliferation of skin cancers, killing wild and domestic animals and making it difficult, it not impossible, to grow many of the crops that provide our food and fiber.

The hypothesis about ozone depletion is the most current and its validity is yet to be established one way or the other. Also, many people still hold exaggerated fears about the fallout radiation and its longer-term effects. . . .

The underlying motive behind these negative hypotheses may be psychological. If everyone "knew" that nuclear war either directly or indirectly would trigger a mechanism for annihilating the human species, somehow the world would appear more secure. No sane person would initiate a series of events that would lead to everyone's death, including his own. Thus to many people the idea of assured destruction contains elements of reassurance.

SOURCE: Defense Civil Preparedness Agency, *Research Report on Recovery from Nuclear Attack*, Information Bulletin No 307, U.S. Government Printing Office, May 10, 1979, pp. 2–3.

Summary considerations in regard to the role of fire are that most forests are remote from expected nuclear targets; approximately half of the lumber in the United States is privately produced and many of these private companies farm—i.e., use stocking-harvesting regimes, maintenance of firebreaks and lookouts—according to methods which provide maximum fire protection to their forests; ... The U.S. Forest Service is continuing its research into providing better methods to provide natural fire control to their forested regions. Hence, forests would not be expected to be extensively damaged, and the outlook is reasonably optimistic that no lack of forest products would keep national recovery from proceeding without serious interruption.

Since severity of erosion would be directly related to the extent of fire damage, and since the consensus of opinion is that fire damage would not materially delay ecological recovery, it follows that erosion problems also would not hamper recovery. ...

As previously stated, the ecological aftermath of a nuclear attack is highly speculative. However, a consensus of opinion of most ecologists who have seriously considered the problem may be summed up by the following:

" ... ecological disturbances would not be such as to prevent recovery"; " ... ecological imbalances that would make normal life impossible are not to be expected"; " ... direct radiation effects from nuclear war on vegetation are not likely to seriously limit man's reconstruction of his renewable resources."

SOURCE: William S. Osburn, Jr., "Forecasting Long-Range Ecological Recovery From Nuclear Attack," in *Postattack Recovery from Nuclear War*, Proceedings of the symposium held at Fort Monroe, Virginia, November 6–9, 1967, Office of Civil Defense, Washington, D.C., 1967, pp. 113, 117.

ECOLOGICAL EFFECTS

Speculation that the attack environment might cause drastic upsets in the "balance of nature" has assumed that changes that exist for a relatively short time can induce permanent ecological damage. Researchers say this is not borne out by experience; and that long-term consequences require continuous pressure over centuries of time, of which the impact of human habitation is the outstanding example.

There could be some significant ecological consequences, such as one cooler growing season, temporarily increased rainfall, forest fires, increased erosion and silting because of dead trees and ground cover, and outbreaks of insect and rodent pests. These could have indirect effects on agriculture and forestry.

But those who have studied potential ecological problems, and other problems that could be expected to result from nuclear attack, feel strongly that Americans would not be helpless—and that they could meet and overcome all the challenges of the postattack environment.

The living would not "envy the dead."

SOURCE: FEMA, *Camera-Ready News Columns,* no. 15, Washington, D.C., December 1980.

To provide perspective on post-attack ecology, it is useful to keep in mind that nature may not be so delicately balanced after all. No logical weight of nuclear attack could induce gross changes in the balance of nature that approach in type or degree the ones that human civilization has already produced. This includes cutting most of the original forests, tilling the prairies, irrigating the deserts, damming and polluting the streams, eliminating certain species and introducing others, overgrazing hillsides, flooding valleys, and even preventing forest fires. Man has radically changed the face of this continent, but should he leave the scene it seems overwhelmingly probable that there would be a gradual return to the original situation or close facsimile thereof rather than violent fluctuation or further change to a new equilibrium state of nature.

SOURCE; Defense Civil Preparedness Agency, *Research Report on Recovery from Nuclear Attack,* Information Bulletin No. 307, U.S. Government Printing Office, Washington, D.C., May 10, 1979, p. 31.

The concept that a crisis relocation program could save a substantial portion of the civilian population of the United States in the event of a nuclear war is rooted in the pervasive ignorance of ecology that has always been endemic in certain circles in Washington. Therefore, in the first part of this chapter, I will outline what every decisionmaker (indeed, every citizen) should know about the ecology of nuclear war. The second part will examine the FEMA point of view on the environmental impacts of a large-scale thermonuclear war and speculate on why that view has not been more vigorously challenged by academic environmental scientists.

ELEMENTS OF NUCLEAR ECOLOGY

Ecology is the discipline concerned with the interactions between organisms and their physical and biological environments. Here we will be primarily concerned with the highest level of ecological organization: ecosystems. Ecosystems consist of the community of plants, animals, and microorganisms in an area (e.g., field, valley, lake, state, continent, entire Earth) and the physical environment of that community. Usually they are systems of appalling complexity that are, at most, partially understood, but there are a few general rules about ecosystems that should be kept in mind through the discussion that follows.

First, with trivial exceptions, ecosystems are driven by the light energy of the sun, which is converted by the process of photosynthesis in green plants into chemical energy that can be used by all organisms. Without photosynthesis, all familiar life forms would disappear, including *Homo sapiens*. The solar energy captured by the plants is used by the plants and by other organisms—herbivores, predators, and decomposers—to power their life processes. A feeding sequence of, say, a snapdragon eaten by a butterfly, eaten in turn by a jay, which is devoured by a hawk, which dies and is decomposed by bacteria, is called a food chain. Food chains are usually woven into food webs, whose complexity is only hinted at in Figure 13–1.

Energy moves along a food chain in one direction only. At each link less usable energy is available than at the previous one; as described by the second law of thermodynamics, every energy "transaction" causes the degradation of some of the energy involved into forms less available for use. This degradation of energy at each step explains why, for example, many fewer people could be supported eating corn-fed cattle than could be fed on the corn itself.

Chemical nutrients, by contrast, move in cycles (Figure 13–2). They are normally taken up by plants as elements or simple molecules and assembled into the large, complex organic molecules characteristic of living systems. Decomposers—mostly small insects, worms, bacteria, and fungi—play a crucial role in restoring the complex molecules of dead organisms and wastes to simple forms available to plants. Without decomposers, all life would soon grind to a halt.

Ecosystems, then, can be thought of as extremely complicated machines with many interdependent living parts. Like other machines, they are vulnerable to disruption in many ways. They can be destroyed outright, or they can be stopped by removing their energy source or by damaging or removing essential parts.

With this background, let us examine the probable effects of a nuclear war of the large scale envisioned by the FEMA[1] and Ambio[2]

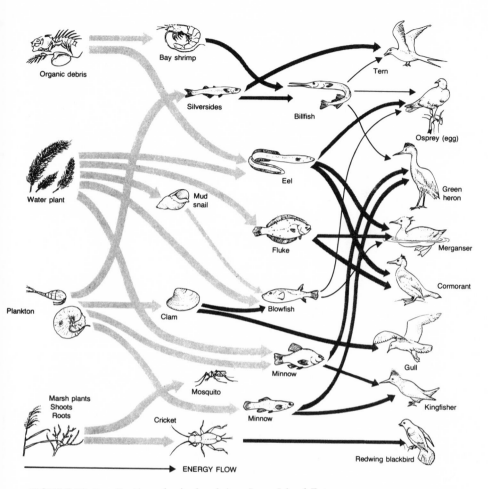

FIGURE 13–1.   *Portion of a food web in a Long Island Estuary.*

scenarios. These scenarios differ in detail. FEMA envisions an attack on the United States in which 1,444 warheads yielding 6,559 megatons are used. Ambio proposes a global war in which 14,747 warheads yielding 5,742 megatons—less than half of the combined U.S.-Soviet arsenals estimated for 1985—are detonated, almost all in the Northern Hemisphere. Because it is both broader in coverage and more in line with modern strategic doctrine, the Ambio scenario is probably more realistic. The differences between them, however, are largely unimportant for the purposes of this discussion. This is especially true in that neither con-

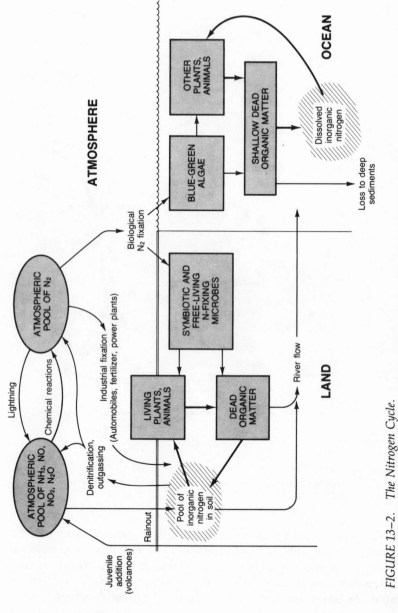

FIGURE 13–2. The Nitrogen Cycle.

SOURCE: From Ehrlich, Ehrlich, and Holdren's ECOSCIENCE: POPULATION, RESOURCES, EN-VIRONMENT, W.H. Freeman and Company, Copyright © 1977.

siders either the likely inaccuracy of both American and Soviet missiles (few independent scientists believe that they will perform to advertised levels of accuracy) or the virtual certainty of retargeting and addition of warheads that would occur if either nation attempted large-scale relocation of its population. Both of these effects would certainly exacerbate ecological effects by assaulting more relatively undeveloped areas without significantly reducing damage in urban centers. In this chapter, the effects of a large-scale war will be discussed without reference to either scenario except where there is a technical reason to do so.

Of course, it is impossible to describe all at once the multidimensional impacts of nuclear war on ecosystems. The following, necessarily linear, description of effects can only hint at the colossal ecological transformation and associated loss of ecosystem services to humanity that would occur in North America, Europe, and Asia after a large-scale nuclear war. It is important to keep in mind that many or all of the effects described would be occurring simultaneously and in many cases would be amplified synergistically. Figure 13–3 presents a necessarily simplified picture of the interrelationships discussed.

There is no direct experimental precedent to provide guidance in projecting the overall consequences. Classic investigations of perturbed ecosystems—such as the Hubbard Brook study of the impact of clearcutting on a temperate forest[3] and Thomas Lovejoy's Minimum Critical Size of Ecosystems Project, which investigates loss of populations from habitat remnants in tropical rain forest[4]—have been concerned with systems that are not subject to any atmospheric, climatic, or radiation stress. George Woodwell's studies of the impacts of radiation did not include any other stresses, such as fire, phytotoxic smog, or acid precipitation.[5]

There is also no body of theory that has attempted to address the impacts of multiple, complex, and poorly understood insults to ecosystems. Interactions in ecosystems are extremely complicated, and building theoretical models to handle even relatively simple subsets of those interactions can be extremely demanding or, at present, impossible.[6] Important topics, such as the ways in which the structure of the ecosystem influences mating systems, are just beginning to be understood.[7] But enough is known to indicate, for example, that many higher organisms that survive the initial impacts of the war will suffer extensive failures when they attempt to breed in highly modified environments.

In short, it is now impossible, and will doubtless remain forever impossible, to predict the environmental effects of thousands of thermonuclear weapons detonations in detail. Indeed, totally unanticipated ecological reactions are likely to occur. One is therefore left with making a projection from partial information about responses of entire ecosystems

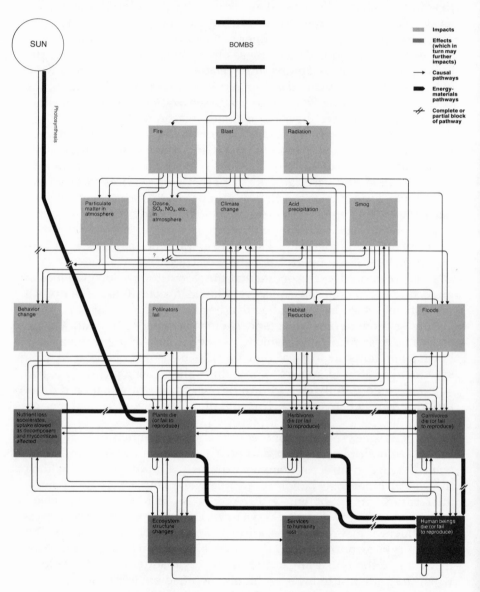

FIGURE 13–3. Human Ecology in a Nuclear War (Simplified Diagram of Probable Effects).

and the behavior of ecosystem components, from theory dealing with simpler situations, and from first principles. In aggregate, these considerations show that, in virtually any large-scale war in the growing season, many or most Northern Hemisphere ecosystems would be changed beyond recognition. Some would disappear totally. In others, many component species would be exterminated, and the survivors would tend to be the least desirable (from the point of view of humanity) "weedy" organisms. For a long time, the remaining systems would be in flux as successional changes took place and new mutualistic, competitive, and predator-prey relationships developed on both ecological time scales (months to decades) and coevolutionary time scales (decades to millennia).

From the standpoint of human survivors of a nuclear holocaust, the environment would be both completely different from today's and incredibly more hostile. As will be detailed in the analysis that follows, delivery of important ecosystem services would be terminated or greatly impaired in many areas, especially in the first few years after the war. Furthermore, for a long time the environment would be extremely unpredictable: there would probably be unusual weather patterns, novel successional sequences (community changes following disturbance), and outbreaks of previously unknown pests and diseases. This would add greatly to the difficulties of survivors, especially those who were attempting to farm.

In short, the ecological effects alone of a large-scale nuclear war that occurred during the spring, summer, or fall could destroy civilization in the Northern Hemisphere. Those of a winter war, when much of the combatant nations would be under snow, almost certainly would be less extensive but still catastrophic. Winter weather conditions would make survival for any people not killed outright by blast, fire, or radiation far more difficult, and those weather conditions could be much more severe because of the war. Even making optimistic assumptions about the season and other variables, the ecological consequences of any sizable nuclear war would be extremely serious and would be a major factor interacting with other impacts to delay or prevent recovery. If pessimistic assumptions are made, a scenario can be constructed that destroys human societies planetwide and even threatens the persistence of our species. Needless to say, the prudent course for society would be to assume that the worst will occur.

NUCLEAR WAR AND ECOSYSTEM SERVICES

Earth's ecosystems provide society with an array of indispensible free services. These include maintenance of the quality of the atmosphere, control of climate, regulation of freshwater supplies, generation and maintenance of soils, disposal of wastes and cycling of nutrients, pest and disease control, pollination, direct supply of foods, and maintenance of a genetic library.[8]

The delivery of services by many ecosystems has already been seriously impaired by human activities,[9] and, even under ideal conditions, substituting for those services is ordinarily impossible.[10] Ecologists and others are concerned about the continued ability of ecosystems to support civilization in the *absence* of nuclear war. But what would happen to ecosystem services in the event of such a war, especially a large-scale one such as is envisioned in the FEMA and Ambio scenarios?

Maintenance of the Quality of the Atmosphere

The mixture of gases in the atmosphere is largely the product of interactions between oceanic processes, geological processes (such as vulcanism), and the living organisms of the planet. Plants, animals, and microorganisms are involved in the movement of oxygen, nitrogen, sulfur, carbon dioxide (CO_2), water vapor, and other components between the atmosphere and other parts of ecosystems. Major concerns today about atmospheric quality include increasing levels of toxic pollutants, reduction of the stratospheric ozone layer, changes in transparency (transmission of both short- and long-wavelength radiation) due to particulate matter, and a steadily climbing concentration of CO_2.

A large-scale nuclear war would enormously increase the quantities of chemical pollutants in the atmosphere.[11] This would occur both from the direct generation of nitrogen oxides by the thermonuclear explosions themselves and from the effects of the gigantic fires that would be ignited by the fireballs. The latter—burning forests, fields, peat bogs (where fires may burn up to two meters deep and are virtually impossible to extinguish), oil and gas wells, oil refineries, tank farms, coal supplies, and the vast array of flammable plastics and other synthetic materials found in cities and towns—would add not only nitrogen and sulphur oxides to the atmosphere, but also a variety of toxic chemicals—many in unprecedented concentrations.

This contamination of the atmosphere would, of course, have a direct health impact on survivors of blast and radiation. A severe photochemical smog might well be generated over the entire planet with the *lowest* levels of ozone (a critical ingredient of smog) anywhere in the Northern Hemisphere about the equivalent of those on a moderately bad day in Los Angeles.[12] In many areas downwind of fires the smog would be worse. This would add respiratory distress to the other problems of many people not killed outright, and there would be *nowhere* for sensitive individuals such as asthma sufferers to seek relief.

The impacts on the ecosystems that normally maintain atmospheric quality cannot be foretold in detail, but some reasonable predictions can be made. Those systems—forests, chaparral and other brushlands, grasslands, etc.—not destroyed outright in huge fires and firestorms would be immediately threatened by smog components such as sulphur dioxide, peroxyacetyl nitrate (PAN), and ozone, all of which are highly toxic to plants.[13] PAN could be present at concentrations as much as 100 times normal, and ozone perhaps five times normal for months after the war.[14] Depending on the concentrations of various toxic components of the smog, the results could include the complete destruction of vegetation in some areas, although this would be unlikely except near and downwind of certain large, persistent fires. One would expect, however, very widespread sublethal changes in trees that would make them susceptible to insect and other enemies[15] and other detrimental impacts on the flora, the ecosystemic implications of which are difficult to predict.

The acidity of rains could increase dramatically for a time because of nitrogen oxides generated by the original thermonuclear explosions and nitrogen and sulphur oxides produced in the widespread fires. Perhaps three months' supplies of fossil fuels (roughly the amount in storage if European reserves are typical) would burn in a matter of days or weeks, and the outflow from decapitated gas and oil wells would continue to burn long after that. The degree of increase in acid precipitation and its duration would, however, depend on complex factors beyond the location, nature, and duration of the oxide sources, such as the distribution and quantity of atmospheric dust, which would tend to neutralize precipitation.

The impacts of the acid rains must be guessed from those already documented. For example, fifty years ago most lakes in the Adirondack Mountains of New York had a pH (the measure of acidity) of between 6 and 8. The pH scale is logarithmic. A pH of 7 is neutral. A pH of 6 is ten times as acid, and 8 is ten times as alkaline, as neutral. By contrast, in 1975 the average pH of Adirondack lakes was around 4.2—roughly 1,000 times more acid than neutral—and fish had disappeared from hundreds of lakes because of it.[16] In Sweden and Norway more than 15,000 lakes are now fishless because of acid precipitation.[17] Snow-melt pools in upstate New York are now too acid to support the breeding of spotted salamanders.[18] There is mounting evidence that acid rains are killing trees in many forests of the Northern Hemisphere.[19]

Following a nuclear attack, increased acidity of precipitation and the increased concentrations of trace metals mobilized by acid from soil and rock could combine with other pollutants and silt to eliminate freshwater fish populations in many areas by killing them outright or inhibiting their reproduction. This would deprive local survivors, if any, of a significant source of accessible protein. The acid rains could induce changes in the chemistry of soils and in populations of soil microorganisms that, in combination with other war-induced ecosystem stresses, might doom surviving forests in many parts of North America, Europe, and northern Asia.[20] The fertility of some soils could be reduced for a long postwar period as a result of the impacts of acid rains on nitrogen-fixing organisms,[21] mycorrhizal fungi, which help higher plants acquire nutrients,[22] and decomposers.[23]

These impacts are especially difficult to judge because of both the uncertainties about the acid precipitation and the differential susceptibility of ecosystems (which depends largely on the characteristics of the soil). Perhaps because of the relatively limited duration of any postwar acid rain "pulse," the most serious disruptions would be seen in ecosystems previously acidified nearly to the threshold of catastrophic biotic effects. For example, a few months of extremely acid rain could use up the remaining buffering capacity of many alpine and subalpine systems in the Rocky Mountains and the Sierra Nevada of California, damaging populations of aquatic organisms and seriously degrading subalpine forest soils.[24]

Acid rain impacts, however, might be dwarfed by those of particulate matter lofted into the atmosphere by blast and fires. Crutzen and Birks, considering the Ambio scenario, conclude: "The fires would create sufficient quantities of airborne particulate matter in the atmosphere to screen out a large fraction of the solar radiation for many weeks, strongly reducing or even eliminating the possibility of growing agricultural crops over large areas of the Northern Hemisphere."[25] And their analysis is conservative, since they did not consider the creation of clouds of dust by ground bursts of hydrogen bombs (of which there might be many if concerted attacks were made on "hardened" military facilities). Such dust in the lower atmosphere could contribute significantly to darkening for up to a month, shutting out as much as 99 percent of the daylight; the dust injected into the stratosphere would last for years.

Neither did Crutzen and Birks consider the addition of fugitive dust from wind erosion of denuded areas—one need only remember the famous dust storms that turned day into night in many areas of the United States during the Great Depression.[26] And finally, the maximum area of forest burn could be as much as twenty times greater than the amount (4 percent of the total) on which they based their calculations.[27] In short, photosynthesis could be considerably reduced for months.

The Ambio scenario was for an early June war. Impacts on crops and natural ecosystems of the screening out of solar radiation would presumably be smaller in, say, a war that occurred in early November. They would probably be greater if the war came earlier in the spring, when annual plants were just germinating and perennials just leafing out—a time when both are also very vulnerable to inclement weather, herbivores, and acid rain, although this might be compensated by reduced fire damage and a thinner veil of pollution.

The precise impact of a drastic reduction of photosynthesis can only be estimated, but it would undoubtedly be an ecocatastrophe causing an epidemic of extinctions unprecedented since the end of the Mesozoic Epoch, some 65 million years ago. Scientists have assembled impressive support for the hypothesis that the massive extinctions at the end of the Mesozoic era were due at least in part to a blackout or brownout and climatic changes caused by dust lofted into the atmosphere by the collison of an asteroid with Earth.[28]

Many species and innumerable local populations of plants in the Northern Hemisphere probably would be lost. Most vulnerable would be those with restricted distributions, since the degree of blackout presumably would be uneven. Perennial plants—trees, shrubs, bulbs—should be able to survive on stored energy, although their reserves for dealing with other stresses (e.g., smog, climate change, herbivore attack) would be reduced. Annual plants, such as many California spring wildflowers, that were growing when the attack occurred would have to depend for their survival on seeds lying dormant in the soil. (Normally all the seeds do not germinate in any one year; there are "seed banks" in the soil.) In order to survive in some areas, they would have to possess seed banks adequate to withstand sudden high levels of soil erosion.

The impact on animals would be much more severe. One could expect billions of local populations and thousands of species of herbivores—many insects, birds, rodents, hooved mammals, etc.—to perish because of the disappearance of their food.[29] Few animals can enter a resting state in response to an unexpected environmental change or have individuals that remain inactive for more than a single season. For example, populations of insects feeding on both annual and perennial plants apparently regularly go extinct if unsatisfactory weather conditions destroy one year's crop of edible material.[30] Carnivores dependent on such vulnerable herbivore populations would quickly follow them to oblivion.

It is important to note that often it is not necessary for a disaster to kill all individuals to drive an animal population or species to extinction. If population size is reduced below a threshold, inability to find mates, loss of genetic variability, changed relationships with predators or competitors, or chance will finish the job. A classic example is that of the passenger pigeon. There were survivors after commercial exploitation of this species ended, and there was still abundant habitat, but it nonetheless continued to decline to extinction.[31]

Control of Climate

Earth's climatic machinery is driven by energy from the sun, and the way in which it operates is primarily a function of the geometric relationship of Earth to the sun and of characteristics of the atmosphere and planetary surface (land and sea) that influence their abilities to reflect, transmit, transport, or absorb energy. The system is extremely complex and, as a result, its reactions are difficult to predict. It is important to keep two things in mind, however. First, climatologists believe that relatively small perturbations in the global system can have very large effects. Second, a general trend does not necessarily dictate a local one; general warming of the planet could change circulation patterns in ways that would cool some areas.[32]

The main determinants of climate would be dramatically altered by a nuclear war. The pollution veil will probably be the overriding change of climatic significance, changing the albedo (reflectivity) and absorbtivity of the atmosphere and preventing energy from reaching the surface. But there would certainly be others. One could be serious depletion of stratospheric ozone due to the injection of nitrogen oxides into the stratosphere from weapons bursts or by giant fires.[33] While ozone is a pollutant in the lower atmosphere, it performs important functions in the stratosphere: by absorbing ultraviolet radiation, it causes heating and creates the temperature inversion that retards vertical mixing between the stratosphere and the troposphere—the layer between the stratosphere and surface. The degree of ozone depletion would vary greatly with the characteristics of the war. Military trends are in the direction of more accurate warheads with smaller yields (from the FEMA toward the Ambio scenario), which would reduce the amount of nitrogen oxides that would reach the stratosphere as a direct result of nuclear fireballs.

Similar uncertainties exist about the precise effect of a war on three other climatically important atmospheric components: water (as clouds), water vapor, and CO_2. But all three could undergo substantial changes. For instance, where vegetation was destroyed, less water would enter the atmosphere. The production by fires of huge numbers of cloud condensation nuclei could alter rainfall significantly. The fires would also produce a large pulse in the atmospheric content of CO_2—a temporary increase that, in the worst case, could be roughly 10 percent of the present content (which is about the magnitude of the increase caused in the twentieth century by the burning of fossil fuels).

Potential climatic transients (changes occurring in the months just following the war) could well be very different from changes taking place over the following decades. The transients could be dramatic and perhaps in the opposite direction from the long-term changes. A likely early effect could be considerable cooling. Temperatures could drop as much as 20° to 30°C for a few months, and influxes of cold air into subtropical and tropical areas could have devastating effects.[34] This phenomenon would add to the stress on both natural and agricultural ecosystems, to say nothing of worsening the lot of survivors, especially in the winter.

After the smoke and dust in the troposphere settled, a significant stratospheric veil, such as that associated with the dust veils from large volcanic explosions, could persist for a year or two.[35] In historic times volcanic veils have cooled the surface and contributed to years "without a summer" in parts of the Northern Hemisphere.[36] A significant increase in atmospheric CO_2 might also persist, tending to warm the surface. (Neither particulate-induced cooling nor CO_2-induced warming would be uniform geographically, and the differences in the spatial patterns of these effects make it extremely unlikely that they would "cancel" each other.) There also could be many surface changes of climatic significance. The albedo could be increased over much of the land surface as a result of blast and fire. For example, forests, in general, have a lower albedo—that is, they reflect less light—than does bare ground. Oceanic albedo would be somewhat changed by pollution from uncapped oceanic oil wells and the runoff of petroleum products and other floating pollutants from coastal areas.

The most dramatic longer term climatic effect might come from the settling of the tropospheric soot load in the Arctic, which, under some conditions, could lead to the melting of the ice pack floating on the Arctic Ocean,[37] lowering the albedo of a huge area and moderating the climate of arctic lands by exposing the (relatively) warm water surface. Thus, in some areas cooling could be followed by warming. But any cascading effects of such a series of changes on global climate are, unfortunately, impossible to predict. There are too many variables, such as season of attack, too many possible effects that may operate in opposite directions, all influencing a poorly understood system. Whether there would be large hemispheric or global effects lasting for many decades would depend heavily on such factors as whether and for how long the floating ice pack disappeared.

Concerning some local effects the prospects are more clear-cut. For instance, where forests were unable to regenerate, there would be deleterious local climatic and other changes. The overall consequences of deforestation have been eloquently summarized by ecologist F.H. Bormann and serve as a reminder of the multiple services supplied by natural ecosystems:

> These natural functions are powered by solar energy, and to the degree that they are lost, they must be replaced by extensive and continuing investments of fossil fuel energy and other natural resources if the quality of life is to be maintained. We must find replacements for wood products, build erosion control works, enlarge reservoirs, upgrade air pollution control technology, install flood control works, improve water purification plants, increase air conditioning, and provide new recreational facilities.[38]

Needless to say, survivors of a nuclear war are unlikely to have the means to make those investments of energy and materials.

Regulation of Freshwater Supplies

The wholesale loss of terrestrial vegetation would have a dramatic effect on flows of rivers. Historically, deforestation has led to increased erosion, runoff, and sedimentation, accompanied by a higher incidence of flooding in wet seasons and decreased flows in dry seasons.[39] A complete loss of vegetation—as opposed to deforestation—would produce even more dramatic hydrological effects,[40] speeding silt-laden runoff to the seas. In addition, large dams are possible targets, as were the Moehne, Sorpe, and Eder dams in Germany during World War II,[41] and one could expect many of the Northern Hemisphere's major dams to be breached. The result would be catastrophic floods followed by less dependable water flows for home consumption, industry, or irrigation—assuming homes, industries, and farms survived and the water distribution system remained more or less intact.

Water *quality* would suffer almost everywhere. Anywhere that sizable human populations survived, the destruction of sanitation systems would inevitably result in fecal contamination of surface waters. A wide range of toxins would also be deposited in rivers, lakes, and streams—some of which (such as some chlorinated hydrocarbons and mercury compounds) would persist for long periods. Deforestation and erosion would contribute to loads of silt and dissolved materials that would further degrade water quality. The degree of toxification of groundwater supplies is difficult to predict, but in recharge areas, ruptured containers would obviously add a wide variety of poisons to underground systems, which are less capable than surface waters of purifying themselves (since they are isolated from sunlight, oxygen, and most decomposers—all of which are important in breaking down toxins).

Generation and Maintenance of Soils

Natural systems manufacture soils at rates measured in inches per millennium. Soils are formed by the disintegration of parent rock by weathering and the action of organisms and evolve into complex ecosystems themselves. Soil contains many plants, animals, and microbes that add organic materials to it and are crucial to fertility—a gram of agricultural soil can contain as many as 30,000 one-celled animals, 50,000 algae, 400,000 fungi, over 2.5 billion bacteria, and numerous tiny insects, mites, and roundworms.[42]

Humanity tends to destroy soils at rates measured in inches per year or decade. In 1977 the coterminous forty-eight states lost some two billion tons of topsoil to water erosion, and in ten Great Plains states alone, nearly 1.5 billion tons to wind erosion.[43] Lester Brown recently wrote: "Civilization can survive the exhaustion of oil reserves, but not the continuing wholesale loss of topsoil."[44] That loss would be enormously accelerated by a large-scale nuclear war. First to go would be the fertile, humus- and seed-containing upper layers upon which regrowth would depend.

Fields and forests would have their cover of vegetation burned away to an extent dependent on the season of the year, among other factors. If an attack hit California in the late summer, for example, one can picture the results by projecting from the common TV scenes of chaparral fires in the Los Angeles area. Most of the state would be ablaze—chaparral in the south and parts of the north, grasslands and crops in the center, forests in the north and in the Sierra. Similarly, the familiar image of mudslides in burned areas during the winter rains would be magnified to include the whole state. Such scenes could characterize the entire Northern Hemisphere. The U.S. Forest Service, for example, made a worst case estimate that a nuclear war could ignite fires *that would burn over 81 percent of the land area of the coterminous United States.*[45]

In general, regrowth of vegetation in burned areas is slow, and it would be even slower after a nuclear war for several reasons. First, most burned areas would be larger and less protected by adjacent unburned areas that normally help to slow water flows and provide shelter from winds. Erosive forces thus would be intensified, with the power in some situations to destroy seed banks and subterranean vegetative structures that had survived. In many cases, the burnover might be so large that reseeding would be extremely slow if the seed bank were destroyed, and the race between revegation and erosion might be lost.

Second, in some forested areas, where fuel supplies were above a critical level (as they probably would be in the taller, denser stands), firestorms might be generated that would virtually sterilize the soil, making revegetation dependent on immigration of seeds from surviving areas.[46] Indeed, even in chaparral (the type of shrub community characteristic of California and other regions with Mediterranean climates), which is adapted to periodic burning, some natural fires create soil temperatures that can kill seed stores and cause loss of soil nitrogen.[47] Exactly what occurs depends, among other things, on the temperature and the moisture content of the soil; wetter soil heats less but moist heat is more lethal than dry. Unfortunately, little or nothing seems to be known about the thermal characteristics of fires in natural ecosystems that do not spread from a single source but are ignited simultaneously over large areas.

Furthermore, the delicate plants sprouting after the fires would, as noted above, likely suffer from radiation, toxic smog, acid rains, insufficient sunlight for photosynthesis, and freezing temperatures. At the very least, these effects would retard revegetation and increase the chances that erosion would destroy the plants before the plants could stabilize the soil. Overall, soil loss is likely to be one of the most serious long-term consequences of a nuclear war.

Disposal of Wastes and Cycling of Nutrients

A critical service provided by ecosystems is the breaking down of the complex organic wastes produced by human beings and other organisms, and their dead bodies, into simple chemical molecules. These "nutrients" are then used in the generation of new plants, animals, and microorganisms. If this process of nutrient cycling by ecosystems ceased, life would cease with it.

A nuclear war would interfere with nutrient cycling in several ways. Nutrient retention is a characteristic of intact ecosystems, nutrient loss of disturbed ones.[48] The widespread burning-erosion situation just described would lead to massive losses of nutrients from many land areas to the oceans, from which they are not ordinarily returned on a human time scale. In addition, as mentioned above, acid rains just after the war might have a serious impact on nitrogen-fixing organisms, damage the all-important nitrogen cycle, further retard succession, and thus promote nutrient loss. A large fraction of the terrestrial areas of the Northern Hemisphere could be impoverished for hundreds of years and their long-term carrying capacity for all forms of life, including human beings, reduced.

Pest and Disease Control

To say the very least, then, ecosystems in a post-attack world would be subjected to a variety of severe stresses. A major insult to them would be increased levels of radiation—a source of ecosystem stress that has been quite thoroughly investigated experimentally.[49] Radiation effects would be differential, damaging or killing many organisms valuable to *Homo sapiens*, such as large trees, and improving conditions for less desirable organisms, such as weeds and cockroaches. As George Wood-well, the ecologist with the most detailed knowledge of radiation effects on ecosystems, put it, "an increased frequency of the small-bodied, rapidly-reproducing organisms that we so often find in competition with man and label 'pests' can be expected."[50]

Responses to the other stresses, individually and in aggregate, can be expected to go in the same direction. Animals and plants that are adapted to colonizing disturbed areas by quickly building large populations will replace those characteristic of more permanent situations—since the entire Northern Hemisphere will be a disturbed area. In a post-attack world, weeds, houseflies, mosquitoes that breed in temporary pools, gypsy moths, corn earworms, mice, rats, starlings, coyotes, and their ilk will make up a much greater proportion of life forms than they do today.

Moreover, one can expect insects not now considered plant pests to achieve pest status (if agriculture continues). The population sizes of previously obscure herbivorous insects will increase greatly. The predators that once kept them under control will have been much more susceptible to extinction than the herbivores because in general their population sizes will have been smaller. The result will be similar to that seen repeatedly after overuse of pesticides: the "promotion" of herbivores to pest status because of decimation of predators.[51] Changed ecological conditions and circumstances of exposure may also result in the appearance of new pathogenic organisms, as has already occurred in such situations with some free-living amoebae.[52]

Pollination

In the United States, at least ninety crops depend upon insects to pollinate them and nine others benefit from insect pollination.[53] Many wild plant species are also insect pollinated. Honeybees, natives of the Old World, which in North America are partially domestic animals, make major contributions to pollination of crops as diverse as cherries and alfalfa. Beekeepers regularly move them from crop to crop. Like other domestic animals, beekeepers' bees would suffer greatly from their association with *Homo sapiens* in the event of a war. In addition, any war-induced change in ultraviolet radiation could alter the behavior of insects, affecting, among other things, their performance as pollinators.[54]

In natural ecosystems, the major impact of the depletion of pollinators would probably be to add another factor that would tend to retard revegetation. Pollinators, like other animals, would in general have more difficulty surviving a catastrophic first post-attack growing season than would plants. But the latter would suffer from a subsequent dearth of pollinators.

Direct Supply of Foods

In the Northern Hemisphere, direct exploitation of natural terrestrial ecosystems for food is minor today. After a nuclear war, it is probable that a much higher proportion of the survivors would attempt to gain food by hunting, both because of shortages of food from agriculture and because survival rates would probably be higher in rural areas, where there are proportionately more hunters. But the large animals in ecosystems would have suffered disproportionately, and hunting would be likely to be poor except, perhaps, in the first weeks after the attack. During that period, deer, coyotes, cattle, dogs, rats, cats, and other wild and domestic animals may be wandering dazed, disoriented, hungry, maimed, and dying of radiation sickness—like the human survivors. Those people in condition to take advantage of them will find a ready source of protein. But it will be a two-way street, with many people (especially the very young, the very old, and the abundant sick and injured) falling prey to carnivores—in particular, rats and packs of dogs.

In contrast to natural terrestrial ecosystems, ecosystems of inland waters and oceans do provide the northern industrial countries with an important source of animal protein today. In a post-attack period, they no longer will. The probable state of bodies of fresh water has already been discussed; their capacity to yield protein will be greatly reduced. So will that of the oceans. Mechanized fishing, which provides most of the yield today, will essentially cease in the Northern Hemisphere. Most of the fishermen will be dead and their boats and equipment destroyed, and fuel will be difficult or impossible to obtain for the few remaining vessels.

Production of human food by oceanic ecosystems would also undoubtedly be reduced. Screening out of solar radiation would have a negative impact on phytoplankton productivity, since they photosynthesize. Reduction of photosynthesis in phytoplankton would reduce productivity at all levels in oceanic food chains. Populations of fishes, whales, and other animals that human beings harvest would decline or disappear. Similar effects could follow depletion of the stratospheric ozone layer, since phytoplankton are sensitive to ultraviolet wavelengths screened out by the ozone. The magnitude of ozone depletion and its effects are highly uncertain, however.

Another major reduction of ocean productivity would occur through the impacts on estuary and shallow water ecosystems of blast, radiation, and, in particular, the runoff of toxic substances and silt. Much of the ocean's productivity is in shallow waters near shore, and many commercially important fisheries are dependent on the health of estuaries and coastal wetlands. These are precisely the ocean associated areas that would bear the brunt of a thermonuclear war.

It is not clear how many bombs might actually be detonated in the oceans. Those directed at American fleet units probably would have the heaviest ecological impacts on the oceans if the ships happened to be deployed in shallow, vulnerable waters (as those close to the east or south coasts of the United States, the North Sea, or in some parts of the Mediterranean). Most of the biological activity of the oceans is concentrated in shallow waters near shore; the open oceans tend to be a "biological desert." Enormous destruction of marine life could occur if U.S. planners decided to bombard the coastal waters of the Soviet Union randomly with H-bombs in attempts to destroy the Russian missile submarines that are deployed there.

Finally, it should be noted that the scattered survivors in many burned out places (such as California is likely to be) may find little to assuage their hunger at the seashore, since silt and chemical pollution is likely to kill or contaminate most of the crabs, mussels, and other easily harvested invertebrates.

Maintenance of a Genetic Library

One of the most important functions of Earth's ecosystems is the maintenance of a vast genetic "library" from which humanity has already drawn the basis of civilization. Species and genetically distinct populations of nonhuman organisms ultimately have provided humanity with all of its foods and many of its medicines, industrial products, and fuels. It is a library whose potential, furthermore, has been barely tapped.[55]

Only the downhill slide toward a nuclear war concerns biologists today more than does the accelerating decay of Earth's biotic diversity. And that decay, at least in the Northern Hemisphere, would be enormously speeded by a nuclear war. Besides all the potential causes of extinctions already discussed, any areas of natural habitat that escaped direct destruction would tend to be reduced in size and increasingly isolated from one another.

Today in the United States, most reserves are islands in seas of human disturbance, and many are subjected to insults such as acid rains and phytotoxic smog. After a nuclear war, they would be much smaller islands in seas of utter desolation, subject to much more severe insults. Reduction of reserve sizes and increases in reserve isolation are by themselves a certain recipe for reducing the capacity of the reserves to maintain populations of various species.[56] Add the other stresses from nuclear war and it is clear that the rate of extinctions of species and populations would skyrocket.

The remaining great reservoirs of diversity are in tropical forests, which probably would suffer little direct damage from a war (assuming minimum "slop-over" of the conflict to the tropics). How they would fare in the long run, however, depends on hard-to-analyze factors such as the amount of global climatic change and the behavior of human populations in tropical countries suddenly cut off from the Northern Hemisphere, with which they have become increasingly interdependent. On one hand, the exploitation of the tropical forests that is generated by rich nations (wood chipping for paper products, clearing for cattle raising) would end. On the other hand, local exploitation for food would be enormously increased, especially since supplies of food, seeds, and chemical fertilizer from industrial countries would be largely cut off.[57] Indeed the entire question of the impacts of a large-scale nuclear war on the largely noncombatant nations of the Northern Hemisphere tropics and the Southern Hemisphere—ecological effects, radiation exposure, technology and trade cutoffs, and so on—remains to be explored in detail. Some atmosphere scenarios, for example, envision below freezing temperatures and little light over the entire planet for extended periods.

One immediate and extremely serious loss in the Northern Hemisphere would be the genetic variability of crops. The genetic base of major crops is already frighteningly narrow.[58] In a war, the "gene banks" (primarily collections of seeds of diverse genetic strains of crops) established by the government and agribusiness would be largely or entirely lost. In addition, many crop strains in the field, especially the less commonly planted ones, would disappear—victims of blast, radiation, fire, smog, darkness, and so on. So would many important genetic reserves represented by populations of wild relatives of crops. Indeed, for many crops the distribution of seed would present a major problem *regardless* of genetics, since most farmers do not now produce their own seed. The overall result, *if* agriculture persisted, would almost certainly be a return for many generations to the sort of subsistence farming practiced a century ago, with crops utterly unsuitable for it and sufficiently depauperate genetically to slow or prevent re-adaptation to pre-mechanized farming without synthetic fertilizers and pesticides.

THE FEMA FANTASY

The views of FEMA quoted at the beginning of this chapter make a stunning contrast to the picture just outlined. FEMA and many important decisionmakers believe that our society can survive an all-out thermonuclear war and recover in a matter of a relatively few years. This assumption and the motivation behind it have been discussed in detail elsewhere (see, e.g., Chapter 1). What concerns me here is why the consistent underrating of the environmental impacts has not attracted the attention of the community of academic ecologists.

One major reason is that most ecologists think it self-evident that a large-scale thermonuclear war would mean the complete or nearly complete destruction of American society. They are no more interested in analyzing in detail the environmental results of the rough equivalent of detonating 500,000 Hiroshima-sized atomic bombs simultaneously in the Northern Hemisphere (Ambio scenario) than medical doctors would be in analyzing the results of putting loaded guns in their mouths and pulling the triggers. That unacceptable damage would be done is crystal clear; that the scientists would not be able to assess how accurate in detail were their estimates of damage is also evident. No questions of *scientific* interest (in the sense of problems being attacked and debated within ecology and medicine) would be involved in either experiment.

Most ecologically informed people still find it difficult to imagine that many powerful decisionmakers have no notion of how the world works and that those decisionmakers accept the "Chipman analysis" of recovery. William Chipman, assistant to the head of FEMA in charge of civil defense, was asked whether he thought American society and democracy would survive a full-scale thermonuclear war with Russia. His reply: "I think they would eventually, yeah. As I say, the ants eventually build another anthill."[59] Unhappily for his analogy, ants, like people, depend on photosynthesis, mineral cycling, climate control, and other ecosystem services for their survival.

The combination of a lack of professional interest and lack of perceived need has resulted in a nearly total ignoring of questions related to the ecological impacts of nuclear war by the main body of population biologists (ecologists, population geneticists, evolutionists, animal behaviorists). Studies of ecological effects have been sponsored repeatedly by the military and other federal agencies, often done by people outside of academic science and mostly published in documents and reports rather than in the referred literature.

Interestingly, some of the earliest ones[60] have presented relatively pessimistic assessments of the more obvious impacts such as widespread fires and erosion and have examined many of the questions dealt with in this chapter.[61] Increasingly, however, those that have followed have either concentrated on the ecological impacts of radioactive fallout[62], or have ignored important sources of ecosystem damage and missed obvious connections, or both. For example, the National Academy of Sciences considered possible climatic effects of the injection of dust into the atmosphere (primarily a very modest stratospheric loading) but did not consider, among other things, the likelihood of changes in the albedo or of reduction of solar radiation by aerosols or the generation of smog as a consequence of widespread fires.[63] Indeed, a sort of "one problem at a time" approach is characteristic of the entire genre.

Furthermore, there has been a general tendency to deemphasize ecosystem effects because of the great difficulties in evaluating them with precision.[64] This problem of emphasizing what is readily analyzable rather than what is likely to be important is endemic to the field of risk assessment.[65] It is especially prominent in the area of environmental problems where the tendency is to focus on readily studied problems of "pollution" while deemphasizing the fundamentally more serious but hard-to-evaluate assaults on ecosystem services.[66]

The end results of ignoring critical ecological effects and decoupling them from one another are exemplified by the remarkable claims of Jack Greene, for years a staff member, associated with post-attack research, of successive federal civil defense agencies. In a 1971 report, he states in a section labeled "The Ecology" that ecological consequences are likely to be trivial in part because "man is now, in peacetime, doing just about everything he can do to upset the ecological balances."[67] Greene recently concluded in an "Information Bulletin" of the Defense Civil Preparedness Agency that the agricultural industry of the United States "is almost immune to significant damage in a nuclear attack."[68] He also contended that there might be "psychological" motives underlying pessimistic evaluations of the results of nuclear war.[69] Motives, of course, are irrelevant. What *is* relevant is the best possible assessment of the consequences, especially—in order to assure that decisionmakers are conservative in their planning—the worst plausible consequences.

The evaluation of the ecological impacts of nuclear war has, so far, largely been left to those ill equipped to do so. It is now critical that the community of academic ecologists and other environmental scientists involve itself deeply in this issue. If the war occurs, and those who deprecate its ecological risks are wrong, we shan't have the opportunity to tell them "I told you so."

ACKNOWLEDGMENTS

I would like to thank the following ecologists, population geneticists, evolutionists, and environmental scientists for reviewing and criticizing this chapter and stating their substantial agreement with its technical conclusions: Kenneth B. Armitage and Charles D. Michener

(Division of Biological Sciences, University of Kansas); Carol L. Boggs, Anne H. Ehrlich, Richard W. Holm, Marcus Feldman, Harold A. Mooney, Dennis D. Murphy, Jonathan Roughgarden, Bruno Streit, John H. Thomas, Ward B. Watt, and Bruce A. Wilcox (Department of Biological Sciences, Stanford University); Daniel B. Botkin and William W. Murdoch (Department of Biological Sciences, University of California, Santa Barbara); Peter F. Brussard and Gene E. Likens (Section of Ecology and Systematics, Cornell University); Thomas Eisner (Section of Neurobiology and Behavior, Cornell University); Lawrence E. Gilbert and Michael C. Singer (Department of Zoology, University of Texas); John Harte and John P. Holdren (Energy and Resources Group, University of California, Berkeley); Robert M. May and John W. Terborgh (Biology Department, Princeton University); Thomas E. Lovejoy (World Wildlife Fund, Washington); Ernst Mayr and Edward O. Wilson (Museum of Comparative Zoology, Harvard University); Kenneth R. McKaye and Svata Louda (Duke University Marine Station); Stephen H. Schneider (National Center for Atmospheric Research); Michael E. Soule (Center for Transcultural Studies); Kenneth E.F. Watt (Department of Zoology, University of California, Davis); and George M. Woodwell (Ecosystems Center, Marine Biological Laboratory, Woods Hole).

Anne Ehrlich, John Harte, John Holdren, Hal Mooney, and Steve Schneider have worked especially closely with me on the manuscript and their efforts are very much appreciated. Darryl Wheye of Stanford helped with various aspects of the project with her usual intelligence and efficiency.

This work was supported in part by a grant from the Koret Foundation of San Francisco.

14

Coming Home: The Urban Environment After Nuclear War

Kevin Lynch

Your country is desolate,
your cities are burned with fire:
your land; strangers devour it in your presence,
and it is desolate,
as overthrown by strangers.

Isaiah 1:7

The choice of debris clearance equipment and the clearance rates that can be attained also depend on the physical characteristics of the debris and its location with respect to the damaged structures and the area to be cleared. Except for tall slender structures that may be toppled, the major components of damaged structures outside the zone of total destruction will generally remain on the building site. Wood frame and wall-bearing masonry structures will either collapse in place or be shattered to strew rubble within and beyond the building bounds. Therefore the debris found off building sites outside the zone of total destruction will generally (but not entirely) be of the type that can be removed by ordinary earthmoving equipment and by hand labor.

The removal of debris remaining or building sites will be hindered by the damaged structures that are still standing. On the other hand, wood frame structures in various states of collapse, and the debris within these structures, will provide only minor difficulties to the removal operation. The removal of debris located within the bounds of steel frame structures that have been damaged or totally destroyed will be greatly hindered by the steel structural members; if these structural members are not removed first, the removal of debris must be carried out by hand. The removal of steel structural members is a piecemeal process. Cutting torches will be required to free the steel members for removal; such operations are very time consuming. . . .

272

At early times after the attack, debris clearance will generally be for the purpose of opening avenues for travel and transport. As stated earlier, this type of operation is ideally suited to bulldozing. Two or more heavy bulldozers, e.g., in the 40,000 lb. class, depending on the width of cleared path desired, operating "blade-to-blade" should be able to make a continuous run through the debris in the streets, spilling it to the sides for later removal. By skirting the zone of total destruction, these bulldozers can clear a swath through the diameter of the debris zone (20 miles for a 10 MT surface burst) in a single day. Because a large portion of the damage area is accessible at early times after the attack, and because the street clearing operation, with the proper equipment in the accessible areas, is rather rapid, this type of debris clearance is useful for operations such as the rescue and evacuation of trapped or non-ambulatory personnel from the damaged areas, as well as for the transport of emergency supplies and equipment. For the same reasons, a cleared narrower path may be useful for laying emergency power lines, emergency communications lines, or a temporary water pipeline. However, the bulk of debris clearance operations during the early postattack period will primarily support damage repair operations, and the emergency supplies and equipment requiring transport over cleared areas will generally be for this purpose.

Operations that require the removal of debris from the general locale are not normally considered to be of an emergency nature. The rate of this type of debris clearance is therefore not of paramount interest to this study. The rate that debris can be loaded into trucks depends on the characteristics of the debris and the tools and equipment available for debris loading. Where the debris consists of relatively fine rubble, the loading rate may be compared to that of loading small irregular aggregates—e.g., the rate of manual loading with a shovel may be estimated at 6 to 8 cubic yards per 8-hour day; also, the loading rate of a 1/2 yard front-end skid loader may be estimated at 200 cubic yards per 8-hour day.

As the size of rubble increases and the shapes become more ungainly and more awkward to handle manually or with light equipment, the loading rate by these methods, and consequently the removal rate, will be reduced. Efficient loading under these more difficult conditions requires the use of larger and more specialized debris handling equipment. Loading rates of 1,000 cubic yards a day are not unusual with heavy equipment.

Within the zone of total destruction, the collapse of steel-frame reinforced concrete structures will provide combinations of distorted and displaced steel members and entire sections of buildings as well as smaller sized debris. Thus, if the total destruction area were predominantly reinforced concrete structures, the type of debris described would be found both on the building site and off the building site. The removal of this type of debris would be very difficult and slow. The removal of debris on the building sites would be most difficult because of the greater number of steel members to be cut loose prior to removal.

SOURCE: Philip D. LaRiviere and Hong Lee, *Postattack Recovery of Damaged Urban Areas*, prepared for the Office of Civil Defense, Stanford Research Institute, Stanford, Calif., 1966, pp. 53, 54, and 55.

A few official studies have considered the world after a nuclear holocaust, when the survivors, shaken but resolute, come back to rebuild America. The thinking about this time at the end of the rainbow is peculiarly thin. Resettlement seems to be a technical problem, something compounded of heavy machines, roads, idle factories, power lines, debris, and such abstract factors as labor, money, food stocks, and managerial skill. But under such awesome conditions, what will resettlement mean to human beings? Who thinks about the links that develop between people and place and how grotesque those links might then become?

One lengthy, careful study[1] considers the likelihood of recovery of the economic system, given nuclear attacks of different dimensions. In the "best" case (one in which less than half of the nation's population might die), the survivors "would have no difficulty in supporting themselves" and in rebuilding the national economic system. This excludes, of course, any such "esoteric" effects as changes in the ecosystem after the burning over of more than 50 percent of the nation's surface and the widespread contamination of its soil and water.

These predictions explicitly put aside any "psychological or organizational effects." The study is a discussion of the *technical* limits of production, not of reality. People are considered to be factors like any other. Space is a nuisance, an "inappropriate distribution" of productive factors, a matter of transport costs.[2] The supreme problem, then, is to rebuild the nationwide market economy while preventing any lapse into barter, self-sufficiency, or the loss of work incentives.

A second report looks more directly at the problem of urban resettlement but does so through an even narrower aperture.[3] Given the probable physical damage in any urban area after a nuclear attack (damage that is described in exquisite detail), what would be the technical problems of clearing off the debris? Within 2.5 miles of ground zero, it would simply not be tried. Up to nine miles out, in the heavily built up zone, the debris might be twenty feet deep and full of steel beams and reinforced concrete, making it difficult to handle. But the main roads could be cleared and the other debris left until later. Any early rescue operation would not be feasible, of course, in all that rubble. However, the heavy machinery necessary to open the main roads and level the strategic locations could probably be recovered and set to work. Farther out, things would be easier.

The reader is left with two concrete images. The first one consists of two large bulldozers, working blade to blade, opening a twenty-foot swathe through the ruined city, pushing the layers of debris into two great ridges at the sides of the road. In the second image, we see a huge power shovel methodically eating away at those piles, loading them into waiting trucks, and thereby opening up a twenty-foot channel without creating great windrows at each edge. In one day, the shovel could clear forty feet; the bulldozers could clear twenty miles. The images are haunting: there is no one there but the big machines and heaps of smashed buildings.

In the final section of a third report, there is a brief consideration of the problem of rehousing the homeless after nuclear attack.[4] Once more, the study draws back from an unsettling reality. The question is reduced to a global, quantitative one: Would enough houses be left, somewhere in a metropolitan region, for the people that remain? The authors assume a "relatively light attack," consider only the larger U.S. metropolitan regions, and further assume that (as if due to the thoughtfulness of the attacker) no nearby regions would be hit if that would preempt houses needed for some larger region. Under those assumptions, they calculate that the survivors in the average U.S. metropolis could be settled in any remaining houses that had received radiation of 2,000 rems per hour or less, by moving these people sixty miles or less (transported how?), and by crowding them into those houses at up to four times the original occupancy rate. But people who move, two weeks after an attack, from shelters into houses that received, one hour after attack, fallout doses of 2,000 rems per hour, will themselves be irradiated by 100 rems per week, assuming protection factors of two and continual occupancy. This is sufficient to cause long-term effects, nausea, and lowered resistence to disease, but probably not sufficient, the authors postulate, to bring on the severe radiation sickness that requires immediate medical treatment. As the authors note, there will be some additional difficulties of allocation, of moving the survivors, and of deciding when to move, how far to move, and what level of contamination to expose people to.

We have two actual experiences of nuclear devastation: Hiroshima and Nagasaki. The record of those assaults focuses on the terrifying physical and medical consequences,[5] but it also has some information to our purpose: a brief account of the days immediately following the explosion and some material on its extended social and psychological effects.

The first days are only sketchily described, since no comprehensive records remain from that chaotic time. But the photographs and personal memories are stark and vivid. One sees the desert of burnt rubble, the blackened corpses and the wounded on the ground, the dazed and mutilated survivors wandering aimlessly over the terrain. Military teams came in early (telephone service for the army was restored on the first day), but they could do little beyond simple first aid and the burning and burying of the dead. Contrary to orders, people from outside streamed into the ruins, looking for kin and friends, even as others stumbled out.

The early entrants into the wreckage themselves fell prey to radiation sickness. A "black rain" fell shortly after the explosion, chilling the weakened people and carrying the radioactive dust back to the earth. Those days made a deep impression on all who survived them, as hundreds of diaries and drawings bear witness.

Almost every family in those two cities lost at least one member. Children remember the successive deaths of their parents and siblings. A blank, indifferent state of mind was followed by deep depression and a sense of guilt for surviving when so many had perished. Orphaned children suffered discrimination, drifted from odd jobs into delinquency, felt conspicuous for their deformities. The "orphaned elderly," bereft of kin, lived in makeshift shacks for years. Adult survivors lost their wealth and social connections and in time became laborers and petty employees, regardless of previous skill and position.

The charred trees sprouted from their roots, and new associations of herbs sprang up in the ruins, but it was a year before people began to return to the edges of the burned out area, and three years before houses were rebuilt. Even by this time, only 50 percent of the original population had resettled in Hiroshima. It was the Korean War that brought the city back to its former size.

The surrender of Japan, shortly after the attack, made it more difficult for the victims, since there then was no possibility of revenge. Their suffering had been converted into a senseless sacrifice. Subsequent suppression of information by the authorities made it difficult for survivors to understand what had happened to them or to find support for their confusions. Only as the antinuclear movement developed could they begin to work out their anger and fear and find common cause with others. They are still a marked group in the Japanese society. Many of them have moved away to other cities, perhaps to lose themselves in more anonymous surroundings.

The official reports, and others like them, have given no thought to the human experience, even as it will rebound directly on their management concerns. In particular, there is no conception of the role of *place*, of the intimate linkages that develop between people and their location.

The issue is neither abstruse nor trivial. To be an active human being, one must know where one is—be able to identify one's present location and know how to get to a neighboring place. Each place has its meanings, some superficial and some profound, that connect it to our everyday lives. This ordinary knowledge will strike back at us whenever we are lost. We are mobile, meaning-creating animals. If we cannot recognize places, know what they mean and how to move through them, we are helpless and disturbed.

It can be a pleasure to wander through a new city looking for surprises, but only if one is certain that a secure order of meaning and location underlies the novel form—that one can refer to a map, or ask one's way, or at least will in time come out on some recognizable feature, whence the way home is clear. To be lost in the woods is not fearful for a trained woodsman; he knows the signs of the woodland and the strategies for coming out. But to be truly lost, unable to recognize anything or any direction, brings us to panic and often to physical nausea.

Being truly lost is for most people an unusual experience, and normally only a temporary one, soon safely buried, if remembered with fear. We have too many resources to fall back upon, social as well as physical, should any one link be severed. In times of great stress, however, the physical environment provides an image of stability to which we will cling, in our grief and inner disorientation. It is our anchor until the inner storm subsides. This is well known in the experience of deep mourning and in neurotic or psychotic disturbance. But if the physical setting is disrupted at the very time that the inner storm is raging, the combined effect can be devastating. In calmer times the environment serves as a religious symbol, or the symbol of a joint culture, or the visible cement of some complex institution. What may seem to be no more than a pleasant landscape may have an important functional role.

In childhood we form deep attachments to the location in which we grew up and carry the image of this place with us for the remainder of our lives. Features of the childhood place have been shown to influence many later decisions—where to live or how to arrange the home, for example. Many people have suffered the shock of finding their childhood home obliterated by some recent development. Even for those long past childhood—effective adults well supplied with social and locational links— the shock is peculiarly disturbing. *Home* is a powerful idea, a fact of which real estate agents are well aware.

In old age, as active social links fall away, we are notoriously dependent on the stability of our physical surroundings. An abrupt move can literally kill an aged person unless it is carefully prepared for and softened by the carriage of personal property and the maintenance of social ties.

Great waves of immigrants have poured into this country. Even when they came voluntarily, they felt the pain of separation. Immigrants dream about home while they struggle to find a place for themselves in the confusion of a new world. Where they can, they settle in landscapes like those they left or reshape places to resemble the lost ones. They never forget "the old country," however miserable their existence there may have been. For the remainder of their lives, most of them never feel that the new country is truly home. And yet these were willing migrants, in the main, coming *to* a place that had meaning and opportunity—a country that they were proud to be part of. They could return if they wished, or at least they thought they could. For many Africans, of course, none of this was true, and the pain and fear of the kidnapping has carried down through the generations.

While we are accustomed to the presence of migrating people (and "looking for roots" is one of our commonplace expressions), we are not familiar with any situation in which *everyone* is uprooted—none willingly, all under stress and without hope of return. Nomadic tribes move en masse, but they keep their social ties intact. It is true enough that a tidal wave of displaced refugees is now sweeping the world, but many of them have maintained their essential social connections or have been able to reestablish them in the camps, where they are supported by outside services. Yet disorientation persists, and effective production is poor.

Major disasters give us some further insight into the role of place. A great fire, earthquake, or inundation will cause much damage and suffering, but society can be reknit if the people and their connections survive: if they still have kin and institutions, if they can return to a familiar landscape. When everyone returns to a customary, recognizable place, they begin from a solid base. Thus the typical rush to return by an evacuated population and its stubborn insistence on rebuilding a place "just as it was." London after the Great Fire and Warsaw after its razing by the Nazis are well-know examples of this phenomenon.

But where the home place has been poisoned—when it is too dangerous to resettle or has been obliterated or made unrecognizable— then the trauma can be deep and lasting. In the Buffalo Creek disaster in West Virginia, a ruptured dam loosed a tidal wave of sludge down a narrow mountain valley. Residents yearning to return were held back by the fear of being trapped in another rush of debris. Those who did go back were always aware of the close valley walls and the single exit far downstream. Many remained afraid to go outside. Their familiar valley had become a place of menace; they were caught between attachment and abandonment.

Making a new place in the wilderness—the recurrent American image that may seem appropriate to the reoccupation of our cities after a holocaust—is a serious business. It involves far more than a functional modification of the landscape. The wild place must be made psychologically safe and familiar: cleared of danger, bounded, named, oriented, given a center, planted and furnished with familiar things. This is a protracted, demanding task requiring the taming of the land and the reorientation of how the newcomers see and feel about the land. Many rituals of blessing and of town founding are used for just that purpose. It is only the second or third generation that begin to feel entirely safe and at home.

Settlement is more disturbing if the ground is studded with the evidence of a previous occupation. The ground must then be conquered and purified. There are frequent historical episodes of razing earlier symbols and of occupying old sites with dominant new symbols. Until the land is psychologically secured, people are uneasy. Interest in the previous remains comes later. To wipe out an enemy, one does not stop with murder; one razes their place as well. Geocide is auxiliary to genocide.

So the role of space in human affairs is far more than the economist's "location space" or "spatial friction," far more than the Cartesian space of the engineer within which machines work on materials. The sense of place is a human experience and will be a crucial ingredient in any resettlement after a nuclear holocaust. To foresee the nature of that experience, we must draw on all these previous experiences: of disaster and immigration, childhood and old age, neurosis and mourning, genocide, refugee camps and place making in the wilderness. Yet coming home after a widespread nuclear war will be unique—not only for its terrifying magnitude but also for the heightened interaction of so many negative features.

It will be a return to a poisoned home, and people will be caught between fear and desire to return. The home place will have been shattered and survivors will know it to be tainted with radiation by the malice of the enemy, and the enemy might return. The environment will be shapeless, largely unrecognizable, bereft of orientation, and yet vast. Most social ties will have been broken by death and the confusion of evacuation and relocation. Ethnic groups will look on each other with suspicious hostility, and government will have lost its legitimacy. There will be no support from outside, since there will *be* no outside. Technically, the survivors are returning, yet psychologically return is impossible. Home is gone; there is no going back to it. Nor is one going to some organized place. The destination is all grey, shapeless, home and not home—a strange, dangerous, uneasy, confusing place.

Survivors will have to cope with this as best they can, but it will be another burden to add to all the medical, social, economic, and technical burdens they must carry. Even in a callous sense, one cannot manipulate these "labor factors" without thought for the interaction of laborer, place, and society. Such an analysis is unreal, not just inhumane. Experiences of this intensity are unpredictable, but one can at least make an attempt to imagine oneself there:

* * * * * *

We had walked in from Northfield. Much of the countryside had been burned away, but I knew the general direction to the city, and we found the main road. Others were moving with us, since orders to return had been announced. Everyone seemed too tired to be dangerous. A few were coming the other way. We asked them why and got confused answers.

We had already decided to return, when we came out of our burrow. Northfield was hostile to the refugees, and the locals had gotten control of the food supply. They said that there was food and work in the city, it was time to get out. I was glad to go, but my older son was sure that it was still too dangerous in the city and said that he would join us later. We appointed a rendezvous, but the place we named proved to be unrecognizable. I never knew what became of him, after the city people had gone.

Closer in, the smashed buildings had been cleared off the road. By then, a file of people were walking between the piles of debris. Here and there, there were temporary signs pointing to different headquarters. It was like a silent battlefield.

I wasn't sure where I was: probably some northern suburb. It had been my intention to put up a shelter on our own land, but now I knew that I would not find it easily. Everything was covered with shapeless, broken, burnt debris. The few cleared roads were marked with strange numbers. At times, these tracks followed old streets, at others they ran over broken foundations. One cracked pavement looked like another, and, since the sky was overcast, I had no sense of direction. I tried to remember the shape of the ground, but without the buildings and streets I could not connect the litter with my memories of shops and houses and different districts. I had never seen this ground before. An old street sign on a wooden pole said Broadway, which was a street I knew. But how could it be on this side of town? It occurred to me that it might be a joke.

Eventually, we came to a cleared space by the side of the road, where some boards and canvas had been set up to keep off the wind and the rain. We settled there for the time. There was a water tank, and we scavenged in the ruins for some lumber and plastic to patch our roof and make a partition around ourselves.

A mile down the road they were clearing away a shattered building. If you were there early you got bread, cheese, and coffee for helping to lift and load the beams and wall fragments. We worked slowly enough, not very sure what we were doing. The work seemed pointless.

Day and night we could hear the crash of the big machines working nearby, chewing away at the trash, making a clearing or a new road. It wasn't obvious to me which roads led out of the city and which ran in, or if any of them went to any particular place. The world had lost its shape, but luckily the sun still gave me directions. I had a map of the old city, and I worked evenings with it to puzzle out where we might be.

Perhaps it had been a mistake to come. Northfield was hostile, but it was real and recognizable. We had food here and were out of our hole, but we were nowhere, drifting with other people we hardly spoke to.

There were little signs posted here and there, asking about someone who had disappeared. I never found a familiar name. The loose piles of wreckage could shift suddenly when we were out on them. If our shoes wore out, it would be difficult to walk over the sharp-edged trash, so we tied on pieces of wood or rubber to make them last.

We knew that the ground was radioactive, but now how much. What effect was it having on us? We watched for nausea and looked for dark patches on our skin. Once a soldier went by, holding a dosimeter, but he would not tell us what it read. Official communications had been reestablished, but we lived in two worlds as far as information was concerned. Officials used telephones, radios, printed reports, computers. We lived on rumors, handwritten notices, graffiti, and public proclamations. We went hungry for news. Maps and papers were luxuries. I remember that a man came by with a camera, taking pictures of us and our camp. He must have been from some newspaper, though I had never seen one. They smashed his camera, not wanting any pictures taken, and I was just as glad.

Our world was our clearing and the road that passed it by, just as if we lived in the wilderness. From time to time, we moved to some new clearing, closer to work or food, or because they told us to move on. I can't remember all those places, not that they were better or worse. Some people moved out to the far edge of the city, where there were houses still standing. Others came back, because the houses were crowded with strangers, and there was no work nearby. Just south of us, a small group—perhaps they were old neighbors who had found each other—decided to settle on a piece of land. They cleared a lane around it, and then a central street. They marked each corner with stones, and put up a large stone at the entrance. They found a priest and made a procession around their bounds, saying a prayer at every mark. They cut the date on the entrance stone, and so declared the land their own.

I was determined to find our own land. I had a strategy: find the river, which must still be recognizable, and go up it until I reached the place where our street ran down the saddle between two hills. Once that close, I was sure that I could find the clues. So I worked up and down the network of cleared roads, counting turns and distances so that I could make my way back. And I came on the river, full of debris, wandering out of its banks, but still flowing. It was difficult to move along it. There were small hills, or perhaps piles of wreckage, but in the end I came to a familiar slope. When I searched over the rubbish, I found a familiar street corner, exposed by the blast, and then a slate from our neighbor's roof. With that, I located our lot, and I was home.

We moved some bulky things off the top of the litter and packed loose rubbish into the holes. Perched up above the old ground, we put up our poles and roof. It was an uneasy foundation since I did not know what was beneath us. When the city was first evacuated, I had reached my sons at work, but I never found my wife and small daugher. Perhaps they had succeeded in joining each other, perhaps not. Perhaps they were buried in the trash on which we camped.

I could not be sure just how our street ran, but we marked it out as well as we could. Then we laid out our lot, since I didn't want to encroach on my neighbor's land. None of our neighbors had returned, however, and it annoyed me that others camping nearby thought that this was some other street. We argued over the clues and landmarks. But I dug a hole down to the old ground at one point. I felt that I must touch it somewhere. I found the burnt stump of our apple tree, and it released a flood of memories.

Now I felt in place again, and I could look for permanent work. Up till then, I had worked at whatever casual job turned up. Now I looked more systematically, and yet I could never find work where I could use my former experience. Sometimes I heard of such jobs, but they were far away, or their location uncertain. I did not have the energy to chase after them, and so I descended to the unskilled labor that I could find. We stole our food when we could. Organized gangs worked on a larger scale, ambushing convoys or raiding supply dumps to supply the black market.

We had to walk some distance now, over and through the trash, to reach water, food, and even fuel, since the firestorm had burned over this area. To find our way through the waste, we made new landmarks out of odd fragments and gave them names and shapes and histories. Gradually, the cleared roads were being extended to connect the workplaces, camps, and depots. The city was slowly taking on a form: clumps of sheds, clearings in the rubble. When we gave directions, we used turnings and small details, which might shift from day to day. All the historic places were gone. Even the natural features were dismembered. Sometimes I thought of the old view down the river valley but could not connect it to the blocked and flooded land, and the memory of what it once was like was beginning to escape me. I saw desolation.

The city center was Ground Zero, an absolute emptiness, still dangerous to enter, but seemed to draw us as if it were a black hole in space. Cold, wet, and mud were our commonplaces, and so we dreamed about smooth clean floors. Waste water ran down the streets, since the sewers were blocked. People relieved themselves on the debris, or at times in the gutter, like dogs. There were epidemics, and illnesses. People were still dying, one by one, leaving their children or their old ones to go on alone. Unidentified bodies occasionally appeared, and space for proper burial was hard to find. Our cemeteries were buried; we were cut off even from our dead.

"Before the bomb" was long ago, a time that had hardly left a trace. We could not describe it even to ourselves. Any structure saved by some quirk of the explosion, any tree still living, took on an immense importance. We lived in a timeless, endless wasteland and slept on the buried past. Where were the old names? Weren't there hidden dangers down below? We had to develop a science of places: signs of power or safety that could be read in the remains. Some people said that the streets were safe enough, if you kept off the debris. Others said that everything was radioactive. We all knew some specials signs of danger: where rust had flaked off the steel and exposed the bare metal, then you kept your distance. A peculiar weed with spiked, downy leaves was known to thrive in hot spots. We refused to work where such signs appeared. We felt the presence of the enemy, whose power and malice had made all this. Would he come again? Should we stay or go? There were frightening and enticing rumors about other cities.

Surveyors began to lay their invisible lines along the roads. Some squatters paid them bonuses, to confirm their land. When they came to us they found (was it true?) that we were not where we had thought, not even in the same district. For me, it was as if the ground were jerked away. Hills were valleys, and valleys hills; we were in a different city. I felt a confusion of the senses, and that night I was ill again.

As soon as I was up, we moved down to a more convenient, nameless clearing. Then my son said that he was sick of this aimless life, and that he would just walk out to see what was outside. I never saw him again, nor any other member of my family.

So then, it was clear that I would live alone, in empty places. The future went with a flash, and the past was gone. When there was a call for labor to clear destroyed cities overseas, I left without looking back. I could dig out the rubble of a strange city, with all my heart.

* * * * * *

All the above is imaginary, or, to give it a more dignified name, it is a "scenario"—one that emphasizes only a single factor. But imagination may be all we have to use in thinking about stress at such levels, in such a synergism of negative influences. The survivors who return to rebuild production will not only be ill and exhausted; not only lacking in information, shelter, power, and food; not only be separated from their kin, or have seen them die or left them to die. They will have been twice uprooted, subject to further random moves, returning and yet unable to return, since home will be unrecognizable. There will be hostility in the "host" area, and unknown dangers in the burned out city. The city itself will be a chaotic landscape of rubbish—disorienting and without discernible parts. It will be a junkyard and will communicate all that deep aversion in our culture for waste and excrement. It will utterly fail to convey any of that sense of exterior stability so important for people under stress. There will be no outside support moving in to deal with the disaster and no undamaged environment outside. *All* the land will be devastated; everyone will be uprooted.

The survivors will come back to a pulverized, poisoned place and be subject to conflicting emotions of attachment and flight. Clearance will be difficult; for long periods there will be no firm floor underfoot. Beneath the rubble there will be dead bodies, some of them abandoned kin and friends. The psychologically necessary operations of purifying and reclaiming the ground will come slowly. All sacred and meaningful landmarks will have disappeared, and the fear of hidden danger will be reinforced by the fear of renewed attack. These pathologies of place are only additions to all the social and biological stress survivors will encounter. Our fantasy hardly alludes to those other stresses and, thus, it underplays the effect. Anger and alienation may be the best that can be hoped for. For those that remain alive that will be the "healthy" reaction. Only after people have been reduced to that level of despair can they act their part as that neutral, mobile, "labor factor," on which the economic calculation of recovery depends.

Even if we should forget how people will feel, the destruction of place raises serious difficulties for management, on top of all the expected problems of epidemics and food, shelter, and transportation shortages; puzzles of restarting production; finding energy and material resources; directing resettlement; dilemmas of distribution; problems of control. The survivors will be frantic or numbed. They will settle where they should not and shift on rumor. They will have irrational perceptions of places, get lost, and consume time in aimless travel. Authority will be in doubt, official information discounted, rumors abundant. Social disorder, violence, theft, and the wastage of resources may be expected. There may be a tendency to underoccupy the built up city and to squat in the outer fringes, where there is cleared space and some surviving buildings. Transportation and the linkage of labor and production will then be a greater burden. Fuel will be scarce, and usable buildings will be picked apart and burned. Many other disturbances of the recovery process may be imagined. Recovery may not be possible.

The distant results of these dislocations are unfathomable. Would survivors stay for long in the burned areas? How would their underlying attitudes toward the land and toward each other shift? Would the nation become, in the minds of its people, that "dark and bloody ground" that the Cherokee prophesized for us? What would be the repercussions on common neuroses, on childhood, on the family, on our sense of past and future, and on a thousand other things? I cannot answer these questions precisely. But to analyze the reoccupation of cities as if it were an economic redistribution, or a clearing of debris from the streets, or even an heroic resettlement of the wilderness, is surely a stupendous error.

15

The Second Death: Psychological Survival After Nuclear War

Robert Jay Lifton, Eric Markusen, and
Dorothy Austin

Therefore shall the land mourn,
and everyone that dwelleth therein
shall languish.

Hosea 4:3

Generalized disasters—catastrophes encompassing whole societies—are exemplified by destructive wars, famines, revolutions, and pestilences. In the past these have ordinarily taken months or years of time to develop their full effects. Nuclear war would probably combine the suddenness usually characteristic of localized disasters with an enormous scale of generalized effect. So each of the two historical types of calamity is of some revelance.

Economic recovery from localized bombing attacks has, in general, been quite remarkable. In Hiroshima, for example, power was generally restored to surviving areas on the day after the attack, and through railroad service recommenced on the following day. By mid-1949 population was back to the pre-attack level, and 70% of the destroyed buildings had been reconstructed. In general, populations of damaged areas have been highly motivated to stay on, even in the presence of severe deprivation; once having fled, they have been anxious to return. The thesis has even been put forward that a community hit by disaster rebounds so as to attain higher levels of achievement than would otherwise have been possible. While this cannot be proved from the historical record, it is clear that there is a strong tendency to return to previous levels and growth trends. This evidence suggests that disaster in some way liberates springs of energy and unselfish activity not ordinarily called upon in periods of normalcy.

The historical record is not so clear for the larger-scale, slower-developing generalized catastrophes. Cases in recent history are few, and so particularized by special circumstances that it is difficult to draw firm conclusions. Over the broad sweep of history, however, the experience has been on the whole again surprisingly favorable. In the mid-19th century John Stuart Mill commented on:

> ... what has so often excited wonder, the great rapidity with which countries recover from a state of devastation; the disappearance, in a short time, of all traces of the mischiefs done by earthquakes, floods, hurricanes, and the ravages of war. An enemy lays waste a country by fire and sword, and destroys or carries away nearly all the moveable wealth existing in it: all the inhabitants are ruined, and yet in a few years after, everything is much as it was before.

And in the twentieth century the industrial recoveries of Germany and Japan since World War II have continued to excite wonder, as has the impressive progress of Russia despite revolution and exceptionally destructive wars.

SOURCE: Jack Hirshleifer, *Economic Recovery*, Rand Corporation, Santa Monica, California, August 1965, pp. 3–4.

Now picture the U.S. one or two weeks after the attack: The 50 percent of the population that has survived can no longer be described with a high degree of accuracy. There has not been time to acquire reliable census or other statistical data.

However, based on years of research prior to the attack certain assumptions can be made:

> [Among them is:] Widespread panic has *not* occurred. The general behavior pattern among the survivors is adaptive rather than maladaptive. By and large people can be counted on to participate constructively in future efforts to achieve national recovery goals. They will continue to do so as long as there appears to be a leadership that has a plan and knows what it is doing. People will contribute as long as their efforts do not appear wasteful. This behavior pattern assumes that individuals are provided an assured supply of the basic requisites for existence—food, water, shelter, etc.—for themselves and their families.

SOURCE: Defense Civil Preparedness Agency, *Research Report on Recovery from Nuclear Attack*, Information Bulletin No. 307, U.S. Government Printing Office, Washington, D.C., May 10, 1979, pp. 8–10.

A form of shock reaction, called a "disaster syndrome," has sometimes been observed in the aftermath of relatively sudden and extensive disasters. This reaction involves an apathetic response and some disorientation in thinking. However, the "disaster syndrome" does not appear in great numbers of people; seems confined only to the most sudden traumatic kinds of disasters; has been reported only in certain cultural settings; and is generally of short duration, hours only, if not minutes. . . .

In general, disaster victims react in an active manner, and do not wait around for assistance by outsiders or offers of aid from organizations.

SOURCE: Russell R. Dynes, E.L. Quarantelli, and Gary A. Kreps, *A Perspective on Disaster Planning*, prepared for the Defense Civil Preparedness Agency, Washington, D.C., December 1972, p. 20.

A discussion of the psychological dimensions of survival after nuclear war must begin by acknowledging the limits of our understanding. Reports differ on how people behave in disaster situations, and we do not know how previous experience, even if adequately analyzed, might apply in the setting of nuclear war. Much has been written about the psychology of human beings in disasters, but the literature is unevenly relevant.[1]

Because of the singular capacity to destroy both the human and natural environments, nuclear war constitutes a disaster very different from those previously experienced. From the practical standpoint of delivering relief, nuclear war obliterates the reality, relied upon always in the past, of outside aid. Victims who survive will, in the main, have to take care of themselves. This all-encompassing characteristic of nuclear war has significant consequences for the psychological responses of survivors because, from what we can discern in the disaster literature, psychological recovery is closely linked to the speed and abundance of relief.[2]

This destructive capacity of nuclear war might exert other psychological effects as well. Students of normal psychology, observing how normal human beings derive a sense of self-definition and stability in the world, have found consistently that there is no self without attachment. Human beings attain definition by interacting with other people and the natural environment. We apprehend ourselves only as situated in the world. We are raised in families, and we learn and validate patterns of behavior in the context of social groupings.[3] We perceive the outside we inhabit. The landscape of our mind reflects the geography of the world. Nuclear war, in the totality of its effects, can be seen as destroying the matrix of relationships that make us human: our families, our communities, our urban, rural, and wilderness environments. From this psychological perspective, dislocation, flight, and shelter—although they might all appear stratagems that in certain cases would secure short-term biological survival—will do nothing, in the setting of nuclear war, to ensure the persistence of humanness. Wrenched from the matrix that creates meaning, people may well cease to function as caring and conscious beings. To the questions raised already, we would add our concern that nuclear war might tear apart the background we now take for granted: the contextual relationships that confer our sense of ourselves.

In our ignorance we are asked to evaluate assertions about population adaptability in the civil defense research on nuclear war. Based on references to previous disasters, it is posited that in the time period surrounding a nuclear war Americans will remain calm, law abiding, rational, and orderly; come to the aid of others; forge a sense of community in relocated sheltered situations; and retain sufficient psychological stamina to embark on the effort of rebuilding American society.[4]

The literature on disasters contains a wide range of information from which data can be drawn to support any point of view. It is evident that many researchers have attempted to articulate the conditions that favor adaptive responses and those in which nonadaptive symptoms and behavior supervene. The data appear to be more complex than the upbeat civil defense reading would have us believe. Differences in the duration, scope, or type of calamity, and their consequent effects on psychological adaptation, have not been given sufficient attention by FEMA. Nor has an attempt been made to evaluate in any structured, cumulative sense how the psychological effects seen in previous disasters might be shaped by the multiple, interactive disasters wrought by nuclear war.

In extrapolating from these insights to the scope of destruction after nuclear war, we can begin to raise relevant questions about the probable psychological states of survivors and their relative competence in the face of the stresses imposed by their surroundings.

In his review of the psychosocial effects of disasters, Frederick Hocking suggests an important principle in the relationship between stress and psychological health:

> The common tendency to divide people into "normal" and "predisposed" on the basis of their reaction to a particular stress is a piece of post hoc reasoning that is meaningless and illogical unless one has some indication of the type and degree of stress involved. . . . [A]s the degree of stress becomes more severe, an increasing proportion of individuals break down, so that if the stress is sufficiently intense, virtually all people will develop what would be, in an everyday setting, neurotic symptoms.[5]

Another theme in studies of numerous disasters of disparate types is that the best psychological outcomes are associated with the most rapid and attentive influx of help from outside the disaster area. Put negatively, increasing the time the survivors must spend in disaster limbo decreases their chances of healthy psychological recovery. It is clear that in the event of a nuclear war, there will be no outside therapeutic community with which a survivor can process his experience and reintegrate. There will be no unaffected healers.

Other recurrent factors noted in the literature that influence the degree of ongoing psychological sequelae include: the amount of actual horror experienced by the individual; the extent of displacement from community; the degree of separation from family members; the extent to which necessity forces departure from familiar patterns of daily life, and the duration, severity, and scope of the disaster-imposed stress. In each instance, the conditions caused by nuclear war would lead one to assign to survivors the poorest prognosis for short- and long-term adaptability.

Finally, another factor noted in the literature, which perhaps would not be immediately deducible as significant, is that psychological recovery is impaired if survivors perceive the disaster at hand as "manmade." In settings where human agency is seen to be at fault, observers have found that survivors harbor widespread feelings of betrayal by those whom they trusted. The spiral of resulting recrimination substantially undermines whatever community spirit remained.[6]

In reviewing those instances where survivors of severe disasters have been most extensively studied, we have found that an abiding and powerful variable is the continuity of life structures. If the disaster was perceived as having destroyed the physical and social community, whether or not its extent was geographically limited and help arrived rapidly, the psychological response of survivors was significantly impaired. Anthony Wallace described the psychological effects of the 1953 Worcester tornado, which in one minute leveled a two-mile-square area and left 66 dead, 738 injured, and 1,200 homeless.[7] Although help from the surrounding city began to arrive within thirty minutes of the impact:

> The precipitating factor in the disaster syndrome seems to be a perception ... that practically the entire visible community is in ruins. The sight of a ruined community, with houses, churches, trees, stores, and everything wrecked, is apparently often consciously or unconsciously interpreted as a destruction of the whole world. Many persons, indeed, actually were conscious of, and reported, this perception in interviews, remarking that the thought had crossed their minds that "this was the end of the world," "an atom bomb had dropped," "the universe had been destroyed," etc. The objects with which he has identification, and

to which his behavior is normally tuned, have been removed. He has been suddenly shorn of much of the support and assistance of a culture and a society upon which he depends and from which he draws sustenance; he has been deprived of the instrumentalities by which he has manipulated his environment; he has been, in effect, castrated, rendered impotent, separated from all sources of support, and left naked and alone, without a sense of his identity, in a terrifying wilderness of ruins.[8]

There are indications throughout the disaster literature that, at stress levels incomparably less than what might lie ahead, the human response has faltered and even collapsed. We draw on the following case studies to suggest that we can only hold to the view of nuclear war as a manageable insult if we avoid looking closely at the parameters that in the past have determined human response to major catastrophe and shy away from confronting the distinctive destructiveness of nuclear war.

BUFFALO CREEK, WEST VIRGINIA

In the Buffalo Creek Flood of 1972, an avalanche of coal sludge and debris thundered down the Appalachian hollow and within two hours killed 125 people and left nearly 5,000 homeless. The National Guard arrived hours later and a massive relief effort ensued.[9] Studied extensively by psychiatrists, psychologists, and sociologists, Buffalo Creek survivors provide us with data of particular relevance in attempting to look at patterns of psychological response to disaster. Although of comparatively limited scope and impact, and although response from outside arrived swiftly, this disaster precipitated an intense, pervasive, and prolonged reaction among survivors.

Significant to that response was the fact that the disaster was seen as manmade. Two psychiatrists who evaluated family problems in the aftermath of the flood noted the following:

Every disaster places man at the mercy of forces beyond his control. The feeling of being a pawn of fate is dehumanizing—people feel without appeal, beyond empathy, and cannot be persuaded or assuaged. When the catastrophe is man-made, dehumanization is magnified. In Buffalo Creek, there was the terrible realization that other human beings had planned, built, and maintained an unsound dam and then acted irresponsibly and uncaringly in the resulting disaster. . . . It destroyed pride and joy in being human.[10]

Another report on the disaster observed: "One is again reminded of the general principle mentioned earlier that the more a survivor of a disaster perceives the experience to reflect human callousness (rather than an act of nature or God), the more severe and long lasting are the psychological effects."[11]

Severe psychosocial problems among survivors persisted for years. One study found that many remained listless, apathetic, and less social. They tended to cling to the immediate circle of their own families, to lack ambition, and to lose interest in hobbies and sports. They seemed to have no interest in work or recreation and to despair of ever regaining the lifestyle they once had enjoyed.[12]

Lifton and Olson, in their study of Buffalo Creek survivors, concluded that "the consistent psychological pattern in Buffalo Creek has been a sequence beyond protest or hope, coalescing into a lasting despair. . . . In Buffalo Creek we found despair to be especially widespread and to include a chronic form of depression and a sense that things would never change."[13]

Erikson's sociological study of Buffalo Creek provides a perspective on how the disaster affected the social system. By destroying the hollow, resulting in a situation where "the victims outnumbered the nonvictims by so large a margin that the community itself has to be counted a casualty,"[14] the disaster inflicted a form of "collective trauma":

> By collective trauma, I mean a blow to the tissues of social life that damages the bonds linking people together and impairs the prevailing sense of communality. The collective trauma works its way slowly and even insidiously into the awareness of those who suffer from it; thus it does not have the quality of suddenness usually associated with the word "trauma." It is, however, a form of shock—a gradual realization that the community no longer exists as a source of nurturance and that a part of the self has disappeared.[15]

Collective trauma exacerbates and prolongs the effects of individual trauma. Erikson described several behavioral patterns expressed "by almost everyone in the valley," including demoralization, disorientation, and loss of connection. Demoralization among the survivors was expressed "both in the sense that they have lost much personal morale and in the sense that they have lost (or so they fear) most of their moral anchors."[16] On the communal level, demoralization was expressed in an apparent increase in deviant behavior and in increased suspicion toward one another. The divorce rate increased sharply following the disaster. As Erikson noted:

> The general problem people have in maintaining intimate ties with others extends beyond marriage, beyond families, across the whole hollow. The complaint is heard everywhere that people can no longer get along warmly. Whether people feel distressed because old neighbors seem reluctant to approach them or because they themselves cannot

mobilize the energy or confidence to approach others, the situation is difficult.[17]

In general, people all over the hollow live with a lasting sense of being out of place, uprooted, torn loose from their moorings, and this feeling has long outlasted the initial trauma of the disaster itself.[18]

STRATEGIC BOMBING DURING WORLD WAR II

Studies of conventional bombing of cities during World War II and records of postwar recovery have been used as evidence of population resilience in stressful circumstances.[19] In assessing the relevance of this conventional wartime experience to the setting of nuclear war, it is important to note that in the six years of the war, the destructive potential of all bombs delivered on all sites totaled three million tons, or three megatons. The nuclear war postulated in government scenarios would deliver over 2,000 times that amount, in a very brief time, to the United States alone. Given this disparity in scale, it is especially noteworthy that studies conducted in the immediate aftermath of the war indicate that the individual and social stress caused by the bombings were highly significant. The subsequent recovery of these devastated urban areas and the eventual reconstruction of communities were possible only because of the enormous and sustained infusion of outside assistance. Whether such recovery could have been accomplished without such aid remains an open question.

Between 1940 and 1945, Germany dropped a total of 74,172 tons of bombs on the United Kingdom. During the same period, the Allies dropped nearly 2 million tons of bombs on Germany.[20] As one historian of the war describes it: "The object of the bombing was in the end to bring as large an amount of destruction as cheaply as possible to the enemy homelands, indiscriminately against military and civilian targets."[21] Both high-explosive and incendiary bombs were used. The latter were most effective in creating huge firestorms that reduced the urban landscape to a smoldering rubble and killed people in bomb shelters through a combination of heat and asphyxiation.

The overall physical effects of bombing on Germany were summarized by the United States Strategic Bombing Survey:[22]

Killed	305,000
Wounded	780,000
Homes Destroyed	1,865,000
Persons Evacuated	4,885,000
Persons deprived of utilities	20,000,000

Even greater death and destruction were caused by bombing in Japan:

> As a result of the American air offensive against Japan, 500 separate
> targets were bombed and an average of 43 percent of Japan's 66 largest
> cities were destroyed. More than two-thirds of the civilian population
> experienced air raids, and more than one-third personally experienced
> bombing ... approximately 1,300,000 people were injured and approxi-
> mately 900,000 killed as a result of bombings. Bombing, or the threat of
> bombing, resulted in mass disruption of the lives of countless millions of
> people, including the evacuation of more than 8,500,000 persons from
> cities.[23]

Extending their observations beyond the physical consequences of
the bombings, the U.S. survey team sought as well to describe the
psychological state these bombings had produced among the different
populations affected. They found that, among the Japanese:

> In addition to enormous physical destruction, the strategic bombing of
> the home islands produced great social and psychological disruption
> and contributed to securing surrender prior to the planned invasion.[24]

> The primary reaction to bombing was abject fear and confusion. People
> felt helpless in the face of the raids and could only seek shelter. Few
> remained behind to combat the fires. While some became better adapted
> to continued raids, most civilians either feared them more than ever or
> simply resigned themselves to fate.[25]

This fear or resignation applied to other populations as well:

> Bombing seriously depressed the morale of German civilians. Its main
> psychological effects were defeatism, fear, hopelessness, fatalism and
> apathy. War weariness, willingness to surrender, loss of hope for
> German victory, distrust of leaders, feelings of disunity and demoraliz-
> ing fear were all more common among bombed than unbombed
> people.[26]

> These apathetic reactions were so typical of both English and German
> populations that experienced air raids that physicians in both countries,
> Survey investigators reported, described the Second World War as the
> "war of the vegetative neurosis."[27]

The death and destruction caused by the bombings had a disruptive
impact on the general society—affecting both those who were directly
bombed and those who witnessed the events at some distance. As the
Strategic Bombing Survey Team concluded:

> Continued military adversity is like a cancer in the social body—it attacks
> the whole thing. ... A social event does not make itself felt in a single

direction; rather it is like a stream, with many branches above and below the ground. Shortage of food not only makes man hungry, but causes him to want to seek the food of his neighbor or to turn upon his leaders in anger. The destruction of houses not only puts people out into the cold, but throws them upon the mercies of those whose houses are not destroyed, and directs them to the authorities to ask for help. As adversity grows in magnitude, therefore, the bonds of human relationship are strained. At a certain point they snap.[28]

THE NAZI CONCENTRATION CAMPS

The psychological experience and adjustment of survivors of Nazi death camps stand as awesome historical examples of multifaceted catastrophe. In our effort to anticipate psychosocial problems faced by survivors of nuclear war, an examination of attributes of the death camps that hold particular relevance includes: the large-scale slaughter of millions of people in horrific ways and the fact that only a small proportion survived; the chronic psychological and physical stress coupled with the constant specter of death through time; the long-term absence of an outside world, preventing provision of even rudimentary relief; and return and attempted re-entry to a war-ravaged European world. In spite of eventual release and healing of physical wounds, permanent psychic changes this disaster wrought among survivors have been extensively documented. Since most survivors lost members of their families in the mass killings, surviving victims were seen to carry a double burden: "First, the actual loss, terror, and grief experienced through the impact of the disaster and the extermination of their loved ones; second, the ever present feeling of guilt, accompanied by conscious and unconscious dread of punishment, for having survived the very calamity to which these loved one succumbed."[29]

Lifton has called this "paradoxical guilt" because the victim may experience more of a *psychological* sense of guilt than does the *morally* guilty perpetrator. However widespread that tendency—there is much controversy about it—there is little doubt about the burden of grotesque death imagery survivors carry within them.

A consistent "concentration camp survivor syndrome" has been identified: increased fatigability, failing memory, inability to concentrate restlessness, irritability, emotional lability, disordered sleep, headache, and other vegetative symptoms. This constellation of chronic anxiety and severe depression with recurrent themes of guilt and concomitant physiological changes has been found to persevere through time and represents the final adaptation of many survivors. According to Leo Eitinger, "the effects of captivity are so deep that the vulnerability of the victims remains increased and full recovery does not appear to be possible. The limited sentences that internment in a concentration or prison camp involved have thus become lifelong sentences, affecting both the prisoners' life spans and their health if not their freedom."[30]

The profound depression is associated with inconsolable feelings of despair and meaninglessness. As Bychowski described it:

> If we now try to approach the structure of this depression, applying the existential point of view, we see a picture characterized by the destruction of his world, the destruction of the basic landmarks on which the world of human beings in our civilization is based, i.e. basic trust in human worth, basic confidence, basic hope. Here there is no trust, there is no confidence, everything has been shattered to pieces.[31]

During their concentration camp ordeals, survivors were prone to a kind of "psychic closing off" against the overwhelming pain within and around them. While repression and denial are the most common and the most primitive defenses during periods of intense stress, it is clear that this "psychic numbing" continues to be active in many survivors. They have been unable to work through this trauma and restructure their personality to take this experience into account. Bettleheim, in his essay "Surviving," examines the nature of the adjustments that he and other survivors have made. He cautions the observer to look beneath superficial signs of adjustment to family and work, suggesting that even those victims who no longer show outward signs of the concentration camp survivor syndrome continue to expend energy to keep all feeling and meaning at some psychic distance. He explains that as they continue to deny the impact and meaning of their ordeal, survivors remain haunted that any deep, intense experience might expose the relatively empty existence they are leading.[32] The emptiness he describes is reminiscent of the projection that Lifton and Erikson make about the feeling state of nuclear war survivors: "The question so often asked, 'Would the survivors envy the dead?' may turn out to have a simple answer. They would not so much envy as, inwardly and outwardly, resemble the dead."[33]

In drawing conclusions from what we understand about survivors of concentration camps to help guide our estimates of the aftermath of nuclear war, we must remain aware of an important distinction between the two situations. For the survivors of the death camps, as catastrophic as these camps were and as seemingly endless as the experience proved to be, the world they held to in their dreams and the world they met when they emerged remained essentially the world they had left. Eventually, that world took up the survivors and gathered them into the familiar networks of communal and family life. Unlike the situation that would obtain for survivors of nuclear war, concentration camp victims were not called upon to be themselves the keepers of humanness. They were not required to find within themselves the resources to reweave the fabric of society amid extensive devastation. The question arises: Would the surviving victims of nuclear war, subjected to greater carnage, vaster loss, and unceasing stress, sustained neither by an intact society nor by a recognizable natural environment, be psychologically capable of recreating a human world?

HIROSHIMA AND NAGASAKI

The destruction of Hiroshima and Nagasaki in World War II introduced the three characteristics of nuclear warfare that distinguish it from disasters previously experienced: capacity for massive destruction on an unprecedented scale, occurrence of indiscriminate destruction within a virtually instantaneous time frame, and persistence of pervasive physical consequences for generations. Yet these distinguishing characteristics, evident even to observers at the time, fade to insignificance against the backdrop of what is possible with current nuclear arsenals. Understanding how people fared who experienced these effects on a scale of magnitude and time far greater than anything previously seen, yet far less than what now may occur, may contribute to a discussion of the psychological competence of survivors of contemporary nuclear war.

The sudden, sweeping obliteration of life and environment brought by these two atomic bombs inflicted an initial state of perceptual, cognitive, and emotional shutdown. As observers from the Strategic Bombing Survey Team concluded: "The psychological effects were evident by the mass exodus of the people to the outlying areas with little regard for the care of casualties, the complete apathy of the population, the inability of the public authorities toward restoration of sanitary facilities and the supply of an adequate and safe water supply."[34]

During the first few days, people moved in slow motion, stunned, as if without purpose. In his *Hiroshima Diary*, Dr. Hachiya gives us the following account of survivors:

> What a weak, fragile thing man is before the forces of destruction. After the *pika* (explosion) the entire population had been reduced to a common level of physical and mental weakness. Those who were able walked silently towards the suburbs and distant hills, their spirits broken, their initiative gone. When asked whence they had come, they pointed to the city and said "that way"; and when asked where they were going, pointed away from the city and said "this way." They were so broken and confused that they moved and behaved like automatons. Their reactions had astonished outsiders who reported with amazement the

spectacle of long files of people holding steadily to a narrow rough path, where close by was smooth easy road going in the same direction. The outsiders could not grasp the fact that they were witnessing the exodus of a people who walked in the realm of dreams.[35]

A professor of physics who spent a week walking among corpses searching for the bodies of relatives explained his reaction this way:

> As I walked along, the horrible things I saw became more and more extreme and more and more intolerable. And at a certain point I must have become more or less saturated, so that I became no longer sensitive, in fact insensitive, to what I saw around me. I think human emotions reach a point beyond which they cannot extend—something like a photographic process. If under certain conditions you expose a photographic plate to light, it becomes black; but if you continue to expose it, then it reaches a point where it turns white. . . . Only later can one recognize having reached this maximum state.[36]

In a disaster of this magnitude, the extreme conditions drastically limited the possibilities of cooperation and mutual aid. The basic urge toward self-preservation became the controlling image that dictated human response. The individual's primary and foremost commitment to his or her own survival became vividly apparent. Loss of attachment, of the capacity to care, began to surface. One man said: "Of course I thought much about my children, but egotism was so great that each person was alone. . . . I felt strongly that human beings were animals—even in the case of parents and children, they still fought with one another to get their food.[37]

This instinct toward self-preservation, to the exclusion of giving help to others, served to promote survival, and yet, in the presence of the unattended injured and dying, instilled a profound sense of guilt. Takashi Nagai, a Catholic physician at Nagasaki, wrote:

> In general, then, those who survived the atom bomb were the people who ignored their friends crying out *in extremis;* or who shook off wounded neighbors who clung to them, pleading to be saved. . . . In short, those who survived the bomb were, if not merely lucky, in a greater or lesser degree selfish, self-centered, guided by instinct and not civilization . . . and we know it, we who have survived. Knowing it is a dull ache without surcease.[38]

Survivors remained haunted by remembered scenes of failed responsibility and of assistance not given. One man spoke of these things as he recalled his walk through the city:

> I went to look for my family. Somehow I became a pitiless person, because if I had pity, I would not have been able to walk through the city, to walk over those dead bodies. The most impressive thing was the

expression in people's eyes—bodies badly injured which had turned black—their eyes looking for someone to come and help them. They looked at me and knew that I was stronger than they. . . . I was looking for my family and looking carefully at everyone I met to see if he or she was a family member—but the eyes—the emptiness—the helpless expression—were something I will never forget. . . . There were hundreds of people who had seen me. I often had to go to the same place more than once. I would wish that the same family would not still be there. . . . I saw disappointment in their eyes. They looked at me with great expectation, staring right through me. It was very hard to be stared at by those eyes.[39]

The inescapability of the experience, sustained by a sense of survivor guilt, was augmented by the drawn-out effects of radiation exposure. From a psychological point of view, the presence of such deadly, invisible contamination aroused in the survivors the image of a nuclear weapon that not only killed instantly and on a colossal scale, but left behind the permanent, active presence of death, embedded in the bodies of survivors—a cruel death that could strike at any time without any warning. No manner of psychological formulation or of "naming" helped to give survivors any sense of mastery or any felt degree of safety or preparedness in coping with "A-bomb disease." As soon as the disease was named, it became a symbol of the mysterious death before which everyone was helpless. One man, a Buddhist priest, explained it this way:

We heard the new phrase, "A-bomb disease." The fear in us became strong, especially when we would see certain things with our eyes: a man looking perfectly well as he rode by on a bicycle one morning, suddenly vomiting blood, and then dying. . . . Soon we were all worried about our health, about our own bodies—whether we would live or die. And we heard that if someone did get sick, there was no treatment that could help. We had nothing to rely on, there was nothing to hold us up.[40]

A-bomb disease effected this sense of the pervasiveness of death, a tired conviction that nothing could ever again be healthy, dependable, and restored to a normal state. A man whose parents were killed by the bomb described his reactions to the additional deaths of two family members and his fear at his own permanent, mysterious sense of affliction:

My grandmother was taking care of my younger brother on the fourteenth of August when I left; and when I returned on the fifteenth, she had many spots all over her body. Two or three days later she died. . . . My younger brother, who . . . was just a (five-month-old) baby, was without breast milk—so we fed him thin rice gruel. . . . But on the tenth of October he suddenly began to look very ill, though I had not then noticed any spots on his body. . . . Then on the next day he began to look a little better, and I thought he was going to survive. I was very pleased, as he was the only family member I had left, and I took him to a doctor—but on the way to the doctor he died. And at that time we found that there were two large spots on his bottom. . . . I heard it said that all these people would die within three years . . . so I thought, "sooner or later I too will die". . . . I felt very weak and very lonely . . . with no hope at all . . . and since I had seen so many people's eyebrows falling out, their hair falling out, bleeding from their teeth, I found myself always nervously touching my hair like this (he demonstrated by rubbing his head). . . . I never knew when some sign of the disease would show itself. . . . And living in the countryside then with my relatives, people who came to visit would tell us these things, and then the villages also talked about them—telling stories of this man or that man who visited us a few days ago, returned to Hiroshima, and died within a week. . . . I couldn't tell whether these stories were true or not, but I believed them then. And I also heard that when the *hibakusha* (survivors) came to evacuate to the village where I was, they died there one by one. . . . This loneliness, and the fear . . . the physical fear . . . has been with me always. . . . It is not something temporary. . . . I still have it now.[41]

As one survivor, a physician, described this state of sustained dread: "Take my own case. If I am shaving in the morning and I should happen to cut myself very slightly, I dab the blood with a piece of paper— and then, when I notice that it has stopped flowing, I think to myself, 'Well, I guess I am all right.' "[42]

In a very real sense, survivors of the atomic bombs never fully recovered psychologically:

The original "curse" becomes an enduring taint—a taint of death which attaches itself to one's entire psychobiological organism and, beyond that, to one's posterity as well. *Survivors feel themselves involved in an endless chain of potentially lethal impairment, which, if it does not manifest itself in one year—or in one generation—may well make itself felt in the next.* (Italics in original.)[43]

The Japanese survivors remained immersed in the death experience. As stated by the Mayors' Committee for the Compilation of Materials: "The severity of this shock, along with other disabling conditions, has robbed the victims of their psychological equilibrium; indeed, the psychological damage was so great that it may be said that they were deprived of their 'humanity.' "[44] Contributing to this devastating disruption of psychic capacity was the destruction of community and environment that, above all, characterized the consequences of the atomic bombings for survivors and for those who bore witness to its effects. As the Mayors' Committee observed:

> A-bomb damage, then, is so complex and extensive that it cannot be reduced to any single characteristic or problem. It must be seen overall, as an interrelated array—massive physical and human loss, social disintegration, and psychological and spiritual shock—that affects all life and society. Only then can one grasp the seriousness of its total impact on the biological systems that sustain life and health, on the social systems that enable people to live and work together, and on the mental functions that hold these two dimensions in integrated unity. The essence of atomic destruction lies in the totality of its impact on man and society and on all the systems that affect their mutual continuation.[45]

CONCLUSION

Historical examples of calamity and recovery not only fall short of evoking a realistic image of survival after nuclear war, but the very act of looking to history for information and advice can in itself mislead. The destruction of human beings in Hiroshima and Nagasaki radically exceeded all we had previously learned about disaster effects. Yet Hiroshima and Nagasaki are no more than a transition between prenuclear disaster and that which we face from contemporary nuclear weapons. Nothing we have known begins to suggest the dimensions of such a holocaust. But in our recognition of these dimensions of destruction—of the possibility of a nuclear "end"—lies the beginning of the wisdom we may draw upon to prevent it from taking place.

Notes

INTRODUCTION

1. FEMA, Office of Public Affairs, *News*, Release no. 82–86 (Washington, D.C.: March 30, 1982), p. 2.
2. Louis O. Giuffrida, quotation dated October 9, 1981, as found in "President Reagan's Civil Defense Program," *The Defense Monitor* 11, no. 5 (Washington, D.C.: Center for Defense Information, 1982), p.3.
3. Louis O. Giuffrida, Testimony before the House Committee on Armed Services, Military Installations and Facilities Subcommittee, 97th Congress, 2nd session, March 12, 1982, p. 927.
4. For a description of CRP, see Defense Civil Preparedness Agency, *Questions and Answers on Crisis Relocation Planning*, Information Bulletin No. 305 (Washington, D.C.: April 20, 1979). Population figures have been updated here to accord with 1980 census.
5. Charles F. Estes, Jr., Testimony before the Senate Committee on Armed Services, 97th Congress, 1st session, March 30, 1981, pp. 4380–4381.
6. John McConnell, Testimony before the Senate Committee on Armed Services, 97th Congress, 1st session, March 30, 1981, p. 4382.
7. William K. Chipman, Testimony before the House Committee on Armed Services, Military Installations and Facilities Subcommittee, 97th Congress, 1st session, February 27, 1981, p. 847.
8. Giuffrida, Testimony before the House Committee on Armed Services, p. 939.
9. B. Wayne Blanchard, *American Civil Defense 1945–1975: The Evolution of Programs and Policies*, PhD dissertation, University of Virginia (Ann Arbor, Michigan: University Microfilms International, 1980), p. 501. Table shows civil defense research appropriations, 1962–1976, in millions of 1976 dollars.
10. Chipman, p. 848.
11. Massachusetts Civil Defense Agency, *Crisis Relocation Planning . . . Questions and Answers* (Framingham, Mass.: MCDA, no date), p. 30.
12. Howard M. Berger, *A Critical Review of Survival and Recovery After a Large-Scale Nuclear Attack* (Marina del Rey, Calif.: R & D Associates, December 1978) [Prepared for the Defense Nuclear Agency]; Abe Feinberg, *Civil Preparedness and Post-Attack U.S. Economic Recovery: A State of the Art Assessment and Selected Annotated Bibliography* (Marina del Rey, Calif.: Analytical Assessments Corporation, October 1979) [Prepared for FEMA].

13.   Herbert L. Abrams and William E. Von Kaenel, "Medical Problems of Survivors of Nuclear War," *The New England Journal of Medicine* 305 (November 12, 1981): 1226–1232.

CHAPTER 1: PARADIGMS OF DISASTER PLANNING

1.   Ronald W. Perry, *The Social Psychology of Civil Defense* (Lexington, Mass.: Lexington Books, 1982), p. 79.
2.   Ibid., p. 34.
3.   Ibid., p. 35.
4.   Russell R. Dynes, E.L. Quarantelli, and Gary A. Kreps, *A Perspective on Disaster Planning* (Columbus, Ohio: Disaster Research Center, Ohio State University, 1972) [Prepared for the Defense Civil Preparedness Agency], p. 31.
5.   Perry, p. 40.
6.   Ibid., p. 105.
7.   Ibid., p. 106.
8.   Ibid., p. 79.
9.   Ibid., p. 31.
10.   Dynes, p. iv.
11.   Ibid.
12.   Office of Technology Assessment (OTA), *The Effects of Nuclear War* (Washington, D.C.: U.S. Government Printing Office, 1979), p. 31.
13.   Quoted in Paul Warnke, "On Political Books," *Washington Monthly* (January 1983): 57.
14.   Union of Concerned Scientists, *The Risks of Nuclear Power Reactors* (Cambridge, Mass.: UCS, 1977), pp. 3 and 116–23.
15.   Perry, p. 32.
16.   Ibid.
17.   OTA, pp. 83–86; Leo A. Schmidt, *A Study of Twenty-Four Nationwide Fallout Patterns from Twelve Winds* (Arlington, Va.: Institute for Defense Analyses, 1981) [Prepared for FEMA], pp. 207–8.
18.   Perry, p. 32.
19.   Ibid.
20.   Paul J. Crutzen and John W. Birks, "The Atmosphere after a Nuclear War: Twilight at Noon," *Ambio* 11, nos. 2/3 (1982): 114–25; National Academy of Sciences, *Long-Term Worldwide Effects of Multiple Nuclear-Weapons Detonations* (Washington, D.C.: NAS, 1975), pp. 5–7 and 25–63.
21.   Ibid., p. 31.
22.   Dynes, Quarantelli, and Kreps, p. 6.
23.   James Fallows, *National Defense* (New York: Vintage Books, 1982), p. 147.
24.   Ibid., p. 139.
25.   National Governors Association, *State Comprehensive Emergency Management* (Washington, D.C.: NGA, 1978), pp. 105–24.
26.   Congressional Record, U.S. House of Representatives, Debate of the Committee of the Whole House on H.R. 6030, Washington, D.C., July 29, 1982, pp. II, 4815–4833; Roger J. Sullivan, et al., *The Potential Effect of Crisis Relocation on Crisis Stability* (Arlington, Va.: System Planning Corporation, September 1978) [Prepared for the Defense Civil Preparedness Agency], pp. 99–166, passim; Hearings before the House Committee on Armed Services, Military Installations and Facilities Subcommittee, 97th Congress, 1st session, Washington, D.C., February 26–27, 1981, pp. 771–72, 780, 819–20.

27. Perry, p. 108.
28. Union of Concerned Scientists, pp. 115–116.
29. Perry, p. 34.

CHAPTER 2: SOCIAL SCIENCE RESEARCH AND CRISIS RELOCATION PLANNING

1. Norman Hanunian, *Dimensions of Survival: Postattack Survival Disparities and National Viability* (Santa Monica, Calif.: Rand Corporation, 1966), p. v.
2. Joseph M. Hans, Jr. and Thomas C. Sell, *Evacuation Risks—An Evaluation* (Las Vegas: U.S. Environmental Protection Agency, 1974), p. 3.
3. Ronald W. Perry, *The Social Psychology of Civil Defense* (Lexington, Mass.: Lexington Books, 1982), p. 3.
4. Hanunian, p. 3:
5. Ibid., p. 3.
6. Ibid., p. 115–16.
7. Ibid., p. 119.
8. Ibid., p. 125.
9. Ibid., p. 132.
10. Ibid., p. 67.
11. Ibid., p. 135.
12. Ibid., p. 66.
13. Ibid., p. 134.
14. Ibid., p. 115.
15. Ibid., p. 141.
16. Ibid., p. 140.
17. Ibid., p. 140.
18. Ibid., p. 133.
19. Hans and Sell, p. 1.
20. Ibid., p. 3.
21. Ibid., p. 4.
22. Ibid., p. 5.
23. Ibid., p. 17.
24. Ibid., p. 18.
25. Ibid., p. 24.
26. Ibid., p. 26.
27. Ibid., p. 35.
28. Ibid., p. 32.
29. Ibid., p. 39.
30. Ibid., p. 54.
31. Ibid., p. 47.
32. Ibid., p. 48.
33. Perry, p. 2.
34. Ibid.
35. Ibid.
36. Ibid.
37. Ibid., p. 81.
38. Ibid., p. 3.
39. Ibid., p. 32.
40. Ibid.

41.   Ibid., p. 31.
42.   Ibid., p. 41.
43.   Ibid., p. 48.
44.   Ibid., p. 39.
45.   Ibid., p. 91.
46.   Ibid., p. 92.
47.   Ibid., p. 101.
48.   Ibid., p. 24.
49.   Ibid.
50.   Ibid., p. 78.
51.   Ibid., p. 69.
52.   Ibid., p. 88.
53.   Ibid., p. 103.
54.   Ibid., p. 105.
55.   Ibid., p. 106.
56.   Ibid., p. 108.
57.   Hans and Sell, p. 35.

CHAPTER 5: CITIZEN RESPONSE TO CRISIS RELOCATION

1.   Ronald W. Perry, *The Social Psychology of Civil Defense* (Lexington, Mass.: Lexington Books, 1982), p. 95.
2.   Ibid., p. 107.
3.   Ronald W. Perry, Michael K. Lindell, and Marjorie R. Greene, *The Implications of Natural Hazard Evacuation Warning Studies for Crisis Relocation Planning* (Seattle: Battelle Human Affairs Research Center, 1980) [Prepared for FEMA], p. 89.
4.   Perry, p. 96.
5.   Joseph M. Hans, Jr. and Thomas C. Sell, *Evacuation Risks—An Evaluation* (Las Vegas: U.S. Environmental Protection Agency, 1974).
6.   Ibid., p. 18.
7.   Perry, p. 101.
8.   Paul Slovic, Sarah Lichtenstein, and Baruch Fischhoff, "Images of Disaster: Perception and Acceptance of Risks from Nuclear Power," in G.T. Goodman and W.T. Rowe, eds., *Energy Risk Management* (London: Academic Press Inc., 1979).
9.   James H. Johnson and Donald J. Zeigler, Testimony before the Suffolk County Legislature in the matter of the Shoreham nuclear station emergency planning proceedings, New York, January 24, 1983.
10.   Kai T. Erikson, Testimony before the Suffolk County Legislature in the matter of the Shoreham nuclear station emergency planning proceedings, Hauppaug, N.Y., January 24, 1983.
11.   Susan Saegert, "Psychological Issues in Planning for a Radiological Emergency" (New York: Center for Human Environments, City University of New York, January 1983).
12.   Planning Research Corporation Voorhees, "Preliminary Evacuation Time Estimators for the Shoreham EPZ", Prepared for the Suffolk County Radiological Emergency Response Plan Steering Committee, November 1982, p. 81.
13.   Robert W. Gilmer and Carolyn Kennedy, *The Potential for Relocation of Population under Threat of Nuclear Attack* (Arlington, Va.: Institute for Defense Analyses, 1976) [Prepared for the Defense Civil Preparedness Agency].

14. Note that even Perry finds that data sometimes questionable. See Perry, p. 103, citing the example of a facility planned for 200 but having only two lavatories.
15. Gilmer and Kennedy, p. 23.
16. Ibid., p. 28.
17. Municipality of Anchorage, Office of Civil Defense, "Crisis Relocation" (no date ca. 1981).
18. Beverlee A. Myers, "To Plan a Hoax is a Disservice to the People," *Journal of Public Health Policy* (June 1982): 119–21.
19. Perry, p. 108.
20. Ibid., p. 69.
21. Office of Technology Assessment (OTA), *The Effects of Nuclear War: Summary* (Washington, D.C.: U.S. Government Printing Office, 1980), p. 10.
22. Carla B. Johnston, "State Summary Tally of Activity on FEMA's Civil Defense Plans" (Boston: New Century Policies, July 23, 1982).
23. FEMA, "New Gallup Survey Results on Civil Defense Announced," FEMA *News*, July 3, 1982; "Backgrounder: Result of Second Gallup Civil Defense Survey," October 18, 1982; "Backgrounder: Results of the Third Gallup Civil Defense Survey," December 28, 1982.
24. Russell R. Dynes, E.L. Quarantelli, and Gary A. Kreps, *A Perspective on Disaster Planning* (Columbus, Ohio: Disaster Research Center, Ohio State University, 1972) [Prepared for the Defense Civil Preparedness Agency], p. 24.
25. Erikson, Testimony before the Suffok County Legislature.
26. Slovic, Lichtenstein, and Fischhoff, "Images of Disaster."
27. "President Reagan's Civil Defense Program," *The Defense Monitor* 11, no. 5 (Washington, D.C.: Center for Defense Information, 1982), p. 4.
28. Perry, p. 65.

CHAPTER 6: THE TRANSPORTATION ASSUMPTIONS OF CRISIS RELOCATION PLANNING

1. "President Reagan's Civil Defense Program," *The Defense Monitor* 11, no. 5 (Washington, D.C.: Center for Defense Information, 1982), p. 3.
2. Clark D. Henderson and Walmer E. Strope, *Crisis Relocation of The Population at Risk in the New York Metropolitan Area* (Menlo Park, Calif.: Stanford Research Institute (SRI), September 1978) [Prepared for the Defense Civil Preparedness Agency], p. xiv.
3. Walmer E. Strope, Clark D. Henderson, and Charles T. Rainey, *The Feasibility of Crisis Relocation in the Northeast Corridor* (Menlo Park, Calif.: Stanford Research Institute, December 1976) [Prepared for the Defense Civil Preparedness Agency], p. vi.
4. Henderson and Strope, p. 3.
5. Ibid., p. 109.
6. Strope, Henderson, and Rainey, *The Feasibility of Crisis Relocation*, pp. 38–40.
7. Henderson and Strope, p. 13.
8. Ibid., p. 79–81.
9. Strope, Henderson, and Rainey, *The Feasibility of Crisis Relocation*, p. 49.
10. Henderson and Strope, pp. 42–50.
11. National Academy of Sciences (NAS), *Highway Capacity Manual* Special Report 87 (Washington, D.C.: NAS, 1965).
12. John W. Billheimer and Juliet McNally, *Traffic Control Measures for Crisis Relocation* (Los Altos, Calif.: Systan, Inc., 1983) [Prepared for FEMA], p. 5-1.

13. John W.Billheimer, Gail Fondahl, and Arthur W. Simpson, *Postattack Impacts of the Crisis Relocation Strategy on Transportation Systems, vol. 2, Revised Planning Guidelines* (Los Altos, Calif.: Systan, Inc., 1978) [Prepared for the Defense Civil Preparedness Agency], p. II-52.

14. NAS, *Interim Materials on Highway Capacity*, Transportation Research Board Circular 212 (Washington, D.C.: NAS, 1980), p. 169.

15. NAS, *Highway Capacity Manual*, p. 81.

16. NAS, *Interim Materials on Highway Capacity*, p. 167.

17. NAS, *Highway Capacity Manual*, p. 81.

18. Billheimer and McNally, p. 3-30.

19. NAS, *Interim Materials on Highway Capacity*, p. 170.

20. Billheimer, Fondahl, and Simpson, pp. II-54 and II-56.

21. Henderson and Strope, p. 13.

22. Billheimer and McNally, p. 3–31.

23. Billheimer, Fondahl, and Simpson, p. II-71.

24. Billheimer and McNally, p. 3–19.

25. Ibid.

26. Ibid., Exhibit S.1, p. S-2.

27. Ibid., p. 1-1.

28. Ibid., pp. 3-8 and 3-9.

29. Joseph M. Hans, Jr., and Thomas C. Sell, *Evacuation Risks—An Evaluation* (Las Vegas: U.S. Environmental Protection Agency, 1974), pp. 45, 47, and 48.

30. Henderson and Strope, p. 65.

31. Ibid., p. 84.

32. Billheimer and McNally, p. 3-41.

33. Ibid., p. 3-42.

34. Hans and Sell, pp. 50 and 51.

35. Billheimer and McNally, p. 5-6.

36. Ibid., p. 1-2.

37. Henderson and Strope, p. 84.

38. Billheimer and McNally, p. 5-6.

39. Ibid., p. 4-11.

40. Ibid., p. 3-17.

41. Ibid., p. 5-6.

42. Ibid., p. 3-30.

43. Ibid., app. B, p. 1.

44. NAS, *Highway Capacity Manual*, pp. 267–68.

45. Billheimer and McNally, pp. 3-30–3-31.

46. Strope, Henderson, and Rainey, *The Feasibility of Crisis Relocation*, Table 23, p. 125.

47. JHK and Associates, *Transportation Background for the Guide for Crisis Relocation Contingency Planning* (San Francisco: JHK and Associates, 1974).

48. Strope, Henderson, and Rainey, *The Feasibility of Crisis Relocation*, p. 103.

49. Ibid.

50. Walmer E. Strope, Clark D. Henderson, and Charles P. Rainey, *Draft Guidance for Crisis Relocation Planning in Highly Urbanized Areas* (Palo Alto, Calif.: Center for Planning and Research, Inc., October 1977) [Prepared for the Defense Civil Preparedness Agency], p. 5-14.

51. Strope, Henderson, and Rainey, *The Feasibility of Crisis Relocation*, pp. 42 and 44.

52. Daniel Brand, "Travel Demand Forecasting: Some Foundations and a Review," in *Urban Travel Demand Forecasting*, Daniel Brand and Marvin Mannheim, eds., Transportation Research Board *Special Report 143* (Washington, D.C.: NAS, 1973).

53. Hans and Sell, p. 40.

54. Strope, Henderson, and Rainey, *The Feasibility of Crisis Relocation*, pp. 44–45.
55. Ibid., p. 120.
56. Strope, Henderson, and Rainey, *Draft Guidance*, p. 1-3.
57. Ibid., p. 7-1.
58. Strope, Henderson, and Rainey, *The Feasibility of Crisis Relocation*, p. 40.
59. Ibid.
60. Strope, Henderson, and Rainey, *Draft Guidance*, pp. 5-3–5-4.
61. NAS, *Highway Capacity Manual*, p. 268.
62. Henderson and Strope, p. 65.
63. NAS, *Highway Capacity Manual*, p. 291.
64. Ibid., p. 292.
65. Ibid., Table 10.13, p. 323.
66. Ibid., p. 322.
67. Henderson and Strope, pp. 76–77.
68. Ibid., p. 16.
69. Strope, Henderson, and Rainey, *The Feasibility of Crisis Relocation*, p. 14.
70. Ibid., Table 8, p. 43.
71. Ibid.
72. Ibid., p. 42.
73. Ibid., p. 124.
74. Henderson and Strope, p.17.
75. Ibid.
76. Billheimer and McNally, p. 3-33.
77. Strope, Henderson, and Rainey, *The Feasibility of Crisis Relocation*, Table 8, p. 43.
78. Ibid., p. 14.
79. John W. Billheimer, Robert Bullemer, Arthur Simpson, and Robert Wood, *Impacts of the Crisis Relocation Strategy on Transportation Systems, Final Report, vol. 1, Analysis and Case Study*, August 1976 [Prepared for Defense Civil Preparedness Agency], Exhibit 3–7, p. 3-38.
80. Henderson and Strope, Table 20, p. 110.
81. Strope, Henderson, and Rainey, *The Feasibility of Crisis Relocation*, Table 8, p. 43.
82. Henderson and Strope, pp. 79–81.
83. Strope, Henderson, and Rainey, *The Feasibility of Crisis Relocation*, p. 57.
84. Ibid., Table 13, p. 59.
85. Henderson and Strope, Table 20, p. 110.
86. Strope, Henderson, and Rainey, *The Feasibility of Crisis Relocation*, Tables 9, 10, and 13, pp. 46, 52, and 59.
87. Ibid., p. 54.
88. Henderson and Strope, pp. 81–82.
89. Strope, Henderson, and Rainey, *The Feasibility of Crisis Relocation*, Table 11, p. 55.
90. Ibid., p. 54.
91. Billheimer, Fondahl, and Simpson, p. II-12.
92. Strope, Henderson, and Rainey, *The Feasibility of Crisis Relocation*, p. 47.
93. Ibid., p. 126.
94. Henderson and Strope, Table 20, p. 110.
95. Ibid., pp. 42–50; and Strope, Henderson, and Rainey, *The Feasibility of Crisis Relocation*, pp. 48–49.
96. Henderson and Strope, Table 20, p. 110.
97. Strope, Henderson, and Rainey, *The Feasibility of Crisis Relocation*, Table 10, p. 52.
98. Ibid.
99. Henderson and Strope, p. 46.
100. Strope, Henderson, and Rainey, *The Feasibility of Crisis Relocation*, p. 49.

101. Henderson and Strope, Table 20, p. 110.
102. Strope, Henderson, and Rainey, *The Feasibility of Crisis Relocation*, Table 10, p. 52.
102. Ibid., p. 51.
104. Henderson and Strope, Table 2, p. 25.
105. Ibid., p. 24.
106. Ibid., p. 30.
107. Ibid., p. 53.
108. Ibid., p. 54.
109. Ibid., p. 56.
110. Ibid.
111. Billheimer, Bullemer, Simpson, and Wood, p. 3-14.
112. Ibid., Table 17 and Tables A-1 to A-14. The identifiable two-way exceptions are the two-lane, two-way H-20 and the four- and six-lane H-70, operated one way but having a separate two-lane backhaul route.
113. Ibid.

CHAPTER 7: CHILDREN AND CRISIS RELOCATION

1. Lloyd de Mause, *The History of Childhood: The Evolution of Parent-Child Relationships as a Factor in History* (London: Souvenir Press, 1980), pp. 51–54 and 407–28.
2. For references on children in war, see bibliography in Marianne Kahnert, et al., eds., *Children and War* (Geneva, Switzerland: Geneva International Peace Research Institute, 1983), pp. 244–56; for references on children in disaster, see bibliography in Stewart E. Perry, et al., *The Child and His Family in Disaster: A Study of the 1953 Vicksburg Tornado* (Washington, D.C.: National Academy of Sciences, 1956), p. 4 and passim.
3. Frank W. Lutz, *Special Problems of Children in Civil Defense Planning* (McLean, Va.: Human Sciences Research, Inc., 1967) [Prepared for the Office of Civil Defense]; William W. Pendleton, *A Second Study of the Demography of Nuclear War* (McLean, Va.: Human Sciences Research, Inc., 1967) [Prepared for the Office of Civil Defense], pp. 58–63; and S.D. Vestermark, Jr., "Social Indicators of Social Effects and the Social Inventory after Attack," in *Postattack Recovery from Nuclear War* (Washington, D.C.: Office of Civil Defense, 1967), pp. 327–63.
4. K.S. Gant and C.V. Chester, "Minimizing Excess Radiogenic Cancer Deaths After a Nuclear Attack," *Health Physics* 41, no. 3 (September 1981): 445–63.
5. M.N. Laney, et al., *Management of Medical Problems Resulting from Population Relocation* (Research Triangle Park, NC: Research Triangle Institute, 1976) [Prepared for the Defense Civil Preparedness Agency], pp. I-1–I-26.
6. Fred Iklé, *The Social Impact of Bomb Destruction* (Norman, Oklahoma: University of Oklahoma Press, 1958), p. 119; Richard Titmuss, *Problems of Social Policy* (London: His Majesty's Stationery Office, 1950), p. 186; United States Strategic Bombing Survey, *The Effects of Strategic Bombing on German Morale, Vol. I* (Washington, D.C.: U.S. Government Printing Office, 1947), p. 2.

CHAPTER 8: SHELTERING THE RELOCATED POPULATION

1. Carsten M. Haaland and Betsy M. Horwedel, *Instrumentation Requirements for Radiological Defense for Crisis Relocation Planning* (Oak Ridge, Tenn.: Oak Ridge National Laboratory, December 1979) [Prepared for FEMA], p. 25.
2. U.S. House of Representatives, Hearings before the Committee on Armed Services, 97th Congress, 2nd session, March 12, 1982, p. 947.

3. Haaland and Horwedel, pp. 50–64.
4. House Committee on Armed Services, Hearings, p. 986.
5. Greensboro-Guilford County Emergency Management Assistance Agency, "Status of War Planning, Greensboro-Guilford County," November 4, 1981, (Draft), p. II-1.
6. Haaland and Horwedel, *Instrumentation Requirements for Radiological Defense for Crisis Relocation Planning.*
7. House Committee on Armed Services, Hearings, p. 937.
8. Greensboro-Guilford County, "Status of War Planning," p. II-1.
9. Ibid., p. II-2.
10. House Committee on Armed Services, Hearings, p. 950.
11. Greensboro-Guilford County, "Status of War Planning," p. II-3.
12. FEMA, *Standards for Fallout Shelters* (Washington, D.C.: FEMA, September 1979), pp. 9–10, 12.
13. Greensboro-Guilford County, "Status of War Planning," p. II-3.
14. FEMA, *Standards for Fallout Shelters*, p. 10.
15. Greensboro-Guilford County, "Status of War Planning," p. II-5.
16. Ibid.
17. Ibid.
18. Ibid.
19. George W. Baker and John H. Rohrer, eds., *Human Problems in the Utilization of Fallout Shelters* (Washington, D.C.: National Academy of Sciences, 1960).
20. Haaland and Horwedel, *Instrumentation Requirements for Radiological Defense for Crisis Relocation Planning.*
21. Greensboro-Guilford County, "Status of War Planning," p. V-1.
22. FEMA, *Camera-Ready News Columns*, no. 15 (Washington, D.C., December 1980).
23. Ibid.
24. Ibid.
25. Ibid.

CHAPTER 9: PROBLEMS OF GOVERNANCE AND SOCIAL CONTROL

1. See, e.g., Stanley Milgram, "Behavioral Study of Obedience," *Journal of Abnormal and Social Psychology* 67, no. 4 (1963): 371–78.
2. William G. Gay, et al., *Crisis Relocation: Disrupting Relocated Populations and Maintaining Organizational Viability* (McLean, Va: Human Sciences Research, Inc., April 1974) [Prepared for Defense Civil Preparedness Agency], p. viii.
3. *Relocation Instructions: City of Boston Risk Area* (Plan prepared by the Massachusetts Civil Defense Agency, n.d.), p. 4; and *Relocation Instructions: Greater Boston Risk Area: Suburban West* (Plan prepared by the Massachusetts Civil Defense Agency, n.d.).
4. On the likelihood of people confronting disasters attempting to help their families rather than play community roles, see Arthur M. Katz, *Life After Nuclear War* (Cambridge, Mass.: Ballinger Publishing Co., 1982), pp. 193ff.
5. *Relocation Instructions: City of Boston Risk Area*, p. 4.
6. Ibid.
7. George Quester, *Options for Accelerating Economic Recovery after Nuclear Attack* (Marina del Rey, Calif.: Analytical Assessments Corporation, July 1979) [Prepared for FEMA], p. 33.

8.   "President Reagan's Civil Defense Program," *The Defense Monitor* 11, no. 5 (Washington, D.C.: Center for Defense Information, 1982), p. 6.

9.   Quester, p. 37.

10.   Jonathan Schell, *The Fate of the Earth* (New York: Knopf, 1982).

11.   Bruce C. Allnut, *A Study of Consensus on Psychological Factors Related to Recovery from Nuclear Attack* (McLean, Va: Human Sciences Research, Inc., May 1971) [Prepared for the Office of Civil Defense].

12.   *Special Problems of Blacks and Other Minorities in Large Scale Population Relocation* (Washington, D.C.: National Capitol Systems, January 1981) [Prepared for FEMA].

13.   Quester, *Options for Accelerating Economic Recovery after Nuclear Attack.*

14.   The quest of public agencies for scientific legitimacy is discussed in Michael Lipsky and David J. Olson, *Commission Politics: The Processing of Racial Crisis in America* (New Brunswick, N.J.: Transaction Books, 1975), ch. 5. Crisis relocation planning may be the ultimate manifestation of symbolic reassurance by federal agencies to mass publics. See Murray Edelman, *The Symbolic Uses of Politics* (Urbana, Ill.: University of Illinois Press, 1964).

CHAPTER 10: MEDICAL AND PUBLIC HEALTH PROBLEMS OF CRISIS RELOCATION

1.   FEMA, *Questions and Answers on Crisis Relocation Planning* (Washington, D.C.: FEMA, October 1980), p. 26; Roger Sullivan, et al., *Candidate U.S. Civil Defense Programs* (Arlington, Va.: System Planning Corporation, March 1978) [Prepared for the Defense Civil Preparedness Agency], p. 26; U.S. Senate, Hearings Before the Committee on Armed Services, 97th Congress, 1st session, March 30, 1981, p. 4382.

2.   U.S. Senate, Hearings Before the Subcommittee on Health and Scientific Research Committee on Labor and Human Resources, 96th Congress, June, 19, 1980, p. 60.

3.   Douglas P. Forbes, "Nuclear Civil Protection," statement before the Public Safety Committee, Boston City Council, June 24, 1982.

4.   Sullivan, et al., p. E-25.

5.   National Center for Health Statistics, *Current Estimates from the National Interview Survey: United States, 1981* (Washington, D.C.: U.S. Department of Health and Human Services, 1981).

6.   M.N. Laney, et al., *Management of Medical Problems Resulting from Population Relocation* (Research Triangle Park, N.C.: Research Triangle Institute, May 1976) [Prepared for the Defense Civil Preparedness Agency], Vol. I, p. I-102.

7.   Ibid., p. I-1.

8.   Ibid., p. I-118.

9.   Sullivan, et al., p. E-18.

10.   Ibid., p. E-19.

11.   William M. Brown, *The Nuclear Crisis of 1979, Final Report* (Washington, D.C.: Defense Civil Preparedness Agency, February 1976), p. 26.

12.   Ibid., p. 27.

13.   National Center for Health Statistics, *Inpatient Health Facilities Statistics: United States, 1978*, Series 14, no. 24 (Washington, D.C.: U.S. Department of Health and Human Services, 1978).

14.   Laney, et al., p. I-25.

15.   D.R. Johnston, et al., *Study of Crisis Administration of Hospital Patients and Study of*

Management of Medical Problems Resulting from Population Relocation (Research Triangle Park, N.C.: Research Triangle Institute, September 1978) [Prepared for the Defense Civil Preparedness Agency], p. II-3.

16. Ibid., p. II-4.
17. Laney, et al., Vol. II, p. S-2.
18. M.N. Laney, et al., *Detailed Health and Medical Annexes to Crisis Relocation Plans* (Research Triangle Park, N.C.: Research Triangle Institute, 1979) [Prepared for the Defense Civil Preparedness Agency], p. 14.
19. Johnston, et al., p. ii.
20. FEMA, p. 12.
21. Vergil Fairbanks, M.D., "The Expedient Shelter," personal communication.
22. Johnston, et al., p. I-6.
23. K.S. Gant and C.V. Chester, "Minimizing Excess Radiogenic Cancer Deaths after a Nuclear Attack," *Health Physics* 41, no. 3 (September 1981): 457.
24. Carsten M. Haaland, et al., *Survival of the Relocated Population of the U.S. After a Nuclear Attack* (Oak Ridge, Tenn.: Oak Ridge National Laboratory, March 1976) [Prepared for the Defense Civil Preparedness Agency], p. 92.
25. Ibid., p. 93.
26. Defense Civil Preparedness Agency, *Protection in the Nuclear Age* (Washington, D.C.: DCPA, February 1977), p. 68.
27. Ibid., p. 65.
28. Herbert L. Abrams and William E. Von Kaenel, "Medical Problems of Survivors of Nuclear War," *New England Journal of Medicine* 305 (November 12, 1981): 1226–1232.
29. H.J. Geiger, "The Illusion of Survival," *Bulletin of the Atomic Scientists* 37, no. 6 (June-July 1981): 16–20.
30. Jennifer Leaning, *Civil Defense in the Nuclear Age* (Cambridge, Ma.: Physicians for Social Responsibility, 1982).
31. H.H. Mitchell, *Survey of the Infectious Disease Problem as It Relates to the Post-Attack Environment* (Santa Monica, Calif.: Rand Corporation, August 1966); H.H. Mitchell, *The Problem of Tuberculosis in the Post-Attack Environment* (Santa Monica, Calif.: Rand Corporation, June 1967).
32. H.H. Mitchell, *Plague in the United States: An Assessment of Its Significance as a Problem Following a Thermonuclear War* (Santa Monica, Calif.: Rand Corporation, June 1966); T. Johnson and D.R. Johnston, *Vectorborne Disease and Control* (Research Triangle Park, N.C.: Research Triangle Institute, June 1968).
33. H.H. Mitchell, *Guidelines for the Control of Communicable Disease in the Post-Attack Environment* (Marina del Rey, Calif.: R & D Associates, July 1972).
34. Cited in Ed Zuckerman, "Hiding from the Bomb—Again," *Harper's Magazine* (August 1979): 36.
35. Sullivan, et al., p. E-30.
36. James L. Costanza and Jack A. Marchese, *The Development of a Means for Assessing Emergency Medical Resources* (Chatsworth, Calif.: Serendipity, Inc., August 1969), [Prepared for the Office of Civil Defense], p. vii-3.
37. Ibid., p. iv-5.
38. Ibid., p. vii-4.
39. Ibid.
40. Ibid.
41. Ibid., p. ii-3.
42. J.B. Hallan, "A Simulation Model of an Emergency Medical System," in *PostAttack Recovery from Nuclear War* (Washington, D.C.: Office of Civil Defense, 1967), p. 90.
43. Gant and Chester, pp. 462–63.

44.   Gerard Piel, "The Illusion of Civil Defense," in *The Fallen Sky: Medical Consequences of Thermonuclear War* (New York: Hill and Wang, 1963), p. 83.

CHAPTER 11: RADIATION CONSEQUENCES OF NUCLEAR WAR

1.   Carsten M. Haaland, et al., *Survival of the Relocated Population of the U.S. After a Nuclear Attack* (Oak Ridge, Tenn.: Oak Ridge National Laboratory, March 1976) [Prepared for the Defense Civil Preparedness Agency], pp. 1, 20.
2.   Ibid., p. 21.
3.   Samuel Glasstone and Philip J. Dolan, eds., *The Effects of Nuclear Weapons* (Washington, D.C.: U.S. Government Printing Office, 1977), p. 575.
4.   Leo A. Schmidt, *A Study of Twenty-four Nationwide Fallout Patterns from Twelve Winds* (Arlington, Va.: Institute for Defense Analyses, September 1981) [Prepared for FEMA], p. 3.
5.   Ibid., pp. 1–2.
6.   Ibid., p. 209.
7.   Haaland, p. 37.
8.   Schmidt, p. 119.
9.   Ibid., p. 135, pp. 87–98.
10.   Schmidt, pp. 195–203.
11.   Ibid., p. 209.
12.   Ibid., p. 213.
13.   Joseph Rotblat, *Nuclear Radiation in Warfare*, Stockholm International Peace Research Institute (Cambridge, Mass.: Oelgeschlager, Gunn & Hain, 1981), pp. 82–84; Glasstone and Dolan, eds., pp. 390–404.
14.   Glasstone and Dolan, eds., pp. 604–609; Rotblat, pp. 54–55, 92–94.
15.   Committee on the Biological Effects of Ionizing Radiation (BEIR III), *The Effects on Populations of Exposure to Low Levels of Ionizing Radiation: 1980* (Washington, D.C.: National Academy Press, 1980), pp. 11–35.
16.   *Code of Federal Regulations 10:* Part 20, 1959.
17.   Clarence C. Lushbaugh, "Human Radiation Tolerance," in *Space Radiation Biology and Related Topics*, Cornelius A. Tobias and Paul Todd, eds. (New York: Academic Press, 1974), pp. 494–99.
18.   Ibid., pp. 500–509; National Council on Radiation Protection and Measurements (NCRP), *Radiological Factors Affecting Decision-Making in a Nuclear Attack*, NCRP Report No. 42 (Washington, D.C.: National Council on Radiation Protection and Measurements, November 15, 1974), p. 23.
19.   H. Aceto, et al., "Mammalian Radiobiology and Space Flight," in Tobias and Todd, eds., p. 374; NCRP, Report No. 42, p. 42; Rotblatt, p. 53.
20.   K.S. Gant and C.V. Chester, "Minimizing Excess Radiogenic Cancer Deaths After a Nuclear Attack," *Health Physics* 41, no. 3 (September 1981): 455–63.
21.   Lushbaugh, pp. 485–86. For discussion of whole body irradiation, see: Ibid. pp. 476–88; G.A. Andrews, "The Medical Management of Accidental Total-Body Irradiation," in *The Medical Basis for Radiation Accident Preparedness*, K.F. Hubner and S.A. Fry, eds. (New York: Elsevier/North-Holland, 1980), pp. 297–310; H. Fanger and C.C. Lushbaugh, "Radiation Death from Cardiovascular Shock Following a Criticality Accident," *Archives of Pathology* 83 (1967): 446–60; J.S. Karas and J.B. Stanbury, "Fatal Radiation from an Accidental Nuclear Excursion," *New England*

Journal of Medicine 272 (1965): 755–61; G.E. Thoma, Jr., and N. Wald, "The Diagnosis and Management of Accidental Radiation Injury," *Journal of Occupational Medicine* (1959): 421–47.

22. Andrews, p. 307.
23. For discussion of external contamination, see: International Atomic Energy Agency (IAEA), *Manual on Early Medical Treatment of Possible Radiation Injury*, Safety Series No. 47 (Vienna: IAEA, 1978), pp. 33–36, 60–62; R.V. Leonard and R.C. Ricks, "Emergency Department Radiation Accident Protocol," *Annals of Emergency Medicine* 9 (1980): 462–70; National Council on Radiation Protection and Measurements (NCRP), *Management of Persons Accidentally Contaminated with Radionuclides*, NCRP Report No. 65 (Washington, D.C.: National Council on Radiation Protection and Measurements, 1980) pp. 113–19; G.A. Poda, "Decontamination and Decorporation: The Clinical Experience," in Hubner and Fry, eds., pp. 327–32.
24. For discussion of internal contamination, see: IAEA, pp. 39–42; NCRP, Report No. 65, pp. 20–29; G.L. Voelz, "Current Approaches to the Management of Internally Contaminated Persons," in Hubner and Fry, eds., pp. 315–16.
25. Rotblat, p. 38.
26. IAEA, pp. 4–32. NCRP, Report No. 65, pp. 125–58.
27. Luther J. Carter, "National Protection from Iodine-131 Urged," *Science* 206 (1979): 201–206. Frank Von Hippel, "Available Thyroid Protection," *Science* 204 (1979): 1032.
28. NCRP, Report No. 42, p. 19.
29. Lushbaugh, p. 502.
30. Aceto, et al., p. 411; Glasstone and Dolan, eds., p. 589.
31. Committee for the Compilation of Materials, *Hiroshima and Nagasaki: The Physical, Medical, and Social Effects of the Atomic Bombings* (New York: Basic Books, 1981), p. 121; Glasstone and Dolan, eds., p. 582; E.H. Vogel, Jr., "Management of Burns Resulting from Nuclear Disaster," *Journal of the American Medical Association* 171 (1959): 205–208.
32. Aceto, et al., pp. 411–12; Glasstone and Dolan, eds., pp. 589–90.
33. BEIR III, pp. 497–98.
34. Ibid., p. 499.
35. Committee for the Compilation of Materials, p. 73, pp. 152–53.
36. Patricia Ash, "The Influence of Radiation on Fertility in Man," *The British Journal of Radiology* 53, no. 628 (1980): 271–73; Lushbaugh, p. 510.
37. Committee for the Compilation of Materials, pp. 153–54.
38. Robert A. Good and David W. Fisher, *Immunobiology* (Sunderland, Mass.: Sinauer Associates, 1971), pp. 240–41.
39. Robert H. Rubin, "Infection in the Immunosuppressed Host," in *Scientific American Medicine*, Edward Rubenstein and Daniel D. Federman, eds. (New York: Scientific American, Inc., 1981), vol. 2, section 7, chapter 10, p. x–3.
40. Aceto, et al., p. 382.
41. Glasstone and Dolan, eds., p. 585; E. Haus, et al., "Circadian Rhythmometry of Mammalian Radiosensitivity," in Tobias and Todd, eds., pp. 464–66; Rotblat, p. 56.
42. Patricia J. Lindop and J. Rotblat, "Consequences of Radioactive Fallout," in *The Final Epidemic*, Ruth Adams and Susan Cullen, eds. (Chicago, Ill.: Educational Foundation for Nuclear Science, 1981), pp. 148–49.
43. NCRP, Report No. 42, p. 40.
44. Aceto, et al., p. 406.
45. Ibid., p. 407.
46. BEIR III, pp 481–85.

47. Committee for the Compilation of Materials, pp. 152–56.
48. BEIR III, pp. 21–23.
49. Hiroo Kato and William J. Schull, "Studies of the Mortality of A-Bomb Survivors: 7: Mortality, 1950–1978: Part 1. Cancer Mortality," *Radiation Research* 90 (1982): 395–432.
50. Stuart C. Finch, "The Study of Atomic Bomb Survivors in Japan," *The American Journal of Medicine* 66, no. 6 (1979): 900.
51. Eliot Marshall, "New A-Bomb Studies Alter Radiation Estimates," *Science* 212 (1981): 900–903; Warren K. Sinclair and Patricia Failla, "Dosimetry of the Atomic Bomb Survivors: A Symposium," *Radiation Research* 88 (1981): 437–47.
52. BEIR III, p. 84.
53. William J. Schull, et al., "Genetic Effects of the Atomic Bombs: A Reappraisal," *Science* 213 (September 11, 1981): 1220–1227.
54. Beir III, pp. 73–75.
55. Ibid., p. 85.
56. Clark D. Henderson and Walmer E. Strope, *Crisis Relocation of the Population at Risk in the New York Metropolitan Area* (Menlo Park, Calif.: Stanford Research Institute, 1978) [Prepared for the Defense Civil Preparedness Agency], p. xv.
57. Rotblat, p. 84.
58. G.E. Pugh, et al., *Estimating the Behavioral Degradation of Fallout Protection Factors for Use in Damage Assessment Calculations* (Arlington, Va.: Decision-Science Applications, Inc., June 1980) [Prepared for the U.S. Arms Control and Disarmament Agency], p. A-6.
59. Schmidt, p. 195; Pugh, et al., pp. A-20–A-22.
60. Lindop and Rotblat, pp. 147–48; Lushbaugh, p. 505.
61. Pugh, et al., pp. A-6–A-9.
62. Lindop and Rotblat, p. 149; Lushbaugh, p. 505.
63. Louis O. Giuffrida, Testimony before the House Committee on Armed Services, Military Installations and Facilities Subcommittee, 97th Congress, 2nd session, March 12, 1982, pp. 930–31.
64. Carsten M. Haaland and Betsy M. Horwedel, *Instrumentation Requirements for Radiological Defense for Crisis Relocation Planning* (Oak Ridge, Tenn.: Oak Ridge National Laboratory, December 1979) [Prepared for FEMA], pp. 11–12, 20, 38–39, 60; Haaland, et al., pp. 89–93; Schmidt, p. 202.
65. Haaland and Horwedel, p. 60.
66. Schmidt, pp. 205–206, 213.
67. Ibid., pp. 123, 135, and fallout maps for May, p. A-11–12; June, pp. A-13–14; and August, pp. A-17–18.
68. Giuffrida, pp. 941–42; Haaland, et al., pp. 93–129.
69. Haaland and Horwedel, pp. 6–8.
70. Giuffrida, p. 972.
71. Haaland and Horwedel, p. 12.
72. NCRP, Report No. 42, pp. 16–17.
73. Pugh, et al., pp. A-20–A-30.
74. Pugh, et al., pp. 1–15, A-22–A-33.
75. Haaland, et al., p. 46.
76. Schmidt, *The Use of the ADAGIO Computer Program in Strategic Evacuation Analysis* (Arlington, Va.: Institute for Defense Analyses, October 1974) [Prepared for FEMA].
77. *1970 Census of U.S. Population*, U.S. Department of Commerce, vol. 1 (Washington, D.C.: U.S. Government Printing Office, May 1972), p. 1–41.
78. Pugh, et al., pp. A-20–A-30.
79. Lushbaugh, p. 487.

80. Ibid., pp. 476–86; Rotblatt, pp. 35–36.
81. Rotblat, p. 36.
82. Vital Statistics of the U.S., 1978, cited in *CA, Cancer Journal for Clinicians*, American Cancer Society, New York, vol. 32, no. 1 (Jan–Feb, 1982): 16.
83. Robert Jay Lifton, *Death in Life* (New York: Simon and Schuster, 1967).
84. C.M. Cipolla, *The Economic History of World Population* (Baltimore, Md.: Penguin Books, 1972), pp. 81–82; E.A. Wrigley and R.S. Schofield, *The Population History of England 1541–1871* (Cambridge, Mass.: Harvard University Press, 1981), pp. 332–36; T.H. Hollingsworth, *Historical Demography* (Ithaca, N.Y.: Cornell University Press, 1969), p. 356; W.H. McNeill, *Plagues and Peoples* (Garden City, N.Y.: Anchor, 1976), pp. 51, 149, 176–85.
85. Ronald W. Perry, *The Social Psychology of Civil Defense* (Lexington, Mass.: Lexington Books, 1982), p. 34.

CHAPTER 12: AGRICULTURAL POTENTIAL AFTER NUCLEAR WAR

1. Based on a comparison between current consumption patterns as reported in Table 12–1 and on the National Emergency Food Consumption Standards described in John W. Billheimer and Arthur W. Simpson, *Effects of Attack on Food Distribution to the Relocated Population*, vol. 1 (Los Altos, Calif.: Systan, Inc., September 1978) [Prepared for the Defense Civil Preparedness Agency], p. 4-2.
2. Ibid., p. 2-1.
3. U.S. Bureau of the Census, *Census of Manufactures and Annual Survey of Manufactures* (Washington, D.C.: U.S. Government Printing Office, 1976).
4. U.S. Bureau of Labor Statistics, *Employment and Earnings* (Washington, D.C.: U.S. Government Printing Office, 1978).
5. Billheimer and Simpson, p. 2-2.
6. U.S. Department of Agriculture, Crop Reporting Board, Statistical Reporting Service, *Cattle, Hogs and Pigs, Eggs, Chickens and Turkeys* (Washington, D.C.: U.S. Government Printing Office, 1983). Cattle inventory as of January 1, 1983; chicken (excluding commercial broilers) and swine inventory as of December 1, 1982.
7. Carsten M. Haaland, et al., *Survival of the Relocated Population of the U.S. After a Nuclear Attack* (Oak Ridge, Tenn.: Oak Ridge National Laboratory, 1976) [Prepared for the Defense Civil Preparedness Agency], p. 27.
8. Haaland, et al., p. 109; Billheimer and Simpson, p. 2–5, 4–7, 4–8; Stephen L. Brown and Ulrich F. Pilz, *U.S. Agriculture: Potential Vulnerabilities* (Menlo Park, Calif.: Stanford Research Institute, January 1969) [Prepared for the Office of Civil Defense], pp. 36–46; Richard L. Goen, et al., *Potential Vulnerabilities Affecting National Survival* (Menlo Park, Calif.: Stanford Research Institute, September 1970) [Prepared for the Office of Civil Defense], pp. 55-57.
9. See Billheimer and Simpson, pp. S–2, 2-11–2-12; Goen, et al., pp. 1–7; A.F. Shinn, "Food Crops and Postattack Recovery," in *Postattack Recovery from Nuclear War* (Washington, D.C.: Office of Civil Defense, 1967), p. 31; Bernard Sobin, *A Model of Technological Capacity to Support Survivors of Nuclear Attack* (McLean, Va.: Research Analysis Corporation, September 1968) [Prepared for the Office of Civil Defense], pp. 1-2.
10. Stephen L. Brown, et al., *Agricultural Vulnerability to Nuclear War* (Menlo Park, Calif.: Stanford Research Institute, February 1973) [Prepared for the Defense Civil Preparedness Agency].

11. Ibid., p. 18.
12. M.C. Bell, "Livestock and Postattack Recovery," in *Postattack Recovery from Nuclear War*, p. 48; Report of Committee One, "Vulnerability of Livestock to Fallout Beta and Gamma Irradiation," Appendix A, in *Survival of Food Crops and Livestock in the Event of Nuclear War*, David W. Bensen and Arnold H. Sparrow, eds. (Oak Ridge, Tenn.: U.S. Atomic Energy Commission Technical Information Center, December 1971), pp. 627–29.
13. Report of Committee Two, "Vulnerability of Crops to Fallout Beta Irradiation," in Bensen and Sparrow, eds., pp. 630–31; Sparrow, et al., "The Effects of External Gamma Radiation from Radioactive Fallout on Plants, with Special Reference to Crop Production," in Bensen and Sparrow, eds., pp. 670–711.
14. Report of Committee Two; Sparrow, et al.; Brown, et al., pp. B-19–B-21; Shinn, pp. 26–27.
15. Bell, pp. 48–49; Bell, et al., "Simulated Fallout Radiation Effects on Livestock," in Bensen and Sparrow, eds., pp. 193–207.
16. Bell, p. 50.
17. Shinn, pp. 34–37.
18. Haaland, et al., pp. 109–115; Haaland, "Availability and Shipment of Grain for Survival of a Nuclear Attack," *American Journal of Agricultural Economics*, May 1977, p. 361.
19. Haaland, et al., p. 110.
20. J. Carson Marks, "Global Consequences of Nuclear Weaponry," *Annual Review of Nuclear Science* 26 (1976): 72–73.
21. Billheimer and Simpson, pp. 4-7, 4-9, 4-41.
22. Haaland, et al., p. 145.
23. Ibid., pp. 146–47.
24. Haaland, p. 364.
25. Ibid.
26. Brown and Pilz, pp. 23–28, 36.

CHAPTER 13: ECOLOGICAL EFFECTS OF NUCLEAR WAR

1. Carsten M. Haaland, et al., *Survival of the Relocated Population of the U.S. after a Nuclear Attack* (Oak Ridge, Tenn.: Oak Ridge National Laboratory, 1976) [Prepared for the Defense Civil Preparedness Agency].
2. Ambio Advisors, "Reference Scenario: How a Nuclear War Might Be Fought," *Ambio* 11, nos. 2/3 (1982): 94–99.
3. G.E. Likens, et al., "Effects of Forest Cutting and Herbicide Treatment on Nutrient Budgets in the Hubbard Brook Watershed-Ecosystem," *Ecological Monograph* 40(1970): 23–47; and F.H. Bormann and G.E. Likens, *Pattern and Process in a Forested Ecosystem* (New York: Springer-Verlag, 1979).
4. T.E. Lovejoy, "Discontinuous Wilderness: Minimum Areas for Conservation," *Parks* 5(1980): 13–15; S. Iker, "Islands of Life in a Forest Area," *Mosaic* 13(1982): 24–30; and T.E. Lovejoy, et al., "Ecological Dynamics of Forest Fragments," *Proceedings of Leeds Tropical Forest Symposium* (in press).
5. G.M. Woodwell, "Radiation and the Patterns of Nature," *Science* 156(1967): 461–70; and Woodwell, "Effects of Pollution on the Structure and Physiology of Ecosystems," *Science* 168(1970): 429–33.

6. See J. Roughgarden, *Theory of Population Genetics and Evolutionary Ecology: An Introduction* (New York: Macmillan, 1979).
7. See, for example, S.T. Emlen and L.W. Oring, "Ecology, Sexual Selection, and the Evolution of Mating Systems," *Science* 197(1977): 215–23.
8. J.P. Holdren and P.R. Ehrlich, "Human Population and the Global Environment," *American Scientist* 62(1974): 282–92; and P.R. Ehrlich and A.H. Ehrlich, *Extinction: The Causes and Consequences of the Disappearance of Species* (New York: Random House, 1981).
9. See P.R. Ehrlich, A.H. Ehrlich, and J.P. Holdren, *Ecoscience: Population, Resources, Environment* (San Francisco: W.H. Freeman and Co., 1977).
10. P.R. Ehrlich and H.A. Mooney, "Extinction, Substitution, and Ecosystem Services," *BioScience:* 33(1983): 248–254.
11. Paul J. Crutzen and John W. Birks, "The Atmosphere after a Nuclear War: Twilight at Noon," *Ambio* 11, nos. 2/3 (1982):114–25.
12. Ibid.; Council on Environmental Quality (CEQ), *Environmental Quality* (Washington, D.C.: U.S. Government Printing Office, 1978).
13. Environmental Protection Agency (EPA), *Air Quality Criteria from Ozone and Other Photochemical Oxidants* (Washington, D.C.: USEPA, 1978); T.T. Kozlowski, "Impacts of Air Pollution on Forest Ecosystems," *BioScience* 30(1980): 88–93.
14. Crutzen and Birks, pp. 120–121.
15. R.W. Stark, et al., "Photochemical Oxidant Injury and Bark Beetle (Coloptera: Scolytidae) Infestation of Ponderosa Pine. I. Incidence of Bark Beetle Infestation in Injured Trees," *Hilgardia* 39(1968): 121–26.
16. C.L. Schofield, "Acidification of Adirondak Lakes by Atmospheric Precipitation: Extent and Magnitude of the Problem," Project F-28-RO4 (New York: N.Y. Environmental Conservation Department, Fish and Wildlife Division, 1976).
17. Norman R. Glass, Gary G. Glass, and Peter J. Rennie, "Effects of Acid Precipitation in North America," *Environment International* 4, nos. 5/6(1980): 443–452.
18. F.H. Pough, "Acid Precipitation and Embryonic Mortality of Spotted Salamanders, *Ambystoma maculatum*," *Science* 192(1976): 68–70.
19. T.G. Siccama, M. Bless, and H.W. Vogelmann, "Decline of Red Spruce in the Green Mountains of Vermont," *Bulletin of the Torrey Botanical Club* 109(1982): 162–68; H.W. Vogelmann, "Catastrophe on Camels Hump," *Natural History*, (November 1982): 8–14.
20. F. Pearce, "The Menace of Acid Rain," *New Scientist*, August 12, 1982.
21. E.B. Cowling and R.A. Linthurst, "The Acid Precipitation Phenomenon and Its Ecological Consequences," *BioScience* 31(1981): 649–54.
22. Kozlowski, "Impacts of Air Pollution on Forest Ecosystems."
23. M. Alexander, *Introduction to Soil Microbiology* (New York: Wiley, 1977).
24. Personal communication with J. Harte.
25. Crutzen and Birks, p. 120.
26. See Ehrlich et al., *Ecoscience: Population, Resources, Environment*, figure 4–31A.
27. Federation of American Scientists (FAS), "One Bomb—One City," *F.A.S. Public Interest Report* 34, no. 2(1981): 3.
28. See, for example, L.W. Alvarez, et al., "Extraterrestrial Cause for the Cretaceous-Tertiary Extinction," *Science* 208(1980): 1095–1108.
29. P.H. Raven, "Ethics and Attitudes," in J.B. Simmons, et al., eds., *Conservation of Threatened Plants* (New York: Plenum), pp. 155–81.
30. See P.R. Ehrlich, et al., "Extinction, Reduction, Stability and Increase: The Responses of Checkerspot Butterfly Population to the California Drought," *Oecologia* (Berlin) 46(1980): 101–105; P.R. Ehrlich and D.D. Murphy, "The Population Biology of Checkerspot Butterflies (*Euphrydryas*)," *Biologische Zentrelblatt* 100(1981): 613–29.

31.   Ehrlich and Ehrlich, *Extinction: The Causes and Consequences of the Disappearance of Species.*

32.   S.H. Schneider and L.E. Mesirow, *The Genesis Strategy: Global Climate and Survival* (New York: Plenum, 1976); Ehrlich, et al., *Ecoscience: Population, Resources, Environment.*

33.   Crutzen and Birks, pp. 121–122.

34.   Personal communication with S. Schneider.

35.   H.H. Lamb, *Climate: Present, Past, and Future* (London: Methuen, 1972); J.B. Pollack, et al., "Volcanic Explosions and Climatic Change: A Theoretical Assessment," *Journal of Geophysical Research* 81(1976): 1071–1083; C. Mass and S.H. Schneider, "Statistical Evidence on the Influence of Sunspots and Volcanic Dust on Long-term Temperature Records," *Journal of Atmospheric Science* 34(1977): 1995–2004; R.A. Bryson and B.M. Goodman, "Volcanic Activity and Climatic Changes," *Science* 207(1980): 1041–44; Bryson and Goodman, "The Climatic Effect of Explosive Volcanic Activity: Analysis of the Historical Data," 1981. (Mimeo.)

36.   H. Stommel and E. Stommel, "The Year without a Summer," *Scientific American* (June 1979): 176–86.

37.   Lamb, *Climate: Present, Past, and Future;* and S.H. Schneider and L.E. Mesirow, *The Genesis Strategy: Global Climate and Survival.*

38.   F.H. Bormann, "An Inseparable Linkage: Conservation of Natural Ecosystems and Conservation of Fossil Energy," *Bioscience* 26(1976): 754–60.

39.   J.T. Curtis, "The Modification of the Mid-Latitude Grasslands and Forests by Man," in W.L. Thomas, Jr., ed., *Man's Role in Changing the Face of the Earth* (Chicago: University of Chicago Press, 1956); D.N. Swanston, "Principal Mass Movement Processes Influenced by Logging, Road Building, and Fire," in *Proceedings of the Symposium on Forest Land Use and the Stream Environment* (Corvallis: Oregon State University, 1971), pp. 29–39; E.P. Eckholm, *Losing Ground* (New York: Norton, 1976); T. Dunn and L.B. Leopold, *Water in Environmental Planning* (San Francisco: W.H. Freeman and Co., 1978).

40.   See, for example, F.J. Swanson, "Fire and Geomorphic Processes," in H.A. Mooney, et al., eds., *Fire Regimes and Ecosystem Properties*, General Technical Report WO-26 (Washington, D.C.: Forest Service, U.S. Department of Agriculture, 1981).

41.   G. Gurney, *The War in the Air* (New York: Crown, 1962).

42.   Ehrlich and Ehrlich, *Extinction: The Causes and Consequences of the Disappearance of Species.*

43.   P.R. Ehrlich and A.H. Ehrlich, "A Resource Down the River," *Mother Earth News*, July/August 1980, pp. 136–37.

44.   L.R. Brown, *Building a Sustainable Society* (New York: Norton, 1981), p. 3.

45.   FAS, "One Bomb—One City."

46.   M. Caidin, *The Night Hamburg Died* (New York: Ballantine, 1960).

47.   P.H. Dunn and L.F. DeBano, "Fire's Effect on Biological and Chemical Properties of Chaparral Soils," in H.A. Mooney and C.E. Conrad, eds., *Proceedings of the Symposium on the Environmental Consequences of Fire and Fuel Management in Mediterranean Ecosystems* (Washington, D.C.: Forest Service, U.S. Department of Agriculture, 1977).

48.   Bormann and Likens, *Pattern and Process in a Forested Ecosystem.*

49.   Woodwell, "Radiation and the Patterns of Nature"; Woodwell, "Effects of Pollution on the Structure and Physiology of Ecosystems"; Woodwell, "The Biotic Effects of Ionizing Radiation," *Ambio* 11, nos. 2/3(1982): 143–48; and Woodwell and A.L. Rebuck, "Effects of Chronic Gamma Radiation on the Structure and Diversity of an Oak-Pine Forest," *Ecological Monograph* 37(1967): 53–69.

50.   Woodwell, "The Biotic Effects of Ionizing Radiation," p. 147.

51. Ehrlich and Ehrlich, *Extinction: The Causes and Consequences of the Disappearance of Species.*
52. See, for example, R.J. Dumar, et al., "Meningoencephalitis and Brain Abscess Due to a Free-Living Amoeba," *Annals of Internal Medicine* 88(1978): 468.
53. United States Department of Agriculture (USDA), *Agricultural Statistics* (Washington, D.C.: U.S. Government Printing Office, 1977).
54. Personal communication with T. Eisner.
55. N. Myers, *The Sinking Ark* (New York: Pergamon); Ehrlich and Ehrlich, *Extinction: The Causes and Consequences of the Disappearance of Species.*
56. R.H. MacArthur and E.O. Wilson, *The Theory of Island Biogeography* (Princeton, N.J.: Princeton University Press, 1967); M.E. Soule and B.A. Wilcox, eds., *Conservation Biology* (Sunderland, Mass.: Sinauer, 1980).
57. Schneider and Mesirow, p. 204.
58. National Academy of Sciences (NAS), *Genetic Vulnerability of Major Crops* (Washington, D.C.: NAS, 1972); and Ehrlich, et al., *Ecoscience: Population, Resources, Environment.*
59. R. Scheer, *With Enough Shovels: Reagan, Bush and Nuclear War* (New York: Random House, 1982), p. 3.
60. For example, H.H. Mitchell, *Ecological Problems and Postwar Recuperation: A Preliminary Report from the Civil Defense Viewpoint* (Santa Monica, Calif.: Rand Corporation, 1961).
61. R.U. Ayres, *Environmental Effects of Nuclear Weapons* Volumes 1 and 2 (Croton-on-Hudson, N.Y.: Hudson Institute, 1965).
63. National Academy of Sciences, *Long-Term Worldwide Effects of Multiple Nuclear-Weapons Detonations* (Washington, D.C.: NAS, 1975).
64. Ibid.; Office of Technology Assessment (OTA), *The Effects of Nuclear War* (Washington, D.C.: OTA, 1979).
65. J.P. Holdren, "Energy Hazards: What To Measure, What To Compare," *Technology Review* 85(April 1982): 32–38, 74–75.
66. W.E. Westman, "How Much Are Nature's Services Worth?" *Science* 197(1977): 960–64.
67. Jack C. Greene, "Introductory Remarks," in David W. Bensen and Arnold H. Sparrow, eds., *Survival of Food Crops and Livestock in the Event of Nuclear War* (Oak Ridge, Tenn.: U.S. Atomic Energy Commission Technical Information Center, December 1971), p. 6.
68. Defense Civil Preparedness Agency, *Research Report on Recovery from Nuclear Attack.* Information Bulletin No. 307 (Washington, D.C.: May 10, 1979), p. 23.
69. Ibid., p. 3.

CHAPTER 14: THE URBAN ENVIRONMENT AFTER NUCLEAR WAR

1. S.G. Winter, Jr., *Economic Viability after Thermonuclear War: The Limits of Feasible Production* (Santa Monica, Calif.: Rand Corporation, September, 1963).
2. Most economists look on space as an exotic cost that disturbs their balancing equations. In that tradition, Winter believes that space would have no economic consequences at all, if only transport were free and instantaneous (p. 142). This observation turns its back on human experience. We depend on the "friction of space" just as we depend on the friction between our shoes and the ground. Imagine a world in which anyone could instantly, and without cost, be anywhere they wished to be! A nightmare.

3.   P.D. LaRiviere and Hong Lee, *Postattack Recovery of Damaged Urban Areas* (Menlo Park, Calif.: Stanford Research Institute (SRI), November 1966) [Prepared for the Office of Civil Defense].

4.   Richard L. Goen, et al., *Potential Vulnerabilities Affecting National Survival* (Menlo Park, Calif.: SRI, September 1970) [Prepared for the Office of Civil Defense].

5.   Committee for the Compilation of Materials, *Hiroshima and Nagasaki: The Physical, Medical, and Social Effects of the Atomic Bombings* (New York: Basic Books, 1981).

CHAPTER 15: PSYCHOLOGICAL SURVIVAL AFTER NUCLEAR WAR

1.   See, for example: Allen H. Barton, *Communities in Disaster* (Garden City, N.Y.: Doubleday, 1970); Russell R. Dynes, E.L. Quarantelli, and Gary A. Kreps, *A Perspective on Disaster Planning* (Columbus, Ohio: Disaster Research Center, Ohio State University, 1972) [Prepared for the Defense Civil Preparedness Agency]; Kai T. Erikson, *Everything in its Path: Destruction of Community in the Buffalo Creek Flood* (New York: Simon and Schuster, 1976); National Research Council, *Disaster Studies Nos. 1, 3, 4, 19* (Washington, D.C.: National Academy of Sciences, 1956–1963); Klaus Hartmann and James Allison, "Expected Psychological Reactions to Disaster in Medical Rescue Teams," *Military Medicine* 146(May 1981): 323–27; David K. Kentsmith, "Minimizing the Psychological Effects of a Wartime Disaster on an Individual," *Aviation, Space, and Environmental Medicine*, April 1980, pp. 409–13; Warren Kinston and Rachael Rosser, "Disaster: Effects on Mental and Physical State," *Journal of Psychosomatic Research* 18: 437–456; Group for the Advancement of Psychiatry, Committee on Cooperation with Governmental (Federal) Agencies, "An Introduction to the Psychiatric Aspects of Civil Defense," Report No. 19, American Psychiatric Association, April 1951; Ronald Perry, *The Social Psychology of Civil Defense* (Lexington, Mass.: Lexington Books, 1982).

2.   Goldine C. Gleser, et al., *Prolonged Psychosocial Effects of Disaster: A Study of Buffalo Creek* (New York: Academic Press, 1981), pp. 148–49.

3.   See, for example: J. Bowlby, *Attachment and Loss*, vol. 1 (London: Hogarth Press, 1969); D.W. Winnicott, *The Maturational Processes and the Facilitating Environment* (London: Hogarth Press, 1965).

4.   Dynes, Quarantelli, and Kreps, passim; Defense Civil Preparedness Agency, *Questions and Answers on Crisis Relocation Planning*, Information Bulletin No. 305 (Washington, D.C.: April 20, 1979), pp. 1–34; DCPA, *Research Report on Recovery From Nuclear Attack*, Information Bulletin No. 307 (Washington, D.C.: May 10, 1979), pp. 8–10.

5.   Frederick Hocking, "Psychiatric Aspects of Extreme Environmental Stress," *Diseases of the Nervous System* 31(1970): 544–45.

6.   For further discussion of these factors, see: Charles E. Fritz and Harry B. Williams, "The Human Being in Disaster: A Research Perspective," *The Annals of the American Academy of Political and Social Sciences* 309(January 1957): 47–48; Gleser; Irving L. Janis, *Air War and Emotional Stress* (New York: McGraw-Hill, 1951), pp. 16–17; Robert L. Leopold and Harold Dillon, "Psycho-Anatomy of a Disaster: A Long Term Study of Post-Traumatic Neuroses in Survivors of a Marine Explosion," *American Journal of Psychiatry*, 119 (April 1963): 919 ff; Martha Wolfenstein, *Disaster: A Psychological Essay* (New York: Arno Press, 1977).

7. Anthony F.C. Wallace, *Tornado in Worcester: An Exploratory Study of Individual and Community Behavior in an Extreme Situation*, Committee on Disaster Studies, Disaster Study No. 3 (Washington D.C.: National Academy of Sciences, National Research Council, 1956), pp. 49–52.

8. Ibid., p. 127.

9. Erikson, *Everything in Its Path*, pp. 40–41.

10. James L. Titchner and Frederick T. Kapp, "Family and Character Change at Buffalo Creek," *American Journal of Psychiatry* 133(March 1976): 299.

11. Robert Jay Lifton and Eric Olson, "The Human Meaning of Total Disaster," *Psychiatry* 39(February 1976): 13.

12. Titchner and Kapp, p. 297.

13. Lifton and Olson, p. 13.

14. Erikson, *Everything in Its Path*, p. 202.

15. Erikson, "Loss of Communality at Buffalo Creek," *American Journal of Psychiatry* 133(March 1975): 302.

16. Ibid., p. 303.

17. Erikson, *Everything in Its Path*, p. 222.

18. Ibid., p. 212.

19. Janis, p. 78; Fred Iklé, "The Social Versus the Physical Effects from Nuclear Bombing," *The Scientific Monthly*, March 1954, p. 186; Richard Titmuss, *Problems of Social Policy* (London: His Majesty's Stationery Office, 1950), p. 186.

20. R.J. Overy, *The Air War 1939–1945* (New York: Stein and Day, 1980), p. 120.

21. Ibid., p. 125.

22. United States Strategic Bombing Survey (USSBS), *The Effects of Strategic Bombing on German Morale*, vol. 1 (Washington, D.C.: U.S. Government Printing Office, May 1947), p. 1.

23. USSBS, *The Effects of Strategic Bombing on Japanese Morale* (Washington, D.C.: U.S. Government Printing Office, June 1947), p. 1.

24. Ibid.

25. Ibid., p. 37.

26. USSBS, *The Effects of Strategic Bombing on German Morale*, p. 1.

27. Larry J. Bidinian, *The Combined Allied Bombing Offensive Against the German Civilian 1942–1945* (Kansas: Coronado Press, 1976), p. 57.

28. USSBS, *The Effects of Strategic Bombing on Japanese Morale*, p. 27.

29. William G. Niederland, "The Psychiatric Evaluation of Emotional Disorders in Survivors of Nazi Persecution," in *Massive Psychic Trauma*, Henry Krystal, ed. (New York: International Universities Press, 1976), p. 14.

30. Leo Eitinger, "The Concentration Camp Syndrome and Its Late Sequelae," in *Survivors, Victims, and Perpetrators: Essays on the Nazi Holocaust*, Joel Dimsdale, ed. (New York: Hemisphere Publishing Co., 1980), pp. 156–57.

31. Gustav Bychowski, "Permanent Character Changes as an Aftereffect of Persecution," in Dimsdale, ed., p. 81.

32. Bruno Bettleheim, *Surviving and Other Essays* (New York: Knopf, 1979), p. 34.

33. Robert Jay Lifton and Kai T. Erikson, "Nuclear War's Effect on The Mind," in *Indefensible Weapons*, by Robert Jay Lifton and Richard Falk (New York: Basic Books, 1982), p. 278.

34. USSBS, *The Effects of Atomic Bombs on Health and Medical Services in Hiroshima and Nagasaki* (Washington, D.C.: U.S. Government Printing Office, March 1947), p. 84.

35. M. Hachiya, *Hiroshima Diary*, (Chapel Hill, N.C.: University of North Carolina Press,), pp. 54–55.

36. Robert Jay Lifton, *Death in Life: Survivors of Hiroshima* (New York: Simon and Schuster, 1967), p. 33.

37.   Ibid., p. 45.
38.   Ibid., p. 48.
39.,   Ibid., p. 36.
40.   Ibid., p. 60.
41.   Ibid., p. 58.
42.   Lifton and Falk, p. 43.
43.   Lifton, *Death in Life*, p. 130.
44.   Committee for the Compilation of Materials, *Hiroshima and Nagasaki: The Physical, Medical, and Social Effects of the Atomic Bombings* (New York: Basic Books, 1981), p. 584.
45.   Ibid., pp. 337–38.

Index

323

also Radiation; Radioactivity. reconstruction after, 58, 178–82, 184–85; resettlement after, 274–75, 278–84; and sanitation system, 262; scope of impact, 9–10, 23; secondary impacts of, 11, 23; societal effects of, 28–32, 38–39, 119; surge period preceeding, 55–56, 78; soils, effect on, 263–64, 274; as survivable, 42, 186, 229; survival after, xiv, xviii, xx, 7, 17, 24, 40, 57–59, 134, 142–43, 184–85, 228–29, 232, 255, 295, 300; survivalist view of, 27; temperature, effect on, 268; threat of, 4, 5, 23, 37, 66, 70, 76–77, 152; transportation, effect on, 58, 142, 231. *See also* Transportation. vegetation regrowth, effect on, 263–64; warning of, xviii, 36–37, 39, 57, 82, 135; water quality, effect on, 11, 262, 264. *See also* Nuclear explosion
Nuclear weapons, 13, 21–22; safeguarding of, 61; use of, 61–62

Office of Technology Assessment, 10, 73
Ozone layer, 13; depletion of, 247, 256, 260, 266; levels, 256–57

Packaged ventilation kits (PVKs), 137
Particle beams, 59–60
Perry, Ronald W., 6–11, 16–17, 22, 28, 33–41, 42–44, 65–67, 72
Phony war, 151–53, 157
Polar ice pack, 261
Political legitimacy, 148–49, 153, 155
Population growth rate, 119
Post-attack phase medical problems, 178–79. *See also* Evacuation/relocation; Medical problems
Potassium iodide, 207
Preemptive or disarming nuclear strike, 60–61
Projected absorbed dosages (PAGs), 33
Psychiatric patients: disposition during evacuation, 164–67; disposition during shelter period, 174–76
Psychiatric responses: to disasters, 285–86, 287, 288–90. *See also* Bombing during World War II study; Buffalo Creek, West Virginia disaster study; Hiroshima; Nagasaki; Nazi concentration camps. to evacuation, 161, 164; to nuclear war, 175–76, 287–90, 295–96, 296–300
Psychological response studies, 285–300

Quarantelli, E.L., 6, 9, 69, 75

Rad (radiation absorbed dose), 194–98, 217, 220

Radiation/radiation exposure, 9, 11, 13, 25, 70, 173, 185–86, 188–98, 201–207, 208–209, 215–17, 224, 264, 279; absorbed dose, 194–98, 217, 220; biological effects of, 198–215; and biological repair rate, 215–17; cancer caused by, 200–201, 228–29; and children, 123, 181; chronic, 208–209, 228; contamination of food chain by, 30, 197–98, 201; cumulative dose of, 191, 194–97, 200, 215, 216, 218, 224–26; deaths from, 199–200, 202, 209–210, 224–30; decontamination procedures, 205–206; detection instruments, 139; dose/dose rate, 141, 199–200, 215, 216, 221–22, 224; and ecosystem, 265; energy from, 198; and evacuation/relocation, 90, 176; external contamination from, 205–206, 220; and fatigability, 211, 227; and fetal development, 211–12; and fertility, xxiii, 210, 227; gamma, 188–90; gastrointestinal effects of, 203; genetic effects of, 213–15, 229; hazard, 183–84; health consequences of, 187–88, 222; hematopoetic effects of, 202–203; hot spots of, 193, 197, 221; and immune response, 210–11, 227; initial, 188–90; injury, 176; and insects, 245; intermediate-term effects of, 208–212; internal contamination from 206–207, 220; levels, 142, 169, 176–78, 182; linear energy transfer (LET), 200; and livestock, 241–43; long-term effects of, 212–15, 247; neurovascular effects of, 203–205; neutron, 188; from nuclear attack, 186–87, 188–98; populations exposed to, 199; in post-shelter period, 193; protection factor (PF), 131–32, 154–55, 215–20, 222, 226; quality, 200; residual, 190; sickness, 138, 178, 182, 185, 202, 227, 275–76; solar, 270; symptoms, 202; threats of, 25, 35–37, 76–77; treatment of, 204, 207; ultraviolet, 247, 265; and vegetation, 248; wavelength, 256. *See also* Fallout; Irradiation, whole body; Radioactivity
Radiation Effects Research Foundation, 213
Radioactive iodine, 207
Radioactivity, xxiii; evacuation involving, 25; in food chain, 30, 197–98, 201, 240–41; ingestion/inhalation of, 201, 206. *See also* Fallout; Radiation
Radiological defense sets (RADEF), 220–21
Radiological Defense System, 139
Radionuclides, 197

About the Editors

Jennifer Leaning is a clinical instructor in medicine at Harvard Medical School; attending emergency physician in the department of medicine at Mount Auburn Hospital, Cambridge, Massachusetts; and research affiliate on the faculty of the Laboratory of Architectural Sciences and Planning at M.I.T. A graduate of Radcliffe College with a masters of science in demography and human ecology from the Harvard School of Public Health, she received her M.D. from the University of Chicago Pritzker School of Medicine and her residency training in internal medicine and emergency medicine at Massachusetts General Hospital. Since 1979 she has been a member of the executive committee and board of directors of Physicians for Social Responsibility and has written and lectured extensively on issues of disaster management, civil defense, and survival after nuclear war. Her background includes rural development work in East Africa, population research in Taiwan, and community health planning on Chicago's southside. Her current research focuses upon disaster management strategies in urban and rural societies.

Langley Keyes is a professor of city planning in the Department of Urban Studies and Planning at M.I.T., where he has taught since 1967. He is a graduate of Harvard University; Oxford University, where he was a Rhodes Scholar; and M.I.T., from which he received his doctorate. The author of *The Rehabilitation Planning Game* and *The Boston Rehabilitation Program*, his research interests are in the areas of public housing, neighborhood planning, and the history of housing reform. In 1978 he was awarded a German Marshall Fellowship to study social aspects of public housing in England, Sweden, and the Netherlands. Currently on leave from M.I.T. and serving as Special Assistant for Policy Development in the Massachusetts Executive Office of Communities and Development, he is also supervising a research project on the impact of funding cutbacks upon human service providers in Massachusetts.

About The Contributors

Dorothy Austin is a lecturer in psychology at Harvard Medical School and director of the Clinical Program in Psychology and Religion at the Harvard Schools of Medicine and Divinity. An ordained minister and psychotherapist, she has lectured and written extensively on issues of nuclear consciousness and the religious imagination.

Daniel Brand is vice president of Charles River Associates, responsible for the work of this consulting firm in the areas of urban transportation and land use. The author or co-author of more than forty professional articles on all phases of urban transportation, he has taught at Harvard and M.I.T. In the mid-1970s, he was under secretary of the Executive Office of Transportation and Construction of the Commonwealth of Massachusetts. He is editor of *Urban Transportation Innovation* and co-editor of *Travel Demand Forecasting*.

Paul Ehrlich is professor of Biological Sciences and Bing Professor of Population Studies at Stanford University. His research on the ecology and evolution of natural populations has involved field work throughout the world. His work in the natural sciences—as well as his policy research on human population, resources, and environmental predicaments—is reflected in over 20 books, 140 scientific articles, and more than 200 articles in the general press. Among these publications are his best-selling book, *The Population Bomb*; *Ecoscience*, the standard textbook in environmental studies, co-authored with Anne Ehrlich and John Holdren; and his latest, *Extinction*. He is a recipient of the John Muir Award, the Sierra Club's highest honor.

Admiral Noel Gayler is a veteran of forty-five years in the U.S. Navy, including service during World War II as a carrier fighter pilot and an experimental test pilot. His sea commands have included the *U.S.S. Greenwich Bay*, the *U.S.S. Ranger* (carrier), and *Carrier Division 20*. From 1972 to 1976, he was Commander of All U.S. Forces in the Pacific. Former director of the National Security Agency and deputy director of the Joint Strategic Target Planning Staff, he has extensive experience in research and development and in nuclear targeting, and has carried substantial responsibility for a major segment of U.S. intelligence. The recipient of three Navy Crosses and the Distinguished Service Medal, since retirement he has been active in the fields of technology and foreign affairs. He currently serves as chairman of the Deep Cuts Campaign of the American Committee on East-West Accord, in Washington, D.C.

H. Jack Geiger is the Arthur C. Logan Professor of Community Medicine at the School of Biomedical Education, City College, City University of New York. He is currently on leave as the Henry J. Kaiser Senior Fellow at the Center for Advanced Study in the Behavioral Sciences at Stanford, California. The author of over sixty articles and book chapters on issues of medical ethics, primary health care, and social aspects of public health, he has received the Distinguished Public Service Award from the National Association of Community Health Centers and the first annual APHA-Rosenhaus Foundation Award for Excellence from the American Public Health Association.

Philip B. Herr is an associate professor in the Department of Urban Studies and Planning at M.I.T., where he has taught for over twenty years. In addition, he is the founder and a principal in Philip B. Herr & Associates, Boston, a planning consulting firm in environmental, economic, and land-use issues. His recent consultant work includes specialization in emergency planning that has focused on nuclear power stations: Shoreham in New York, Seabrook in New Hampshire, and Pilgrim in Massachusetts. He is the co-author of *Evaluating Development Impacts*, a publication of the M.I.T. Laboratory of Architecture and Planning.

Howard Hjort is a partner in Economic Perspectives, Inc., a food and agricultural consulting firm in McLean, Virginia. In this position, and while vice president and partner in an economic consulting firm in Washington, D.C., he has monitored performance of the world agricultural and food system; conducted economic studies for food and agricultural clients; and provided consulting services to the U.S. government, the Food and Agricultural Organization, and the World Bank. His extensive experience in agricultural economics includes 2½ years with the Ford

Foundation in India and fourteen years with the U.S. Department of Agriculture. As the chief economist for the U.S. Department of Agriculture from 1977 to 1981, he served as principal departmental spokesman on policy matters. A charter member of the senior executive service since 1978, he received a Presidential Award during the Carter administration for exemplary executive performance.

Robert Jay Lifton holds the Foundations' Fund for Research in Psychiatry Professorship at Yale University. In the course of his career he has examined the problems of nuclear weapons and their impact on death symbolism, Chinese thought reform and the Chinese Cultural Revolution, and the Vietnam war experience and Vietnam veterans. In addition, he is engaged in research on medical behavior in Auschwitz, and specifically the role of Nazi doctors. Among his books are *Death in Life: Survivors of Hiroshima,* winner of the National Book Award; *The Broken Connection: On Death and the Continuity of Life;* and *Indefensible Weapons,* co-authored with Richard Falk.

Michael Lipsky, a specialist in American politics and public policy, is a professor of political science at M.I.T. His most recent publication, *Street Level Bureaucracy* (1980), won awards from both the Society for the Study of Social Problems and the American Political Science Association. He has been a consultant to federal and state agencies on human service issues, particularly youth services and public welfare. He was for several years director of policy analysis at the Legal Services Institute in Boston. He is presently a consultant to the Massachusetts Department of Public Welfare.

Kevin Lynch, planner, urban designer, author, and teacher, is currently a principal of Carr Lynch Associates, an environmental design consulting firm in Cambridge, Massachusetts. He was for over thirty years professor of city design in the Department of Urban Studies and Planning at M.I.T. Recipient of the Boston Society of Architects' Urban Design Award, the American Institute of Architects' Allied Professions Medal, and the American Institute of Planners' 50th Anniversary Award, he has authored numerous books and articles, including *Image of the City* and *A Theory of Good City Form.*

Eric Markusen is instructor in sociology at the University of Minnesota and co-director of the Nuclear War Education Project of the Federation of American Scientists. His lectures and publications address problems of death and bereavement, with particular focus on the sociological significance of nuclear war.

Irwin Redlener is a pediatrician, director of the Special Care Nursery at St. Luke's Memorial Hospital Center in Utica, and clinical assistant professor of pediatrics at Upstate Medical Center, State University of New York at Syracuse. Prior to entering private practice, he worked as director of the Pediatric Intensive Care Unit at the University of Miami Jackson Memorial Hospital. His publications include papers on Reye's syndrome, pediatric cardio-pulmonary resuscitation, and child abuse. Since 1981 he has served as chairman of a task force advisory to members of the New York State Assembly on the issue of nuclear war evacuation planning.

John Haj Ross is professor of linguistics and philosophy in the Department of Linguistics and Philosophy at M.I.T., where he has taught since 1966. His central areas of research have been syntax, semantics, and phonology. In addition to many articles, he is the author of *Infinite Syntax* and co-author of the series, *Language and Being*. He has held visiting professorships at Brown University, Barnard College, and the State University of New York at Buffalo, and has taught at institutes in Sweden, Japan, Egypt, Tunisia, and Brazil.

Donald A. Schön is Ford Professor in the Department of Urban Studies and Planning at M.I.T. As an industrial consultant, governmental administrator, and president of a nonprofit social research consulting organization, he has worked as a researcher and practitioner on the problems of technological innovation, organizational learning, and professional effectiveness, and has written extensively in these areas. His most recent book, *The Reflective Practitioner*, was published in January 1983. He has done extensive consulting in Europe and Israel and was invited in 1970 to deliver the Reith Lectures on the BBC.

Lawrence E. Susskind is professor of urban and environmental planning in the Department of Urban Studies and Planning at M.I.T. He is currently acting executive director of the Program on Negotiation at the Harvard Law School— an inter-university consortium devoted to improving the theory and practice of conflict resolution. His publications include numerous articles and monographs on environmental planning and land use. His most recent book, *Proposition 2½: Its Impact on Massachusetts*, is the result of an extensive research project on the cutback of real estate in Massachusetts.

Jerome B. Wiesner is President Emeritus of M.I.T. and currently Institute Professor. He was science advisor to President John F. Kennedy, and from 1976 to 1979 he served as chairman of the Advisory Council of the Office of Technology Assessment of the U.S. Congress. During World War II he was a leader in the development of radar. In addition to his national role in matters of science policy and technical education, he is recognized as an authority on microwave theory, communications science and engineering, and radio and radar propagation phenomena.